G000097790

WebSphere Studio Application Developer 5.0: Practical J2EE Development

IGOR LIVSHIN

Apress™

WebSphere Studio Application Developer 5.0: Practical J2EE Development
Copyright ©2003 by Igor Livshin

All rights reserved. No part of this work may be reproduced or transmitted in any form or by any means, electronic or mechanical, including photocopying, recording, or by any information storage or retrieval system, without the prior written permission of the copyright owner and the publisher.

ISBN (pbk): 1-59059-120-8
Printed and bound in the United States of America 12345678910

Trademarked names may appear in this book. Rather than use a trademark symbol with every occurrence of a trademarked name, we use the names only in an editorial fashion and to the benefit of the trademark owner, with no intention of infringement of the trademark.

Technical Reviewer: Jeff Miller
Editorial Directors: Dan Appleman, Gary Cornell, Martin Streicher, Jim Sumser, Karen Watterson, John Zukowski
Assistant Publisher: Grace Wong
Project Manager: Sofia Marchant
Development Editor: Tracy Brown
Production Editor: Janet Vail
Proofreader: Lori Bring
Compositor: Diana Van Winkle, Van Winkle Design Group
Indexer: Ann Rogers
Artist and Cover Designer: Kurt Krames
Production Manager: Kari Brooks
Manufacturing Manager: Tom Debolski

Distributed to the book trade in the United States by Springer-Verlag New York, Inc., 175 Fifth Avenue, New York, NY, 10010 and outside the United States by Springer-Verlag GmbH & Co. KG, Tiergartenstr. 17, 69112 Heidelberg, Germany.

In the United States: phone 1-800-SPRINGER, email orders@springer-ny.com, or visit http://www.springer-ny.com. Outside the United States: fax +49 6221 345229, email orders@springer.de, or visit http://www.springer.de.

For information on translations, please contact Apress directly at 2560 Ninth Street, Suite 219, Berkeley, CA 94710. Phone 510-549-5930, fax 510-549-5939, email info@apress.com, or visit http://www.apress.com.

The information in this book is distributed on an "as is" basis, without warranty. Although every precaution has been taken in the preparation of this work, neither the author(s) nor Apress shall have any liability to any person or entity with respect to any loss or damage caused or alleged to be caused directly or indirectly by the information contained in this work.

The source code for this book is available to readers at http://www.apress.com in the Downloads section.

To my family, Bella, Julia, and Ethan

Contents at a Glance

Contents

Part Two
Working with J2EE:
The Distributed Application Framework............*105*

Part Three
Working with Enterprise Messaging *445*

About the Author

Igor Livshin is a J2EE senior architect with extensive experience in developing large-scale distributed applications. He specializes in WebSphere and WebSphere MQ (MQSeries) IBM products. He has written communication-related articles for *Web Informant* and *Windows Tech Journal.* Igor has a master's degree in computer science from the Institute of Technology in Odessa, Russia.

About the Technical Reviewer

Jeff Miller is an e-business architect and member of the dragonslayers team with IBM Developer Relations Technical Consulting. He has more than 20 years of software development experience as an electrical engineer, software developer, and architect. Jeff has worked for MultiMate, Ashton-Tate, and Lotus, among others, and was a founding partner and vice president of international development at Software By Design, a software consulting company. His current focus at IBM is Web and enterprise application architecture, design, development, and particularly security. He works with partners and customers, consulting, mentoring, coding, and teaching. Jeff is an IBM-certified e-business solution designer and solution technologist and is IBM certified on WebSphere Application Server and WebSphere Studio Application Developer. He received his master's degree in computer science from Rensselaer Polytechnic Institute.

Acknowledgments

I WOULD LIKE TO THANK John Zukowski and Gary Cornell, Apress editorial directors, for helping me make this project a reality.

Special thanks to Ryan Cox, IBM WebSphere WebSpeed (SWAT) team; Sree A. Ratnasinghe, IBM advisory software engineer; Jeff Miller, e-business architect for IBM Developer Relations; Roland Barcia, IBM Software Services for WebSphere; Willy Farrell, IBM Developer Relations Technical Consulting; and Sheldon Wosnick, IBM WebSphere advisory software developer. All were generous with sharing their knowledge.

Lots of thanks to a wonderful Apress team: Grace Wong, assistant publisher; Sofia Marchant, project manager; Jeff Miller, technical editor; Tracy Brown, development editor; and Janet Vail, production editor. All contributed greatly to the technical accuracy and style of the book.

My thanks also go to Lori Doherty, CNA insurance company, and Debbie Cabell, Kemper Insurance, for their help and encouragement.

Introduction

SEVERAL YEARS AGO, my job requirements changed and I had to switch from Borland JBuilder to IBM WebSphere Studio Application Developer (WSAD). At that time, WSAD was a new product, and I was pleased with the elegance of its design and the power it provided to Java 2 Enterprise Edition (J2EE) developers. At the same time, I was amazed by the absence of detailed documentation about the product. The online help was simply inadequate for learning how to use the product (and was not intended for that purpose). Several WebSphere-related books available at that time targeted WebSphere Application Server (WAS), but they included little or no information about WSAD.

Thus, I started researching and eventually was able to collect a lot of valuable information about WSAD (although it took substantial time and effort). The process of collecting different pieces of information swamped my office with numerous folders, and soon it became a challenge to find what I needed among them. I began to realize the need for an organized repository of WSAD information.

Now, several years later, WebSphere is one of the industry-dominant J2EE development/runtime tools. However, the lack of WSAD documentation has not changed much. With the exception of several IBM Redbooks written about narrow topics, no retail book has been specifically written for WebSphere developers—until now. This book teaches you how to use the latest version of WSAD 5.0 for developing J2EE 1.3–compliant enterprise applications.

This practical, how-to book documents many types of J2EE development tasks with WebSphere 5.0. The step-by-step approach includes plenty of examples, screen shots, and explanations to facilitate your learning experience. I hope that this book eases your WebSphere learning process and helps you quickly become more productive.

What This Book Covers

This book covers the latest release of WSAD—version 5.0—and shows how to use it for developing J2EE 1.3–compliant distributed enterprise applications. It also shows how to deploy J2EE 1.3 applications on WAS 5.0. J2EE is a large and relatively complex technology that handles many different aspects of developing distributed applications. It is practically impossible to cover the entire J2EE technology in one book without just scratching the surface of each aspect. Rather than doing that, this book concentrates on several important topics that are applicable to any large J2EE development project:

- Enterprise JavaBean (EJB) 2.0 development, including Container Managed Persistence (CMP) and Bean Managed Persistence (BMP) entity beans and stateless and stateful session beans

- Web development, including servlets 2.3 and JavaServer Pages (JSP) 1.2

- Extensible Markup Language (XML) development, including XML namespaces, Document Type Definitions (DTDs), XML schema, and XML transformations

- Asynchronous communication, including Java Message Service (JMS) and Message Driven Beans (MDBs), and the integration of the WebSphere and WebSphere MQ products

- Deployment of J2EE 1.3–compliant applications on WAS 5.0

No learning process can be successful (regardless of how detailed the information provided) without practice. Therefore, each topic discussed in this book comes with corresponding examples of practical development, debugging, and selective application installation (deployment) on WAS 5.0. Many development steps include screen shots to make the learning process easier and more productive. The source code for all examples and the exported applications' EAR files are available for download on the Apress Web site (http://www.apress.com) in the Downloads section. (For more information, see the next section.)

 NOTE *All examples in this book were developed on the Windows 2000 platform. All software packages necessary to follow the book examples are available for free download (and 60-day evaluation) from the Internet. All software packages are resource intensive and require a decently equipped Windows 2000 machine. I recommend 768MB of RAM (minimum 512MB), a 1.5MHz processor, and about 30GB of disk space.*

Downloading the Book's Sample Code

All of the code for this book is available in the Downloads section of the Apress Web site (http://www.apress.com). It is broken up into chapters, and each chapter contains three folders. The Source folder includes all the source code files, the Export folder contains all the exported applications, and the Server folder contains the exported server project. If additional information is necessary, a readme.txt file will be present in the chapter folder.

Who This Book Is For

This book is for professional Java developers who are familiar with the basic aspects of the J2EE technology but who do not have much practical experience. The book is also for experienced J2EE developers who would like to quickly learn the WSAD 5.0 development environment and see how to use it to develop the latest J2EE 1.3–compliant applications.

The book does not teach J2EE, but it covers many of the new features introduced in the latest J2EE 1.3 specification and explains how to use these new features when working with the WebSphere family of products. The book also discusses several advanced topics of J2EE 1.3 development.

Contacting the Author

This book should facilitate your WebSphere learning process and help you become more productive. I hope that you find it useful and that it serves as an essential part of your WebSphere toolkit. If you have any questions or comments related to the book, you can contact me at ilivshin@apress.com.

Part One

Getting Started with WebSphere Studio Application Developer (WSAD) 5.0

CHAPTER 1

Introducing WSAD 5.0

IBM WEBSPHERE STUDIO Application Developer (WSAD) is an Integrated Development Environment (IDE) for building and testing Java 2 Enterprise Edition (J2EE) distributed applications. Being a member of the WebSphere family of products, WSAD is tightly integrated with IBM WebSphere Application Server (WAS), which is the runtime environment for J2EE applications.

Although it is possible to run non-WSAD-developed applications on WAS and to run WSAD-developed applications on other J2EE application servers, running WSAD-developed applications on WAS is the easiest and the most straightforward way of deploying and running J2EE applications because the products are so tightly integrated.

WSAD is a relatively new J2EE development tool that replaces the IBM VisualAge for Java package. WSAD is built on top of Eclipse—an open-source, Java-based framework for building Java application development tools. Originally developed by IBM, Eclipse was released to the open-source development community, which includes such software vendors as Fujitsu, Serena Software, Sybase, Borland, Merant, Rational Software, Red Hat, and many others. The Eclipse plug-in architecture allows software vendors to develop their products as plug-ins to Eclipse.

WSAD runs on a variety of operating systems including different flavors of Windows and Linux. This book covers the recently released 5.0 versions of both the WSAD and WAS packages. This chapter introduces WSAD 5.0 and its major features: role-based architecture, the Workbench and workspaces, perspectives, views, and so on. This chapter also introduces the features new to WSAD 5.0. In addition, the chapter explores the WebSphere Studio family of products.

Why Learn WSAD?

The popularity of WebSphere as a development and runtime J2EE environment has grown rapidly. In 2002, the WebSphere family of products won numerous awards from various magazines, awarded by readers and editors, in the categories of Enterprise, Web Services, Java, and Extensible Markup Language (XML). Furthermore, more than 11,000 readers cast their votes in 2002 in the first annual *Web Services Journal* Readers' Choice Awards, naming WebSphere products as the winner in four categories and the first runner-up in 11 more. Together with WAS, WSAD is quickly becoming the dominant J2EE development tool. According to IBM, WebSphere has become the most successful software development product in the history of IBM, and it continues to gain market share faster than any other J2EE-related commercial product. Some of the largest Web sites on the Internet are developed and hosted by WebSphere products. The use of the WebSphere family of products has increased about 500 percent in 2002.

By learning WSAD, you equip yourself with an extremely powerful development tool and make yourself more marketable as a J2EE specialist. Consider that about 50,000 companies and about one million developers are currently using WebSphere technology. Another important reason for selecting WSAD as your development tool is the product integration. When developing distributed enterprise applications in Java, you typically work with a variety of products that facilitate access to legacy data and integration of legacy applications (such as the J2EE application server runtime environment, databases, communication middleware, and so on). IBM is the only vendor capable of proving the entire supporting infrastructure.

Imagine that all the products you need for developing and running your J2EE applications come from different vendors. At your first serious production problem, you will need to communicate with different vendors, each blaming the others for your problem. On top of this, software releases coming from different vendors are uncoordinated and are not necessarily able to work together.

WSAD distinguishes itself from other development tools with its elegant and innovated design, which is based on role-based architecture. J2EE development is a complex process that involves specialists in many different professions such as Java, servlets, and JavaServer Pages (JSP) developers; graphic artists; Enterprise JavaBean (EJB), Java Database Connectivity (JDBC), Java Naming and Directory Interface (JNDI), and Java Message Service (JMS) developers; and application assemblers and deployers. By incorporating a role-based architecture, WSAD adjusts its development environment by optimizing it for each developer's role and, therefore, increasing development productivity.

Understanding the Major Features of WSAD 5.0

WSAD 5.0 is a major product release that introduces two important features and includes a multitude of equally important enhancements. The two new features are as follows:

- WSAD 5.0 supports the J2EE 1.3 and EJB 2.0 specifications, including the EJB component's new local interface in addition to the traditional remote interface; it also supports a new persistence model for entity beans.

- WSAD 5.0 supports JMS Message Driven Beans (MDBs).

The following sections explain the significance of these additions and enhancements.

Supporting the J2EE 1.3 and EJB 2.0 Specifications

Until release 5.0, WSAD supported only a remote interface mechanism, which provided invocation of EJB components over the network. The remote interface is a foundation of distributed applications that allows processing to be spread between multiple platforms, which in turn facilitates scalability and reliability.

However, with the remote interface, communication over the network is slow, which negatively impacts application performance. Many best-practice patterns can somewhat minimize this negative impact. The EJB 2.0 specification introduced the local interface mechanism with the main goal of substantially improving the performance and responsiveness of J2EE applications. For EJB components and their clients that run in the same address space—that is, in the same Java Virtual Machine (JVM)—the local interface allows local component invocation that is substantially faster than network-based component invocation.

Another important difference between remote and local interfaces is the way in which method parameters are passed. In the remote interface, parameters are passed by value. In other words, remote methods work with a local copy of passed parameters, so the original parameters are not modified even if the remote method changes their values. It also takes longer and requires more network resources to copy and pass large parameters over the network. In contrast, the local interface passes parameters by reference. It is faster, and the called methods can directly modify the original parameters.

WSAD 5.0 supports both remote and local interfaces. EJB components can provide remote interfaces, local interfaces, or both. In the case when an EJB component supports both local and remote interfaces, it is up to the EJB client to decide how to invoke the EJB component. Chapter 5 covers this WSAD 5.0 feature; you will develop several EJB components that use local and remote interfaces.

Supporting JMS Message-Driven Beans

The J2EE 1.2 specification originally introduced Java Message Service (JMS), which is now included as a default in J2EE 1.3. To support JMS, J2EE 1.3 introduced a new type of EJB: the MDB that is part of the EJB 2.0 specification. WSAD 5.0 now fully supports JMS.

JMS is a vendor-neutral Java messaging Application Programming Interface (API) that supports J2EE asynchronous communication. It is similar in concept to JNDI or JDBC, which are vendor-neutral APIs for accessing different naming and directory servers and various databases. Before the introduction of MDBs, there was a major technical issue with EJB components executing JMS on the receiving side of communication. Specifically, the problem was with using the Send/Receive mode of JMS communication. EJB components never have problems just sending asynchronous messages.

In the Send/Receive mode, an EJB component sends a message and then waits for a response. Because of the nature of the asynchronous communication, there is no reasonable time limit for when the response should be expected. The EJB component can continue sending messages even when the opposite side of communication is not running. A J2EE application server is an object-based, distributed, transaction-processing monitor developed and tuned for processing a large number of short tasks—conceptually similar to the Custom Information Control System (CICS). An EJB component that has sent a message cannot afford to stay active for a long time waiting for a response and monitoring a queue for the arrival of an expected response message.

This message listening service should be removed from the component and delegated to a server. That was the main design purpose of the MDBs introduced in the EJB 2.0 specifications. In WSAD and WAS versions 4.0*x*, IBM supported a proprietary listener; however, starting from release 5.0, it fully supports JMS. This is an advanced part of J2EE development, covered in Chapters 9, 10, and 11. Again, this book uses a practical, step-by-step approach to explain the intricate details of developing JMS applications with WSAD 5.0.

Understanding Other Significant WSAD 5.0 Enhancements

Version 5.0 includes other important enhancements, most of which are covered in more detail throughout this book:

- A new visual editor for Java that supports the Abstract Window Toolkit (AWT) and Swing-based graphical user interface for applets and applications.

- Support for J2EE 1.3, servlets 2.3, and JSP 1.2 (Filters, Listeners, Events, etc). This part is covered in Chapter 5 with practical development examples in Chapters 6 and 7.

- Full support for Struts-based Web application development.

- Support for Enterprise JavaBean Query Language (EJB QL)—covered in Chapter 5.

- Simplified build and runtime CLASSPATH support (see Chapter 3).

- A new Java Archive (JAR) generation utility and support for Javadoc.

- Pluggable runtime support for the Java Runtime Environment (JRE) and multiple runtime environments switching (see Chapter 3).

- The ability to run code with errors in methods.

- Java template support.

- Enhanced Web Service support.

- Enhanced XML support—covered in Chapter 8.

- New support for views, a stored procedure builder, a Data Definition Language (DDL) remote export, and DDL commitment to the database.

- Support for additional databases (Cloudscape 5.0 and Informix 9.3) and new database releases (Sybase Adaptive Server Enterprise 12.5 and Oracle 9i).

- New server support tools (WebSphere Log Analyzer).

- Extensible HTML (XHTML) support and custom JSP tags (taglib) support for JSP 1.2 (see Chapter 5).

- A new library view to catalog reusable objects.

- A TCP/IP monitoring server.

- Enhanced integration with Rational ClearCase LT and support for name-space and project versioning.

- New Web page designer (implemented in Java). See Chapter 7 for more information.

- The EJB 1.1 (J2EE 1.2) internal project structure in WSAD 5.0 is different from it was in WSAD 4.0*x*. This simplifies the tool's usability and is not related to J2EE 1.2 vs. J2EE 1.3. See Chapter 6 for more information.

- Enhanced Java Testing Framework (JUnit) and Apache Java-based build tool (ANT) integration.

- The Database Web Pages Wizard now allows development of Web pages that perform update, edit, and delete database operations (version 4.0*x* supported only the read operations). See Chapter 6 for more information.

- Enhanced profiling and log analyzing.

In addition to supporting the standard EJB QL specification (EJB 2.0), Web-Sphere also provides numerous extensions to the EJB QL language (such as ORDER BY, date/time expressions, subqueries, GROUP BY, HAVING, EXISTS, and multiple elements for the SELECT clauses) that make the EJB QL language much more powerful. WebSphere also introduces the new *dynamic queries*, which are query strings accepted at runtime rather than queries accepted statically at development time.

Exploring the WebSphere Studio Family of Products

WebSphere Studio comes in several flavors, discussed in the following sections. This book covers WSAD.

WebSphere Studio Site Developer (WSSD)

WSSD is a subset of WSAD; it provides tools for building Web and Struts applications but does not support EJBs. WSSD includes the integrated WAS software (versions 4 and 5) used for unit testing. Also, you can integrate Apache Tomcat and use it for testing.

WebSphere Studio Application Developer (WSAD)

WSAD contains all the WSSD functionality (including WAS) and provides full support for J2EE development: servlets, JSPs, EJBs, Web Services, major database access, XML, JMS, and other J2EE technologies.

WebSphere Studio Application Developer Integration Edition (WSAD IE)

WSAD IE includes all the functionality in WSAD plus the following:

- J2EE connector architecture support

- Visual editing of service-oriented architecture workflows

- A wizard for complex Web Services and EJBs

- WebSphere Application Server Enterprise Edition (WAS EE) support

WebSphere Studio Enterprise Developer (WSAD EE)

WSAD EE includes all the functionality of WSAD IE plus the following:

- Enterprise Generation Language

- z/OS and OS/390 support

- WebSphere Studio Asset Analyzer

- Developer resource portal

Understanding the Resource Requirements

WSAD is a powerful tool that requires substantial machine resources to run:

- Intel Pentium II processor minimum (Pentium III 500MHz or faster recommended)

- 512MB RAM minimum (768MB recommended)

- 800MB available disk space

Referring to the WSAD 5.0 Migration Guide

WSAD 5.0 supports WSAD 4.0*x* and VisualAge for Java migration. The *WSAD 5.0 Migration Guide* contains detailed information for various product versions and operating systems. Be aware that migration from version 4.0*x* to version 5.0 does not automatically change the project level. To change the Web project level, right-click the project and select Properties ➤Web ➤J2EE Level.

Changing the EJB project level is more involved. You need to create a new EAR project, open the META-INF/Application.xml deployment descriptor, select Modules, and then select Add ➤myModules. You can find the *WSAD 5.0 Migration Guide* at `http://www.ibm.com/websphere/developer/zones/studio/transition.html`. In addition, you can refer to the IBM Redbook *Migrating to WebSphere V5.0: An End-to-End Migration Guide* at `http://www.redbooks.ibm.com/redbooks/SG246910.html`.

Targeting WAS 4.0x, WAS 5.0, and WAS Express

Most applications that have been developed and subsequently tested on WAS 4.0*x* will run unchanged on WAS 5.0. However, if the application uses newer specification-level features (J2EE 1.3, servlets 2.3, JSP1.2, and so on), then that application will only run on WAS 5.0.

If you develop applications with WSAD 5.0 that you want to deploy and run on WAS 4.0*x*, you should be aware that some WSAD 5.0 wizards create projects and resources that default to J2EE 1.3. To change the default to J2EE 1.2, select Windows ➤Preferences ➤J2EE. Then select the highest J2EE 1.2 version.

The WAS Express environment is the only test environment included in the WAS Express development product. WAS Express is similar to WAS 5.0 but does not support EJBs.

After this brief introduction to the relevant WebSphere products, you are ready to start building your development environment.

Summary

This chapter briefly introduced you to WSAD 5.0—one of the most popular J2EE development tools from IBM. You learned that WSAD 5.0 is fully compliant with the J2EE 1.3 specification and provides full support for EJB 2.0, servlets 2.3, and JSP 1.2. The chapter also described numerous new features and enhancements of version 5.0 and highlighted the most important ones: local interfaces, a new CMP entity bean model, and JMS MDBs.

The following chapters explore many of these features in detail by building step-by-step examples.

## CHAPTER 2

Setting Up the Development Environment

THE DEVELOPMENT ENVIRONMENT requires the installation of WebSphere Studio Application Developer (WSAD) 5.0 and the DB2 Universal Database (UDB) 7.2 with Fixpack 6 database. You will install WebSphere MQ (MQSeries 5.3.1) in Chapter 9 where enterprise messaging is covered. This chapter covers how to set up the development environment for the Windows 2000 platform (other platforms require a similar installation process). The Windows 2000 platform requires Service Pack 2 or later to be installed.

NOTE *At the time of this book's publication, Service Pack 3 is currently available for download from the Microsoft Web site (*http://www.microsoft.com*). The cumulative update includes Service Pack 2, so Service Pack 3 is all you need to download and install. Please check the documentation for other Windows platforms.*

In this chapter, you will first download and install the DB2 database and then download and install the WSAD 5.0 files.

Downloading and Installing the DB2 Database

If you do not have the DB2 installation CD-ROM, you can download a trial version of the DB2 UDB Personal Edition 7.2 from the Internet. At the time of this book's publication, you can download the package from the IBM Web site at http://www.software.ibm.com/data/db2.

Setting Up Your System for DB2 Installation

The trial version is a single-user version of the DB2 product. Once you download the latest available version of DB2 and read the installation instructions, create a temporary directory and unzip the downloaded file in this directory. Follow these steps before starting the DB2 installation:

1. Log on as an administrator on the local machine. Create a new local user account called `db2admin` and make it a member of the Administrators group. The password must be DB2 compatible. (In other words, it should be eight characters or fewer, and it should not include the < or > characters.)

2. Next, assign special rights to this account by selecting `Start` ➤ `Control Panel` ➤ `Administrative Tools` ➤ `Local Security Policy` ➤ `Local Policies` ➤ `User Rights Assignment`.

3. Assign the following special rights to this account:

   • Act as part of the operating system.

   • Log on as a service.

   • Create a token object.

   • Increase quotas.

   • Replace a process-level token.

4. Log off and log in again locally as `db2admin`. Launch `setup.exe` to begin the DB2 package installation. Finally, follow the installation instructions.

NOTE *Avoid installing DB2 in the subdirectory of the* `<Windows-installation-drive>` `\Program Files` *directory for two reasons. First, writing in this directory (or its subdirectory) requires the user to have an account with administrative rights. In addition, try to avoid a long-name installation directory because the CLASSPATH and PATH environment variables have a length limit. On my development machine, I installed the DB2 package in the* `g:\sqllib` *directory.*

When prompted to enter a username and password, enter `db2admin` and the corresponding password for this account. When the DB2 setup is complete, the `First Steps` window will appear. Close it and reboot the machine. When the system restarts, log in locally again as `db2admin` to configure DB2 as explained in the next section.

Configuring DB2 to Use JDBC 2.0 Drivers

DB2 (by default) supports Java Database Connectivity (JDBC) 1.0 drivers, which is not acceptable for Java 2 Enterprise Edition (J2EE) development. You need to change the DB2 configuration to support JDBC 2.0 drivers. You must make this configuration change when the DB2 JDBC Applet Server is not running. To stop the DB2 JDBC Applet Server (it runs as a Windows service), enter the following command:

```
net stop DB2 JDBC Applet Server
```

Now, you can switch DB2 to the mode that supports JDBC 2.0 drivers. In the command-line window, switch to the directory g:\sqllib\java12. Enter the following command:

```
usejdbc2.bat
```

Next, verify that you receive the "file copied" message. Finally, start the DB2 JDBC Applet Server by entering the following command:

```
net start "DB2 JDBC Applet Server"
```

To make your work more convenient, create a DB2 shortcut. Right-click Start ➤ Explore, expand All Users in the Document and Settings directory, expand Start Menu, and click Programs. Right-click IBM DB2 and drag it onto your desktop. This creates the DB2 shortcut for easy DB2 invocations. Finally, log in as a network user and build a DB2 shortcut for the network user account using the same steps.

Downloading the WSAD 5.0 Installation Files

If you do not have the WSAD 5.0 installation CD-ROM, you can download a trial version for free 60-day evaluation from the IBM WebSphere Developer Domain site at http://www7b.software.ibm.com/wsdd/downloads/WSsupport.html.

Picking the Files to Download

From the same site, you can also get 30-day free-trial support with installation, configuration, and deployment. For the current WSAD 5.0 release, you need to download nine required core files. The rest of the files (called *parts*) are optional. You download or ignore them depending on your specific development environment.

The following parts are optional:

Part 10: This contains the remote Agent Controller installation. Agent Controller is no longer installed automatically (as it was for WSAD 4.0*x*). Agent Controller is a daemon process that helps the client application launch new host processes or attach to agents that exist within existing host processes. You need to install Agent Controller if you plan to perform the following tasks: profile your applications, use logging tools to import remote WebSphere activity log files, or remotely debug your applications. I recommend you install this part.

Part 11: This contains the Rational ClearCase LT Source Configuration Management (SCM) package. Download this file if you intend to use ClearCase LT for your SCM. Currently, WSAD comes with support for two source-control management packages that allow developers to work as a team: Concurrent Versions System (CVS) and ClearCase LT.

CVS is an open-source control management package from Concurrent Versions System. It is available for free from http://www.cvsnt.org. ClearCase LT is a limited release of the full ClearCase version from Rational Software. The LT version comes with WSAD (on CD-ROM) or is downloadable from the Internet as a part of the WSAD trial version. CVS is a simple SCM package. Its main problem is the lack of change-control mechanisms (mechanisms that allow a developer to lock the source in the repository for the duration of source modification). ClearCase LT is a more sophisticated package that supports source locking in local streams, but it still lacks source locking in external streams.

NOTE *You can postpone this decision by selecting* Other *when prompted for the SCM package during installation. Keep in mind that selecting the* CVS, ClearCase, *or* Other *option merely installs the WSAD support for the corresponding package. You must install the actual package separately. You also need to be aware that selecting the* Other *option is compatible with CVS. You do not need to reinstall WSAD should you decide later to use the CVS package. On the other hand, you have to reinstall WSAD to use ClearCase LT if you did not select this option during installation.*

TIP *With WSAD 4.x, there was an easier way to switch between SCM packages and avoid WSAD reinstallation. However, at the time of publication, this facility was not included in WSAD 5.0. In case this facility does become available again, I've included this tip. Be sure to check availability before using the tip. There are two procedures located in the* <WSAD_Install_Directory>\plugins\com.rational.clearcase *directory called* enable_clearcase.bat *and* enable_vcm.bat *(you need to close WSAD before executing either of these procedures).*

Part 12: This contains the embedded messaging client and server. You do not need this part if any of the following are true:

- You do not plan to build Java Message Service (JMS) applications.

- You plan to test your JMS application on WAS.

- You plan to use WebSphere MQ as a WSAD 5.0 JMS provider.

Should you decide that you need the messaging support, download this part.

Download the nine required files (plus any optional files that you need) and unzip them in the same directory. All files are self-extracting, so click each file and specify the same target directory for extraction. Before installing WSAD 5.0, you may want to print two files: install.pdf and readme.html. Both documents provide useful installation information.

Starting from this point, the installation process is identical to the CD-ROM installation. The only difference is that the CD-ROM installation has the autorun feature, which automatically launches the setup.exe program (with the image files, you need to launch the setup.exe program manually).

Understanding the Installation Requirements

Before you start installing WSAD on Windows 2000, you need to understand the following installation requirements.

WSAD's workspace is a directory where WSAD keeps all user development activity organized in the form of projects. WSAD is capable of working with multiple workspaces. When first started after installation, WSAD 5.0 creates a new workspace in the Windows Document and Settings directory. You can change the location of this first workplace. In addition, if you check the Use This Workspace as a Default and Do Not Show This Dialog Again box, this workspace will become the default workspace, and it will be used any time you start WSAD. In this case, to start WSAD with another workspace, create another shortcut for starting WSAD and modify the command that invokes WSAD. Add the -data WSAD_workspace parameter to this command. For example:

```
G:\WSAD\wsappdev.exe  -data WSAD_workplace
```

where WSAD_workplace indicates the workspace directory to be used by WSAD.

Figure 2-1 shows the WSAD Windows shortcut that has been set to use the workspace_Developer1 directory as the default workspace.

Figure 2-1. WSAD shortcut specifying the workspace directory

On the other hand, if you uncheck the Use This Workspace as a Default and Do Not Show This Dialog Again option, WSAD will always prompt you at startup for the workspace location. WSAD will create a new workspace directory if the directory you specified does not exist. If you start WSAD with a new (nonexisting) workspace directory defined as a subdirectory of the <Windows-installation-drive> \Program Files directory, the user starting WSAD needs to have an account with administrative rights.

WSAD (by default) is installed in the <Windows-installation-drive>\ProgramFiles directory, which (again) requires the user installing WSAD to have an account with administrative rights. In addition, be aware of the following: Your development environment, especially if you are going to use JMS, will require a substantial number of JAR files to be included in your CLASSPATH environment variable. The CLASSPATH environment variable in the Windows environment has a length restricted to 256 bytes. I strongly recommend you install WSAD in a directory with a shorter name (say, g:\WSAD). Otherwise, you will end up with a CLASSPATH environment variable that exceeds 256 bytes. This way of installation also helps deal with another Windows 2000 problem—the value of the PATH environment variable must be fewer than 820 characters.

Considering all options, the best way to install WSAD (and any other software packages) is by logging in locally as an administrator, installing the package outside the Program Files directory, and using a relatively short name for the installation directory (such as g:\WSAD). Select Customized (when prompted) to install WSAD in a nonstandard directory.

After WSAD installation, log in as a network user, right-click Start ➤ Explore, expand All Users in Document and Settings, expand Start Menu, and click Programs. Finally, right-click the icon for IBM WebSphere and drag it onto your desktop. This will create a shortcut for easy WSAD invocation.

 TIP *Specifying different workspace locations for different WSAD shortcuts allows a developer to conveniently work on different WSAD projects. This is a useful option for organizing your work.*

If you have already used WSAD 4.0*x* and have projects that need to be converted to WSAD 5.0, you can use two methods to migrate your projects to WSAD 5.0:

- Use one of the available SCM systems, such as CVS or Rational ClearCase LT. This is the recommended way.

- Export your projects from the WSAD 4.0*x* workspace and import them to the WSAD 5.0 workspace. This method migrates everything except the Project BuildPath, which needs to be entered manually.

As mentioned, the migration from version 4.0*x* to version 5.0 does not automatically change the project level. To change the Web project level, right-click the project and select Properties ➤ Web ➤ J2EE Level. Changing the EJB project level is more involved. You need to create a new EAR project and then open the META-INF/ Application.xml Deployment Descriptor, select Modules, and then select Add ➤ myModules. Once in WSAD 5.0, you can migrate a J2EE 1.2 project to J2EE 1.3 using the Migration wizard. Right-click the project and select Migrate ➤ J2EE Migration Wizard to start the wizard.

Do not install WSAD on High Performance File System (HPFS) files because Windows 2000 has a problem handling long filenames on HPFS files. You are now ready for WSAD installation.

Installing WSAD 5.0

With all the files extracted, start the WSAD installation by executing setup.exe, which is located in the directory where all the files have been extracted. You will see the screen shown in Figure 2-2.

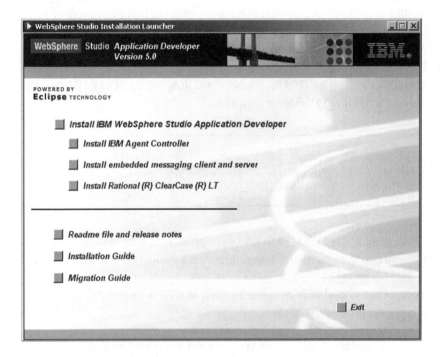

Figure 2-2. WSAD installation screen

From the screen shown in Figure 2-2, you can select several installation options (from the full WSAD installation to the installation of several optional parts of WSAD). Several additional options allow you to display, read, and print certain parts of the WSAD documentation. To install the WSAD package, follow these steps:

1. Click `Install IBM WebSphere Studio Application Developer`. Select `Custom Installation` and indicate a short-named WSAD installation directory (on my machine, I installed WSAD in the `g:\WSAD` directory). Follow the installation instructions. After successful WSAD installation, reboot the machine.

2. Run `setup.exe` again. This time, select `Install IBM Agent Controller`. Specify the installation directory (on my machine I installed it in the `g:\WSAD\AgentController` directory). When prompted to indicate the Java runtime, click `Browse` and navigate to the `<WSAD-install-directory>\eclipse\jre\bin` directory. When prompted, select `Disable Security`.

Optionally, repeat the same steps to install ClearCase LT. (Chapter 9 discusses the installation of the embedded messaging client and server.)

Finally, start WSAD. The first screen will prompt you for the location of WSAD's workspace directory (see Figure 2-3).

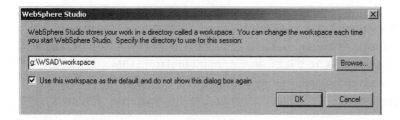

Figure 2-3. Setting the WSAD workspace

On my machine, I specified: g:\WSAD\workspace. I also checked the box (making this the default workspace directory and requesting not to show this dialog box again). If you need to use another workspace, you can build a separate WSAD shortcut. The last installation screen should indicate that WSAD has been successfully installed.

··

Installing WSAD on the Server

Large WSAD installations typically require installing WSAD executables on the server but storing the workspace on a local drive or on a mapped home directory. Assuming that all the company software packages are installed on a server drive locally mapped to the s: drive, use the following command for the shortcut to start WSAD from the server:

```
S:\wsad\wsappdev.exe -data g:\local_workspace_directory
```

This concludes setting up the development environment. Chapter 9 covers additional development environment setup that is necessary for processing JMS applications.

··

Summary

This chapter covered the process of building the development environment necessary to follow the book examples. You learned how to download and install the DB2 database and the WSAD 5.0 J2EE development tool from IBM.

In the next chapter, you will start exploring the WSAD 5.0 Integrated Development Environment (IDE), so make sure your development environment is ready.

CHAPTER 3

Working with the
WSAD 5.0 Workbench

THIS CHAPTER INTRODUCES you to the WebSphere Studio Application Developer (WSAD) 5.0 Workbench, which is WSAD's graphical user interface. This chapter explores a rich set of features, tools, and wizards that simplifies Java 2 Enterprise Edition (J2EE) development and substantially increases your productivity as a developer.

In this chapter, you will learn about the role-based development architecture of WSAD. Specifically, the chapter covers the following topics:

- Using Perspectives and Views

- Creating projects and folders

- Developing and debugging programs

- Exporting and importing wizards

- Customizing the Workbench

You will also develop your first project with WSAD in this chapter; specifically, you will create a "Hello World" Java application. The chapter begins by exploring the Workbench, which is the main graphical user interface window.

Understanding the Workbench Window Layout

You can invoke the Workbench by selecting Start ➤ Programs ➤ IBM WebSphere Studio ➤ Application Developer 5.0.

However, this method is a little bit involved. You probably remember that during the WSAD 5.0 installation you developed a shortcut for fast WSAD activation. Double-click the shortcut now to start WSAD. The screen that appears is the main interface of the WSAD Workbench (see Figure 3-1).

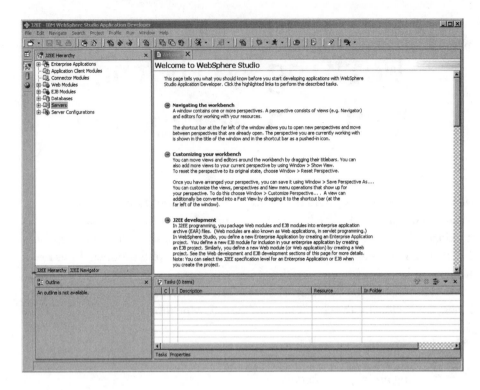

Figure 3-1. The WSAD Workbench

You will see the main menu and toolbar at the top of the Workbench window. The vertical bar on the left is the Perspective Bar. It contains buttons that are shortcuts for the quick activation of already opened Perspectives (you will learn about Perspectives in a moment).

You can divide the Workbench layout roughly into two areas. The area on the left is the Navigation Pane, which presents a hierarchical view of the *workspace*. A more detailed discussion of the workspace follows, but for now it is important to understand that the *workspace* is a directory where WSAD keeps all of your development projects.

The area on the right is the Content Pane, which displays different content depending on the type of development work being done. In Figure 3-1, a welcome screen for the Help Perspective appears in this area. The bar on top of the Content Pane shows mini-bars for files opened in the Content Pane. Each mini-bar has an X button for closing the corresponding window. These windows are *Editor Views*.

Although you can open multiple windows in the Content Pane, only one window is visible at a time (with the rest being hidden behind it). The visible window is the *active window* and its bar is highlighted. You can click the X button on the active window's mini-bar to close the window.

On the top of the WSAD Workbench is the main window title bar. To the left of the program's title, you should see the name of the currently active Perspective; in Figure 3-1, it is J2EE. The active Perspective's name is always displayed in the left part of the title bar. The next section discusses Perspectives and Views—two fundamental parts of the Workbench.

Using WSAD Perspectives and Views

A WSAD *Perspective* is a set of tools made available for a particular type of development. For example, when you develop a stand-alone Java application, you do not need the Web development tools (such as the Art Editor, HTML Editor, and so on). Therefore, the Java Perspective displays only the tools you need for effective Java development.

You can use Perspectives to adjust the WSAD development environment for a particular development role in accordance with the main notion of the WSAD architecture—as a role-based development tool. Switching to a certain Perspective causes the corresponding changes to occur in the Workbench internal configuration (together with visible changes of the Workbench content).

J2EE is a complex technology that requires the involvement of many specialists, such as Web developers, Java coders, Enterprise JavaBean (EJB) developers, application assemblers, and so on. The WSAD Perspective architecture allows WSAD to adjust its development setting and the layout of its main window to provide the best combination of tools for each developer's role.

Each WSAD tool appears inside the WSAD Workbench as a *View*. Each *View* displays the data that a specific tool visually presents to the developer. One tool can be presented by multiple Views, such as the Java Editor tool being presented by the Editor View, Outline View, Tasks View, and Properties View. You will learn more about Perspectives and Views shortly, but for now you should get an idea of how they look.

To select a particular Perspective, click Window ➤ Open Perspective from the main menu. Then, select the Perspective you want to open; for example, select Window ➤ Open Perspective ➤ Java.

If the Perspective you need is not in the menu list, select Other. You will see a full list of Perspectives (see Figure 3-2).

Figure 3-2. Perspective selection list

Select the Perspective from the list and click OK. Figure 3-3 depicts the Web Perspective. (You can even create and name your own Perspectives by choosing and arranging a group of Views and providing a name for a new Perspective. The new Perspective will then be available from the list.)

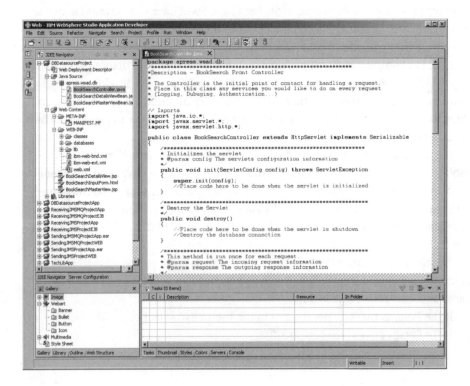

Figure 3-3. The Web Perspective

When the Web Perspective is open, an icon for the Web Perspective appears on the Perspective Bar (a vertical bar located on the left of the upper part of Workbench). In the Navigation Pane in Figure 3-3, the Web project called DBProject is expanded. The BookSearchController.java servlet module is in the Java Source directory (in the subdirectory that corresponds to this program's Java package name, apress.wsad.db). Double-clicking the BookSearchController.java module opens its source code in the Java Editor View (in the Content Pane).

The Web Perspective also displays many additional Views. On the left-lower part of the Workbench, the Gallery View presents a set of Web art and images that you can use when designing Web page graphics. Clicking the Illustration folder displays available graphics files in the Thumbnail View (see Figure 3-4).

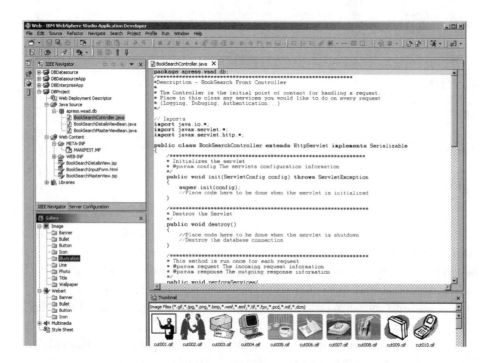

Figure 3-4. The Thumbnail View

In the same pane where the Gallery View displays, you should see several tabs at the bottom (Library, Outline, Web Structure, and Attributes). Clicking the Outline tab shows the outline of the currently displayed Java code: the package name, the import declaration, and the methods (see Figure 3-5).

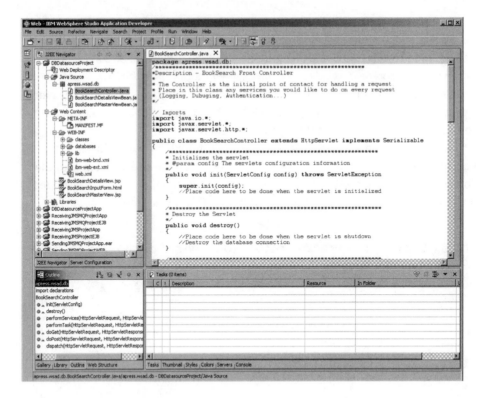

Figure 3-5. The Outline View

At the bottom of the Content Pane, you will see the tab for the Tasks View displayed. All error and other messages found in the entire Workbench appear in the Tasks View (see Figure 3-6). You can also filter tasks displayed in the Tasks View based on type, status, a particular set of resources, priority, or problem severity. You can also add your own tasks as reminders and optionally associate them with a set of resources.

Clicking any message displayed in the Tasks View highlights the corresponding line in the source code (the code this message references). If you modify some code, saving the file (by selecting Save from the main menu or clicking the icon that looks like a floppy disk) automatically triggers the Java compilation process. You can control this WSAD behavior by selecting Window ➤ Preferences from the main menu. On the screen that appears, you can change the way the Workbench behaves in certain situations (see the "Customizing the Workbench" section for more information).

Figure 3-6. The Tasks View

Learning Multiple Ways to Select Perspectives

WSAD provides several ways for selecting Perspectives. Say you want to switch to the Java Perspective. One way to do this is to select `Window ➤ Open Perspective` from the main menu.

Another way is to click the first icon located on the top of the vertical Perspective Bar. If you put the cursor on top of this icon, the help message displays the text `Open a Perspective`. Click this icon and select the Java Perspective from the list. The Workbench switches to the Java Perspective (see Figure 3-7).

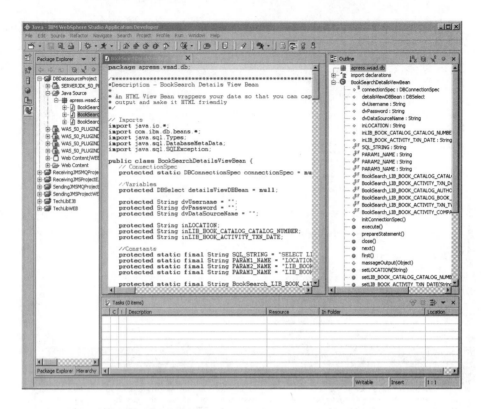

Figure 3-7. The Java Perspective

Now, the icon of the opened Java Perspective appears on the Perspective Bar. The third way for switching the Workbench to another Perspective is to use the icons on the Perspective Bar, which displays the icons of all the opened Perspectives. Moving a cursor over each icon displays a description of the selected Perspective. Simply clicking an icon switches the Workbench to the selected Perspective.

TIP *Keeping many Perspectives concurrently opened (displayed on the Perspective Bar) is not a good idea. First, each opened Perspective consumes additional resources. Second, if several concurrently opened Views point to the same file, then all such Views must be synchronized—a process that also consumes resources. This extra processing slows down WSAD execution.*

Working with Commonly Used Perspectives

The following sections briefly describe the most frequently used Perspectives. The book provides more detailed Perspective-related information in later chapters.

Using the Java Perspective

The Java Perspective is most useful for developing Java applications. It shows Java classes and interfaces grouped by packages. It also provides the Java Editor, Outline, and Tasks Views. In this Perspective, the Workbench toolbar contains several icons to add new packages, new Java classes, new Java interfaces, and so on. (You already saw the Java Perspective in Figure 3-7.)

In Figure 3-7, the first Java Editor View displays the `BookSearchController.java` file. You see only the module name on the top bar of the Java Editor View because this View is not active. The second Java Editor View displays the `BookSearchDetailsViewBean.java` file (the active View). Clicking the X icon of the active Java Editor View closes this View, and the pane automatically displays the next open Java Editor View that was previously hidden. Now, this View becomes the active View with its tab highlighted.

Using the Web Perspective

The Web Perspective is preconfigured for developing static pages—consisting of Hypertext Markup Language (HTML) and images—and dynamic pages—consisting of servlets and JavaServer Pages (JSPs). Figure 3-8 depicts the Web Perspective with the HTML Editor View previewing the file being edited.

The HTML Editor View can display the HTML file content in three different Views: Design (shows the page as a set of HTML controls), Source (shows the HTML code), and Preview (shows how the page looks in a browser). Clicking one of three tabs at the bottom of the HTML Editor View switches the pane to the corresponding View. Figure 3-8 shows the Preview View (how the user will see the page at runtime).

Figure 3-8. The Web Perspective's Preview View

At the bottom of the Workbench, several tabs show different Views that can be displayed (depending on the type of file displayed in the upper pane). Clicking one of these tabs will display a Tasks, Links, Thumbnail, Styles, Colors, or Servers View.

As you can see, the Links View is displayed in Figure 3-8. It shows the relationship between different files that comprise the Web project. If a file refers to an HTML page that the Workbench is unable to locate, the link will appear as broken.

Using the J2EE Perspective

You use the J2EE Perspective for developing the EJB components (entity and session beans). The toolbar displays the icons for building enterprise applications; building entity, session, and Message Driven Beans (MDBs); generating EJB deployed code; mapping Container Managed Persistence (CMP) entity bean properties to the database record fields; and so on. Double-clicking a bean file in the Navigation Pane opens it in the Java Editor View. Also displayed are the Outline and Property Views (for working with bean properties). The J2EE View shows all the J2EE modules present in the workspace. The Navigator View shows your projects as folders and files.

You can also use the J2EE Perspective for packaging the J2EE applications and preparing the projects for deployment. It provides editors for editing the Deployment Descriptor files (setting transaction properties, security, and so on). You will frequently use this Perspective when developing this book's examples. To open the project's Deployment Descriptor, right-click the project and select Open With ➤ Deployment Descriptor Editor (see **Figure 3-9**).

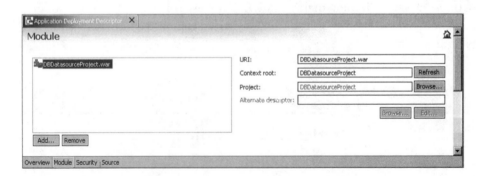

Figure 3-9. The project's Deployment Descriptor in the J2EE Perspective

 NOTE *To open the Deployment Descriptor for the Web projects, right-click the* web.xml *file and select* Open With ➤ Deployment Descriptor Editor, *or just double-click* web.xml.

The application-level Deployment Descriptor screen displays the context root of the Web module as well as many other fields. This information determines the Uniform Resource Locator (URL) structure for activating the application. To construct a URL that would invoke the components of this Web module, the context root should be concatenated with the component filename (typically an HTML or JSP file). Chapter 7 shows how to do this.

Using the Data Perspective

You can use the Data Perspective for working with relational databases, schemas, and tables. The DB Servers View shows connections to the databases. If the plus (+) sign appears in front of the connection, you can expand it to show the hierarchical structure of the database, schema, tables, and fields. This View also shows remote procedures, table views, aliases, triggers, and so on. To create a new connection, right-click anywhere in the DB Servers View area and select New Connection. You can use the Data Definition View for building a new database, schema, table, and so on. To do this, right-click anywhere in the Data Definition View and select New Connection (see Figure 3-10).

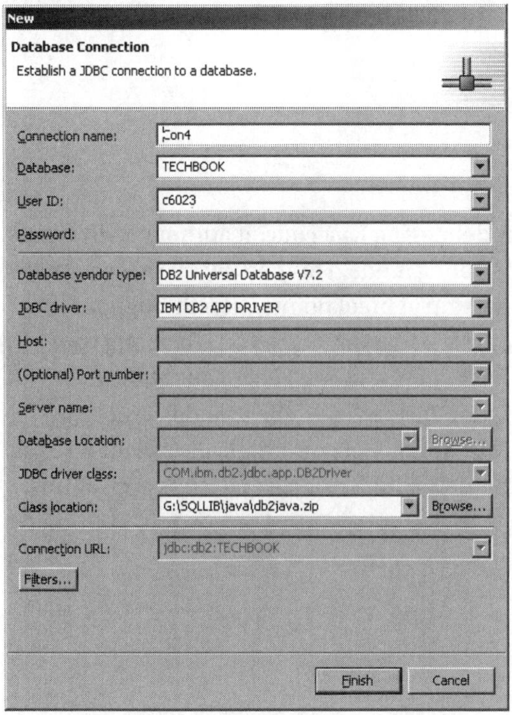

Figure 3-10. The Database Connection *screen*

Using the XML Perspective

You can use the XML Perspective for developing the XML-related applications. It presents several editors for building and modifying Extensible Markup Language (XML), Extensible Stylesheet Language (XSL), Document Type Definitions (DTDs), and XML Schema files. The Outline View displays XML tags of the open XML file. You can also use this Perspective for integrating XML with relational databases (see Figure 3-11).

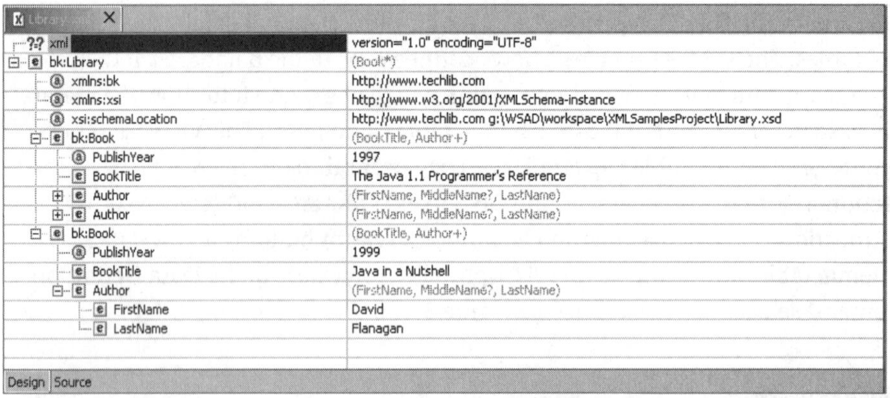

Figure 3-11. The XML Perspective

Using the Debug Perspective

You can use the Debug Perspective for debugging Java code. It automatically opens when you run a Java application in the debug mode. This Perspective allows you to set simple and conditional breakpoints, stop at breakpoints, step throughout the code, examine and modify the value of Java variables, and so on. To debug your application, the server needs to start in the debug mode. Next, you set the necessary breakpoints and run the application (also in the debug mode). When the executing code reaches a breakpoint, the Workbench automatically switches to the Debug Perspective (see Figure 3-12). In the Debug View, several icons appear on the toolbar that allow you to perform Step Over, Step Into, Step Return, and other typical debugging steps.

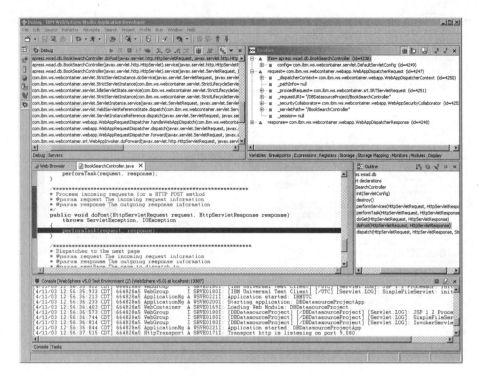

Figure 3-12. The Debug Perspective

Using the Server Perspective

You can use the Server Perspective to run (and optionally debug) J2EE applications and J2EE clients. This Perspective allows you to define and configure servers and server configurations and to attach your project to a specific server configuration. The Server Configuration View shows available server configurations. The Servers View shows available server instances and their status: Stopped, Started, The server should be republished, or Server is synchronized.

To start the server, right-click it in the Servers View and select Start. To stop the server, right-click it and select Stop. Alternatively, just highlight the server and click the corresponding icon (Start or Stop) on the Servers View toolbar. In a similar way, you can select Profile, Restart, and Republish. Starting the server automatically republishes and synchronizes it. Starting the server in the debug mode automatically switches the Workbench to the Debug Perspective. This Debug Perspective is similar to the Debug Perspective of the regular Java application (see Figure 3-13).

The Workbench automatically switches to the Debug Perspective when you right-click a module within an EJB or Web project and select Run on Server.

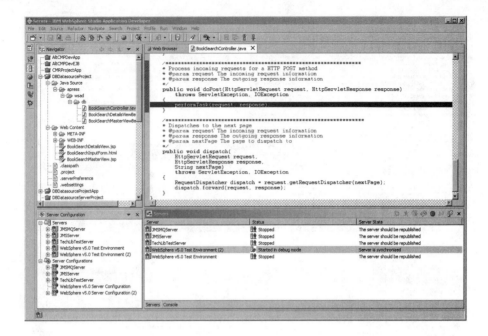

Figure 3-13. The Server Perspective

Setting the server configuration for each server instance allows you to control the runtime environment for each executed application; it is similar to some degree to the WebSphere Application Server (WAS) setting. To open a particular server configuration file, double-click that server in the Server Configuration View (see Figure 3-14).

This Server Configuration View has many tabs at the bottom. Clicking these tabs presents screens that display different parts of the server configuration file. Click the Paths tab. The screen that appears allows you to control the ability of different Java classloaders to find your project classes and Java Archive (JAR) files.

On the Paths screen, shown in Figure 3-15, you can control two CLASSPATH variables—the global system Java CLASSPATH variable and the ws.ext.dirs variable (the extended CLASSPATH-like variable) that is used by the WAS 5.0 as an additional global system CLASSPATH. You can add external and internal JAR files and folders to these CLASSPATH variables. JAR libraries and files included in both of these CLASSPATH variables are not reloadable, meaning that any changes made to them require the server to be restarted for the changes to take effect.

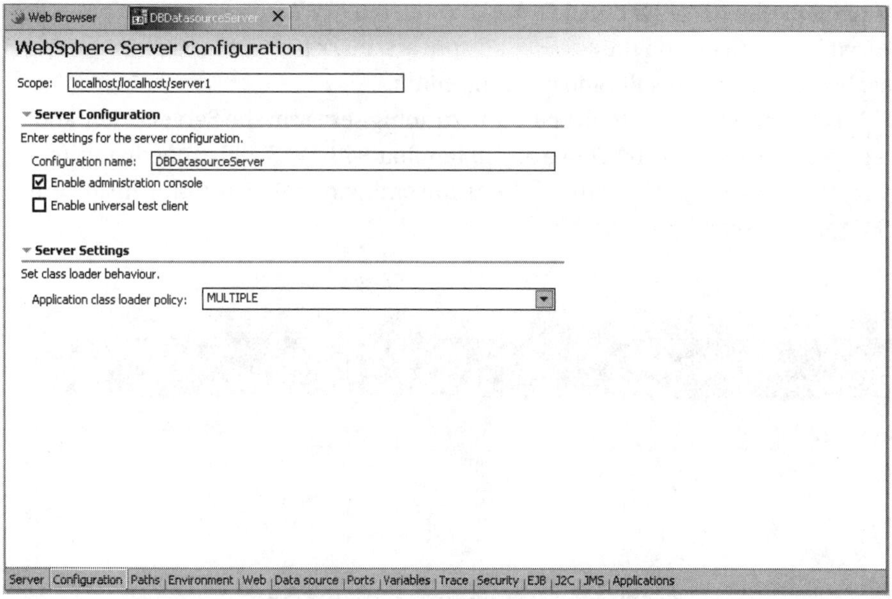

Figure 3-14. The opened server configuration

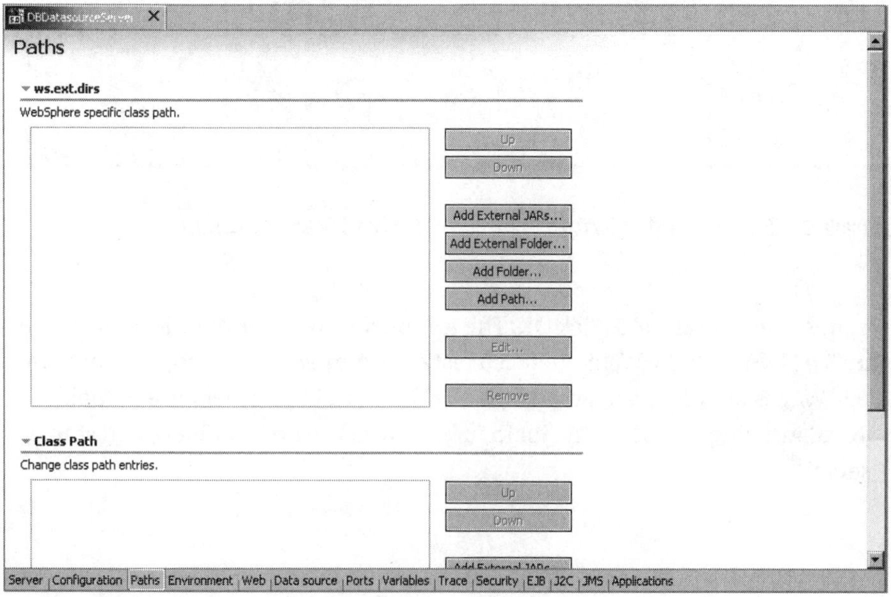

Figure 3-15. Setting the CLASSPATH and `ws.ext.dirs` *environment variables*

Actually, the test server is an embedded version of WAS (the base version). Click the Configuration tab; on the screen that appears, mark the Enable Administration Console box. Save the results and close the editor.

Next, start the server. Right-click the running server in the Servers View and select Start Admin Console. Those of you familiar with WAS will immediately recognize it (see Figure 3-16). Indeed, this is the embedded WAS running inside the WSAD environment.

Figure 3-16. Embedded WAS running inside the WSAD environment

Enter your user ID and click OK. The Administrative Console will launch (see Figure 3-17). Having the WebSphere 5.0 test environment server implemented by the real WAS is an important advantage of WSAD as a J2EE development tool.

Next, just click Logout on the main menu, close the Browser View, and stop the server.

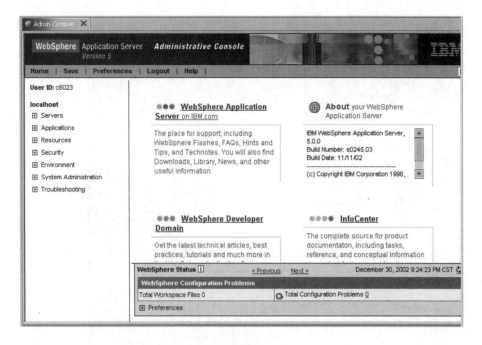

Figure 3-17. Embedded WAS Administrative Console

Using the Profiling Perspective

The Profiling Perspective allows you to preset the way of launching certain Java processes—specifically, the command-line parameters to be used with the launching Java process and the environment variables that the process uses.

If the host Java process resides on the machine where the Workbench is installed, do the following to set the environment variables:

1. Switch to the Profile Perspective and then click the Profile icon in the main toolbar. This opens the Launch Java Process wizard.

2. Indicate the project, the main class, and the command-line parameters and then click the Environment Variables button. On the dialog that appears, click Add.

3. On the next dialog, enter the name and value pairs of the environment variables you want to add (see Figure 3-18).

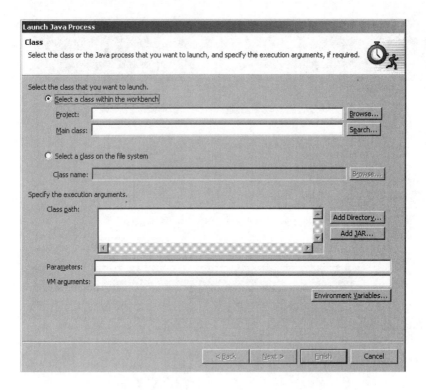

Figure 3-18. Launching a local Java process

4.   If the host Java process resides on the remote machine, you need to switch to the Profile Perspective, click the List button (the arrow to the right of the Profile icon) on the main toolbar, and select Launch ➤ Remote Process. This opens the Launch Remote Java Process wizard.

5.   Indicate the remote machine. Any remote management requires the Agent Controllers running on both machines. You can highlight the host and click the Check Connection button to check the communication session. Then click Next.

6.   On the next page, select a Java class. Then follow the same steps stated for the local process (see Figure 3-19).

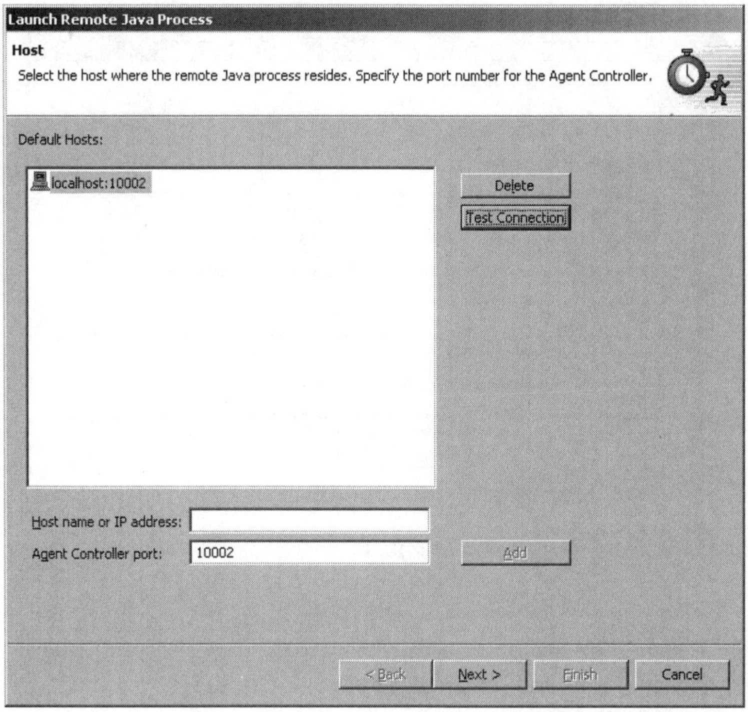

Figure 3-19. Launching a remote Java process

Using the Help Perspective

The Help Perspective displays online help information. The Search tab allows you to search for a specific topic. You can invoke the Help Perspective like any other Perspective or from the main menu by clicking Help ➤ Help Contents. Figure 3-20 shows the result of the search for Java help topics.

Selecting Help ➤ Software Update searches the IBM WSAD-related Web site for available updates and fixes. Selecting Help ➤ About IBM WebSphere Studio Application Developer displays the dialog that shows the details of the installed WSAD release.

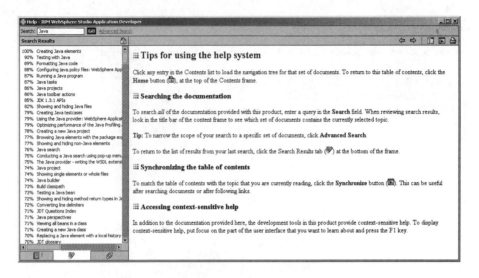

Figure 3-20. Results of a search for Java help topics

Selecting Help ➤ About IBM WebSphere Studio Application Developer displays the official WSAD release (5.0.0); the screen also shows the Build ID (which is currently 20021125_2118). This is important information when communicating with the IBM WSAD technical support. The dialog also provides three buttons for displaying additional information: Feature Details, Plug-in Details, and Configuration Details. On the Configuration Details page, you can find useful information about your WSAD environment (such as the boot class path, the library boot path, the library path, the temp directory WSAD uses, and so on).

Selecting Help ➤ Cheat Sheets displays a menu list where the help information is organized by the type of development activity. Selecting Create a Web application from this menu list displays a concise list of topics that walk you through the process of developing Web applications (see Figure 3-21).

Clicking a black arrow icon displays the WSAD screen used in the topic. Clicking the icon on the right (which looks like a question mark in a balloon) presents a catalog of help documents relevant to the topic (see Figure 3-22).

Finally, WSAD provides content-sensitive help. When you need help understanding the meaning of some field on the WSAD screen, just place the cursor in the field and press the F1 key. The related help information will appear.

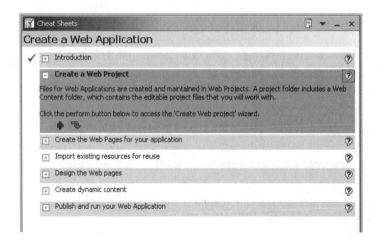

Figure 3-21. The Create a Web Application *help screen*

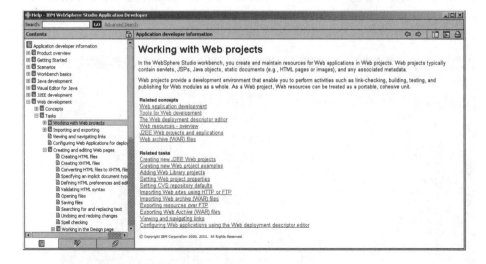

Figure 3-22. The Working with the Web projects *help screen*

Customizing Perspectives

You can customize the Workbench default Perspectives permanently or temporarily. If you work under some Perspective and you need to display a View that is not a part of the default Perspective, select Window ➤ Show View and then select the View from the list of available Views.

Customizing a Perspective Permanently

This section describes how to customize a Perspective permanently. Say you are working in J2EE as the current Perspective, and you would like to always have a Servers View as part of the J2EE Perspective. From the main menu, select Window ➤ Show View and select the Servers View. The Servers View will appear on the Workbench. Next, from the main menu, click Window ➤ Save Perspective As... and give the modified Perspective a new name (say, J2EE_with_Servers_View). To get back to the original default Perspective content, select Window ➤ Perspective Reset.

Making a Fine-Grained Perspective Customization

WSAD also allows you to customize a Perspective in a fine-grained way. For any open Perspective, select Window ➤ Customize Perspective... from the main menu. On the screen that is displayed, select the items to be displayed on the current Perspective (see Figure 3-23).

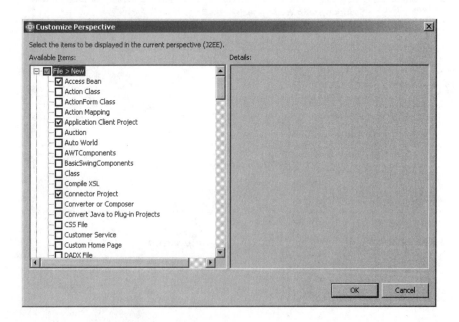

Figure 3-23. Customizing Perspectives

Understanding WSAD Projects

A WSAD *project* is an organization structure that combines all the resources necessary for developing and running J2EE and J2EE client applications. The J2EE specification defines the project types discussed in the following sections.

Web Project

You use the Web project for developing Web modules that combine HTML, servlet, JSP, JavaBean, JavaScript, and graphics files. It is also used for packaging the result in the Web Archive (WAR) file. WAR modules are considered stand-alone until they are assembled into an EAR Application project. Once you have created the Web project, you can import various Web resources in the Web project. You can import resources from the local file system or via HTTP/FTP protocols.

EJB Project

You use an EJB project for developing EJB modules that combine session, entity, and MDB files and for packaging the result in the EJB JAR file. EJB modules are considered stand-alone until they are assembled into an EAR Application project.

Application Client Project

You use the Application Client project for developing Application Client modules that run on the client machine outside the WebSphere environment. They typically combine user interface presentation files that run within the client container on the client machine. They can also include applets. Files are packaged in the Application Client archive files (JAR) files. Client archive files are assembled into an EAR Application project.

J2EE Project

Used for developing enterprise applications, the J2EE project is the top-level project that can include one or more EJB, Web, and Application Client modules. The J2EE project packages the result in the EAR file suitable for application deployment.

All WAR, EJB JAR, client application JAR, and EAR files include corresponding Deployment Descriptor files that instruct WAS containers how to install and run them.

Additional Project Types

WSAD defines additional project types specific to the WSAD environment, discussed in the following sections.

Java Projects

Used for building Java applications, the Java project consists mostly of Java classes and interfaces. The project packages the result in a JAR file. Java applications are stand-alone tasks running outside WAS under the control of the Java Virtual Machine (JVM). Web, EJB, or J2EE projects can also use them as utility code.

Server Projects

The Server project is built for setting the WSAD test server environment. Any server-side J2EE application runs on the WAS inside the appropriate container. WSAD includes WAS for creating a runtime environment that is close to the production runtime environment. WSAD allows local and remote testing using WAS as a runtime environment or only local testing using the Apache Tomcat application server as a runtime environment. The "Creating a New Java Project" section discusses the Server project in more detail.

Simple Projects

A Simple project is a Java-type project, but the project folder serves as a source container. For this type of project you have no choice of placing the source files in a different folder.

Plug-in Projects

WSAD is a plug-in-based Integrated Development Environment (IDE) in which you can develop plug-ins for WSAD! The plug-in project is used for plug-in development and is beyond the scope of this book.

Three project types (Web, EJB, and Application Client) are always added to one of the existing EAR projects. If at the time of creating a Web, EJB, or Application Client project, the EAR Enterprise project is not present in the Workspace, you have to build a new EAR project that will contain these new Web, EJB, and Application Client projects. You can do this automatically by selecting New ➤ Enterprise Application.

Customizing the Workbench

You can change the behavior of the Workbench and many of its tools by selecting Window ➤ Preferences from the main menu. The Preferences dialog will appear (see Figure 3-24).

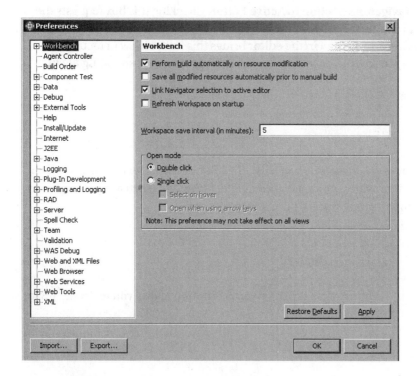

Figure 3-24. Customizing the Workbench

The majority of the options are self-explanatory, so the following sections discuss only the options that require some additional information.

Workbench

The following options exist in the Workbench's Preferences dialog:

- **Perform Build Automatically on Resource Modification**: If this box is checked, every time you save your changes, WSAD performs a build. The build is incremental and quick (only resources that have been changed since the last build are rebuilt).

- **Save All Modified Resources Automatically Prior to Manual Build**: If this box is checked, the Workbench saves all modified resources before performing the Rebuild All function.

- **Link Navigator Selection to Active Editor**: Checking this box requests the editors and the corresponding Navigator Views to interact—selecting a file that is already opened in the editor brings this Editor View in focus. The reverse is also true—selecting an editor brings the corresponding file in focus.

Perspectives

The Perspectives section shows you a list of all Perspectives, including any custom Perspectives. It provides options for opening Perspectives (such as opening a new Perspective in the same window or in a new window).

External Tools/Internet

If you access the Internet via a proxy server, this option allows you to set the proxy server.

Java

The following Java options control the appearance of the generated Java code and the version of the installed Java support environment:

- **Code Formatter**: This option allows you to adjust the way WSAD formats the generated Java code. All new Java code will be generated according to this formatter. However, if you have a Java class that is formatted differently, display it in the Editor View, right-click, and select Format. The code will be reformatted in accordance with the preferences you have set. A similar formatter is available for XML code.

- **Installed JREs**: This option allows you to replace the Java runtime version used by WSAD. Keep in mind that WSAD always uses the Java compiler with which it is shipped. Be careful if you decide to replace the Java Runtime Environment (JRE).

- **Server**: This option provides settings for Apache Tomcat, audio, publishing, TCP/IP monitoring, and so on.

One important option is J2EE. It controls the default level of the J2EE specifications that WSAD supports. If you want to develop your projects to follow the J2EE 1.3 newest specifications, then the value of this field should read 1.3.

Another useful feature when you are typing the Java code is Code Assist. You invoke Code Assist by pressing the Control+spacebar key combination. For example, type some method and press the Control+spacebar key combination to display a list of parameters that you can use with the method. You can select a parameter from the menu list to insert in the correct place in your code. You can control the auto-activation of this feature by selecting Window ➤ Preferences ➤ Java ➤ Editor ➤ Code Assist.

Options that you select under Window ➤ Preferences are not limited to a specific Perspective but are global for the Workbench. You will explore the Perspectives in more detail throughout the book.

Web Browser

This option allows you to select an external or internal Web browser. It also provides optional settings for each browser.

 NOTE *If you make any changes in this section, you need to restart the Workbench for the changes to take effect.*

Building a Simple "Hello World" Java Application

In accordance with the industry tradition, you will build your first project as a "Hello World" application. This is a simple Java project to demonstrate the way applications are developed with WSAD. This first example is simple, but the examples that follow will gradually become more complex.

Creating a New Java Project

To create a new project, click File ➤ New from the main menu. A list of project types displays for your selection. If the type of the project you want to create is not in the list, select Project.... A new dialog displays a list of all the available WSAD project types. Select Java on the left pane and Java Project on the right pane (see Figure 3-25).

Figure 3-25. Building a Java project

Click Next. The New Project wizard displays the screen that prompts you to specify the name and the location of the project. Enter HelloWorldProject in the Project Name field and check the Use Default box (meaning the new project will be created inside the workspace), as shown in Figure 3-26.

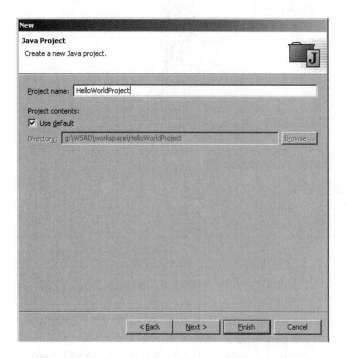

Figure 3-26. The New Java Project wizard

Click Next. The Java Setting dialog displays. Four tabs on the top of the dialog (Source, Projects, Libraries, and Order and Export) control the active page (the page currently visible). On the Source tab, you can specify the location of the project source files. The default option is to use the project directory as a source folder. Accept the default and click the Projects tab.

On the Projects tab, you can select other projects that this Java project may require. Projects marked on this page will be included in your project's Build Path. The Build output folder field enables you to specify the location of the compiled source files. By default, compiled files will be placed in the project folder, the same location where the source files are placed (see Figure 3-27).

Figure 3-27. The Projects *tab*

This Simple project does not require any other projects. Accept the defaults and click the Libraries tab (see Figure 3-28).

This page allows you to include all internal and external JAR files and folders that this project may need in the Build Path. Your Simple project does not require an additional library to be included in the Build Path.

> **NOTE** *For many frequently used libraries, WSAD provides environment variables. It is always preferable to add an environment variable to the* Build Path *instead of including the full path to the resource location. It makes the environment less location dependent. To use WSAD-provided environment variables, click the* Add Variable... *button.*

Next, click the Order and Export tab. On this tab, you can indicate the order of libraries in the Build Path. WSAD builds resources sequentially. So, if there are resources that are dependent on other resources, the dependent resources must be included in the Build Path after the resources they depend upon (see Figure 3-29). This page allows you to reorder libraries in the Build Path.

Figure 3-28. The Libraries *tab*

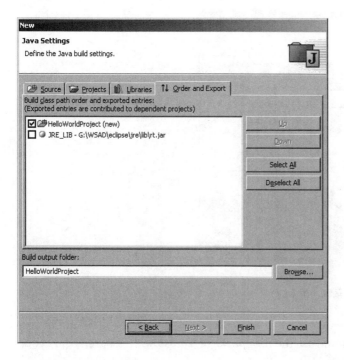

Figure 3-29. The Order and Export *tab*

Again, you do not need to do anything on this tab. Finally, click `Finish`. WSAD will generate `HelloWorldProject`. You should be able to see it in the Package Explorer View.

Creating a New Package

Next, you will create a Java package. Java packages combine related processing in one place within a project. As usual, WSAD provides several ways to create Java packages:

- Right-click `HelloWorldProject` and select `New` ➤ `Package`.

- From the main menu, select `File` ➤ `New` ➤ `Package`.

- Click the `Create a Java Package` toolbar icon.

The first way is preferable because the next screen appears with the `Folder` field already populated. Enter `apress.wsad.sample` as the package name (see Figure 3-30).

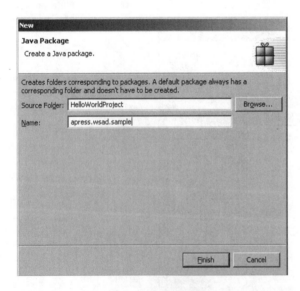

Figure 3-30. Building a Java package

Click `Finish`. You should see the new package (`apress.wsad.sample`) inside your project.

Creating a New Java Class

Create a new Java class by right-clicking apress.wsad.sample and selecting
New ➤ Class. Again, this is the preferable way of creating a new class because
the next screen appears with a prefilled Package field. Enter HelloWorld in the
Name field and request to generate the main() method and a call to a superclass
constructor (see Figure 3-31).

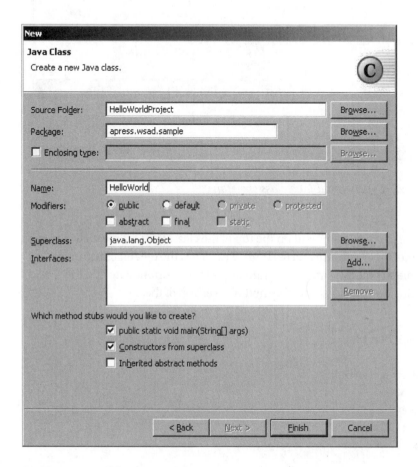

Figure 3-31. Building Java class

Click Finish. WSAD will generate the skeleton of the Java class and open it in
the Java Editor View. Right-click anywhere inside the Java Editor and select Format.
This will reformat your Java code in accordance with the setting made on the
Windows ➤ Preferences dialog for Java ➤ Code Formatter.

Figure 3-32. WSAD-generated Java class skeleton

Notice the package statement on the top of the class. The Outline View displays two methods of the class: main and HelloWorld (which is the default constructor). Modify this file so that this simple program displays the current date and the "Hello World" greeting. Listing 3-1 shows the modified version of the file.

Listing 3-1. HelloWorld.java

```
package apress.wsad.sample;
import java.io.*;
import java.text.SimpleDateFormat;
import java.util.Date;
public class HelloWorld
{
    // Constructor for HelloWorld
    public HelloWorld()
{
 super();
}
public static void main(String[] args)
{
```

```
    Date today;
    SimpleDateFormat sFormat;
    String currentDate = "";
    HelloWorld hwInstance = new HelloWorld();
    today = new Date();
    sFormat = new SimpleDateFormat("MM-dd-yyyy");
    currentDate = sFormat.format(today);
    System.out.println("Date: " + currentDate);
    System.out.println("Hello World!");
  }
}
```

When typing modifications to update the Java skeleton class, you can use the auto-completion feature that WSAD provides to help build Java code. For example, say you get to the point where you want to type the following statement:

```
currentDate = sFormat.format(today);
```

Just type `currentDate = sFormat.` (stop typing after entering the dot character). Then press the Control+spacebar key combination. A pop-up window displays a list of available methods for this class instance. Scroll this list to the point where it displays `format(Date)`. Double-click it to insert the method in your source. Next, replace the parameter `Date` with `today` and you are done.

Debugging the "Hello World" Application

Let's debug the program. Set a breakpoint on the line that reads "Hello World." As always, there are several ways of doing this. The simplest way is to position the cursor on the line where the breakpoint needs to be set and double-clicking the vertical bar on the left of the Editor View. A green dot appears confirming the breakpoint. Another way of setting a breakpoint is to select `Run ➤ Add/Remove Method Breakpoint` to toggle the breakpoint. You can also double-click a breakpoint to remove it.

The Breakpoints View allows you to set conditional breakpoints. You will find the Breakpoints View in the Debugger Perspective, or you can add it yourself to the Java Perspective or another Perspective. In the Breakpoints View, right-click a breakpoint and select `Hit Count`, which tells the debugger to stop at the breakpoint after the specified number of hits. To launch the test, highlight the "Hello World" program and on the main toolbar click the list arrow icon (located to the right to the bug-like debug icon). From the menu list, select `Debug As ➤ Java Application`. The Workbench switches to the Debug Perspective and the debugger starts. You should see your Java program stopped at the breakpoint.

On the upper-left side of the Workbench, you should see the Debug View. The toolbar of the Debug View contains several icons that look like curved arrows. These are the navigation icons for debugging. They allow you to perform Step Into, Step Over, and Step Return actions. Click the Step Over icon (or press F6). You should see the cursor move down to the next line (the previous command has been executed).

Click the Step Over icon three more times until the cursor is on the following line:

```
System.out.println("Date: " + currentDate)
```

Put the cursor over the currentDate variable and WSAD will display the variable value.

On the upper-right side of the Workbench, you should see the Variables View. If it is not displayed, click the Variables tab. You can also see the value of the currentDate variable.

Press F8 to run the program to the end. The Console View displays the execution results (see Figure 3-33). You should see the following in the Console View:

```
Date =  12-31-2002
Hello World!
```

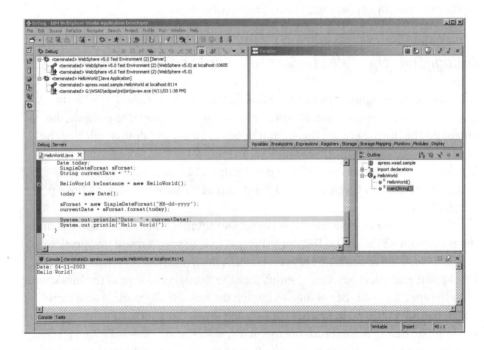

Figure 3-33. Debugging a Java program

During execution in the debug mode, when stopped at the breakpoint, it is possible not only to examine the value of variables, but also to change the value of some variables and continue execution. Follow these steps:

1. From the main menu, click Run ➤ Debug Last Launched (or just press the F11 key). The program starts executing again. It stops at the same breakpoint. Click the Step Over icon until the cursor reaches the same statement as before.

2. Make sure that the Variables View is displayed (if not, click the Variables tab). Locate the currentDate variable in the Variables View. Right-click it and select Change Variable Value. Enter some other data, and click outside the updated field so the change takes effect.

3. Press F8 to continue the program execution. You should see a different date displayed in the Console View.

Working in the WSAD Testing Environment

The first Java project that you just built is a simple Java application; however, it is not the typical application that WSAD was designed to develop. All J2EE enterprise applications are server based and require an application server to run. As already mentioned, the WSAD test environment supports local and remote testing on WAS Advanced Single Server Edition 4 and WAS 5. In addition, the Apache Tomcat server supports testing, but only local testing of Web projects that contain servlets and support JSPs.

Remote testing allows testing of the WebSphere applications running under WAS on a remote machine. To enable remote testing, you must have the following software installed on the remote machine:

- WAS

- Agent Controller

The following software must be installed on your local machine:

- WSAD

- Agent Controller

When you test a project, you can control how the test server starts. It can be started automatically when you right-click a module and select Run on Server. If this is the first time you are testing a project, the system will prompt you to select the type of server (WAS version 4.x or 5.x) to be used. After your selection, the server will be automatically configured and started.

Click the Advance button during this prompt to have more detailed control of the type of server to run. In this case, you will be presented with a dialog that lists available servers. You can select Use an existing server. If the test server you choose has not been configured yet, it will be automatically configured and started; otherwise, it will just restart. Alternatively, you can choose Create a new server. In this case, the server and server configuration will be created automatically before starting the server.

If your project is attached to multiple servers, you can select a particular server as a preferred server for the project. To do this, you right-click the project and select Properties ➤ Server Preferences.

Alternatively, you can start the test server manually in the Servers View. To start the server manually, highlight the server and click one of the following icons located on the Servers View's toolbar: Start the server (a running man icon), Start the server in debug mode (a bug icon), or Start the server in profiling mode (a running man with the clock icon).

In the previous example, you tested your project as a Java application by selecting the project and selecting Run As ➤ Java Application from the icon bar.

Let's explore the steps necessary for manually starting test servers.

Creating a New Server Project

First, create a new Server project. Switch to the Server Perspective. From the main menu, select File ➤ New ➤ Project. On the dialog that appears, select Server ➤ Server Project. Name the project as MyServerProject and click Finish. WSAD will create a new Server project called MyServerProject.

Right-click the new MyServerProject and select New ➤ Server and Server Configuration. In the resulting dialog, enter MyServer in the Server name field. Make sure you select the MyServerProject in the Folder field. For the Server type field, select the server type you need. Figure 3-34 shows the WebSphere version 5.0 Test Environment, which is the local WebSphere server.

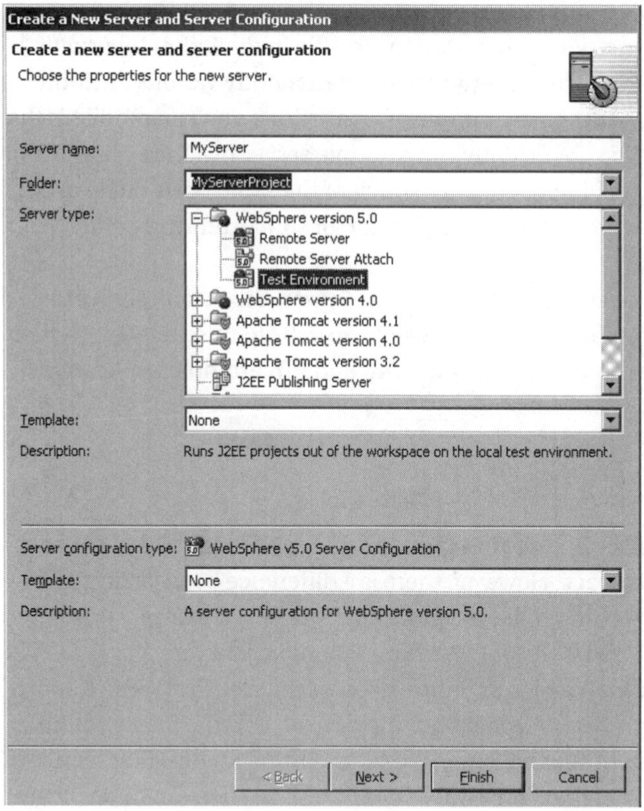

Figure 3-34. Selecting the test server

Click Next. The next screen allows you to set the port number on which the
server will listen. Accept the defaults and click Finish. WSAD will generate a new
Server in the Servers View and a new Server Configuration in the Server Configuration View. The server and server configurations are just XML files that keep
specific configuration data. The Server represents the *type* of server—Tomcat or
WebSphere 4 or 5, for example—and the Server Configuration stores specific configuration information about the server, such as its name, classloader policy, data
sources, and so on.

Finally, you need to attach an existing EAR project to the server. For this
example, you will attach the DBEnterpriseApp EAR project. You have not built this
project yet, so there is no DBEnterpriseApp in your environment. For now we just
show you how to attach an existing EAR project to the server. In the Server Configuration View, right-click MyServer and select Add Project ➤ DBEnterpriseApp. Now, if
you expand MyServer in the Server Configuration View, you should be able to see
that the DBEnterpriseApp and DBProject projects have been added to the MyServer
server configuration.

You can attach an EAR project to many Server Configurations. Double-clicking the Server Configuration instance opens the file in the Editor View with multiple tabs at the bottom of the View (where you can modify various attributes of the test server environment). One example of an attribute you can modify is the port number. If you want to concurrently run multiple server instances, or if WAS is installed on the same machine, there is a conflict of the same ports being used by multiple servers. You need to change the port for all concurrently running server instances.

By right-clicking a project and selecting Run on Server, the default server to which the project is attached starts automatically. You will later use the Test Server environment quite frequently for testing your WAR and EJB example applications.

Importing Resources into WSAD

You can import various Java resource files (Java, images, XML, JAR, WAR, EAR, and so on) into the WSAD workspace. However, there is a difference between importing simple resource files (such as Java files, images, and XML files) and importing archive files (such as WAR, EJB-JAR, and EAR files) that represent projects.

You import regular resource files into the existing projects. The WSAD Import wizard lets you indicate the resource location, the project, and the folder within the project of where to import the resource. When importing archive files, you enter the name of the project that you want to use for the application that you are going to import. To import a resource, click File ➤ Import…. The Import screen appears (see Figure 3-35).

Finally, select the type of resource, click Next, and follow the Import wizard's instructions.

WSAD allows you to import regular resource files locally (select File System) or download them from the Internet (using the HTTP or FTP protocols). The archive-type resources must be local to be imported.

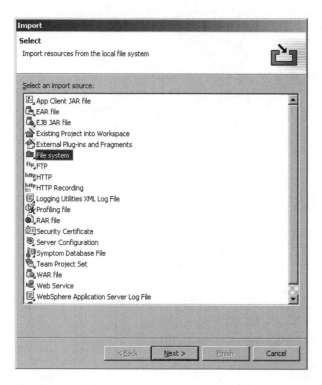

Figure 3-35. Importing resources in the WSAD environment

Summary

This chapter introduced you to the most frequently used features and tools of the WSAD 5.0 Workbench. It showed you the role-based architecture of the Workbench, its Perspectives, Views, projects, the server test environment, and other artifacts of the Workbench. You also developed and tested a simple Java project.

In the chapters that follow, you will continue exploring WSAD and its rich J2EE development environment.

CHAPTER 4

Developing Database Applications

IN THE PREVIOUS CHAPTER, you briefly learned about the WebSphere Studio Application Developer (WSAD) 5.0 Workbench as a development environment. This chapter builds on this initial knowledge and presents the first J2EE development example with WSAD 5.0. The following chapters expand your knowledge of WSAD 5.0 as a development tool by discussing more specific areas of development and providing much more detailed information about the WSAD 5.0 Workbench functionality that supports this type of development.

No learning process can be successful (regardless of how much detailed information is provided) without practice. Thus, each topic discussed in this book comes with the corresponding examples of practical development as well as figures that illustrate the development process.

All examples presented in this book are J2EE 1.3 applications (or application fragments) developed for a hypothetical library that rents technical books to its clients—software vendors. The database-related examples use the TECHBOOK database that you will build in this chapter. Later chapters concentrate on specific aspects of J2EE development.

This chapter starts with building the TECHBOOK database and its three tables: BOOK_CATALOG, BOOK_ACTIVITY, and BOOK_NOTIFY. Next, you will develop your first example that demonstrates how to use databases in WSAD 5.0. In the appendix, you will install this example on the WebSphere Application Server (WAS) 5.0. Now, it is time to start building the TECHBOOK database.

Understanding the TECHBOOK Database

For this book's examples, you will want your simple database to keep the following information:

- A list of all library books with a brief description of each book (the book title, the book author, and so on)

- The book rental activity (the company that rented or returned the book)

- Communication between the library and its clients

Subsequently, the TECHBOOK database consists of three tables:

- The BOOK_CATALOG table represents a library's book catalog.

- The BOOK_ACTIVITY table records book rental and return activity.

- A librarian uses the BOOK_NOTIFY table to communicate with the customers (informing them about new book arrival and so on).

Table 4-1 describes the structure of the BOOK_CATALOG table, Table 4-2 describes the structure of the BOOK_ACTIVITY table, and Table 4-3 describes the structure of the BOOK_NOTIFY table.

NOTE *The user ID account c6023 is set as the Windows 2000 domain administrator, local machine administrator, and the DB2 administrator in my development environment.*

Table 4-1. The BOOK_CATALOG Table

DATABASE TABLE FIELD	DESCRIPTION	FORMAT
CATALOG_NUMBER	A unique number assigned to the book by the library.	CHAR(5)
AUTHOR	The book's author.	VARCHAR(50)
BOOK_TITLE	The book's title.	VARCHAR(100)
LOCATION	Where the book is currently located. The value Library means it is available for renting. Otherwise, the company name that has rented the book should be coded here.	VARCHAR(50)
PLATFORM	Two-digit number indicating the platform for which the book is written: 00 means cross-platform; 01 means Unix (AIX); 02 means Unix (Solaris); 03 means Unix (HP), 04 means Windows NT/2000, and 05 means Linux.	CHAR(2)
LANGUAGE	Two-digit number indicating the development language: 01 means Java, 02 means C/C++, 03 means Delphi, 04 means Cobol, 05 means PLI, and 06 means Assembler.	CHAR(2)

Table 4-2. The BOOK_ACTIVITY Table

DATABASE TABLE FIELD	DESCRIPTION	FORMAT
TXN_DATE	The day of the book rental or return.	CHAR(10)
TXN_TIME	The time of the book transaction.	CHAR(8)
TXN_TYPE	The type of book transaction: RENT means book rental, and RETR means book return.	CHAR(4)
BOOK_CAT_NUM	A unique number assigned to the book by the library.	CHAR(5)
COMPANY_NAME	The name of the company that rented or returned the book.	VARCHAR(50)

Table 4-3. The BOOK_NOTIFY Table

DATABASE TABLE FIELD	DESCRIPTION	FORMAT
MESSAGE_KEY	Unique key used to look up message.	CHAR(20)
MESSAGE_BODY	The message sent to the customer.	CHAR(250)

Building the TECHBOOK Database

You are now ready to start building the TECHBOOK database. First, log in locally as the database administrator (in my environment, it is c6023) and select Start ➤ Programs ➤ IBM DB2 ➤ Command Window. Second, you can use the file shown in Listing 4-1 as input to the DB2 command, which builds the TECHBOOK database and your tables. You can find the BuildTextbookDatabase.sql file on the Apress Web site (http://www.apress.com) in the Downloads section.

NOTE *All book titles (and their authors) used in all this book's examples are fictitious and do not represent any published commercial books.*

Listing 4-1. BuildTextbookDatabase.sql

```
-- Build TECHBOOK database and tables --

-- Create the TECHBOOK database

DROP DB TECHBOOK;
CREATE DB TECHBOOK;
```

```
UPDATE DB CFG FOR TECHBOOK USING APPLHEAPSZ 256;
-- Commit to save work
COMMIT WORK;
GRANT ALL ON TECHBOOK TO PUBLIC;
CREATE SCHEMA LIB;
-- Commit to save work
COMMIT WORK;
CONNECT RESET;
-- Create the BOOK_CATALOG table
CONNECT to TECHBOOK;

-- DROP TABLE LIB.BOOK_CATALOG;
CREATE TABLE LIB.BOOK_CATALOG
  (CATALOG_NUMBER CHARACTER(5) NOT NULL,
   AUTHOR VARCHAR(50) NOT NULL,
   BOOK_TITLE VARCHAR(100) NOT NULL,
   LOCATION VARCHAR(50) NOT NULL,
   PLATFORM CHARACTER(2),
   LANGUAGE CHARACTER(2),
   PRIMARY KEY(CATALOG_NUMBER));

-- Commit to save work
COMMIT WORK;

-- Load BOOK_CATALOG table data
INSERT INTO LIB.BOOK_CATALOG (CATALOG_NUMBER, AUTHOR, BOOK_TITLE,
 LOCATION, PLATFORM, LANGUAGE)
VALUES('00001', 'Developer Journal', 'Windows NT Programming in Practice',
 'Library', '04', '02');

INSERT INTO LIB.BOOK_CATALOG (CATALOG_NUMBER, AUTHOR, BOOK_TITLE,
 LOCATION, PLATFORM, LANGUAGE)
VALUES('00002', 'Chris Hare', 'Inside Unix', 'AAA_Company', '00', '02');

INSERT INTO LIB.BOOK_CATALOG (CATALOG_NUMBER, AUTHOR, BOOK_TITLE,
 LOCATION, PLATFORM, LANGUAGE)
VALUES('00003', 'David Flanagan and a team', 'Java Enterprise in a Nutshell',
 'Library', '00', '01');

INSERT INTO LIB.BOOK_CATALOG (CATALOG_NUMBER, AUTHOR, BOOK_TITLE, LOCATION,
 PLATFORM, LANGUAGE)
VALUES('00004', 'Danny  Ayers and a team', 'Java Server Programming',
 'BBB_Company', '00', '01');
```

```
INSERT INTO LIB.BOOK_CATALOG (CATALOG_NUMBER, AUTHOR, BOOK_TITLE, LOCATION,
 PLATFORM, LANGUAGE)
VALUES('00005', 'Bill McCarty', 'Learn Red Hat Linux', 'Library', '05', '01');

INSERT INTO LIB.BOOK_CATALOG (CATALOG_NUMBER, AUTHOR, BOOK_TITLE, LOCATION,
 PLATFORM, LANGUAGE)
VALUES('00006', 'Lisa Donald and a team', 'MCSE Windows 2000 Professional',
 'BBB_Company', '04', '02');

INSERT INTO LIB.BOOK_CATALOG (CATALOG_NUMBER, AUTHOR, BOOK_TITLE, LOCATION,
 PLATFORM, LANGUAGE)
VALUES('00007', 'Harry M. Brelsford', 'Windows 2000 Server Secrets',
 'BBB_Company', '04', '02');

-- Commit to save work
COMMIT WORK;

-- Create the BOOK_ACTIVITY table

-- DROP TABLE LIB.BOOK_ACTIVITY;

CREATE TABLE LIB.BOOK_ACTIVITY
   (TXN_DATE      CHARACTER(10) NOT NULL,
    TXN_TIME      CHARACTER(8) NOT NULL,
    TXN_TYPE      CHARACTER(4) NOT NULL,
    BOOK_CAT_NUM CHARACTER(5) NOT NULL,
    COMPANY_NAME VARCHAR(50) NOT NULL,
    PRIMARY KEY(TXN_DATE,TXN_TIME));

-- GRANT ALL ON BOOK_ACTIVITY TO PUBLIC;

-- Commit to save work
COMMIT WORK;

-- Load the BOOK_ACTIVITY table data
INSERT INTO LIB.BOOK_ACTIVITY (TXN_DATE, TXN_TIME, TXN_TYPE , BOOK_CAT_NUM,
 COMPANY_NAME)
VALUES('01-01-2002', '09:17:25', 'RENT', '00001', 'AAA_Company');

INSERT INTO LIB.BOOK_ACTIVITY (TXN_DATE, TXN_TIME, TXN_TYPE , BOOK_CAT_NUM,
 COMPANY_NAME)
VALUES('01-10-2002', '10:11:66', 'RETR', '00001', 'AAA_Company');
```

```
INSERT INTO LIB.BOOK_ACTIVITY (TXN_DATE, TXN_TIME, TXN_TYPE , BOOK_CAT_NUM,
COMPANY_NAME)
VALUES('02-20-2002', '11:12:55', 'RENT', '00002', 'AAA_Company');


INSERT INTO LIB.BOOK_ACTIVITY (TXN_DATE, TXN_TIME, TXN_TYPE , BOOK_CAT_NUM,
COMPANY_NAME)
VALUES('01-15-2002', '12:12:12', 'RENT', '00003', 'BBB_Company');


INSERT INTO LIB.BOOK_ACTIVITY (TXN_DATE, TXN_TIME, TXN_TYPE , BOOK_CAT_NUM,
COMPANY_NAME)
VALUES('01-31-2002', '13:26:33', 'RETR', '00003', 'BBB_Company');


INSERT INTO LIB.BOOK_ACTIVITY (TXN_DATE, TXN_TIME, TXN_TYPE , BOOK_CAT_NUM,
COMPANY_NAME)
VALUES('03-05-2002', '14:22:11', 'RENT', '00003', 'CCC_Company');


INSERT  INTO LIB.BOOK_ACTIVITY (TXN_DATE, TXN_TIME, TXN_TYPE , BOOK_CAT_NUM,
COMPANY_NAME)
VALUES('04-05-2002', '15:44:31', 'RETR', '00003', 'CCC_Company');


INSERT INTO LIB.BOOK_ACTIVITY (TXN_DATE, TXN_TIME, TXN_TYPE , BOOK_CAT_NUM,
COMPANY_NAME)
VALUES('02-11-2002', '16:32:33', 'RENT', '00004', 'BBB_Company');


INSERT INTO LIB.BOOK_ACTIVITY (TXN_DATE, TXN_TIME, TXN_TYPE , BOOK_CAT_NUM,
COMPANY_NAME)
VALUES('02-17-2002', '17:12:22', 'RENT', '00005', 'BBB_Company');


INSERT INTO LIB.BOOK_ACTIVITY (TXN_DATE, TXN_TIME, TXN_TYPE , BOOK_CAT_NUM,
COMPANY_NAME)
VALUES('03-11-2002', '18:23:44', 'RETR', '00005', 'BBB_Company');


INSERT INTO LIB.BOOK_ACTIVITY (TXN_DATE, TXN_TIME, TXN_TYPE , BOOK_CAT_NUM,
COMPANY_NAME)
VALUES('03-15-2002', '19:27:11', 'RENT', '00005', 'DDD_Company');


INSERT INTO LIB.BOOK_ACTIVITY (TXN_DATE, TXN_TIME, TXN_TYPE , BOOK_CAT_NUM,
COMPANY_NAME)
VALUES('04-12-2002', '20:43:21', 'RETR', '00005', 'DDD_Company');


INSERT INTO LIB.BOOK_ACTIVITY (TXN_DATE, TXN_TIME, TXN_TYPE , BOOK_CAT_NUM,
COMPANY_NAME)
VALUES('05-01-2002', '20:11:21', 'RENT', '00006', 'BBB_Company');
```

```
INSERT INTO LIB.BOOK_ACTIVITY (TXN_DATE, TXN_TIME, TXN_TYPE , BOOK_CAT_NUM,
 COMPANY_NAME)
VALUES('05-02-2002', '21:11:21', 'RENT', '00007', 'BBB_Company');

-- Commit to save work
COMMIT WORK;

-- Create the BOOK_NOTIFY table

-- DROP TABLE LIB.BOOK_NOTIFY;

CREATE TABLE LIB.BOOK_NOTIFY
  (MESSAGE_KEY CHARACTER(20) NOT NULL,
   MESSAGE_BODY CHARACTER(250) NOT NULL,
   PRIMARY KEY(MESSAGE_KEY));

-- GRANT ALL ON BOOK_NOTIFY TO PUBLIC;

-- Commit to save work
COMMIT WORK;

-- End the connection
CONNECT RESET;
```

Download this file from the Apress Web site and copy it to the g:\sqllib\bin directory (where g:\sqllib is the DB2 installation directory in your environment). Make the appropriate adjustments if you installed DB2 in a different location.

From the DB2 command line, enter the following:

```
db2 -tf BuildTechbookDatabase.sql
```

and press Enter. Listing 4-2 shows the execution results.

Listing 4-2. Execution Results

```
G:\SQLLIB\BIN>db2 -tf Build_Database\BuildTechbookDatabase.sql

DB20000I  The DROP DATABASE command completed successfully.
DB20000I  The CREATE DATABASE command completed successfully.
DB20000I  The UPDATE DATABASE CONFIGURATION command completed successfully.
DB21026I  For most configuration parameters, all applications must disconnect
from this database before the changes become effective.
```

```
SQL1024N  A database connection does not exist.  SQLSTATE=08003
DB21034E  The command was processed as an SQL statement because it was not a
valid Command Line Processor command.  During SQL processing it returned:
SQL1024N  A database connection does not exist.  SQLSTATE=08003

DB21034E  The command was processed as an SQL statement because it was not a
valid Command Line Processor command.  During SQL processing it returned:
SQL1024N  A database connection does not exist.  SQLSTATE=08003
SQL1024N  A database connection does not exist.  SQLSTATE=08003
SQL1024N  A database connection does not exist.  SQLSTATE=08003


Database Connection Information

Database server        = DB2/NT 7.2.3
SQL authorization ID   = C6023
Local database alias   = TECHBOOK


DB20000I  The SQL command completed successfully.
DB20000I  The SQL command completed successfully.
DB20000I  The SQL command completed successfully.
DB20000I  The SQL command completed successfully.
DB20000I  The SQL command completed successfully.
DB20000I  The SQL command completed successfully.
DB20000I  The SQL command completed successfully.
DB20000I  The SQL command completed successfully.
DB20000I  The SQL command completed successfully.
DB20000I  The SQL command completed successfully.
DB20000I  The SQL command completed successfully.
DB20000I  The SQL command completed successfully.
DB20000I  The SQL command completed successfully.
DB20000I  The SQL command completed successfully.
DB20000I  The SQL command completed successfully.
DB20000I  The SQL command completed successfully.
DB20000I  The SQL command completed successfully.
DB20000I  The SQL command completed successfully.
DB20000I  The SQL command completed successfully.
DB20000I  The SQL command completed successfully.
DB20000I  The SQL command completed successfully.
DB20000I  The SQL command completed successfully.
DB20000I  The SQL command completed successfully.
DB20000I  The SQL command completed successfully.
DB20000I  The SQL command completed successfully.
DB20000I  The SQL command completed successfully.
```

```
DB20000I  The SQL command completed successfully.
DB20000I  The SQL command completed successfully.
DB20000I  The SQL command completed successfully.
DB20000I  The SQL command completed successfully.
SQL1024N  A database connection does not exist.  SQLSTATE=08003
G:\SQLLIB\BIN>
```

Checking the Database and Tables in the Control Center

It is always a good idea to check the execution results. To check the database and tables you have just created, start the DB2 Control Center utility. This utility displays the database metadata (the structure of database tables and their keys, foreign keys, database aliases, triggers, and so on) by selecting Start ➤ Programs ➤ IBM DB2 ➤ Control Center. The screen shown in Figure 4-1 will appear.

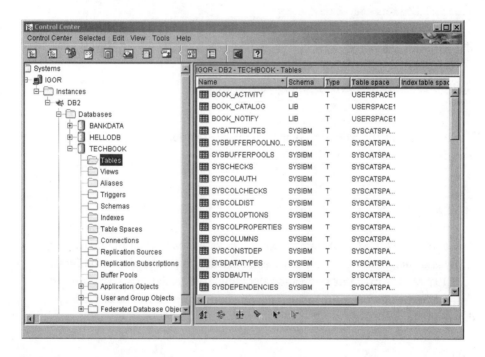

Figure 4-1. The DB2 Control Center

 NOTE *IGOR is the name of my development computer.*

Expand the IGOR computer node (or whatever your computer is called) all the way down by clicking the plus (+) sign. You should see the TECHBOOK database and your three tables. To see a table structure, double-click the BOOK_CATALOG table and click the Columns tab. Figure 4-2 shows the structure of the BOOK_CATALOG table.

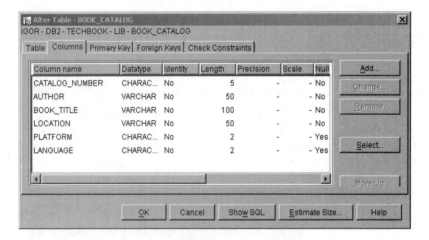

Figure 4-2. The BOOK_CATALOG table structure

You can click different tabs (such as Primary Key, Foreign Keys, and so on) to see additional information about the table.

Checking the Table Data

To see the BOOK_CATALOG table records, activate the DB2 Command Center utility and click the Interactive tab. Next, click the box at the end of the Database field. Expand the machine node and select the TECHBOOK database. The tool will connect to the database. Enter the following command in the Command field, as shown in Figure 4-3:

```
Select * from LIB.BOOK_CATALOG
```

NOTE *The LIB prefix is the database schema name.*

Command Center
Command Center Interactive Edit Tools Help
Interactive
Script
Query Results
Access Plan
Database connection
IGOR - DB2 - TECHBOOK
Command history
connect to TECHBOOK
Command
select * from LIB.BOOK_CATALOG
SQL Assist
Append to Script
------------------------------ Command Entered ------------------------------
connect to TECHBOOK
Database Connection Information
Database server = DB2/NT 7.2.4
SQL authorization ID = C6023
Local database alias = TECHBOOK

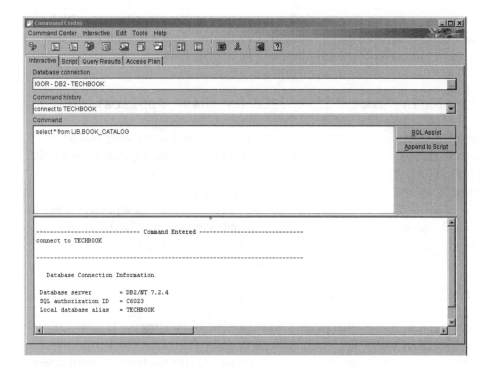

Figure 4-3. Entering the command

Next, highlight the entered text and select `Interactive` ➤ `Execute` from the main toolbar. Figure 4-4 shows the execution results.

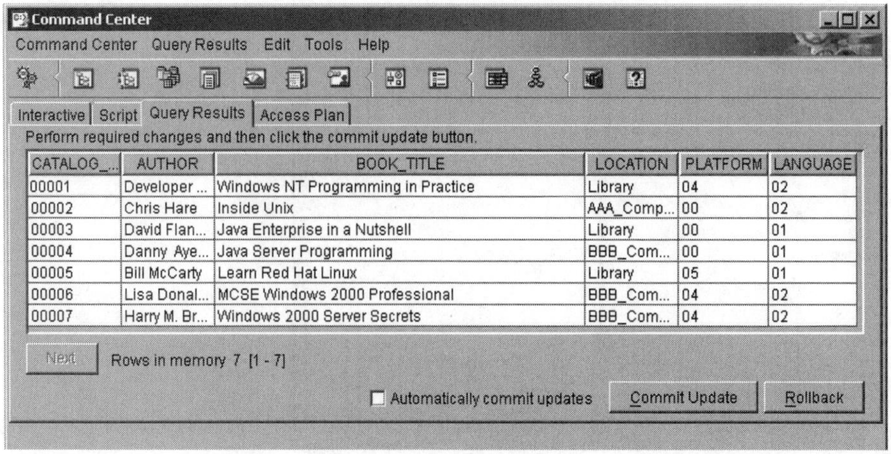

Command Center
Command Center Query Results Edit Tools Help
Interactive
Script
Query Results
Access Plan
Perform required changes and then click the commit update button.
CATALOG_... AUTHOR BOOK_TITLE LOCATION PLATFORM LANGUAGE
00001 Developer... Windows NT Programming in Practice Library 04 02
00002 Chris Hare Inside Unix AAA_Comp... 00 02
00003 David Flan... Java Enterprise in a Nutshell Library 00 01
00004 Danny Aye... Java Server Programming BBB_Com... 00 01
00005 Bill McCarty Learn Red Hat Linux Library 05 01
00006 Lisa Donal... MCSE Windows 2000 Professional BBB_Com... 04 02
00007 Harry M. Br... Windows 2000 Server Secrets BBB_Com... 04 02
Next
Rows in memory 7 [1 - 7]
Automatically commit updates
Commit Update
Rollback

Figure 4-4. The contents of the BOOK_CATALOG table

In the same way, you can display the content of the rest of the tables. With the TECHBOOK database built, you are now ready to start developing your first WSAD 5.0 database-related application.

Developing Your First J2EE Database Application

As mentioned, you will develop an application for a fictitious library that lends technical books to its clients. You will develop this database application as a Web application (Web *module* in J2EE 1.3 terminology), so you will not use any Enterprise JavaBean (EJB) development in this first example.

When creating a database connection, you should create a separate project to store the generated database files, as in the following section. This facilitates deployment by making it easier to use the database in multiple projects.

Creating the Database Project

In this section, you will first create a simple project for building the TECHBOOK database. Start WSAD (if it is not running yet) and switch to the Web Perspective. From the main menu, select File ➤ New ➤ Project. On the New Project wizard screen, select Simple on the left pane and Project on the right pane, as shown in Figure 4-5.

Figure 4-5. Creating a simple project

Click Next. On the subsequent screen, name the project DBUtilityProject (see Figure 4-6).

Figure 4-6. Naming the project

Next, click Finish. WSAD will create the new DBUtilityProject, and you should see it in the Navigator View. Notice that the Workbench automatically switches to the Resource Perspective, and the Perspective's icon appears on the Perspective Bar.

Building the Database Connection

Now, you will create a database connection. To switch to the Data Perspective, select Window ➤ Open Perspective ➤ Other from the main menu. In the Select Perspective dialog, select Data and click OK. Right-click inside the DB Servers View and select New Connection. The Database Connection screen will appear. Enter Con1 in the Connection name field and TECHBOOK in the Database field. Also, enter the user ID and password of the account capable of connecting to the TECHBOOK database. The rest of the fields are already filled in correctly (see Figure 4-7).

New

Database Connection
Establish a JDBC connection to a database.

Connection name:	Con1
Database:	TECHBOOK
User ID:	c6023
Password:	******
Database vendor type:	DB2 Universal Database V7.2
JDBC driver:	IBM DB2 APP DRIVER
Host:	
(Optional) Port number:	
Server name:	
Database Location:	Browse...
JDBC driver class:	COM.ibm.db2.jdbc.app.DB2Driver
Class location:	G:\SQLLIB\java\db2java.zip Browse...
Connection URL:	jdbc:db2:TECHBOOK
Filters...	

Finish   Cancel

Figure 4-7. The Database Connection *screen*

Finally, click Finish. The new connection Con1 is displayed in the DB Servers View. Expand the Con1 connection in the DB Servers View to see the entire hierarchical view of the TECHBOOK database (see Figure 4-8).

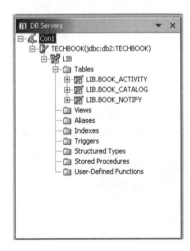

	DB Servers

Con1
  TECHBOOK(jdbc:db2:TECHBOOK)
    LIB
      Tables
        LIB.BOOK_ACTIVITY
        LIB.BOOK_CATALOG
        LIB.BOOK_NOTIFY
      Views
      Aliases
      Indexes
      Triggers
      Structured Types
      Stored Procedures
      User-Defined Functions

Figure 4-8. The TECHBOOK database hierarchical view

The main reason for developing this project is to bring the TECHBOOK database into the WSAD Workbench, so other projects can use it. Now, you need to build the project that will use the TECHBOOK database and include the database processing logic. That is what you will do in the next section.

Creating a New Web Project

Now, you will create the Web project. Switch to the Web Perspective and select File ➤ New ➤ Web Project from the main menu. On the Create a Web Project dialog, enter DBDatasourceProject in the Project name field. Uncheck the Create a default CSS file box in the "Web Project features" section. Make sure that the J2EE Web Project box is selected (see Figure 4-9).

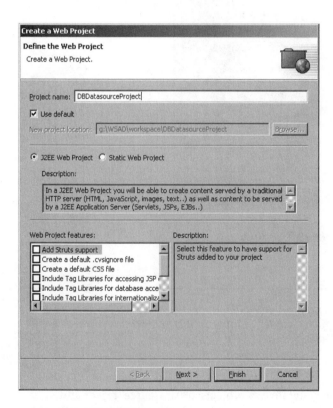

Figure 4-9. Creating a new Web project

Click Next. On the next screen, indicate that you want to create a new enterprise application project and name it DBDatasourceProjectApp. Make sure that the J2EE Level field shows 1.3 (see Figure 4-10).

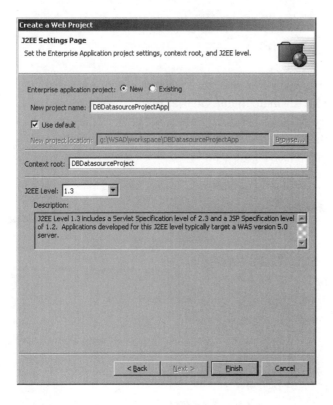

Figure 4-10. Working with the J2EE settings

 NOTE *If you select J2EE 1.2, you will only be able to add J2EE 1.2 modules to the application. You could deploy and run such applications on both application servers: WAS 4.0x and WAS 5.0.*

Click Finish. WSAD will generate two projects: DBDatasourceProject and DBDatasourceProjectApp. In the next section, you will import the TECHBOOK database into your DBDatasourceProject.

Importing the Database in the Web Project

Every project that uses a database needs the database to be imported inside the project's structure. That was the main reason for creating DBUtilityProject—to facilitate the import of the TECHBOOK database in the projects that use this database. To import the TECHBOOK database in your project, switch to the Data Perspective by simply clicking its icon on the Perspective Bar. In the DB Servers View, right-click the TECHBOOK database and select Import to Folder. You should perform this step in any other project that needs to use the TECHBOOK database. That is the main reason for creating the database in a separate project and then importing it in any other project that needs it. On the next screen, click the Browse button and navigate to the DBDatasourceProject (see Figure 4-11).

Figure 4-11. Importing the TECHBOOK database into DBDatasourceProject

Click OK. On the original screen, click Finish. A message will display informing you that the folder does not exist and prompting you to create the folder. Click Yes. This will import the TECHBOOK database into DBDatasourceProject (see Figure 4-12).

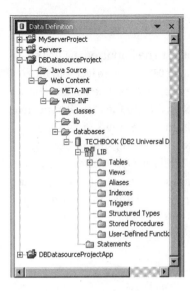

Figure 4-12. Confirming the TECHBOOK import

Building the SQL Statement

Next, you will build the SQL statement and the Web pages that allow the user to enter a database search request and see the database processing results. Switch to the Web Perspective, expand `DBDatasourceProject`, and right-click `Web Content`. Next, select `New` ➤ `Other` ➤ `Web Database` ➤ `Web Pages` (see Figure 4-13).

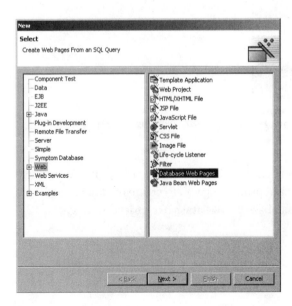

Figure 4-13. Building database Web pages

Click Next. The Database Web Pages wizard opens. Enter apress.wsad.db in the
Java package field and then choose Select Statement in the SQL Statement Type
field and IBM Database Access Java Beans—Master-Details Pattern in the Model field
(see Figure 4-14).

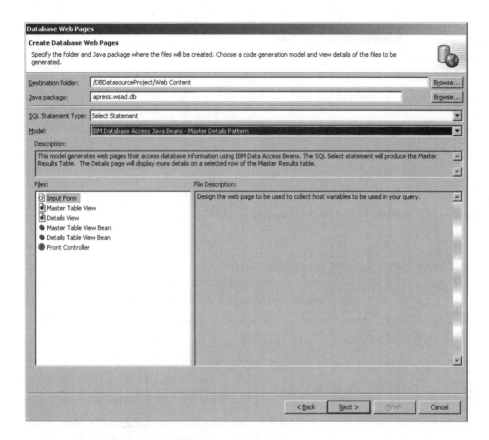

Figure 4-14. Generating the database Web pages

NOTE *Notice the* SQL Statement Type *field. It allows you to select different
types of SQL statements (*select, update, insert, *and* delete*). This feature is
available starting with release 5.0. In the previous releases, only one SQL type
(*select*) was available in this field.*

Click Next. On the next screen, select Be guided through creating an SQL
statement (you will build the SQL statement by using the visual SQL builder tool).
Also, select Use existing database model because you already have the database
and do not need to build a new one. Click the Browse button and navigate to the
TECHBOOK database by extending DBDatasourceProject (see Figure 4-15).

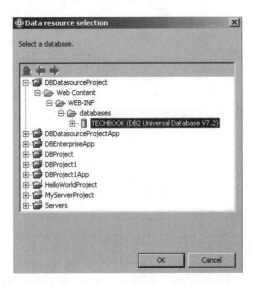

Figure 4-15. Selecting an existing database model

Click OK. You will return to the original screen.

Notice that WSAD allows you to save the SQL statement in a file and reuse it later in other projects. Next, you want to visually construct the SQL statement. Click Next. The next screen is a graphical editor that facilitates visual construction of SQL statements.

Visually Constructing SQL Statements

Expand the database schema by clicking the plus (+) sign in front of LIB. Next, expand Tables. For this project, you need to select only two out of the three available database tables, and the order of the selection is important because it impacts the order of processing in the generated SQL statement. On the left pane, select the LIB.BOOK_CATALOG table first and click the > button to move it to the right pane. Next, select the LIB.BOOK_ACTIVITY table and click the > button to move it to the right pane. The SQL query will be built against these two tables (by selecting certain fields from both tables). The BOOK_CATALOG table will be processed first (see Figure 4-16).

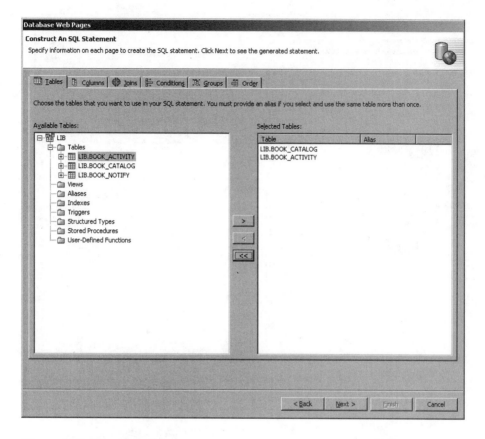

Figure 4-16. Selecting tables

Notice that the screen has several tabs near the top (Columns, Joins, Conditions, and so on). Clicking any of these tabs opens a page that helps you visually construct the corresponding part of the SQL statement. For example, clicking the Columns tab allows you to control the table's columns that will be included in the SQL statement. That is what you want to do, so click the Columns tab, hold the Control key, and highlight the columns that need to be displayed on the output user screen. Click the > button to move them to the right pane (see Figure 4-17).

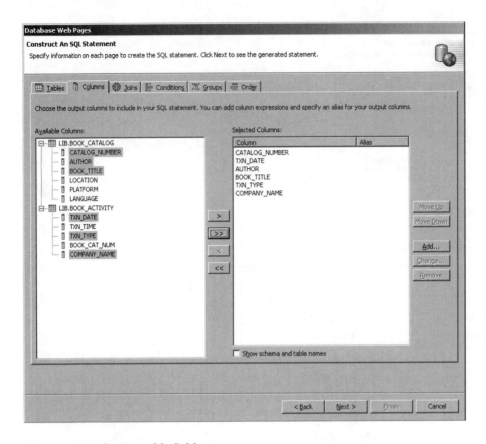

Figure 4-17. Selecting table fields

Next, click the Conditions tab. Set the following for the first row by clicking in each column and then selecting or entering the appropriate values:

1. In the Column field, select LIB.BOOK_CATALOG.LOCATION.

2. In the Operator field, select the not-equal (<>) sign.

3. In the Value field, enter the :location variable name.

4. In the And/Or field, select AND.

Enter the following in the second line:

1. In the Column field, select LIB.BOOK_ACTIVITY.BOOK_CAT_NUM.

2. In the Operator field, select the equals (=) sign.

3. In the Value field, select LIB.BOOK_CATALOG.CATALOG_NUMBER.

Your screen should look like Figure 4-18.

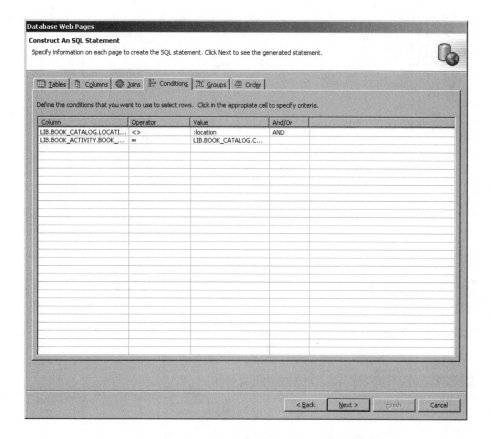

Figure 4-18. Selecting column values

Click Next. The subsequent screen shows the constructed SQL statement (see Figure 4-19).

On this screen, you will search for the books that are currently not in the library possession and return certain fields from both tables. WSAD sets the value of the :location variable to the string Library programmatically. Click the Execute button to test the constructed SQL statement. Click Execute again on the next screen. You will be prompted to give the value to the :location variable. Enter 'Library' using single quotes (see Figure 4-20).

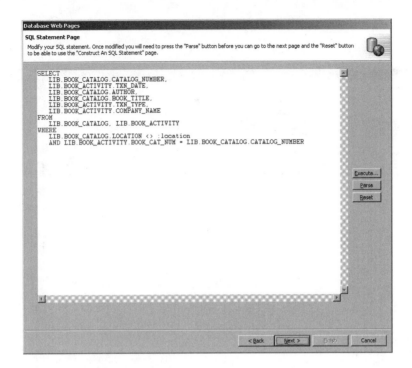

Figure 4-19. The constructed SQL statement

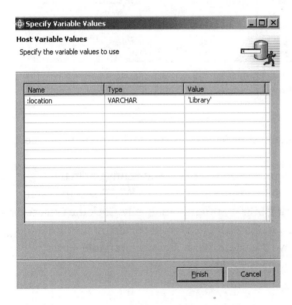

Figure 4-20. Setting the variable value

Click Finish. The next screen shows the SQL processing results (see Figure 4-21).

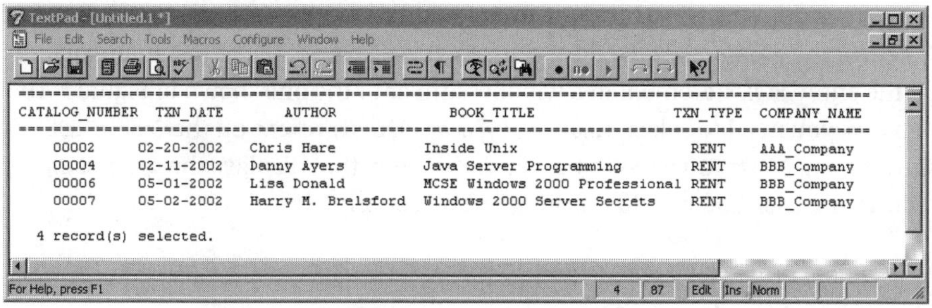

Figure 4-21. The SQL processing results

Click Close to return to the original screen. Then click Next. The subsequent screen prompts you to configure how to connect to the database at runtime. You can select Use driver manager connection, but it is better to select Use data source connection because the Datasource automatically provides a pool of connections. Connections that are no longer used are not closed but are instead returned to the pool of connections and later reused (substantially improving application performance). Select Use data source connection (see Figure 4-22).

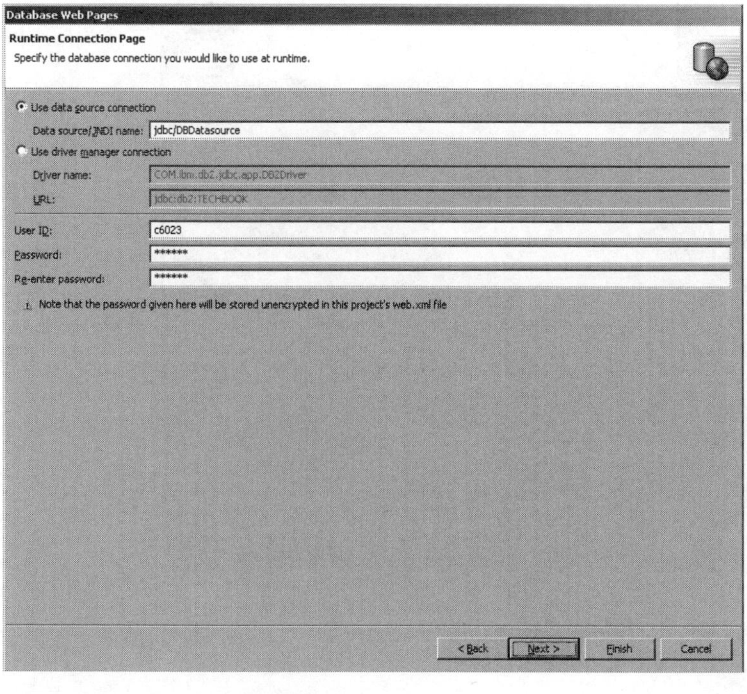

Figure 4-22. Selecting the connection pool

In this section, you visually constructed and tested the SQL statement with the help of the graphical SQL editor screens. It is also possible to just manually type the entire SQL statement in a window similar to the one shown in Figure 4-19. To do this, you need to select Manually type an SQL statement on the Choose SQL Method screen. Next, you want to build a Web screen that displays the processing results to the user. You will do this in the next section.

Building the User Interface Screens

The next screen lets you define certain properties of building Web pages. Specifically, you can specify the error page for displaying processing errors. You can also specify where to store the results. Leave the Request box selected because the user interaction will require a single screen (for the user multiscreen conversation, you should choose the Session option). Finally, select Create a new Front Controller option (see Figure 4-23).

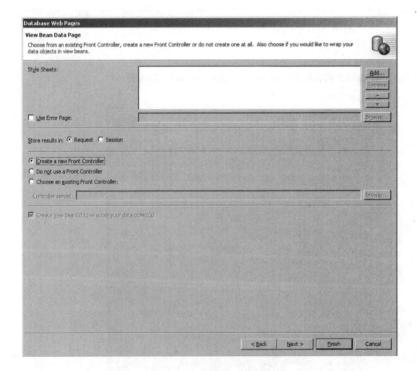

Figure 4-23. The View Bean Data Page *screen*

Click Next. The input screen displays on the next page. The screen that WSAD automatically generates is really only suitable as the skeleton or the first draft of a professional-looking screen. Therefore, you need to customize the WSAD-generated screen. Using creativity, you can greatly improve the crude-looking original screen. That is what you will do in the next section.

Customizing the Input Screen

WSAD-generated screens are highly customizable. To go to the extreme, you can even completely redesign them. Typically, though, you rearrange some fields, change their titles and other attributes, replace the screen title with an image, and so on. There are two tabs, Page and Fields, located at the left side near the bottom of the screen. Clicking the Page tab displays the dialog that allows you to customize the overall screen look and feel (screen title, background and foreground colors, and so on). Clicking the Fields tab displays a dialog for customizing the screen fields.

To customize the input screen, first select the Page tab, then click the Page Title and replace the text Input Form with the text Enter Book Location. Click the next line for the change to take effect. Next, click the Fields tab. Select the LOCATION field, click the Label field and replace the text LOCATION with Book location. Also, increase the field size to 35 and the maximum size to 50. Your screen should look like Figure 4-24.

Figure 4-24. The input screen design

Click Next. The subsequent screen displays the output page. Notice the red stars. They mark the key fields. Click the Page tab. Change the form title to Search Results. Click the Fields tab and change all the column labels by removing the schema name—in other words, the table name prefix. Also, unmark two fields: TXN_DATE and TXN_TYPE (you will not display these fields here but on the Detail page). Your screen should look like Figure 4-25.

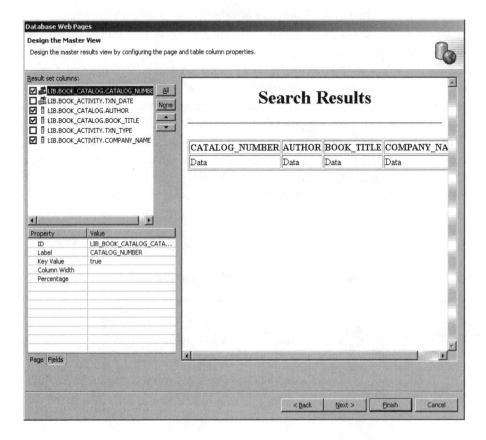

Figure 4-25. The output screen design

Click Next. The subsequent screen is for designing the Detail View output screen. Click the Page tab. Change the form title to Details View. Remove the schema and the table names coded as a suffix in the field names (see Figure 4-26).

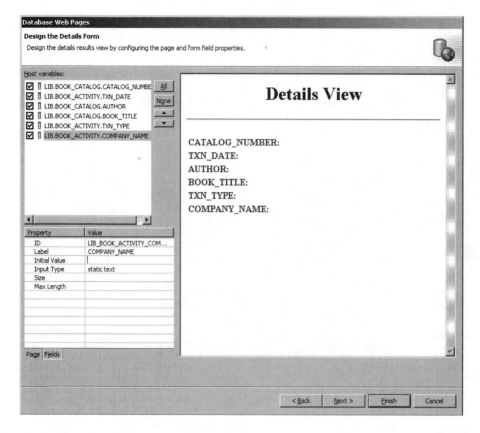

Figure 4-26. The Details Views *page design*

Click Next. This design will build the Model-View-Controller pattern for the Web application. It will be implemented by the several modules listed on the next screen. The system asks you to come up with a common prefix for all these modules that replaces the inconvenient LIB_BOOK_ACTIVITY prefix generated by WSAD. Change the Prefix field to BookSearch (see Figure 4-27).

Click Finish. WSAD will generate six modules: BookSearchController.java, BookSearchDetailsViewBean.java, BookSearchMasterViewBean.java, BookSearchDetailsView.jsp, BookSearchInputForm.html, and BookSearchMasterView.jsp (see Figure 4-28).

Click Finish. Your first database project is practically ready. The still-missing part is the Deployment Descriptor, which you will build in the next section.

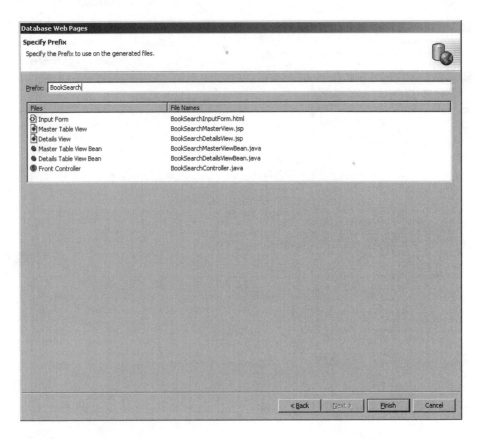

Figure 4-27. Setting the common prefix

Figure 4-28. The generated modules

Setting the Application Deployment Descriptor

WSAD provides several ways of building the Deployment Descriptor. In the J2EE Perspective, you can double-click a project to have its Deployment Descriptor open in the Editor View. Alternatively, you can right-click a project and select Open With ➤ Deployment Descriptor Editor. The third way is to locate the project's Deployment Descriptor file (web.xml located in the WEB-INF folder for Web projects or ejb-jar.xml located inside the META-INF folder for the EJB projects) and double click it.

Now, it is time to set the Deployment Descriptor for your project. In the J2EE Navigator View, right-click DBDatasourceProject and select Open With ➤ Deployment Descriptor Editor.

On the screen that appears, click the References tab. Select Resource at the top of the screen and click the Add button. Then click the Browse button next to the Type field to display the Type Selection screen (see Figure 4-29).

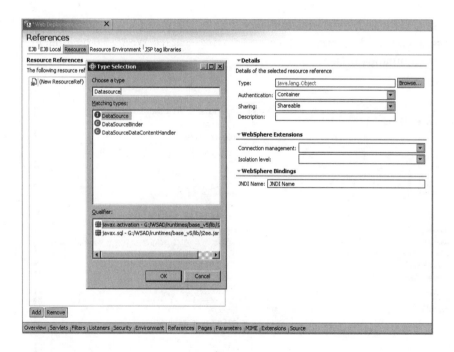

Figure 4-29. Selecting a Datasource

Select Datasource and click OK. On the next screen, change the Datasource name to DBDatasource. Click the Browse button and select the javax.activation.DataSource package. In the "WebSphere Bindings" section, enter jdbc/DBDatasource in the JNDI Name field. In the "WebSphere Extensions" section, select TRANSACTION_READ_COMMITTED (no dirty reads) for the Isolation Level field (see Figure 4-30).

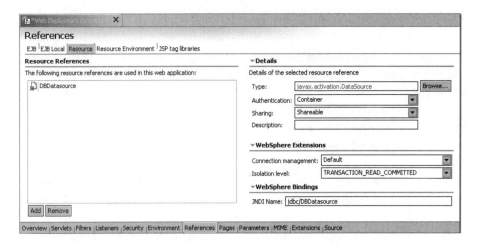

Figure 4-30. Configuring the Datasource

Next, click the Extensions tab and check these two boxes: Automatic Request Encoding enabled and Automatic Response Encoding enabled. WSAD 5.0 no longer does this automatically (see Figure 4-31).

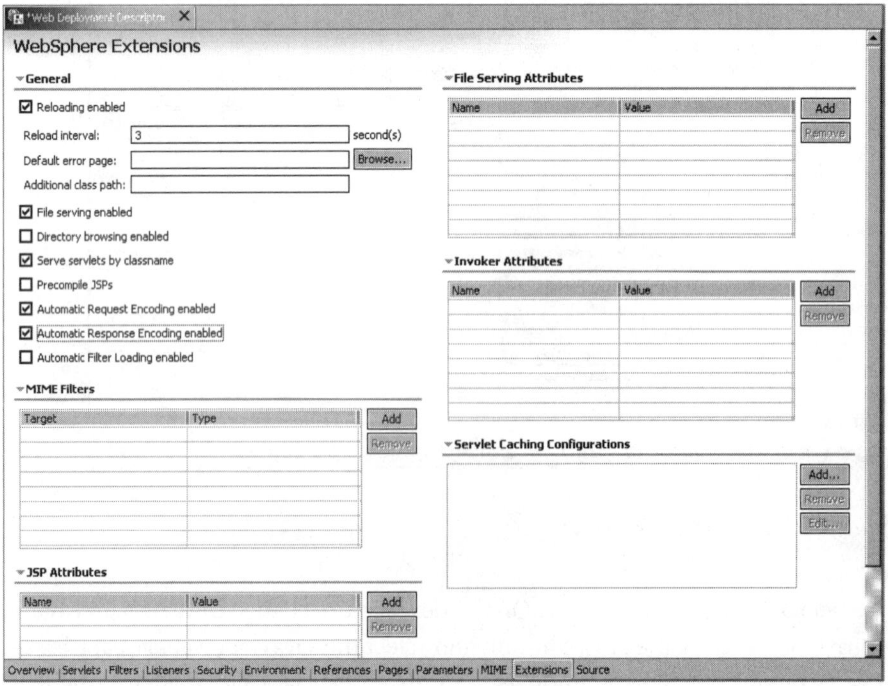

Figure 4-31. Setting WebSphere extensions

Next, click the `Servlets` tab and select `BookSearchMasterView`. Make sure that the `username`, `password`, and `dataSourceName` fields are set correctly (see Figure 4-32).

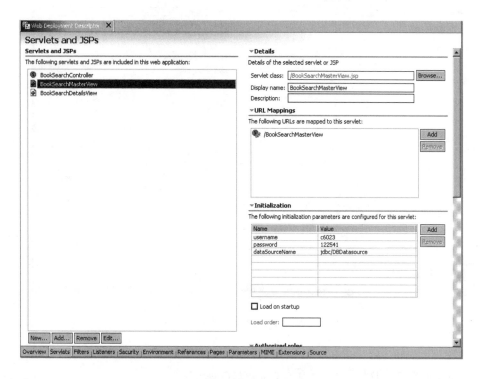

Figure 4-32. Setting a `Datasource` *for* `BookSearchMasterView`

Next, select `BookSearchDetailsView`. Make sure that the `username`, `password`, and `dataSourceName` fields are set correctly (see Figure 4-33).

Save the Deployment Descriptor file and close the editor. Any project that needs to be debugged or simply executed inside the WSAD development environment requires you to set a Unit Test Server (UTS) environment. UTS is actually an embedded WAS provided here for the purpose of the WSAD project's unit testing. Because this unit testing environment closely mimics the runtime environment, WSAD testing is performed under conditions that are close to a real production runtime environment.

This close integration of WSAD and WAS also facilitates future project deployment. Setting UTS requires you to create a separate server project and server configuration. The server configuration is the place where you configure the runtime WSAD environment that is (as mentioned) close to a real production environment. In the next section, you will set the UTS environment for your project so that you will be able to run and test it.

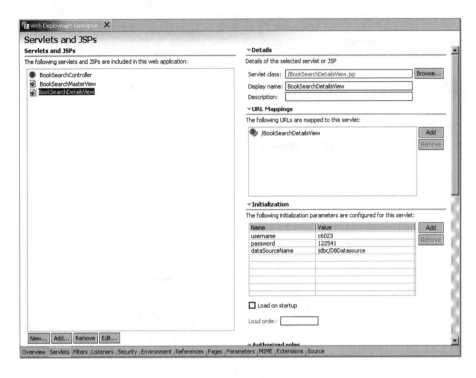

Figure 4-33. Setting the Datasource *for* BookSearchDetailsView

Setting the Unit Test Server Environment

In this section, you will create a new server project and set the server configuration (specifically, you will set the Datasource for the UTS environment). Switch to the Server Perspective and select File ➤ New ➤ Server Project. On the next screen, enter DBDatasourceServerProject in the Project name field (see Figure 4-34).

Finally, click Finish. WSAD will build a new server project called DBDatasourceServerProject. Next, right-click DBDatasourceServerProject and select New ➤ Server and Server Configuration. On the screen that appears, enter DBDatasourceServer in the Server name field. Also, expand WebSphere version 5.0 and select Test Environment in the Server type field (see Figure 4-35).

Finally, click Finish. WSAD will create the server instance and server configuration. In the Server Configuration View, right-click DBDatasourceServer and select Add ➤ DBDatasourceProjectApp to make this server the default server for the DBDatasourceProjectApp application.

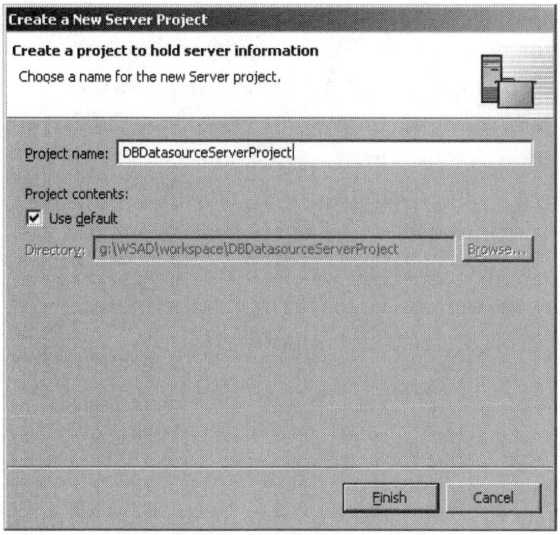

Figure 4-34. Creating the server project

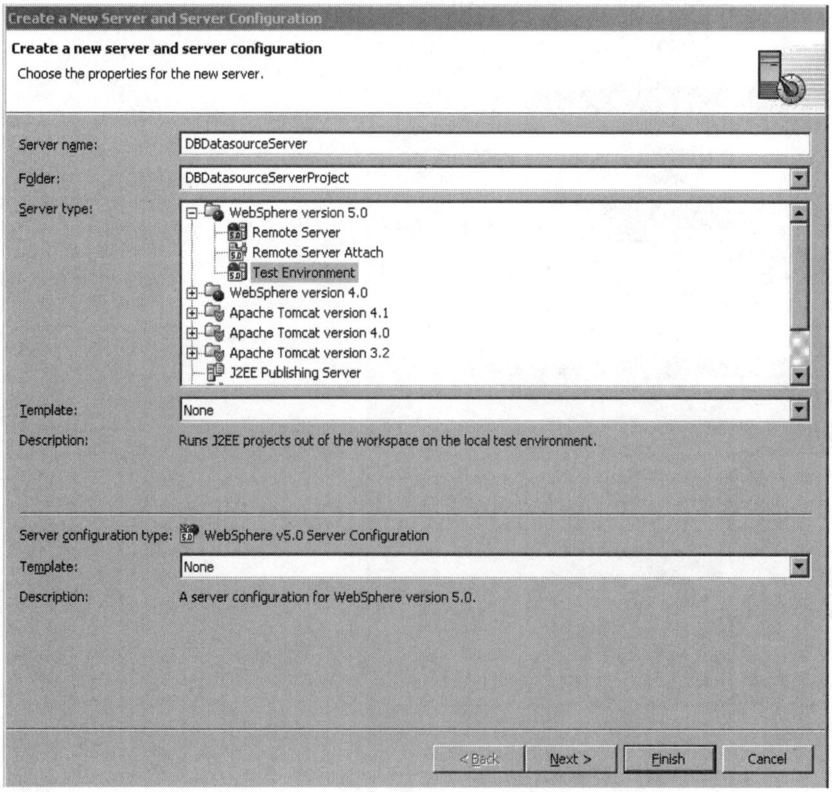

Figure 4-35. Creating the server project configuration

The last step in the process of configuring the server environment is to build the Datasource object for the TECHBOOK database. The advantage of using the Datasource object (instead of directly manipulating the database driver) is that the Datasource object maintains a pool of connections to the underlying database that it represents. When an application that uses a Datasource object closes the database connection, the connection is not physically closed but simply returned to the pool of database connections. Conversely, when an application opens a database connection, an available connection is taken from the pool and reused. That process substantially improves the application performance. In the next section, you will build the Datasource object for your application.

Configuring the Datasource Connection

Under the Server Configuration View, double-click DBDatasourceProjectApp to open the server configuration file in the Editor View. Click the Data Source tab. Highlight Default DB2 JDBC Provider in the JDBC Provider list field and click the Add button near the Data Source list field. On the next screen, select DB2 JDBC Provider and select Version 5.0 data source (see Figure 4-36).

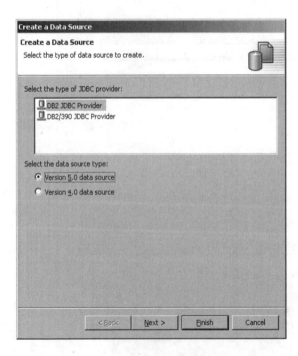

Figure 4-36. Setting server configuration

Click Next. On the subsequent screen, you can configure the Datasource for the server. Enter DBDatasource in the Name field and enter jdbc/DBDatasource in the JNDI name field. Also, uncheck the Use this data source in container managed persistence box (see Figure 4-37).

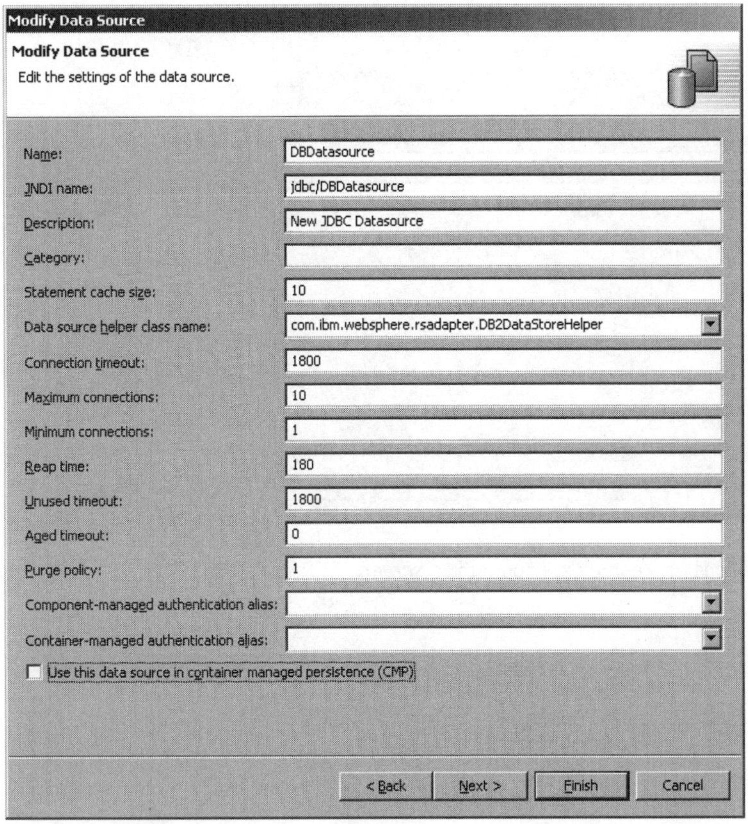

Figure 4-37. Modifying the Datasource

Click Next. On the subsequent screen, select databaseName in the Resources Properties list and enter TECHBOOK as the database name in the Value field (see Figure 4-38).

Click Finish. WSAD will create the new Datasource (see Figure 4-39).

Save the results (click the main toolbar icon that looks like a floppy disk) and click the X button to close the editor. You are ready to test your application.

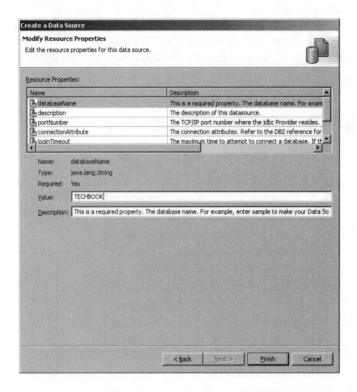

Figure 4-38. The `Modify Resource Properties` *screen*

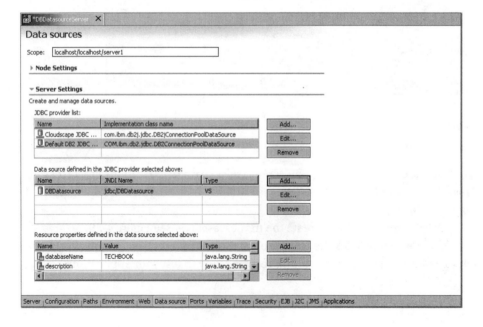

Figure 4-39. The `Datasource` *setting screen*

Testing the Application

In the Server Perspective (the Servers View), right-click the DBDatasourceServer server and select Start (see Figure 4-40).

Figure 4-40. Starting the server

Wait until the server displays the message "Server is ready for e-business." In the Servers View, the ready server will display the status Started. Now, switch to the Web Perspective. Right-click BookSearchInputForm.html and select Run on Server. The Enter Book Location screen will appear. Enter Library in the Book location field (see Figure 4-41).

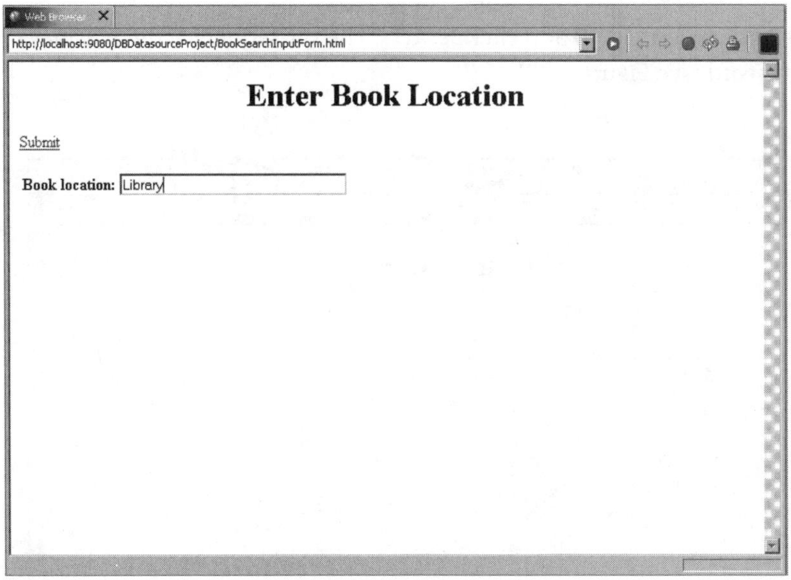

http://localhost:9080/DBDatasourceProject/BookSearchInputForm.html

Enter Book Location

Submit

Book location: Library

Figure 4-41. Testing the project

Click Submit. The next screen shows the processing result (see Figure 4-42).

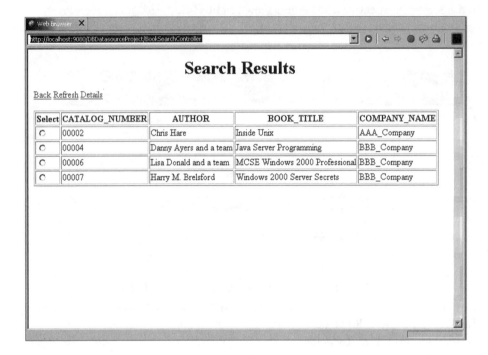

Figure 4-42. The processing results screen

Next, select the first record and click Details. The subsequent screen displays the detailed record (see Figure 4-43).

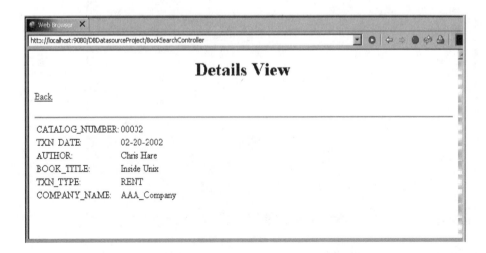

Figure 4-43. The Details View *results screen*

Close the Web Browser View and stop the server. To learn how to deploy this application, refer to the appendix.

Summary

In this chapter, you achieved two results. First, you built the TECHBOOK database that the rest of the book examples will use. Second, you learned how to develop J2EE database-aware applications in the WSAD 5.0 environment. The chapter also discussed the reasons for using the Datasource instead of directly using the database drivers.

In the next chapter, you will start exploring the development of J2EE 1.3 applications.

Part Two

Working with J2EE: The Distributed Application Framework

## CHAPTER 5

J2EE Development

THIS CHAPTER CONCENTRATES on some of the new features of the latest Java 2 Enterprise Edition (J2EE) 1.3 and Enterprise JavaBean (EJB) 2.0 specifications and how you can use them in the WebSphere Studio Application Developer (WSAD) 5.0 and WebSphere Application Server (WAS) 5.0 family of tools. This chapter also includes some advanced topics of J2EE development.

NOTE *You should be familiar with basic concepts of the J2EE technology. J2EE is a large topic that cannot be adequately covered in one chapter. A large number of J2EE books are available; I recommend* Enterprise JavaBeans 2.1 *(Apress, 2003).*

Quick Introduction to J2EE

Developed by Sun Microsystems, J2EE is a component-based framework for developing of server-based enterprise applications. J2EE offers a multitiered distributed application model that provides a multitude of services necessary for enterprise applications: distributed component architecture, remote object execution, network communication, standardized access to databases and other resources, asynchronous messaging, unified security, transaction processing, platform independence, load balancing, and so on.

The multitiered distributed model allows developers to build highly scalable applications by dividing the application logic between multiple machines and executing different parts of application processing on the most suitable processing platforms. A J2EE multitiered application typically consists of four tiers: the client tier, the Web tier, the EJB (business) tier, and the enterprise tier.

NOTE *The enterprise tier can consist of database servers, enterprise messaging, enterprise namespaces, Custom Information Control System (CICS), IBM's IMS-based legacy applications, and so on.*

J2EE applications consist of the following J2EE modules:

- Client modules of the J2EE applications typically run on the client machine in the client container and directly communicate with the EJB tier of the J2EE application. In WSAD, a client module is presented as a client project.

- Web modules—servlets and JavaServer Pages (JSP)—run in the Web container and are typically responsible for the application presentation logic. In WSAD, a Web module is presented as a Web project.

- EJB modules—session, entity, and Message Driven Beans (MDBs)—run in the EJB container and are typically responsible for the application's business processing logic. In WSAD, an EJB module is presented as an EJB project.

All J2EE components (Web, EJB, and J2EE client) run inside their corresponding containers—application server software that provides a necessary interface between the J2EE components and the underlying operating system. Containers represent an environment for providing J2EE services to their components.

Understanding JNDI

You use the J2EE framework for developing distributed enterprise Java-based applications. Components of such applications are typically spread between multiple tiers on the network. Any distributed application needs a mechanism for locating its components regardless of where they live on the network. J2EE's Java Naming and Directory Interface (JNDI) facilitates locating distributed EJB components and calling their interfaces exposed to the EJB clients.

Many directory service packages are available from different vendors, such as Lightweight Directory Access Protocol (LDAP), Sun Microsystem's Network Information Services (NIS+), Microsoft's Active Directory for Windows-based networks, and so on. Each directory package requires a proprietary set of Application Programming Interfaces (APIs)—a situation similar to databases. JNDI is a set of standard (vendor-independent) APIs, classes, and interfaces that allows the J2EE developer to use many proprietary (but JNDI compliant) directory service packages in a standard (vendor-independent) way.

JNDI is a common framework for locating enterprise components (not only EJBs but also remote resources such as databases, enterprise messaging, and so on). By using JNDI, J2EE developers should not be concerned about the underlying specifics of the directory service they use, and their code stays the same if migration between different packages is necessary. The same standardization is achieved in the J2EE environment with the databases by using Java Database Connectivity (JDBC).

Using JNDI for Locating EJB Components

The clients of the EJB components are typically another EJB component, a servlet, a JSP, a J2EE client application, or a stand-alone Java-based application. There are several naming and directory service software packages available.

- LDAP: This is a hierarchical repository of entries and attributes.

- NIS+: This is a naming system developed by Sun. It allows users to access systems on other hosts with a single user ID and password.

- COS Naming Service: This is the CORBA naming service.

- Domain Naming Service (DNS): This is mostly used on the Internet to translate human-readable addresses into binary TCP/IP address.

All these software packages use a different set of APIs and classes. By providing standard APIs, classes, and interfaces, Sun Microsystems made JNDI work the same way as JDBC, Java Message Service (JMS), and other standard framework interfaces. All vendors of naming services that support the JNDI standard can be used via JNDI. WSAD's test server and WebSphere Application Server (WAS) provide a CORBA-based JNDI naming services, which you will use for your development and testing examples in this chapter.

There are several basic steps necessary for locating an EJB component via JNDI. Before using JNDI, the JNDI client needs to specify the context environment properties. That helps the client to build the InitialContext pointing to the JNDI namespace. The context environment is represented as a hashtable that is used as a parameter in the InitialContext class constructor. The following three attributes are provided in the hashtable parameter: context factory class name, location of the server where the naming service is implemented, and security preferences (YES, NO). If the security preference property is omitted, the default is NO. You use different context factory classes for different naming systems.

Listing 5-1 shows the meta-code for constructing the InitialContext for different naming service providers. (For the sake of simplicity, I dropped the try/catch blocks that should surround this logic.)

Listing 5-1. Meta-Code for Constructing the JNDI InitialContext

```
// Import necessary packages
import  java.util.*;
import  javax.naming.*;
import  javax.naming.Directory*;

// Create the InitialContext variable
InitialContext jndiContext = null;

// Create a Hashtable Property Object
Hashtable prop = new Hashtable(2);

// Use the following code for WebSphere-based Naming Service
prop.put(INITIAL_CONTEXT_FACTORY,
    com.ibm.websphere.naming.WsnInitialContextFactory);
prop.put(Context.PROVIDER_URL, "iiop://localhost/");

// Use the following code for LDAP-based Naming Service
prop.put(Context.INITIAL_CONTEXT_FACTORY,
         "com.sun.jndi.ldap.LdapCtxFactory");
prop.put(Context.PROVIDER_URL, "//polaris/o=ibm,c=us");

// Use the following code for the File-based Naming Service
prop.put(Context.INITIAL_CONTEXT_FACTORY,
      "com.sun.jndi.fscontext.RefFSContextFactory");
prop.put(.Context.PROVIDER_URL,
                        "/C:/JNDI-Directory");

// Construct the InitialContext object
jndiContext = new InitialContext(prop)

// Look up for an EJB remote object
Object obj = jndiContext.lookup(JNDI_name_of_EJB_component);

// Returned stub is a generic java.lang.Object that has no idea
// of how to be our home interface. The narrow method allows us to
// cast it to the appropriate type.

// Get the Home Interface of the remote object
MyEJBComponentHome componentHome =
(MyEJBComponentHome)
      PortableRemoteObject.narrow(obj, MyEJBComponentHome.class);
```

```
// Having the Home interface we can call the create() method
// (the container will call the corresponding ejbCreate() method
// to create an object).
MyEJBComponent componentRemote =
    componentHome.create([arguments]);

// Obtain a Remote interface of the EJB component. Having a Remote
// Interface, an EJB client can call the remote
// object's methods.
String catalogNumber = componentRemote.getCatalog_number();

// If an EJB client calls a statefull session bean, always
// clean up when the session bean is no longer needed
// by calling the remove method componentHome.remove();
```

In the WSAD environment, the EJB client that runs inside the container (another EJB component, servlet, or JSP) does not need to prepare the HashTable parameters to create the InitialContext object. WSAD takes care of this automatically. Such EJB clients create the default InitialContext object in the following simplified way:

```
jndiContext = new InitialContext();
```

The EJB 2.0 specification introduced the Local Interface (Local Client View) for EJB components. You will learn about it in detail later in this chapter and build several examples that use Local Interfaces in Chapter 6. For now, I only want to mention that the lookup method for EJB components with the Local Client View are coded differently and the narrow method is not used.

Starting from EJB 1.1, it is recommended that all EJB references be bound to java:comp/env—the JNDI environment context that the application server must maintain. This is only a recommendation and not a requirement. The following lookup code shows how to perform a lookup for the bookCatalog object in the JNDI environment context:

```
Object objRef = jndiContext.lookup("java:comp/env/bookCatalog");
```

Applications that do not run in the container cannot use the java: lookup namespace because it is the container that sets the java namespace for the application. Instead, an application of this type must look the object up directly from the name server. Each application server contains the name Server. System components such as EJB homes are bound relatively to the server root context in that name server. The form of the constructed lookup name depends on whether the qualified name is a topology-based name or a cell-scoped-fixed name.

The following example shows how the topology-based `lookup` name is constructed for the single server `MySingleServer`:

```
Java.lang.Object ejbHome = initialContext.lookup
("cell/nodes/Node1/servers/MySingleServer/com/
myCompany/AccountEJB")
```

The following example show how the topology-based `lookup` name is constructed in the cluster `MyCluster`:

```
Java.lang.Object ejbHome = initialContext.lookup
("cell/clusters/MyCluster/com/myCompany/AccountEJB")
```

The following example shows how the cell-scoped-fixed-name `lookup` name is constructed:

```
Java.lang.Object ejbHome = initialContext.lookup
("cell/persistent/com/myCompany/AccountEJB")
```

For more information, search the WAS 5.0 Info Center for the "Looking Up an EJB with JNDI" topic.

Using the JNDI dumpSpace Utility

WAS provides a JNDI-based utility that allows you to dump the content of the `InitialContext` maintained by WAS. It is typically used to diagnose the naming service–related problem. To run the utility, execute the following command from the command line:

```
<WAS_Install_Directory>/bin/dumpNameSpace.bat [-keyword value]
```

The keywords and values include the following:

- The host name is the WebSphere host whose namespace you want to dump. The default is the local host.

- `-report [short | long | help]`

  - `short` means dump the binding name and bound object type, which is essentially what JNDI `Context.list` provides.

  - `long` means dump the binding name, bound object type, local object type, and string representation of the local object.

  - `help` prints the help information for the command.

Exploring the New Features of the J2EE 1.3 Framework

This section concentrates on three of the most important new features of the J2EE 1.3 release: Local Interfaces, the new model of Container Managed Persistence (CMP) entity beans, and a new type of EJB component—the MDB. In the following chapters, you will see how they are implemented in WSAD 5.0. Chapter 6 presents several examples of using the Local Interface and new model of CMP entity bean. Chapters 9–11 discuss MDBs, and the appendix shows how to deploy the corresponding examples.

Understanding the EJB 2.0 Tier of the J2EE 1.3 Application

The discussion starts with the EJB component Local Interface (also called Local Client View). This is a new feature introduced by the EJB 2.0 specification.

Using a Local Reference to EJB Objects

In addition to providing the Remote Interface (Remote Client View), EJB components can now provide the Local Interface (Local Client View). An EJB client can communicate with an EJB component via the Local Client View in only one situation—when both the EJB client and the corresponding EJB component are *co-located*, meaning they run on the same machine and on the same Java Virtual Machine (JVM). If multiple WAS instances are installed on the same node (machine), the EJB client running on one WAS instance cannot use the Local Client View to communicate with the EJB component that runs under another WAS instance because both components run under different JVMs and they are not co-located.

Therefore, the Local Interface is quite restricted. It is also sensitive to component movement from one location to another because this movement can make the component and its client no longer co-located. On the other hand, the Local Interface provides substantial benefits. The first is performance. Because co-located objects do not need to communicate over the network, a lot of processing is saved here (there is no need to marshal parameters and send them over the network).

Apart from saving resources by eliminating the network communication, the Local Interface provides an additional important advantage. With the Remote Interface, parameters were passed by value. This meant that the remote method receives the copy of the parameter objects and not their reference. There are two implications of this. The first is that the copy of large parameter objects must be sent over the network, which is a resource-intensive process. The second is that the remote method is unable to modify the objects sent as parameters because it deals only with copies of the actual objects.

In contrast, the Local Interface passes parameters by reference, meaning that only a reference of the object is sent to the method, and the method is now capable of modifying the objects it receives as parameters. The performance benefits of the Local Interface are so significant that you need to come up with strong architectural reasons for not using the Local Interface.

One of the J2EE best-practice recommendations is that an EJB client never calls entity beans directly but rather utilizes the Session Facade pattern. The Session Facade is a session bean that implements the business logic and calls multiple entity bean methods necessary for executing the business function. This pattern provides several benefits.

Using Session Facade and Transfer Objects

First, the Session Facade session bean is typically co-located with the entity bean it calls. Because all calls are local here, the interaction is fast even for quite complex interaction logic and multiple method calls. The result of the business process obtained by the Session Facade session bean can be returned to a remotely located client as one network call (which is much faster), and the local client can get the result over the Local Interface. Typically, Session Facade session beans are designed to have both Local and Remote Interfaces, so they can be called efficiently by the local and remote EJB clients.

Second, you typically need to execute the business logic under a single transaction so that the processing results are all committed or all backed out. You achieve this goal by designing the business processing in a way that all entity beans run under a single transaction context of the Session Facade session bean. The alternative (when each entity bean runs under its own transaction context) would lead to a data integrity problem. One entity bean that successfully completed its transaction would update the database, when another entity bean with failed processing would not update the database.

Another widely used J2EE development pattern is to use transfer objects typically designed as JavaBeans. The transfer object allows you to group multiple processing results and to return this single object over the network to the client (instead of returning multiple objects over the network). This technique substantially reduces the network and other overhead and improves the application performance for the Remote Interface of communication. For the clients with Local Views, the performance benefits of this pattern are not so significant, but this is still a clean architectural design that facilitates maintenance and should be used even with the Local Interface in place.

From the EJB client point of view, the Local Interface is similar to the Remote Interface. The EJB component that exposes the Local Interface has a similar basic structure. Instead of the Home Interface, it has a Local Home Interface with the same meaning. Finally, instead of promoting EJB bean methods to the Remote Interface, you promote them to the Local Interface.

Understanding Local and Remote Interfaces

Still, you need to be aware of several differences. The lookup call to locate the object with the Local Interface is slightly different. The following is an example of lookup for the Local Interface (the try/catch block has been removed for simplicity):

```
Javax.naming.Context jndiContext = new InitialContext();
Book_catalogLocalHome catalogLocalHome =
   (Book_catalogLocalHome)
            jndiContext.lookup("javaLcomp/env/ejb/Book_catalogLocalHome");
```

Notice that you do not use the PortableRemoteObject.narrow method. There is no need to use it here because you are not communicating over the network. The second difference is related to the Handle object, which is discussed in the next section.

Setting Local Interface and Conversational Processing

If a business function consists of several user screens, you have to design such a business function as a conversation. In other words, there is a need to maintain the state of conversation between multiple method invocations. On the Web side of the J2EE application, the conversation state is saved in the session object. Objects that can be saved in the session are wrappers of primitive Java types (Integer, Short, Long, Float, Double, and Boolean), String, Date, and any Java object that implements the java.io.Serializable interface.

Other Java objects must be serializable (objects that implement the Serializable interface) to be properly saved in the session object. There are two reasons for this requirement. First, the container can passivate the session (when the container needs to reduce its memory requirements) and subsequently activate it. Second, the session objects can be distributed over the network between multiple machines in the network cluster. The process of swapping the session object out of memory and subsequently bringing it back is done by the container by using the object serialization and converting the state saved in the session to bit-blob for saving it on disk.

Because the remote stub itself cannot be serialized, references to the Home and Remote Interfaces cannot be put in a session. The solution is to use the Handle object, which is a serializable reference to the remote EJB object. The Handle object allows you to re-create an EJB object remote reference. The following code is the example of using the Handle object. Having the remote object reference, you can create a Handle to this object and put it in the session object:

```
Handle catalogHandle = catalogRemote.getHandle();
session.putValue("Catalog_Handle", catalogHandle);
```

To get back the remote reference to the object, get the Handle object from the session and use the getEJBObject method. Note that because anything you get out of the session is java.lang.Object, you must cast the returned object to its proper type, Handle:

```
Handle catalogHandle = (Handle) session.getValue("Catalog_Handle");
Catalog catalogRemote = (Catalog) catalogHandle.getEJBObject();
```

That is how it works with the Remote Interface. Objects that expose the Local Interface are different. Because the network is not involved here, the references to the Local Home and Local Interfaces are special objects that are allowed to be saved in the session. No Handle object is needed, and, actually, no Handle object is even defined for the Local Interface (because no network is involved). You will see an example of saving references to the Local Home and Local Interface objects in the session in Chapter 7.

Using EJB 2.0 Entity Beans

The EJB 2.0 specification made dramatic changes to the CMP entity bean compo-
nents. The extent of these changes is so serious that EJB 2.0 CMP beans are no longer backward compatible with EJB 1.1 CMP entity beans. To handle CMP entity bean migration from EJB 1.1 to EJB 2.0, J2EE vendors are required to maintain two separate types of EJB containers (one for EJB 2.0 and another for EJB 1.1 entity beans).

Understanding EJB 2.0 CMP Entity Bean Persistence Fields

A CMP entity bean is now an abstract class that implements the javax.ejb.EntityBean interface. All persistence fields are now virtual fields (meaning that they are no longer physically present in the CMP class. They are declared by the CMP developer as abstract assessors. The following is an example of the EJB 2.0 CMP class:

```
public abstract class TechLibBook_catalogBean
                       implements javax.ejb.EntityBean
{
 public abstract String getCatalog_number();

 public abstract void setCatalog_number(String newCatalog_number);


       ------------------
       ------------------
       ------------------

}
```

As you can see, a persistant field (catalog_number) is not defined in the class. It is represented by its abstract accessories getCatalog_number and setCatalog_number. Based on this abstract class and the information present in the Deployment Descriptor, the container generates the real CMP entity bean class. What is the advantage of this new arrangement? The main benefit is that now the container has full control of the CMP entity bean (the generated CMP source files are typically hidden from the developer).

Having full control over the CMP entity bean class allows the container to better optimize CMP processing. It no longer has to load the state at the beginning of module execution (or at the beginning of a new transaction), postponing the state load until the first call to one of the getter classes is issued. It no longer has to load the entire state of the bean on the ejbLoad callback method. By controlling the persistence fields, the container now knows which of these fields needs to be updated.

Persistant fields are called *CMP fields*. They can be represented by Java primitive types (int, short, long, float, byte, and boolean) or by the wrappers of Java primitive types (Integer, Short, Long, Float, Bite, and Boolean). In addition, you can use the Java String and Date classes as the CMP fields. They all are serializable objects and map naturally to fields in the relational databases. Again, the serialization requirement for the state field of CMP beans is because the container can passivate and activate CMP beans, and it uses the serialization mechanism to do this.

Understanding EJB 2.0 CMP Entity Bean Dependent Value Classes

In addition, Java objects that implement the serializable interface can also be used as state beans. These types of beans are called *dependent value classes*. Listing 5-2 shows an example of a dependent value class.

Listing 5-2. Dependent Value Class

```
public class Publisher implements java.io.Serializable
 {
    // Abstract accessor methods
    private String publisherName;
    private String publisherAddress;

    // Constructor
    public Publisher (String pubName, String pubAddress)
     {
        publisherName = pubName;
        publisherAddress = pubAddress;
      }
    public String getPublisherName()
    {
      return publisherName;
     }
    public String getPublisherAddress()
     {
      return publisherAddress;
     }
 }
```

Listing 5-3 shows how this class can be set as a dependent value class for the CMP entity bean.

Listing 5-3. CMP Entity Bean with the Dependent Value Class

```
public abstract class TechLibBook_catalogBean
                      implements javax.ejb.EntityBean
{
    // Abstract accessor methods
    public abstract String getPublisherName();
    public abstract String getPublisherAddress();

    // Business method
    public Publisher getPublisher()
     {
        Publisher publisher =
            new Publisher(getPublisherName(), getPublisherAddress())
        return publisher;
}
```

You should use dependent value classes as CMP fields carefully because they do not naturally match the database fields. These types of classes should be mostly used as transfer objects (defined earlier). With Remote Interface parameters passed by value, it makes sense to make these transfer objects immutable because the method that receives them cannot change the original object value. By not implementing the setter method, the transfer objects become immutable.

Understanding EJB 2.0 CMP Entity Bean Relationship Fields

A CMP entity bean can now maintain relationships with other CMP entity beans. Attributes coded within the CMP entity bean that point to other entity beans are called *container relationship fields*. Listing 5-4 shows an example of two CMP entity beans with a relationship.

Listing 5-4. Publisher.java *CMP Entity Bean*

```
public abstract class Publisher implements javax.ejb.EntityBean
 {
   // Abstract accessor methods
   public abstract String getPublisherName();
   public abstract String getPublisherAddress;

   // Constructor
   public Publisher (String pubName, String pubAddress)
    {
      publisherName = pubName;
      publisherAddress = pubAddress;
    }
   public String getPublisherName()
   {
     return publisherName;
   }
   public String getPublisherAddress()
    {
     return publisherAddress;
   }


        ---------------------
        ---------------------
        ---------------------

}
```

The Publisher CMP entity bean exposes the Local Home and Local Interfaces and its getter methods are promoted to the Local Interface.

Listing 5-5 shows how the second CMP entity bean will use the container relationship fields that point to the first CMP entity bean.

Listing 5-5. Book.java *CMP Entity Bean*

```java
public abstract class Book implements javax.ejb.EntityBean
{
  // Persistent relationship fields (CRP)
  public abstract PublisherLocal getHomeAddress();
  public abstract PublisherLocal getPublisherAddress();

  // Business method
  public Publisher getPublisher()
   {
      Publisher publisher =
           new Publisher(getPublisherName(), getPublisherAddress())
      return publisher;
}
```

 NOTE *Only the Local Interface is allowed to expose the relationship fields.*

Based on the abstract classes and information provided in the Deployment Descriptor, the container generates the necessary code and SQL statements needed to persist and navigate the relations. Relationships can be unidirectional and bi-directional and can be one of three types: one-to-one, one-to-many, and many-to-many. The container also takes care of maintaining referential integrity.

In this section, you will see two entity beans that are set in a unidirectional relationship of one-to-many. In this example, you will not go through the entire process of the entity bean development. (Chapter 6 shows detailed examples of the entity bean development.) Here, you will look at the source code of two entity beans and discuss the logic to be written to maintain these two entity beans' relationship. This chapter also discusses the WSAD tools that you should use to establish the entity bean relationship.

The two entity beans are called Book_catalog and Book_activity. The Book_catalog entity bean maintains books available in the library, and the Book_activity entity bean keeps each book-related transaction (companies borrowing and returning books). Of course, each book can have multiple transactions; therefore, the Book_catalog-Book_activity relationship is the one-to-many unidirectional relationship.

 NOTE *You won't be able to actually follow this exercise because the* TechLibEJB *project is not built yet in your environment.*

The goal here is just to show you how it is done in WSAD.

First, you will build the container relationship field between these two entity beans. In the J2EE Perspective, right-click the TechLibEJB project and select Open With ➤ Deployment Descriptor Editor. On the screen that appears, scroll down to the "Relationship 2.0" section and click the Add button. On the next screen, select Book_catalog in the left pane and Book_activity in the right pane (see Figure 5-1).

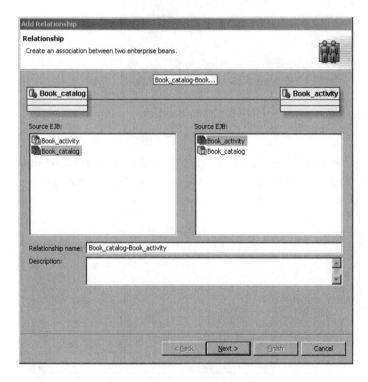

Figure 5-1. Setting an entity bean relationship

Click Next. On the next screen, select Many in the Multiplicity field for the Book_activity entity bean and One in the Multiplicity field for Book_catalog (see Figure 5-2).

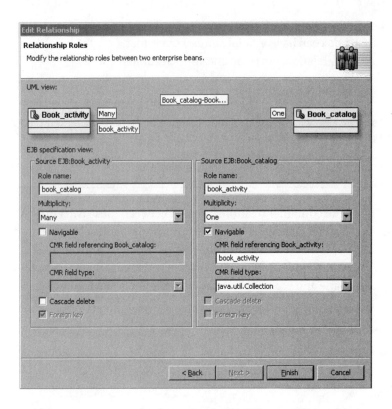

Figure 5-2. Setting multiplicity for the CMP bean relationship

Note the `Cascade delete` field. Checking this field will set the database's Cascade Delete feature. Click `Finish`. Figure 5-3 shows the `Book_catalog-Book_activity` relationship set in the Deployment Descriptor.

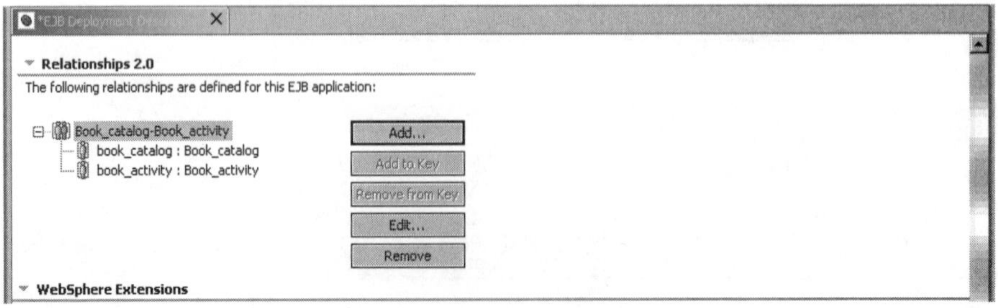

Figure 5-3. Relationship set in the Deployment Descriptor

The wizard also created the necessary EJB references. Click the `References` tab, extend `Book_catalog` bean, and click `EjbLocalRef` (see Figure 5-4).

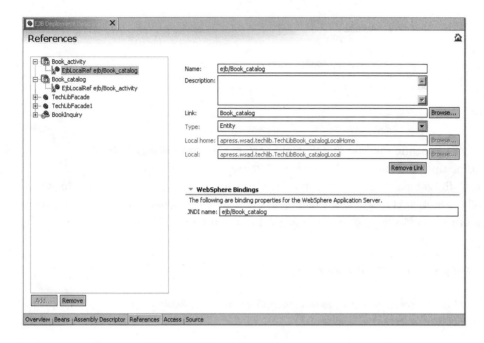

Figure 5-4. Local reference to the `Book_catalog` *CMP bean*

Now, save the results and close the Deployment Descriptor. Next, you need to generate the deployment and Remote Method Invocation Code (RMIC). So, right-click the `TechLibEJB` project and select `Generate` ➤ `Deploy` and `RMIC` code. On the next screen, select `Book_activity` and `Book_catalog` and press `Finish`.

Next, you need to edit the source code. Double-click `TechLibBook_catalog` to open it in the Java Editor View. Note the container relationship field being set by its abstract assessors:

```
public abstract
 TechLibBook_activityLocal getBook_activity();
public abstract void
 setBook_activity(TechLibBook_activityLocal aBook_activity);
```

You add the `addBookActivity` method here. It allows the `Book_activity` entity bean to add the book activity transaction to `Book_catalog` whenever a new book transaction is created:

```
// This method is used by the Book_activity bean to add a new book transaction
// to the Book_catalog whenever a new book transaction is built
public void addBookActivity(TechLibBook_activityLocal bookActivity)
 {
  if(bookActivity != null)
   {
    getBook_activity().add(bookActivity);
   }


 }
```

The second method that you add here, getAllCompanyNames, lists all companies that have this book-related transaction. Notice that this method calls the getBook_activity container relationship field's accessory method to get all the Book_activity beans attached to this Book_catalog bean. This is an abstract method, and its logic is maintained by the container (see Listing 5-6).

Listing 5-6. The getAllCompanyNames *Method*

```
// list all companies that made transactions for this book
public Vector getAllCompanyNames()
 {
  Vector allBookCompanyNames = new Vector();
  Collection allBookActivities = getBook_activity();

  Iterator iterator = allBookActivities.iterator();

   while (iterator.hasNext())
    {
     TechLibBook_activityLocal localBookActivity =
         (TechLibBook_activityLocal) iterator.next();
     String activityCompanyName = (String)
         localBookActivity.getCompany_name();

     // Form the vector to return the results
     allBookCompanyNames.add(activityCompanyName);
    }

    return allBookCompanyNames;
  }
```

You need to make these methods visible to other EJB clients; therefore, you promote these two methods to the Local Interface. In the Outline View, right-click each of these methods and select Enterprise Bean ➤ Promote to Local Interface. Save the update and close the editor.

Next, you need to modify the Book_activity entity bean. Double-click TechLibBook_activity to open it in the Java Editor View. Here, you need to build the ejbPostCreate method. Creating the ejbPostCreate method processing logic is the developer's responsibility. Listing 5-7 shows the ejbPostCreate method code.

Listing 5-7. The ejbPostCreate *Method*

```
/**
 * ejbPostCreate. Whenever a new Book_activity bean is created
 * add it to the Book_catalog bean.
 */
public void ejbPostCreate(String txn_date,
                          String txn_time,
                          String txn_type,
                          String book_cat_num,
                          String company_name
                          )
        throws javax.ejb.CreateException
{

  try
   {
    // Get the LocalReference to this object
    // This can be done only in the ejbPostCreate method (not in
    // ejbCreate method)
    TechLibBook_activityLocal thisBean =
         (TechLibBook_activityLocal)
                   getEntityContext().getEJBLocalObject();

    InitialContext initContext = new InitialContext();
    TechLibBook_catalogLocalHome bookCatalogLocalHome =
            (TechLibBook_catalogLocalHome)
              initContext.lookup("java:comp/env/BookCatalog");

    // Get the Book_catalog bean for the specified book catalog number.
    TechLibBook_catalogLocal bookCatalogLocal =
      bookCatalogLocalHome.findByPrimaryKey( new
                   TechLibBook_catalogKey(book_cat_num));
```

```
    //Add this book transaction to the Book_catalog bean
    bookCatalogLocal.addBookActivity(thisBean);

  } // End of try
 catch(Exception e)
  {
   e.printStackTrace();
   throw new CreateException(e.getMessage());
  }


}
```

Let's discuss the processing logic written in this method. This method ensures that whenever a new book activity is processed, it is also added to the Book_catalog bean. The first statement of the method gets the local reference to this bean:

```
TechLibBook_activityLocal thisBean =
        (TechLibBook_activityLocal)
                   getEntityContext().getEJBLocalObject();
```

This can be done only in the ejbPostCreate method and not in the ejbCreate method (where the local reference to the creating bean is not available until the ejbCreate method is finished). Next, create the default InitialContext and lookup for the Book_catalog bean. You keep the Local Home reference to the Book_catalog bean in the bookCatalogLocalHome variable.

With the Local Home reference, you execute the findByPrimaryKey method using the book_cat_num attribute of the Book_activity bean as a key (it is actually a foreign key to the BOOK_CATALOG table). The result of executing the findByPrimaryKey method is held in the bookCatalogLocal variable. Finally, you add this bean instance to the Book_catalog bean:

```
bookCatalogLocal.addBookActivity(thisBean);
```

This is the end of this example.

Using the FIND and SELECT Methods of CMP Entity Beans

You know that `findByPrimaryKey` is a mandatory method of any CMP entity bean. You can also define customer `find` methods that can return single-entity or multi-entity results. For example:

```
public Book_catalogLocal findByBookTitle(String bookTitle)
throws javax.ejb.FinderException, javax.rmi.RemoteException;
```

This code returns a single reference to the `Book_catalog` Local Interface object. On the other hand, the next example returns multiple references to Local Interface objects. In this case, the returned results should be coded as a collection of objects:

```
public Collection findByPlatform(String bookPlatform)
throws javax.ejb.FinderException, javax.rmi.RemoteException;
```

The `select` methods are similar to `find` methods, but they have several distinct features. The `select` methods are in the format of `select<METHOD_NAME>()`, and each `select<METHOD_NAME>()` declared in the Deployment Descriptor must have a corresponding `ejbSelect<METHOD_NAME>()` method in the implementation class. They also should be declared as abstract methods. For example:

```
public abstract String ejbSelectBookTitle(String bookTitle)
throws FinderException;
```

This `select` method can return the value of a single CMP field or a collection of CMP fields. Several features distinguish `select` methods from `find` methods:

- The `select` methods are not limited to the CMP fields of any specific entity bean; they can query across multiple entity beans declared in the same Deployment Descriptor.

- The `select` methods execute in the transaction context of the business or callback method that invoked them, and the `find` methods execute in their own transaction context.

- The `select` methods are private methods that can be used only inside the CMP entity bean and should never be exposed to a client. They can be called from the `find` method of an entity bean.

Using EJB Query Language

The EJB Query Language (EJB QL) is designed to abstract the data processing language from the relational database structure, making it object oriented and independent of the type of the database (relational or object oriented). The EJB QL syntax is similar to that of SQL, but it introduces many different constructs. EJB QL is now mandatory to use in implementation of the finder methods (you will see some examples of using EJB QL in the development examples in Chapter 7).

A QJB QL statement can consist of three clauses: the SELECT clause, the FROM clause, and the optional WHERE clause. The WHERE clause determines which entity bean types will be included in the SELECT statement. Notice that you process an entity bean and not the database table:

```
SELECT OBJECT(o) FROM Book_catalog AS o
```

In this code, the FROM clause defines that the Book_catalog type will be processed. The identifier variable o located after AS (AS is optional and can be omitted) identifies the Book_catalog entity bean. The identifier variable is not case sensitive. The SELECT clause determines the type of values that will be returned (the Book_catalog entity bean, in this case). The OBJECT operator indicates that the single-entity bean is returned. The SELECT clause can return a single CMP or container relationship field. The following is an example of returning the bookTitle CMP field:

```
SELECT o.bookCatalog.bookTitle FROM Book_catalog AS o
```

If the CMP or container relationship fields have a complex structure, the field at the path end can be as follows:

```
SELECT o.bookCatalog.bookNumber FROM Book_catalog AS o
```

In addition, for the CRM field, the path can lead to a specific CMP field within another entity bean. For example:

```
SELECT o.bookCatalog.bookActivity.txnDate FROM Book_catalog AS o
```

The path must always end with the single type (not a collection type). It is also illegal to navigate across the collection of returned values. If authors is a returned collection of author objects, the following statement is illegal:

```
SELECT o.autors.author FROM Book_catalog AS o
```

To return an element in the collection, you should use the IN operator. For example in the following::

```
SELECT Object(a) FROM Book_catalog AS o, IN(o.authors) AS a
```

This statement returns all author fields in the authors collection. You can use the DISTINCT keyword to ensure that the query does not return duplicate statements:

```
SELECT DISINCT Object(a) FROM Book_catalog AS o, IN(o.authors) AS a
```

You use the WHERE clause to express some search condition that limits the returned results:

```
SELECT OBJECT(o) FROM Book_catalog AS o WHERE o.catalogNumber = "00005"
```

The following is another example of the WHERE clause:

```
SELECT  Object(o) FROM Book_catalog AS o, IN(o.authors) AS a
WHERE a.authorSalary > 50000
```

The a.authorSalary construct will iterate over all the values of the collection authors, selecting those with the indicated authorSalary condition.

Instead of literals, you can use input parameters of the corresponding ejbSelect statement. Say you have the following ejbSelect method that returns the bookLocation field and the corresponding SELECT statement:

```
Public abstract String
 ejbSelectByBookTitleAuthor(String bookTitle,
 String bookAuthor)
Throws FinderException;
SELECT o.bookLocation FROM Book_catalog AS o
WHERE c.bookTitle = ?1 and c.bookAuthor = ?2
```

The ?1 prefix indicates the first parameter, and ?2 indicates the second parameter.

Now let's discuss how to set the find and select methods in WSAD 5.0. Say you want to set a finder method called findByAuthor for the Book_activity CMP entity bean. First, you double-click the bean's Local Home class module (for a bean with the Local Interface) or Home module (for a bean with the Remote Interface) to open the module in the Java Editor View. Second, you add the finder method (see Figure 5-5).

```
EJB Deployment Descriptor        TechLibBook_activity...          X
package apress.wsad.techlib;

import java.util.*;

/**
 * Local Home interface for Enterprise Bean: Book_activity
 */
public interface TechLibBook_activityLocalHome extends javax.ejb.EJBLocalHome
{
    /**
     * Creates an instance from a key for Entity Bean: Book_activity
     */
    public apress.wsad.techlib.TechLibBook_activityLocal create(
        java.lang.String txn_date,
        java.lang.String txn_time)
        throws javax.ejb.CreateException;

    /**
     * Creates an instance from a key for Entity Bean: Book_activity
     */
    public apress.wsad.techlib.TechLibBook_activityLocal create(
        java.lang.String txn_date,
        java.lang.String txn_time,
        java.lang.String txn_type,
        java.lang.String book_cat_num,
        java.lang.String company_name)
        throws javax.ejb.CreateException;

    /**
     * Finds an instance using a key for Entity Bean: Book_activity
     */
    public apress.wsad.techlib.TechLibBook_activityLocal findByPrimaryKey(
        apress.wsad.techlib.TechLibBook_activityKey primaryKey)
        throws javax.ejb.FinderException;

    public Collection findByAuthor(java.lang.String workAothor)
        throws javax.ejb.FinderException;

    public Collection findByBook(java.lang.String workBookCatNum)
        throws javax.ejb.FinderException;

    public java.util.Collection findByCompany(java.lang.String workCompanyName)
```

Figure 5-5. Creating a new filter in a chain

Next, you open the EJB project's Deployment Descriptor. In the J2EE Perspective, you right-click the EJB project and select Open With ➤ Deployment Descriptor Editor. You highlight the CMP entity bean where you want to set the method and scroll down to the "Queries" section. Click the Add button. On the screen that appears, check Existing and specify whether this is a find method or ejbSelect method (see Figure 5-6).

Click Next. On the next screen, you select the type of query that most closely matches the query you want to create. This query appears in the Query statement area where you can modify it. Modify the query and click Finish (see Figure 5-7).

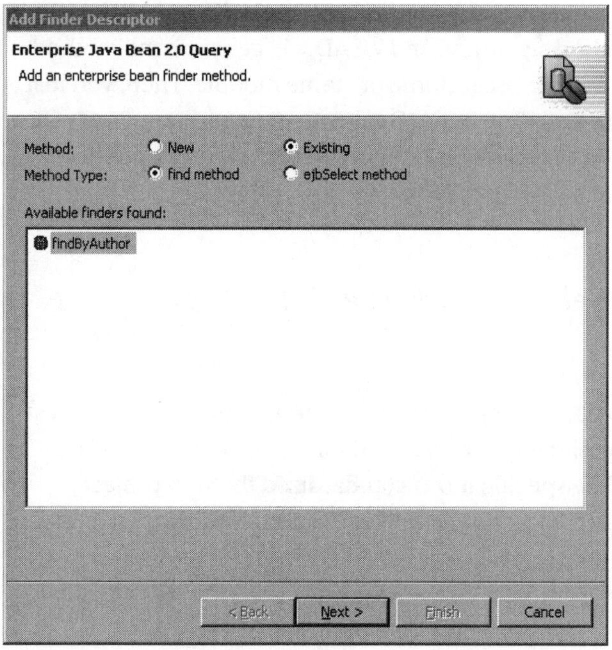

Figure 5-6. Creating a finder *method*

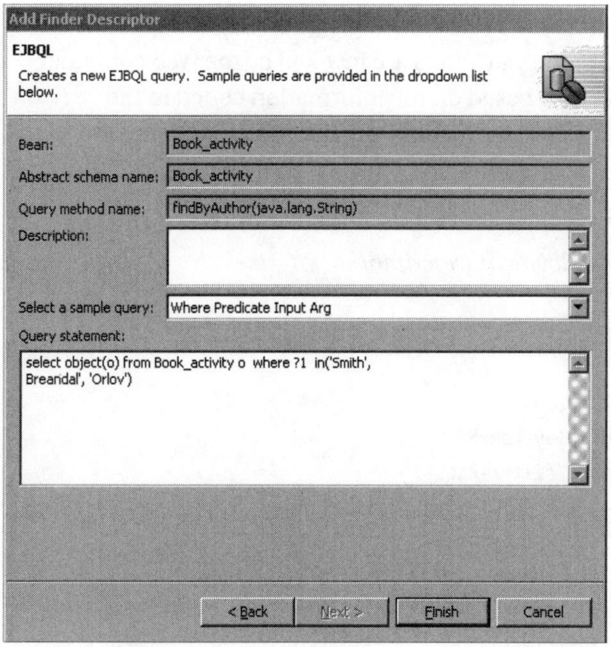

Figure 5-7. Building the EJB QL query

Alternatively, you can indicate that the method is new on the screen depicted in Figure 5-6. Specify the method signature, and WSAD will generate the method and include it in the corresponding Local Home or Home module. Then, you just follow the same steps to set the method in the Deployment Descriptor. (You will use the EJB QL language in the Chapter 6 development examples. Chapter 9 covers the new type of EJB 2.0 bean, the MDB.)

Understanding the Web Tier of the J2EE 1.3 Application

Two main blocks of any Web tier J2EE application are servlets and JSP. In contrast with the EJB 2.0 major changes, the servlets 2.3 and JSP 1.2 specifications introduced only minor changes. The specifications standardized the Web project structure (discussed in Chapter 7 where you will build several Web applications).

Understanding Filters

The servlet 2.3 specification introduced filters that are based on the old "servlet chaining" concept. Filters are preprocessors of the request before it reaches a servlet and postprocessors of the response returned by a servlet.

Filters allow decoupling of some processing logic from the servlet, making it declarative. That has to do with the way filters are invoked by the Web container. The Web container activates filters based on the information coded in the Deployment Descriptor. Listing 5-8 shows the fragment of the Deployment Descriptor related to the filter activation.

Listing 5-8. Fragment of the Deployment Descriptor

```
<web-app>
  <filter>
    <filter-name>MyFilter</filter-name>
    <display-name>MyFilter</display-name>
    <filter-class>MyFilterClass</filter-class>
  </filter>
  <filter-mapping>
    <filter-name>MyFilter</filter-name>
    <uri-pattern>MyFilter</uri-pattern>
    <filter-class>*.html</filter-class>
  </filter-mapping>
</web-app>
```

The <filter-mapping> section of each particular filter controls filter activation. In this example, the Web container is instructed to activate MyFilter any time it receives the Hypertext Transfer Protocol (HTTP) request. This is the way the processing flow works. The Web container intercepts the HTTP request and calls the filter init method where the filter initialization is done. Each filter implements the javax.servlet.Filter interface that defines the three methods shown in Listing 5-9.

Listing 5-9. The javax.servlet.Filter *Filter Interface*

```
void setFilterConfig(FilterConfig config);
FilterConfig getFilterConfig();
Public void doFilter (ServletRequest request,
              ServletResponse response,
              FilterChain chain)
```

The container calls the init and setFilterConfig methods only once to initialize the filter environment. The FilterConfig interface has methods to retrieve the filter's name, its init parameters, and the active servlet context. If the container passes null to the setFilterConfig method, this indicates that the filter is being taken out of service. Next, the container invokes the doFilter method, which is similar to the servlet's service() method. The following is the doFilter method signature:

```
Public void doFilter (ServletRequest request,
              ServletResponse response,
              FilterChain chain)
  Throws IOException, ServletException
  {
  }
```

The FilterChain parameter passed to the doFilter method allows the servlet to instruct the container to invoke the next servlet in the chain, as in the following:

```
Chain.doFilter(request, response);
```

How does the container know the next filter in the chain? It gets the information from the Deployment Descriptor. Listing 5-10 shows a fragment of the Deployment Descriptor and how the filter chain is defined.

Listing 5-10. Fragment of the Deployment Descriptor with the Filter Chain Definition

```
<filter-mapping>
    <filter-name>MyFilter1</filter-name>
    <uri-pattern>MyFilter1</uri-pattern>
    <filter-class>/book/catalog</filter-class>
</filter-mapping>
<filter-mapping>
    <filter-name>MyFilter2</filter-name>
    <uri-pattern>MyFilter2</uri-pattern>
    <filter-class>/book/catalog</filter-class>
</filter-mapping>
```

For every request starting from /book/catalog, a chain that consists of two filters (MyFilter1 and MyFilter2) is defined in this fragment. That is why filters provide a declarative processing. By simply changing the Deployment Descriptor (without changing any program), it is possible to change the processing logic. The processing flow executes all filters in the chain and then passes control to the original resource that has been requested (say, a servlet). When the servlet has done its processing, the control is returned to the chain of the filters but in reverse order (so that the last filter in the chain gets control first). When the chain of filters is executed before the resource, it typically works with the request data. On the way back after the resource finished processing, the chain of the filters works with the response data. If the filter wants to halt the request processing and gain full control of the response, it can intentionally *not* call the next filter.

Filters are typically used to validate HTTP requests, modify Request and Response objects before or after servlet and JSP processing, check client's authorization, logging, and so on. They are mainly used to handle preprocessing and post-processing on the Web tier side of the J2EE application (see Listing 5-11).

Listing 5-11. Logging Filter Code Example

```
import javax.servlet.Filter;
import javax.servlet.FilterConfig;
import javax.servlet.FilterChain;

public class LogFilter implements Filter
  {
  FilterConfig config;
```

```
  public void setFilterConfig(FilterConfig config)
{
    this.config = config;
  }


  public FilterConfig getFilterConfig()
{
    return config;
  }


  public void doFilter(ServletRequest req,
                       ServletResponse res,
                       FilterChain chain) {
    ServletContext context = getFilterConfig().getServletContext();
    long bef = System.currentTimeMillis();
    chain.doFilter(req, res); // no chain parameter needed here
    long aft = System.currentTimeMillis();
    context.log("Request to " + req.getRequestURI()
    + ": " + (aft-bef));
  }
}
```

This filter shows how long it takes to process a request. Let's see how to control filter processing flow in WSAD 5.0. Switch to the J2EE Perspective, right-click some Web project, and select Open With Deployment Descriptor Editor. Click the Filters tab. Click the New button. On the screen that appears, enter MyFilter in the Filter Name field (see Figure 5-8).

Click Next. On the next screen, you can add the init parameters and set the servlet mapping. Click the Add button attached to the Servlet Mappings field (see Figure 5-9).

Select the servlet. This creates the <filter-mapping> entry in the Deployment Descriptor, controlling when this filter chain should be invoked by the container. Click OK. You will return to the original screen. Click Finish. The skeleton of the filter will be generated. Now, when you have the first filter in the filter chain, you can click the Add button and add the next filter to the chain.

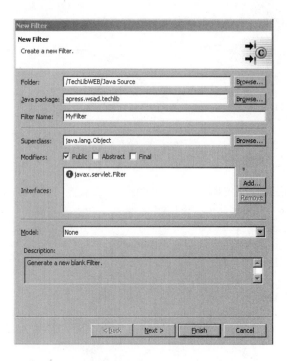

Figure 5-8. Creating a new filter in a chain

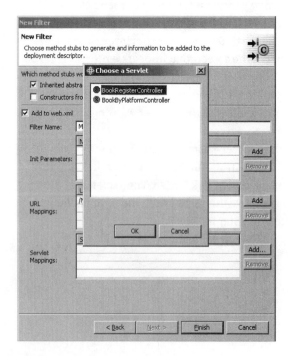

Figure 5-9. Servlet mapping

Understanding HTTP Session Event Listeners

Another new feature that has been introduced by the servlet 2.3 specification is session event listening. A *listener* is an object that is called when a specified event occurs. This is similar to the concept of Swing event listeners. A class interested in observing the session events should implement an appropriate listener interface. The following sections discuss the interfaces provided for processing session events.

Using the HTTPSessionListener Interface

This interface tracks when a new session is created or an existing session is destroyed. It provides the following methods:

```
public void  sessionCreated (HttpSeeionEvent event);
public void  sessionDestroyed (HttpSeeionEvent event);
```

The `HttpSessionEvent` class passed as a parameter to those methods has only one `getSession` method that returns the session being created or destroyed.

A class that implements this interface should include the previous respective methods that will be called by the container when a session is created or destroyed. For this to work, the object to be notified about these events must be registered in the Deployment Descriptor:

```
<listener>
 <listener-class>MySessionListenerClass</listener-class>
</listener>
```

You can do any processing that needs to be done before the session is created or destroyed within the `sessionCreated` and `sessionDestroyed` methods. One example of using this event is to track all new users that use conversation in a Web application.

Using the HTTPSessionActivationListener Interface

This interface tracks session passivation and activation. It provides the following methods:

```
public void  sessionDidActivate (HttpSeeionEvent event);
public void  sessionWillPassivate (HttpSeeionEvent event);
```

A class that implements this interface should include the previous respective methods that will be called by the container before the session will be activated or passivated. For this to work, the object to be notified about these events must be registered in the Deployment Descriptor. This listener can handle sessions that migrate from one server to another. The methods of this interface give an application the chance to persist non-serializable data across different JVMs. The sessionDidActivate and sessionWillPassivate method calls will occur on two different servers.

Using the HTTPSessionBindingListener Interface

This interface notifies an object when it is being placed into a session or removed from the session. It provides the following methods:

```
public void valueBound(HttpSessionBindingEvent event);
public void valueUnbound(HttpSessionBindingEvent event);
```

When an attribute implements this interface, it will be notified when it is added to the session object or removed from the session object.

Using the HTTPSessionAttributeListener Interface

This interface is similar to the HTTPSessionBindingListener interface except that it is intended for any object that can implement it and is notified when the state of the session is changed. It provides these three methods:

```
public void attributeAdded(HttpSessionBindingEvent event);
public void attributeRemoved(HttpSessionBindingEvent event);
public void attributeReplaced(HttpSessionBindingEvent event);
```

The last method is called when one attribute replaces another attribute in a session. The HttpSessionBindingEvent class extends HTTPSessionEvent and adds two methods: getName and getValue.

Listing 5-12 shows an example of a session listener that puts a database connection in the servlet context, making it available to all servlets in the application. The listener closes the connection before the servlet context is closed.

Listing 5-12. Fragment of the Listener Code

```
public class MyConnection implements ServletContextListener
 {
  public void contextInitialized(ServletContextEvent e) {
    Connection con = // create connection
    e.getServletContext().setAttribute("con", con);
  }

  public void contextDestroyed(ServletContextEvent e)
   {
    Connection con = (Connection) e.getServletContext().getAttribute("con");
    Try
     {
       con.close();
     }
    catch (SQLException ignored)
     { } // close connection
   }
}
```

The MyConnection listener class must be registered in the Deployment Descriptor as a listener. The container creates an instance of the listener class and uses introspection to determine the listener interface the class implements:

```
<listener>
    <listener-class>
        MyListener
    </listener-class>
</listener>
```

Understanding ServletContext Event Listeners

The listeners concept is also applicable to the ServletContext events. The idea is similar to the session events. A class interested in observing the ServletContext events should implement an appropriate listener interface. The ServletContextListener interface is provided for processing ServletContext events. The interface has two methods:

```
void contextInitialized(ServletContextEvent event);
void contextDestroyed(ServletContextEvent event);
```

The first method is called when a Web application is first ready to process a request. The second method is called when the ServletContext is about to be closed by the container. The ServletContextEvent class passed to those methods has one method, getServletContext, that returns the context being initialized or destroyed.

Understanding Character Encoding

This improvement is important for processing foreign languages that are different from Western European languages. Character encoding maps bytes to characters. If a request is submitted—say, in Japanese—a servlet needs to know how to process the request parameters. By setting a proper charset, it knows how to do it:

```
Req.setCharacterEncoding ("Shift_JIS");
// Now, read parameters in Japanese
String bookTitle = req.getParameter()
```

Understanding JAR Dependence

Application classes are loaded at runtime by the JVM classloaders. Classloaders impact the visibility of classes. Each separately deployed application is assigned a separate classloader. Therefore, separately deployed WAR and EJB applications are unable to see each other's classes. Before the EJB 2.0 specification, J2EE did not fully standardize how application components could share common code. That left a lot of flexibility to J2EE vendors, which led to many proprietary interpretations and the implementation of class visibility.

After the EJB 2.0 specification, class visibility (and the associated issue of classloaders) has finally been standardized. All classloaders are organized in a hierarchy. Each EAR file (application level) has its own classloader. The EJB classloader is a child of the EAR classloader. All EJB JAR classes are loaded by a single classloader.

Each Web module gets its own classloader, and all Web classloaders are children of the EJB classloader. This makes all EJB classes visible to the Web applications, which is what allows the Web classes to function as EJB clients. From the structure of a Web project, you know that classes placed in the WEB-INF/lib directory are locally visible to all classes of this Web application.

To place a JAR file in the WEB-INF/lib directory, right-click the Web project in the J2EE Perspective and select Properties. On the screen that appears, click Web Library Projects. Click the Add button and navigate to JAR project to be included in the list. All JAR projects listed here are treated as JARs in the WEB-INF/lib folder (see Figure 5-10).

Figure 5-10. Including a JAR file in the `WEB-INF/lib` *folder*

Click OK. On the same dialog, you can specify other projects in the Workbench that this Web application needs to access. Click the `Project References` link; the next screen presents a list of projects in the Workbench available for selection (see Figure 5-11).

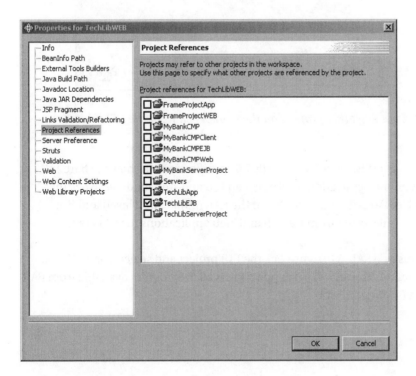

Figure 5-11. Accessing other projects on the Workbench from the Web project

To specify other projects referenced by the EJB project, right-click the EJB
project and click the Project References link. The next screen presents other
projects in the Workbench that can be referenced by this project (see Figure 5-12).

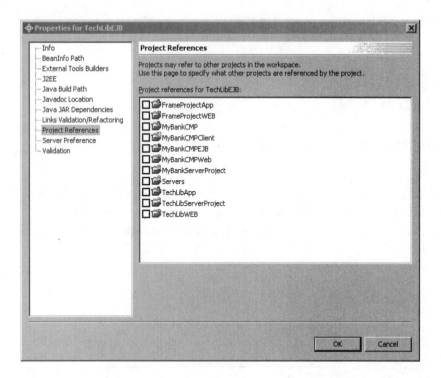

Figure 5-12. Accessing other projects on the Workbench from the EJB project

Still, the biggest issue before the EJB 2.0 specification was how to share JAR
files located on the application level between EJB and Web modules. Now, that
issue is resolved. You place the JAR file in the EAR (application level) and use
the MANIFEST.MF file available in the EJB and Web applications to indicate the
dependencies.

To do this in WSAD 5.0, right-click the EJB project and select Open With JAR
Dependency Editor. The screen that appears lists all the JAR files available from EAR
for selection (see Figure 5-13).

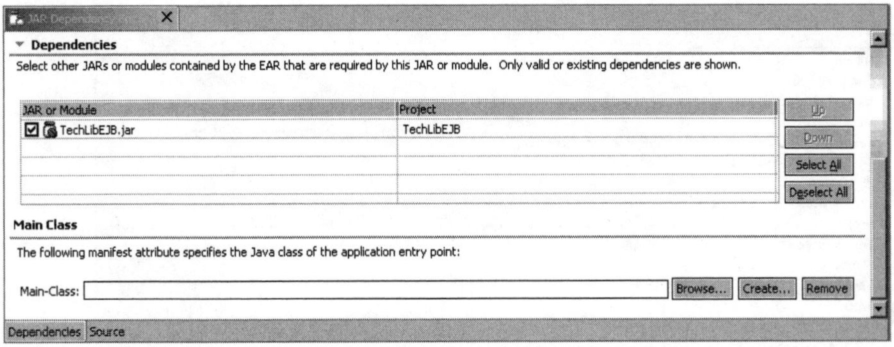

Figure 5-13. Specifying dependent JAR files for the Web project

Use similar steps to specify dependent JAR files for the EJB projects (see Figure 5-14).

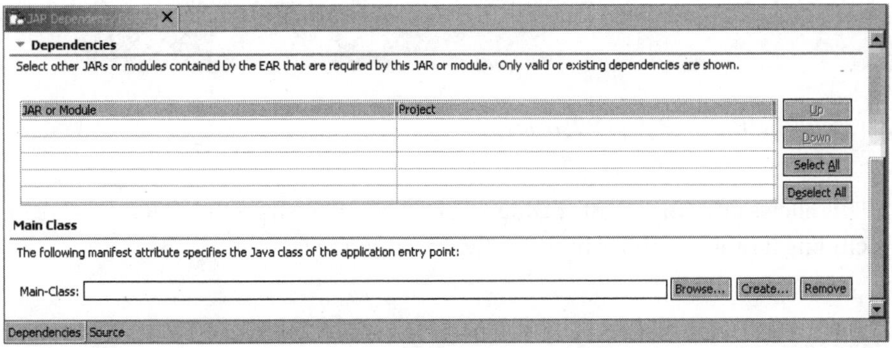

Figure 5-14. Specifying dependent JAR files for the EJB project

Another way of setting JAR-dependent files is right-clicking the Web or EJB project and selecting Attributes. On the page that appears, click Java JAR Dependencies. Select the JAR file on which this Web or EJB project depends. Selected files will be included in the Manifest CLASSPATH (see Figure 5-15).

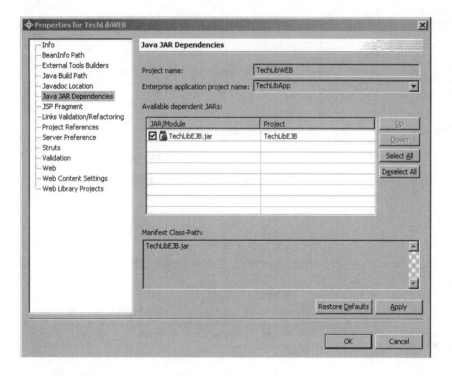

Figure 5-15. Setting JAR dependencies

This allows all components inside an application to share this JAR file (instead of including it multiple times in the individual modules).

Understanding Classloaders

This section discusses how classloaders work in the WSAD 5.0/WAS 5.0 environments. In the J2EE 1.3 specification, classloaders are hierarchically organized. This is how it is done in WebSphere 5.0: At the top is a global classloader (which is actually a Java system classloader). This classloader searches classes to be loaded in the CLASSPATH environment variable. On the next level is the WebSphere-specific classloader. It is responsible for loading necessary WebSphere classes. This classloader searches for classes based on the ws.ext.dirs environment variable.

The application classloader is located on the next level and is a child of the WebSphere-specific classloader. The EJB classloader is located below the application classloader and is a child of the application classloader. All classes used inside the EJB module are linked inside the EJB JAR file. Web classloaders are located below the EJB class loader and are children of the EJB classloader. The Web classloader searches for classes to be loaded in two directories: WEB-INF/classes and WEB-INF/lib.

The classloader hierarchy is set in a parent-child relationship. Children classloaders can delegate a search for classes to their parent classloaders (but not the
other way around). In other words, the direction is always from children to parents.
The sequence of the search depends on the Delegation Mode. A classloader can
have Delegation Mode turned ON or OFF.

Java system classloader and WebSphere-specific classloaders have Delegation
Mode turned ON. The rest of the classloaders have Delegation Mode turned OFF. Therefore, an effective search is from application classloader to Java system classloader
to WebSphere classloader. After a class is loaded by a classloader, any new classes
that this tries to load will reuse the same classloader.

For each application server, you can set the application classloader policy:
SINGLE or MULTIPLE. This setting controls the application isolation level. When the
SINGLE policy is selected, a single application classloader loads classes for all applications and their modules. Effectively, applications are not isolated from each
other. When the MULTIPLE policy is selected, then each application receives its own
classloader, which is used for loading that application's EJB modules, dependency
JAR files, and shared libraries. Effectively, applications are separated from each
other.

To set this policy in WSAD 5.0, double-click the server configuration to open it
in the Editor View. Then, click the Configuration tab. You should see the "Server
Settings" section, which allows you to select the SINGLE or MULTIPLE values (see
Figure 5-16).

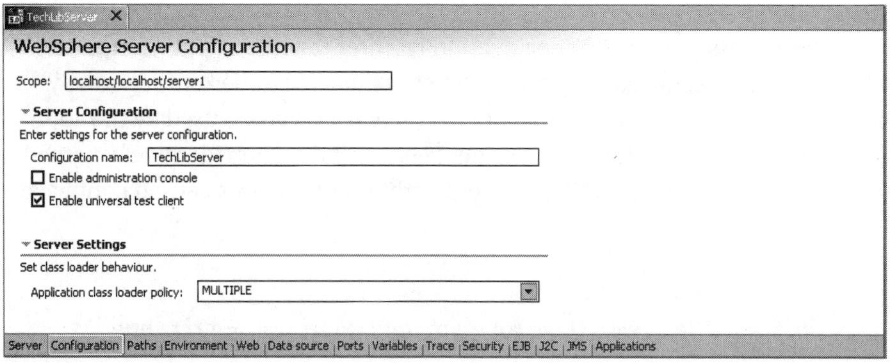

Figure 5-16. Setting policies

When the Web module policy is set to APPLICATION, the application classloader
will be loading the Web module classes. On the other hand, if the Web module
policy is set to MODULE, then each Web module receives its own classloader. If the
application classloader policy is SINGLE, then there are two additional classloader
settings: PARENT_FIRST and PARENT_LAST.

PARENT_FIRST causes the classloader to delegate the loading of classes to its parent classloaders before attempting to load the classes from its local path. PARENT_LAST causes the classloader to attempt loading classes from its local CLASSPATH before delegating the class loading to its parent; this allows an application classloader to override classes that exist in the parent classloader and use its own classes. To set it in WSAD 5.0, double-click the server configuration to open it in the Editor View (if it is not opened yet). Then, click the Application tab. You should see the section that allows you to set the Classloader mode and WAR classloader policy (see Figure 5-17).

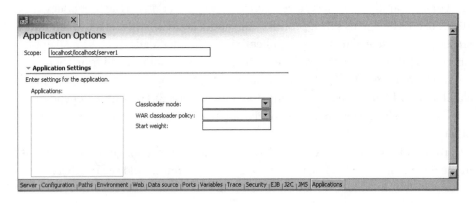

Figure 5-17. Setting the classloader policy and WAR classloader mode

In addition, the servlet 2.3 specification requires that the application classloaders and classloaders used by the server containers must be kept separately. This ensures that application classes are not able to see classes used by the application server. In the past, this was the source of conflicts when identically named classes or classes of the same packages but of different versions caused conflict at runtime.

Understanding the WSAD Development and Runtime Environments

WSAD has two environments: development and runtime. During development, you need to make sure that the WSAD tools that build the project have access to all the required resources. To do this, you right-click the EJB or Web project and select Properties.

On the screen that appears, select Java Build Path. There are four tabs at the top of the screen. The Source tab displays a page that allows you to specify additional folders that WSAD will use as a source folder. The Projects tab displays a page that allows you to include necessary projects in the Java Build Path. The Libraries tab displays a page that allows you to include additional libraries in the Build Path. You can include JAR files present in the Workbench and external JAR files (located outside the Workbench). You can also include environment variables that point to additional JAR libraries. The Order and Export tab displays the page that allows you to control the order of library in the Build Path (see Figure 5-18).

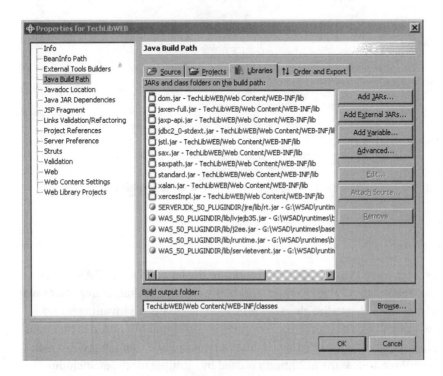

Figure 5-18. Setting the development environment

The Build Path constructed here is used by the WSAD development environment only and is completely meaningless for the runtime environment. At runtime, the server has no idea about the project and its environment. The server deals with the deployed EAR application file and its EJB and Web parts.

Therefore, a separate setting is required for the runtime environment. You set this on the server configuration. Switch to the Server Perspective and double-click the server that is attached to your application project (to open it in the Editor View). On the screen that appears, click the Paths tab (see Figure 5-19).

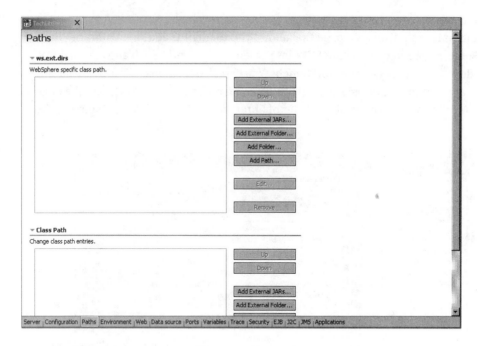

Figure 5-19. Setting the runtime environment

This screen allows you to add JAR libraries to the Java standard CLASSPATH and/or the WebSphere CLASSPATH. You probably remember that adding your own application-related files to the global CLASSPATH has many disadvantages and should be avoided. The best practice is to put the additional JAR libraries that your Web module requires in the WEB-INF/lib directory or include them in the EJB JAR file for the EJB module. If the JAR library is used by multiple modules, include them in the EAR (application level) and use the JAR Dependence screen to set them in your module's MANIFEST CLASSPATH variable.

Processing Errors

Servlets 2.2 introduced three request attributes that facilitate the creation of error pages:

```
javax.servlet.error.status_code    (an integer telling the error status code)
javax.servlet.error.exception_type
(a class instance indicationg the type of exception)
javax.servlet.error.error_message    (a string telling the exception message)
```

Still, you are missing two valuable parts of information: the exception stack trace and the Uniform Resource Identifier (URI) of the servlet that caused the problem. Add them to the Request object:

```
javax.servlet.error.exception    (a throwable object thrown by exception)
javax.servlet.error.request_URI (the URI of the servlet caused this problem)
```

Now the error page servlet can display all necessary data on the error page. Listing 5-13 shows the fragment of the error servlet code.

Listing 5-13. Error Page Servlet Source Code

```
import java.io.*;
import javax.servlet.*;
import javax.servlet.http.*;

public class ErrorPageServlet extends HttpServlet
{
  public void doGet(HttpServletRequest req, HttpServletResponse res)
                            throws ServletException, IOException
  {
    res.setContentType("text/html");
    PrintWriter out = res.getWriter();

    String errorCode = null, errorMessage = null, exceptionType = null,
                                              requestURI = null;
    Object statusCodeObj, errorMessageObj, exceptionTypeObj;
    Throwable errorException;

    // Retrieve the three possible error attributes, some may be null
    statusCode = req.getAttribute("javax.servlet.error.status_code");
    errorMessage = req.getAttribute("javax.servlet.error.message");
    exceptionType = req.getAttribute("javax.servlet.error.exception_type");
    errorException = (Throwable)
        req.getAttribute("javax.servlet.error.exception");
    requestURI = (String) req.getAttribute("javax.servlet.error.request_uri");

    if (uri == null) {
      uri = req.getRequestURI(); // in case there's no URI given
    }
```

```
    // Convert the attributes to string values
    if (statusCodeObj != null) statusCode = statusCodeObj.toString();
    if (errorMessageObj != null) errorMessage = errorMessageObj.toString();
    if (exceptionTypeObj != null) exceptionType = exceptionTypeObj.toString();

    // The error reason is either the status code or exception type
    String errorReason = (statusCode != null ? statusCode : exceptionType);

    out.println("<HTML>");
    out.println("<HEAD><TITLE>" + reason + ": " + errorMessage +
                "</TITLE></HEAD>");
    out.println("<BODY>");
    out.println("<H1>" + erroReason + "</H1>");
    out.println("<H2>" + errorMessage + "</H2>");
    out.println("<PRE>");
    if (erroException != null) {
      errorException.printStackTrace(out);
    }
    out.println("</PRE>");
    out.println("<HR>");
    out.println("<I>Error accessing " + requestURI + "</I>");
    out.println("</BODY></HTML>");
  }
}
```

Of course, the servlet must be registered as the application error page in the Deployment Descriptor:

```
<web-app>
    <error-page>
        <exception-type>
            javax.servlet.ServletException
        </exception-type>
        <location>
            /servlet/ErrorPageServlet
        </location>
    </error-page>
</web-app>
```

Follow these steps to set up this servlet as an exception processing servlet in WSAD 5.0: In the J2EE Perspective, right-click the Web project and select `Open With Deployment Descriptor Editor`. Click the `Pages` tab. Locate the "Java Exception Types" section. Click the `Add` button. On the screen that appears, select `javax.servlet.ServletException` in the `Exception Type` field. Enter your `ErrorPageServlet` servlet in the `Location` field. Click `OK`.

The remaining sections discuss several EJB and Web development topics that are not new in the J2EE 1.3 specifications but are important to understand.

Understanding XForms

Starting from release 5.0, WSAD supports Extensible Hypertext Markup Language (XHTML). Currently, this new technology has not been finalized, and no major Web browsers support it. Therefore, XHTML does not currently provide much benefit, except enforcing a strict HTML tag syntax code format. But XHTML is the base for XForms—the next-generation HTML-like language for developing Web pages. XForms uses an Extensible Markup Language (XML) tag language; it supports development of more sophisticated Web pages and can use namespaces. It has been announced that the XHTML 2.0 specification will introduce XForms. For more information about XForms, please read the "Understanding XForms" article by Nicholas Chase (`http://www-106.ibm.com/developerworks/web/edu/wa-dw-waxforms-i.html`).

Creating a Frameset

Framesets allow you to present complex multiple screens in a form convenient to the user. In this section, you will build an Internet site of a fictitious company that provides investment services. Specifically, it maintains several portfolios with investment recommendations. Let's create a new Web project called `FrameProjectWEB` that is part of the new application project `FrameProjectApp` (see Figure 5-20).

Click `Next`. On the next page, enter the new application project name as `FrameProjectApp` (see Figure 5-21).

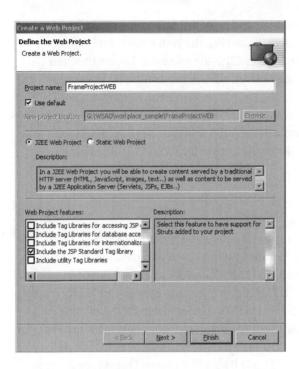

Figure 5-20. Setting up a new Web project

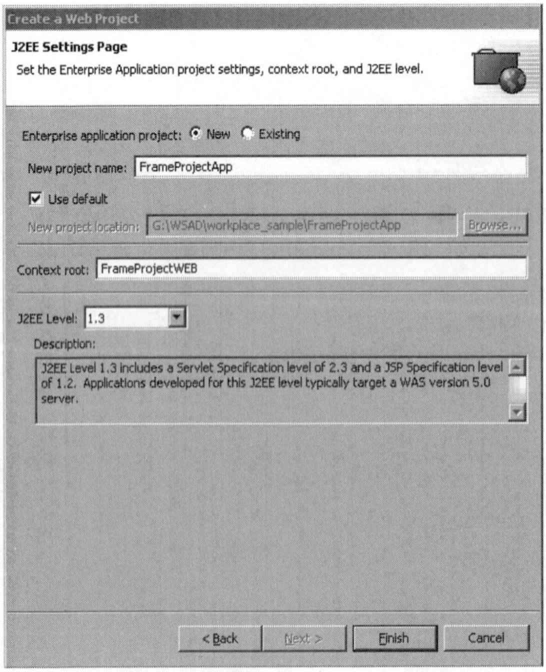

Figure 5-21. Setting up a new application project

Click Finish. WSAD will create two new projects (FrameProjectWEB and FrameProjectApp). Next, you will create a new HTML page. Right-click the Web Content folder and select New HTML/XHTML File. On the next page, enter index.html in the File Name field (see Figure 5-22).

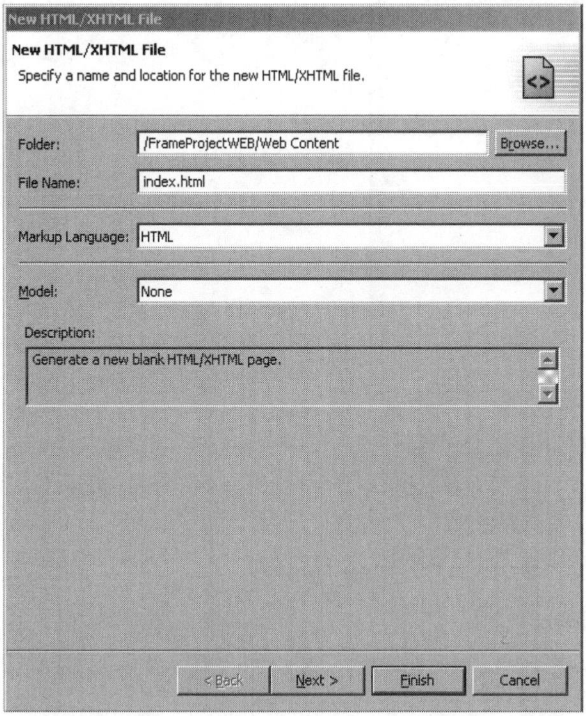

Figure 5-22. Building a new HTML page

Click Finish. WSAD will create a new HTML page called index.html and open it in the Page Editor View. Next, you create a new folder to store the frameset files. Right-click the Web Content folder and select New Folder. Name this new folder Menu (see Figure 5-23).

Click Finish. The index.html file opens in the Page Editor View. Make sure you are on the Design page. Remove the text "Place index.html content here." From the main menu, select Frame Split Frame Split Vertically. On the Split Frame dialog, select In the frameset parent, which means that index.html will be the file that contains the frameset instead of becoming a file called into a frameset (see Figure 5-24).

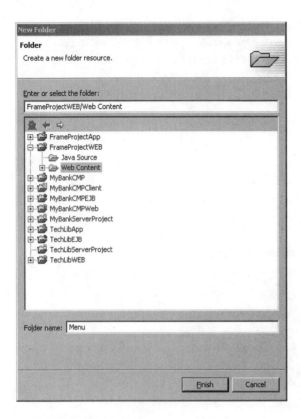

Figure 5-23. Building a new folder

Figure 5-24. Building a new folder

Click OK. You will see a vertical bar splitting your frameset in two vertical frames. Save the results. WSAD created two placeholder pages called newpage1.html and newpage2.html. Save the files by selecting File Save All. On the Save As dialog, replace the newpage1.html name with catalog.html. Click OK. The next Save As dialog will appear. Replace the newpage2.html name with main.html. Click OK.

Move the vertical bar to the left so that your screen will look like the screen depicted in Figure 5-25.

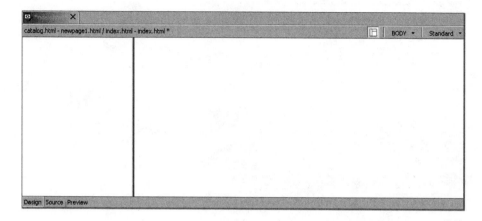

Figure 5-25. The frameset

Click the Links tab. You should see the structure of the frame (see Figure 5-26).

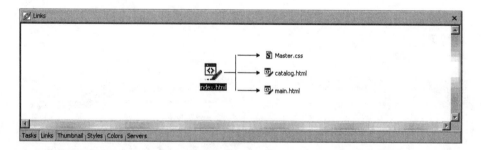

Figure 5-26. The structure of the frameset

You can find a ready-made HTML file to be displayed in the frameset in the Downloads section of the Apress Web site (http://www.apress.com). Copy all files into some temporary directory on your machine (say, c:\Temp). Now, select Import from the main menu. On the screen that appears, select File System and click Next. On the next screen, click Browse and navigate to the c:\Temp directory. Click the Select All button to import all the files in the subdirectory. Check the Overwrite existing resources without warning box and keep the rest of the fields as they are (see Figure 5-27).

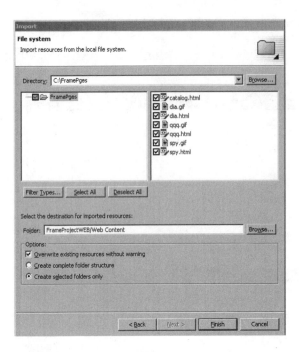

Figure 5-27. The copied files displayed in the frameset

Next, click Finish. Then, click the Preview tab. You should see the screen in Figure 5-28.

Figure 5-28. The already-made frameset page

Click the QQQ link in the left frame. The QQQ portfolio screen will display (see Figure 5-29).

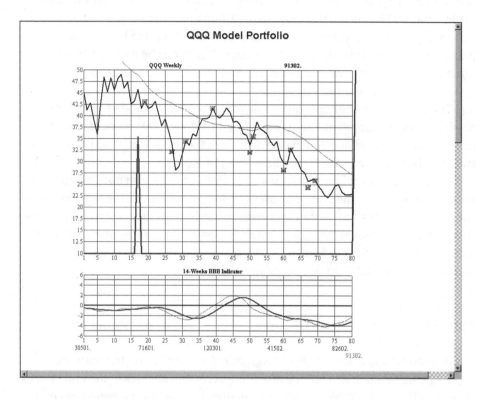

Figure 5-29. The QQQ portfolio screen

Try displaying other portfolios to see how the frame layout works. This is the end of the frame-building example.

Developing Thread-Safe Servlets

If the servlet implements the `SingleThreadModel` interface, the container operates such a servlet in one of two ways:

- **Instance pooling**: The container maintains a pool of servlet instances, and for each request, the container invokes a servlet instance from the pool. After processing is complete, the servlet instance is returned to the pool.

- **Request synchronization**: Only a single instance of the servlet is maintained by the container, and the container synchronizes multiple requests to the same servlet.

Both types of processing consume substantial server resources and should be avoided for applications with many concurrent users. Servlet programmers who don't use the `SingleThreadModel` interface should understand that they are effectively dealing with servlets that run in a multithreaded environment. This means that multiple service requests will be executed by multiple servlet threads. The immediate concern is the class-level variables. If they can be updated by multiple threads, it is the developer's responsibility to make the processing thread-safe by synchronizing access to such variables.

The same consideration is applicable to the `service` method. If there is processing inside the `service` method that is not thread-safe, this block of code needs to be synchronized. However, never synchronize the `service` method itself because you effectively will be in the `SingleThreadModel` processing.

Another point of concern is the session object, which is also not synchronized. If there is a possibility that the same user can access and modify the same attribute concurrently, making the session processing thread-safe is the responsibility of the developer. Concurrent access of session attributes from the same user can happen if the user screen is built in frames. Finally, some collection objects such as `Vector` and `SET` are thread-safe and do not require serialization.

Managing EJB Transactions

A *transaction* is an undivided set of tasks (called a *unit of work*) that must be successfully completed. If at least one task is unsuccessful, all tasks of the unit of work must be rolled back. Local transactions run under a local resource manager on the same machine. Global Java Transaction API (JTA) or two-phase commit transactions involve tasks executed under coordinated efforts of different transaction managers, and these tasks typically span multiple machines. An example of a JTA transaction is accessing multiple databases or a combination of a database and a messaging system.

EJB components can manage the transaction context themselves (bean-managed transactions) or delegate this responsibility to the container (container-managed transactions):

- Session beans can use either container-managed transactions or bean-managed transactions.

- Entity beans use container-managed transactions.

- Web components (servlets) use bean-managed transactions.

Container-managed transactions are controlled by the container and are the easiest way to execute applications within a transactional context. Furthermore, it is suitable in most cases. CMP and BMP entity beans must use container-managed transactions. WSAD and WAS support the following six types of EJB transactions:

Required: The transaction is required to run the application. If a client invokes a bean method in a transaction context, that context is passed to the bean. If a nontransactional client invokes a bean method, a new transaction context is created by the EJB container and committed before the method returns.

Mandatory: If a nontransactional client invokes the bean method, the container throws the `java.jtx.TransactionRequired` exception.

Supports: The client runs within a transactional context, it is passed to the bean. It is okay if the client is not part of the transaction.

RequiresNew: A new transaction will always be created by the container. If a client runs within a transaction, it is suspended and later renewed.

NotSupported: If a client that invokes a method bean has a transaction context, the transaction will be suspended and resumed after the method execution.

Never: If the client calls a bean method from within a transaction context, the container throws the `java.rmi.RemoteException` exception. If the client calls a bean method from outside a transaction context, the container behaves in the same way as if the `Not Supported` transaction attribute was set. The client must call the method without a transaction context.

To set the transaction type, right-click your EJB project and select `Open With Deployment Descriptor Editor`. Click the `Assembly Descriptor` tab. In the "Container Transaction" section, click the `Add` button. On the screen that appears, select one or more EJB bean to set its transaction properties (see Figure 5-30).

Click `Next`. On the next screen, select the type of transaction in the `Container transaction type` field and the corresponding methods of the selected EJB beans that should be assigned this transaction type (see Figure 5-31).

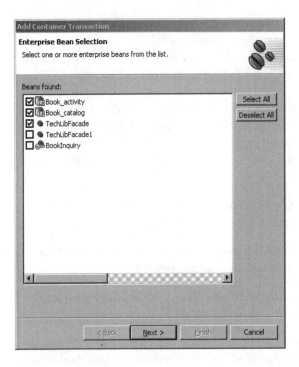

Figure 5-30. Setting transaction properties for EJB beans

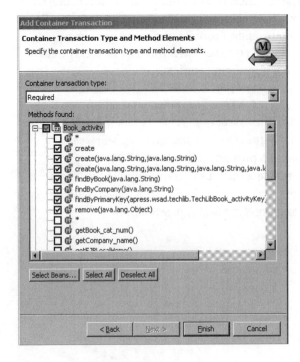

Figure 5-31. Setting transaction properties for EJB bean methods

Click Finish. Repeat the same steps until you have assigned all methods their transaction types.

 NOTE *You can assign a selected transaction type to all bean methods by selecting the asterisk (*) from the list of bean methods.*

Session beans can manage themselves in their transaction context. The stateless session bean can control the transaction for one method only, where the stateful session beans can reuse the transaction context across the methods. In addition, the bean-managed transaction type can be set for the entire class and not for individual methods. To enable a session bean (or servlets) to use the bean-managed transaction, you complete the following two steps:

1. You use the Application Assembly tool and set the Transaction Type attribute to Bean (instead of Container).

2. You write code that uses the javax.transaction.UserTransaction object to explicitly control the transaction demarcation boundaries. Listing 5-14 shows the code snippet.

Listing 5-14. Code of the Bean-Managed Session Bean

```
...
import javax.transaction.*;
...
public class BeanManagedSessionBean implements SessionBean
{
 private SessionContext sessionContext = null;
 ...
 public void setSessionContext (SessionContext ctx)throws EJBException
 {
   sessionContext = ctx;
 }
 ...
 public void processTransaction(int arg1)
   throws FinderException,EJBException
 {
   UserTransaction userTran = (UserTransaction)initCtx.lookup(
        "java:comp/UserTransaction");
```

```
...
// Manage transaction bounderies
userTran.begin ();
creditCardObject.ProcessPayment(payment1);
 creditCardObject.ProcessPayment(payment2);
userTran.commit ();

...

}
...

}
```

Notice that you get the UserTransaction object by using the JNDI lookup method.

Using the Entity Bean Commit Option

The entity bean's Commit Option determines how the state data is loaded to the database or stored in state variables. This option also controls how entity beans are loaded and removed from the cache. Commit Option has a substantial entity bean performance implication and should be carefully considered. The following sections describe the types of Commit Option that entity beans can have.

Understanding the Cached Bean Option

This option requires that an entity bean instance have exclusive access to its data. When the transaction commits, data is written to the database (in other words, ejbStore is called). Because the instance has exclusive access to data, the instance data does not need to be reloaded (in other words, there is no ejbLoad call) at the beginning of the next transaction. Concurrent client requests for the same data are queued by the container.

No other applications can access the data. Concurrency is reduced, but the overall performance improves. This option could be quite dangerous, however. Imagine that at the beginning, there was only one application accessing the data, and this option was set. Several years later, another application is developed that accesses the same data. If at that time no one pays attention that this option was set originally, data integrity will be compromised.

Understanding the Stale Bean Option

It is assumed that no single application has exclusive access to data. When the transaction commits, the ejbStore method is called. Because there is no exclusive access to data, the ejbLoad method is called at the beginning of the next transaction. In the case of concurrent requests, the container assigns a different instance of the entity bean for the second transaction. Concurrency is better in this situation than with the previous option, but more resources are consumed (the extra ejbLoad call and extra instance of the entity bean in memory).

Understanding the Polled Bean Option

No exclusive access to data is assumed here (which is the same as in the previous option). When a transaction commits, the ejbStore method is called and the data is written to the database. The entity bean instance does not stay active in memory but is returned to the pool of instances. The ejbLoad method is called at the beginning of each transaction, so both the ejbLoad and ejbStore methods are called during the life cycle of a transaction.

In addition, the ejbActivate is called at the beginning of each transaction, and the ejbPassivate method is called at the end of each transaction. Both ejbActivate and ejbPassivate are expensive calls depending on the location where they are stored. This option has a potential for less memory usage (in the previous option, entity bean instances remain active in memory after the end of the transaction but are still associated with the same client).

If the same client makes another call, it will reuse the same entity instance. However, a call for the same entity data from another client will be performed by a new instance of the entity bean. After a transaction is committed, the instance of the entity bean is removed from memory as a result of a timeout. Therefore, with a high level of concurrency, the stale bean option could easily consume all available memory.

In contrast with the stale bean option, the polled bean option reduces the memory usage because an instance of entity bean is immediately removed from memory at the end of each transaction. For the stale bean and polled bean options, WSAD performs no database locking and no transaction serialization. Instead, each transaction creates its own copy of entity bean instance. The underlying database handles all locking.

To summarize, the cached bean option provides the best performance and resource utilization, but it can be used only when exclusive access to data from one application is guaranteed. The stale bean option is better than the polled bean option when there is a relatively low level of concurrent processing. The polled bean option is better than the stale bean option when there is a high level of concurrency. In addition, it is desirable for the entity bean to be loaded from the fast storage.

To specify the Commit Option, right-click your EJB project and select Open With Deployment Descriptor Editor. Click the Beans tab. Select the EJB bean and find the "Bean Cache" section. The Activate at field specifies the point at which the bean is activated and placed in the cache. Once means that the bean is activated when it is first accessed and is passivated at the container discretion. Transaction means that the bean is activated at the start of a transaction and passivated (removed from the cache) at the end of the transaction. ACTIVITY_SESSION is bound to the session activity.

The Load At field specifies when the state is loaded from the database. Activate means that the state is loaded at the beginning of transaction and implies exclusive access to data. Transaction means that the state is loaded at the start of the transaction, and it implies shared access to data. In addition, the Enable optimistic locking box controls the selection of pessimistic or optimistic locking. Table 5-1 shows how to set the entity bean Commit Option.

Table 5-1. Transaction Isolation Level

OPTION	ACTIVATE AT FIELD	LOAD AT FIELD
Cached bean	Once	Activation
Stale bean	Once	Transaction
Polled bean	Transaction	Transaction

Figure 5-32 shows an example of setting Commit Option to the polled bean option for the Book_catalog entity bean.

On the Beans page of the Deployment Descriptor, the "Local Transaction 2.0" section provides an IBM extension to the standard J2EE Deployment Descriptor that allows you to control certain local transaction properties (see Figure 5-33).

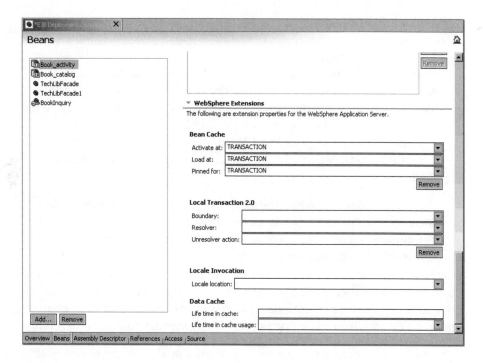

Figure 5-32. Setting Commit Option

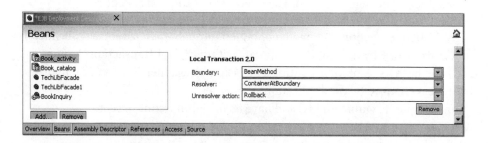

Figure 5-33. The "Local Transaction 2.0" section

The following are additional properties that you can set to control the transaction context:

The Boundary field determines the duration of a local transaction context. When this field is set to ActivitySession, then the local transaction must be resolved within the scope of any ActivitySession in which it was started. If no ActivitySession context is present, then it must be resolved within the same bean method in which it was started. When the field is set to BeanMethod, then the local transaction begins when the method begins and ends when the method ends. This is the default.

The Resolver field specifies how the local transaction is to be resolved before the local transaction context ends: by the application through user code or by the EJB container. The ContainerAtBoundary option means that the container takes responsibility for resolving each local transaction. The user code does not have to handle local transactions. The Application option means that the user code must either commit or roll back the local transaction. If this does not occur, the runtime environment logs a warning and automatically commits or rolls back the connection as specified by the Unresolver action setting.

The Unresolver action field specifies the action that the EJB container must take if resources are uncommitted by an application in a local transaction. This setting is applicable only when Resolution control is set to Application. Rollback is the default action. The alternative is the Commit action.

All JDBC connections, when first obtained through a getConnection call, have AutoCommit = TRUE by default. If you operate within a Local Transaction Context (LTC) and have its resolution-control set to Application, then AutoCommit remains TRUE unless changed by the application.

If you operate within an LTC and have its resolution-control set to ContainerAtBoundary, then the application should not touch the AutoCommit setting. The WAS runtime sets the AutoCommit value to FALSE before work begins and then commits or rolls back the work as appropriate at the end of the LTC scope.

When using a connection within a global transaction, upon first use of the connection, the database ignores the AutoCommit setting so that the transaction service that controls the commit and rollback processing can manage the transaction—regardless of the user changing the AutoCommit setting. After the transaction completes, the AutoCommit value returns to the value it had before the first use of the connection. Therefore, even if the AutoCommit value is set to TRUE before the connection is used in a global transaction, you need not set the value to FALSE because the database ignores the value. In this example, after the transaction completes, the AutoCommit value of the connection returns to TRUE.

If you use multiple distinct connections within a global transaction, all work is guaranteed to commit or roll back together. This is not the case with the LTC scope. Within LTC, work done on one connection commits or rolls back independently from work done on any other connection within the LTC (see Listing 5-15).

Listing 5-15. Setting the AutoCommit *Option for LTC Transactions*

```
public void addAmount(int fromAcct, int toAcct, double amt, DataSource ds)
 throws CreateException, RemoteException
 {
    Connection con = ds.getConnection(user, password);

    // Set autocommit to false
  con.setAutoCommit(false);

    try
     {
       --- Some database processing ----
       con.commit();
       cin.close();
     }
catch(Exception e)
    {
       con.rollback();
    }
}
```

Listing 5-16 shows a code fragment for the JTA transaction.

Listing 5-16. Setting the AutoCommit *Option for JTA Transactions*

```
public void addAmount(int fromAcct, int toAcct, double amt)
 throws CreateException, RemoteException
 {
     ----- Some code here -----
    UserTransaction userTran = (UserTransaction) ejbContext.getUserTransaction();
    try
     {
       userTran.begin();
       ------ processing ----
       userTran.commit();
 }
catch(Exception e)
 {
  userTran.rollback();
 }
}
```

Another IBM extension to the standard J2EE Deployment Descriptor is the Lifetime in cache option. This value is set in seconds and indicates how long the cached data is to exist beyond the end of the transaction in which the data was retrieved. This might avoid another retrieval from persistent storage if the same bean instance were to be used in later transactions. If your application uses CMP beans in which the underlying data changes infrequently, you might gain significantly better performance by using this setting with Lifetime in cache.

Typically, data read from persistent storage is held temporarily in an internal cache until the state of the instance is restored. Cached data normally does not persist beyond state restoration or the end of the transaction in which the finder method was called. By setting Lifetime in cache usage to a value other than Off, you indicate that the cached data is to be held for a longer time, potentially hours or days, before invalidating the version of the data in the cache and fetching a new version. Avoiding a trip to persistent storage greatly speeds up access to such beans by applications. The default value is zero.

In addition, the use of a value other than Off requires that finder methods on the bean have an access type of Read, because EJB applications are not permitted to update such CMP beans. When this value is used, the value of Lifetime in cache is ignored. Beans of this type are cached only in a transaction-scoped cache. The cached data for this instance expires after the transaction in which it was retrieved is completed. When the Elapsed Time is selected, the value of Lifetime in cache is added to the time of the completed transaction (the transaction in which the bean instance was retrieved). The resulting value becomes the time at which the cached data expires. The value of Lifetime in cache can add up to minutes, hours, days, and so on.

When the value Clock Time is selected, the value of Lifetime in cache represents a particular time of day. The value is added to the immediately preceding or following midnight to calculate a future time, which is then treated as Elapsed Time. Using Clock Time enables you to specify that all instances of this bean type are to have their cached data invalidated at, for example, 3 A.M., no matter when they were retrieved. This is important if, for example, the data underlying this bean type is batch updated at 3 A.M. daily.

The selection of midnight (preceding or following) depends on the value of Lifetime in cache. If Lifetime in cache plus the value that represents the preceding midnight is earlier than the current time, the following midnight is used. When you use Clock Time, the value of Lifetime in cache should not represent more than 24 hours. If it does, the cache manager subtracts 24-hour increments from it until it gets a value less than or equal to 24 hours. To invalidate data at midnight, set Lifetime in cache to zero. When the value Week Time is selected, the usage of this value is the same as for Clock Time, except that the value of Lifetime in cache is added to the preceding or following Sunday midnight (11:59 P.M. Saturday plus 1 minute). When Week Time is used, the value of Lifetime in cache can represent more than 24 hours but not more than seven days.

Understanding Concurrency Control and Optimistic/Pessimistic Locking

The Access Intent section of the Deployment Descriptor (click the Access tab) is different for EJB 1.1 and EJB 2.0 entity beans. For EJB 1.1 entity beans, you can set it to For Read Only to eliminate unnecessary load/store operations and improve the performance.

For EJB 2.0 beans, concurrency control is managed by the Pessimistic/Optimistic Access Intent. The Pessimistic scheme locks the data at the early stage of the transaction and does not release it until the transaction is closed. The Optimistic scheme locks the data immediately before a read operation and releases it immediately afterward. Update locks are obtained immediately before an update operation and held until the end of the transaction.

To support optimistic concurrency, WebSphere uses overqualified updates to test whether the underlying Datasource has been updated by another transaction since the beginning of the current transaction. With this scheme, the columns marked for update and their original values are added explicitly through a WHERE clause in the UPDATE statement so that the statement fails if the underlying column values have been changed. As a result, this scheme can provide column-level concurrency control. The Pessimistic scheme controls concurrency at the row level only. Pessimistic and Optimistic concurrency schemes require different transaction isolation levels. Enterprise beans that participate in the same transaction and require different concurrency control schemes cannot operate on the same underlying data connection.

Whether to use Optimistic concurrency depends on the type of transaction. Transactions with a high penalty for failure might be better managed with a Pessimistic scheme. (A *high-penalty* transaction is one for which recovery would be risky or resource intensive.) For low-penalty transactions, it is often worth the risk of failure to gain efficiency with an Optimistic scheme. In general, Optimistic concurrency is more efficient when update collisions are expected to be infrequent. The Pessimistic concurrency is more efficient when update collisions are expected to occur often.

The following values are available for selection:

- wsPessimisticUpdate-WeakestLockAtLoad

- wsPessimisticUpdate

- wsPessimisticRead

- wsOptimisticUpdate

- wsOptimisticRead

- wsPessimisticUpdateNo-Collisions

- wsPessimisticUpdate-Exclusive

The default access intent policy is wsPessimisticUpdate-WeakestLockAtLoad; however, you cannot use this policy with Oracle. In addition, if the Lifetime in cache policy is set to the Bean value, the default value is wsOptimisticRead. You can assign the Access Intent policies to individual methods of the entity beans and their associated Home Interfaces. A policy is acted upon by the combination of the EJB container and a specific persistence manager. IBM advises the following when using this setting:

Start with defaults: The default access intent policy (wsPessimisticUpdate-WeakestLockAtLoad) loads persistent data with the weakest lock that is supported by the persistent store (typically a read lock). Updates are allowed, and the database is permitted to undertake lock escalation when necessary. This option generally works best for most EJB application patterns. After your application is built and running, you can more finely tune certain access paths in your application.

Don't mix access types: Avoid using both pessimistic and optimistic policies in the same transaction. For most databases, pessimistic and optimistic policies use different isolation levels. This results in multiple database connections, which prevents you from taking advantage of the performance benefits possible through connection sharing.

Access intent for the ejbSelect method must be applied indirectly: Because ejbSelect methods are not exposed through a Home, Remote, or Local Interface, you cannot apply a policy to them directly. An ejbSelect method is called by a home or business method, so apply the appropriate policy to the home or business method that governs the behavior of the ejbSelect method.

Take care when applying wsPessimisticUpdate-NoCollision: This policy does not ensure data integrity. No database locks are held, so concurrent transactions can overwrite each other's updates. Use this policy only if you can be sure that only one transaction will attempt to update a persistent store at any given time.

For entity beans that are backed by tables with nullable columns, use an optimistic policy with caution: Nullable columns are automatically excluded from overqualified updates at deployment time; concurrent changes to a nullable field might result in lost updates. WSAD supports selecting a subset of the nonnullable columns that will be reflected in the overqualified update statement that is generated in the deployment code to support optimistic policies.

A method that is configured with a read-only policy that causes a bean to be activated can cause problems if updates are attempted within the same transaction: Those changes will not be committed, and an exception will be thrown because data integrity might be compromised.

 NOTE *Refer to the following two topics in the WSAD Help system for more information: "Frequently Asked Questions: Access Intent" and "Access Intent: Isolation Levels and Update Locks."*

Understanding Data Integrity

J2EE applications are typically driven by remote users. Consider the following scenario: A librarian performs updates of book activity to reflect book rentals by some company. A screen with the book-related data is displayed. The librarian fills in the screen fields and clicks OK. The book-related data is sent to the system and the book-related database record is updated.

To display the original book activity screen, the data should be retrieved by the application from the database. Typically, it is done by the CMP bean, but this is not important here. What is important is that the book-related data is retrieved under transaction context, and when the data is sent to the user, this transaction is closed. All possible data locks are released, and the same book-related information could be modified by another user. The data that the first user sees on the screen is already staled, but the user does not know it.

When the first user sends the updates, the book-related data is updated in the database, replacing the updates made by the second user. The second user's transaction results are mysteriously lost. How do you prevent this data integrity problem? It would be possible to design the system in such a way that the data originally retrieved to be displayed on the user screen remains locked. This is impractical, though, because the time required by the user to complete the screen is highly unpredictable. The user may receive a phone call or take a coffee break. This type of solution is suitable for an application with a low concurrency. For a typical application, this is not a solution.

There are three architectural designs you can use for solving this data integrity problem for high concurrency applications: Timestamp, Version Count, and State Comparison. The main idea of all of them is to retrieve the data again (just before the update) and make sure that the data remains unchanged since it was originally retrieved.

Using the Timestamp

This is an additional field that is added to the state variable to store the time when the data was committed. When the first user receives its data, it has a Timestamp field. When the data is ready for update, the application receives the same data again and compares the timestamps of both records. If they are different, another user managed to update the data and the current update should be terminated (because it is based on staled data). To eliminate the performance impact from reading the data a second time, the SQL query can include the expected value of the Timestamp field in the WHERE clause. In this case, if modifications are already made to the data, the updated record will not be found.

Using the Version Count

A similar idea is implemented here, but the extra field is used not as a timestamp but as a counter. The counter is incremented at each data commit operation. If the counter doesn't match at the update time, the transaction is roll backed.

Using the State Comparison

Before each data update operation, all fields involved in the update are compared against their values saved somewhere when they were originally retrieved. This alternative requires more effort to implement, but it is more flexible by working on the field level. If the fields to be updated are the same, you are not concerned about the rest of the fields (that could be updated), and you can complete the update.

It also should be mentioned that the Timestamp and Version Count alternatives work only if all different applications working with the same data consistently modify the Timestamp or the Version Count field. The best way to ensure this is to include this logic in the CMP bean that every application will use for working with the same data.

Setting the EJB Transaction Isolation Level

The isolation level controls data availability for concurrent data processing from multiple clients. The isolation level controls the following types of database processing: dirty reads, repeatable reads, and phantom reads. These types are as follows:

- A *dirty read* means that the current transaction reads uncommitted results of other transactions. If some of these transactions issue rollback, the current transaction will be processing incorrect data.

- A *phantom read* means that subsequent reads can produce different results (because of some update made during this transaction).

- A *repeatable read* always produces the same results for subsequent reads within the same transaction.

The isolation level values available for selection are Read uncommitted, Read committed, Repeatable read, and Serializable:

- The Read uncommitted option allows dirty reads, nonrepeatable reads, and phantom reads.

- The Read committed option prohibits dirty reads but allows nonrepeatable reads and phantom reads.

- The Repeatable read option prohibits dirty reads and nonrepeatable reads but allows phantom reads.

- The Serializable option prohibits all three: dirty reads, nonrepeatable reads, and phantom reads.

The Serializable level is the most restricted (providing sequential access to the same data). This isolation level leads to the worst performance but the best data integrity. To specify the isolation level in WSAD 5.0, open the Deployment Descriptor and click the Access tab. At the bottom, you should see the "Isolation Level" section. Click the Add button. On the next screen, select the isolation level (see Figure 5-34).

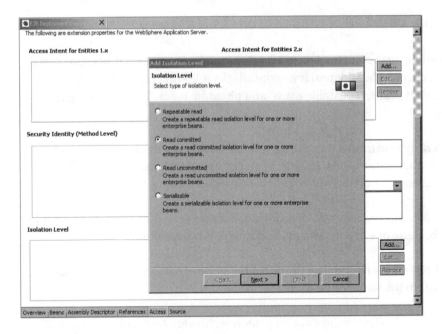

Figure 5-34. Selecting the isolation level

Click Next. On the next screen, select the EJB beans (notice that CMP entity beans are not available for selection) and click Next. On the last screen, expand the selected EJB beans and select the methods to use this isolation level (see Figure 5-35).

Click Finish. Save the results and close the Editor View.

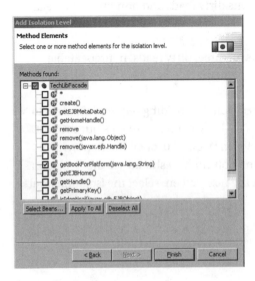

Figure 5-35. Setting the methods for the isolation level

Setting J2EE Application Security

WSAD and WAS support two types of security: declarative and programmatic. You set *declarative security* within the different levels of Deployment Descriptors, and the application code maintains the *programmatic security*.

Declarative security is based on role-based security. A security role is a logical grouping of principles with security authorizations. Security roles are logical entities that are mapped to the operating system users and groups at assembly or deployment time. Global security roles of the J2EE application are stored in the Deployment Descriptor of the EAR application file. Security roles for components are stored in their corresponding Deployment Descriptors inside JAR and WAR files. This allows enterprise applications to be portable among different J2EE-compliant application servers. At runtime, WebSphere checks if the user who is trying to access a restricted method is authorized to access the method.

For the J2EE resources, you typically use a method-level security (protecting methods of EJB components). As mentioned, you set the declarative type of security in the Deployment Descriptor. In this section, you will set security on the application level. Switch to the J2EE Perspective, expand Enterprise Applications, select the TechLibApp project, right-click the EJB Deployment Descriptor, and select Open With Deployment Descriptor Editor.

The application level of the Deployment Descriptor will be displayed. Click the Security tab. On the screen that appears, you should see the "Security" section. You will set two security roles
(Librarian and Director). Click the Add button. On the screen that appears, enter Librarian in the Name field and a description of the Librarian security role in the Description field (see Figure 5-36).

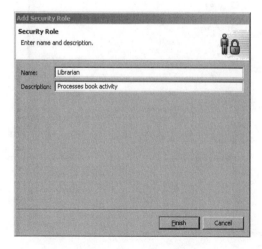

Figure 5-36. Setting the Librarian security role

Click OK. Repeat the same steps to add the second security role, Director. When you are done, you screen should look like the one depicted in Figure 5-37.

Next, you will indicate the method each security role is authorized to access. Highlight the Librarian security role and click the Users/Groups check box in the "WebSphere Bindings" section. Click the Add button in the "Groups" section. On the next screen, enter Library-clerks as a group name and click OK. Highlight the Director security role and repeat the same steps to enter the Library-administration group. When you are done, the screen should look like the one depicted in Figure 5-38.

Save the changes and close the editor.

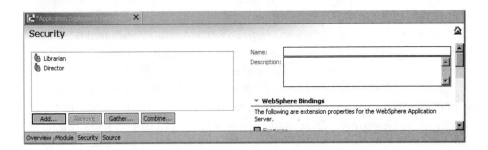

Figure 5-37. Setting the Director security role

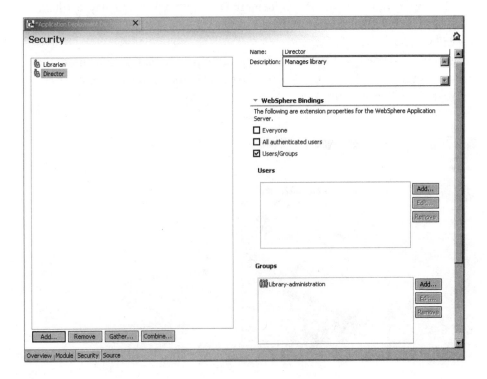

Figure 5-38. Setting security groups

Protecting Web Resources

For Web modules, you protect HTTP commands that access specific methods (typically GET and POST methods of servlets). In this section, you will work on the Web module level. Expand Web Modules, right-click the Web Deployment Descriptor of some Web project, and select Open With Deployment Descriptor Editor. On the next screen, click the Security tab. Highlight the Security Roles tab at the top of the screen. Click the Add button and create the Librarian security role. Click the Add button again and create the Director security role. Scroll to the "Authorized Roles" section.

Click the Security Constrains tab and click the Add button. A new security constrain will appear. Click the Add button in the "Web Resource Collection" section. Enter Web_methods in the Name field and give the description for this name. Check the method that the security role is authorized to access (see Figure 5-39).

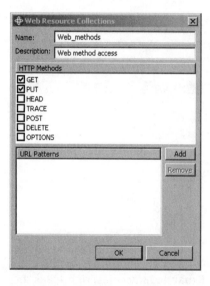

Figure 5-39. Setting security constrains

Click OK. Next, click the Edit button in the "Authorized Roles" section. On the next screen, select the Librarian security role, making it authorized to access the GET and POST methods. Repeat the same steps to select the Web methods that the Director security role is authorized to access.

Click the Servlets tab and select the BookRegisterController servlet. Locate the "Authorized Roles" section. Click the Edit button and select the security roles that are authorized to access BookRegisterController (see Figure 5-40).

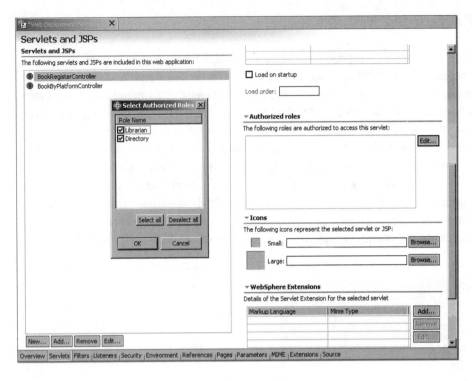

Figure 5-40. Servlet access authorization

Click OK. Save the results and close the editor.

Protecting EJB Resources

For EJB modules, you control the access to EJB components methods. In this section, you will work on the EJB module level. Expand EJB Modules, right-click the EJB Deployment Descriptor of some EJB project, and select Open With Deployment Descriptor Editor. On the next screen, click the Security tab. Click the Assembly Descriptor tab. Click the Add button in the "Security Roles" section and create the Librarian security role. Repeat the same steps and create the Director security role.

Click the Add button in the "Method Permission" section. On the next screen, select Librarian as the security role (see Figure 5-41).

Click Next. On the next screen, select the enterprise beans that the Librarian security role is allowed to access (see Figure 5-42).

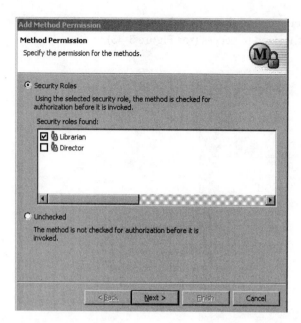

Figure 5-41. Selecting the Librarian security role

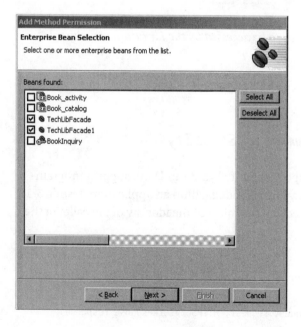

Figure 5-42. EJB modules permitted to be accessed by the Librarian security role

Click Next. On the next screen, expand the selected components and mark the methods this security role is authorized to access (see Figure 5-43).

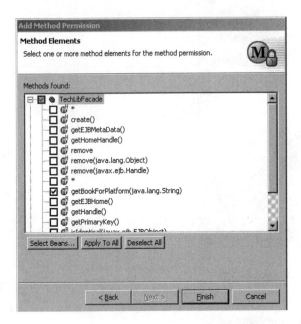

Figure 5-43. EJB method permitted to be accessed by the Librarian security role

Click Finish. Save the results and close the editor.

Understanding Programmatic Security

In addition to the declarative type of security, WSAD and WAS support programmatic security where the security logic is coded within an application. Listing 5-17 shows the code fragment for checking the role and the identity of the caller of the Web tier.

Listing 5-17. Programmatic Security

```
Public void doGet(HTTPServletRequest request, HTTPServletResponse response)
{
    // Get remote user by using getRemoteUser()
    String  remoteUser = request.getRemoteUser();
```

```
    // Get remote user by using the getUserPrincipal()
    java.security.Principal proncipal = request.getRemoteProncipal();
    String remoteUser = principal.getName();

    // Check if remoteUser is granted "Mgr" role
    boolean isMgr = request.isUserInRole("Mgr");
    ---
}
```

The EJB tier developer uses the following two methods to check the role and the identity of the caller:

```
public javax.security.Principal EJBContext.getCallerPrincipal();
public Boolean EJBContext.isCallerInRole(String roleName);
```

Setting Security Delegation

The delegation policy allows an intermediary to perform a task initiated by the client under an identity determined by the delegation policy. By default, if no delegation is specified, the intermediary will use the identity of the client. The delegation policy is specified by setting the Run-as mode for each EJB component or component method. The field can have the following values:

- **Client identity**: Say the session bean calls the method XXX of the entity bean. If the method XXX has the client identity, then the client should be authorized to invoke the XXX method (rather than the identity of the session bean itself).

- **EJB Server identity**: This is the identity of the intermediate module. If the delegation policy for the method XXX is set to the EJB Server identity, then the EJB server must be authorized to call the method XXX.

- **Specific Security Role identity**: The session bean invokes the XXX method under this identity, so this security role must have authorization to call the method XXX.

Right-click the EJB Deployment Descriptor of an EJB project and select Open With Deployment Descriptor Editor. Click the Access method. Two sections control the user identity: one on the bean level and the second on the method level. Clicking the Add button in the user identity (Bean Level) opens the screen shown in Figure 5-44.

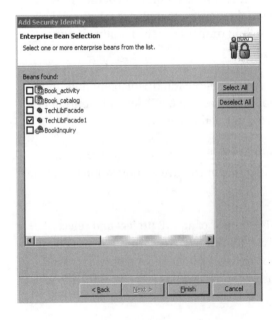

Figure 5-44. Bean-level user identity

Here, you can specify to use the identity of a caller or the identity assigned to a specific role. In the latter case, select the security role and click Next. On the next screen, you select the EJB beans that should use this type of security identity (see Figure 5-45).

Figure 5-45. Selecting beans to use this security identity

Click Finish. Now, click the Add button in the "Security Identity (Method Level)" section. The next screen presents three choices for selection: Use identity of caller, Use identity of EJB server, and Use identity assigned to specific role (see Figure 5-46).

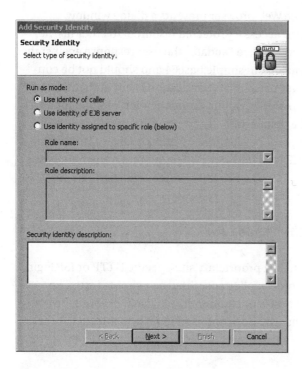

Figure 5-46. User identity of the specific security role

Click Next. The next screens are identical to the previous Security Identity screen, but they allow you to set on the method level. Save the changes and close the editor.

Understanding User Authentication

WAS supports three authentication mechanisms:

- HTTP Basic Authentication

- Form-Based Authentication

- HTTPS Client Certificate Authentication

The following sections describe the first two authentication mechanisms.

Using HTTP Basic Authentication

In HTTP Basic Authentication, the Web browser presents a dialog window prompting the user (attempting to access a protected resource) to enter his/her user ID and password. The security service validates the user response against the user registry. The password is encoded in simple base64 and should not be considered as secure. The target server used for authentication is not authenticated itself. If a security constrain has been set, but no authentication method for a Web module has been configured, the default is to use Basic Authentication.

A more sophisticated variation of Basic Authentication is Digest Authentication, which encrypts the user ID and password when they are transmitted over the network.

Using Form-Based Authentication

Form-Based Authentication permits a proprietary site-specific HTTP or JSP login form. The password is not encrypted at all (transmitted as a simple text). The target server used for authentication is not authenticated itself. Because the container supports single sign on, the user does not need to reauthenticate to other protected resources.

Using HTTPS Client Certificate Authentication

This authentication mechanism requires the client to possess a public key certificate. This is more involved but also the most secured form of authentication. Coverage of HTTPS Client Certificate Authentication is beyond the scope of this book.

Open the Deployment Descriptor for the Web project. Click the Pages tab. You should see the "Login" section on the top of the screen. In this section, you can select the type of user identification, the login page, and the error page (see Figure 5-47).

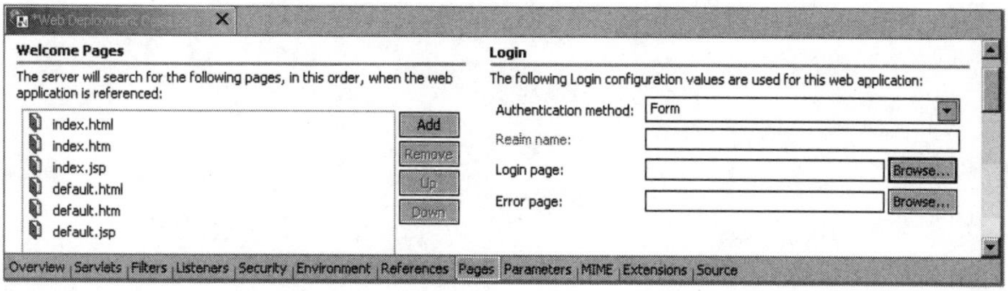

Figure 5-47. Login settings

Use groups rather than individual users when assigning security roles. This will improve the performance of checking the authorization. There are several reasons for that. First, the number of groups is substantially smaller than the number of users. Second, it reduces the administration work. Finally, adding or deleting users from groups outside the WebSphere environment is much more preferable to adding and removing WebSphere security roles because the application must be stopped and reloaded for such changes to take effect.

Summary

In this chapter, you explored the latest J2EE 1.3 specifications, discussed the major features of the EJB 2.0 standard (the Local Interface and the new CMP entity beans model), and learned how to implement them in WSAD 5.0. The third major feature, MDBs, will be covered in Chapters 9, 10, and 11. You also explored many additions and improvements of the J2EE 1.3 specification and how you can use them with WSAD 5.0.

In addition, the chapter covered some advanced topics of EJB and Web development and linked them to the corresponding WSAD 5.0 facilities. In the next two chapters, you will develop a fully functional J2EE 1.3 application and many short examples that demonstrate additional development topics. Refer to the appendix to see how to deploy this application.

J2EE EJB
Development

IN THIS CHAPTER, you will start developing a complete Java 2 Enterprise Edition (J2EE) 1.3 application that consists of the Enterprise JavaBean (EJB) and Web modules. This chapter covers EJB development, and Chapter 7 covers Web development. The EJB module will include entity beans—the Container Managed Persistence (CMP) and Bean Managed Persistence (BMP) types—and session beans (stateless and stateful beans). In Chapter 7, you will build the Web module by following the industry best-practice Model-View-Controller (MVC) pattern, and it will consist of Hypertext Markup Language (HTML), servlets, JavaServer Pages (JSP), and JavaBean files. In this chapter's example, you will use J2EE technology for developing the application used by a hypothetical library that rents technical books to its clients—data processing companies.

The EJB development process typically includes building the entity beans (CMP and BMP) that represent the database records and building the session beans (stateless and stateful) that represent the business processing logic. It also frequently includes building the helper classes.

Understanding the EJB Project Organization

The J2EE 1.3 EJB projects are organized in the following directory structure:

- `ejbModule`: All EJB module folders reside inside the `ejbModule` directory.

- `Java Source`: Java source directories reside inside the `ejbModule` folder according to their package structure.

- `websphere-deploy`: This directory is a child of the corresponding `Java Source` folder. It contains compiled and WebSphere Studio Application Developer (WSAD)–generated classes.

- `WSAD Classes`: Container classes and other project support classes reside in this folder.

- META-INF: This folder also resides inside the ejbModule folder. It contains the EJB Deployment Descriptor file (ejb-jar.xml), two proprietary IBM-extended configuration files (ibm-ejb-jar-bnd.xml and ibm-ejb-jar-ext.xml), and the MANIFEST file.

- backends: This is a subdirectory of the META-INF folder. It contains databases attached to the project. The next section discusses entity bean development.

Developing Entity Beans

You will first develop two CMP entity bean components called Book_catalog and Book_activity. The book's examples use the same TECHBOOK database (developed in Chapter 4). Just as a reminder, the TECHBOOK database consists of three tables: BOOK_CATALOG, BOOK_ACTIVITY, and BOOK_NOTIFY. The BOOK_CATALOG table represents the catalog of the books available in the library. The BOOK_ACTIVITY table keeps the book rental activity. Finally, the BOOK_NOTIFY table is used for communication with the library customers.

You will use the Book_catalog entity bean to maintain the BOOK_CATALOG database table. It should have two business methods: FindByPlatform and FindAllBooks. You will use the Book_activity entity bean to maintain the book rental activity in the BOOK_ACTIVITY database table. It also should have two business methods: findByBook and findByCompany. You will build both of these entity beans with the Local Interface. In the following session bean development example, you will build a stateless session bean with both Local and Remote Interfaces and a stateful session bean with the Local Interface. With this quick introduction, let's start developing the examples.

Developing CMP Entity Beans

First, you need to build a new project. So, switch to the J2EE Perspective. By default, you will also be in the J2EE View. Next, select File ➤ New ➤ EJB Project from the main menu. On the screen that appears, select Create 2.0 EJB Project and click Next. On the next screen, enter TechLibEJB in the Project name field, check New in the Enterprise Application Project field, and enter TechLibApp in the New Project Name field. Each new EJB module should be attached to an EAR application project. If no such project exists yet (such as TechLibApp), the system will automatically build it. The EAR application file is used for subsequent deployment on the WebSphere Application Server (WAS).

Click Finish. Two new projects (TechLibEJB and TechLibApp) will be generated and become visible in the J2EE View.

You probably remember that any project that requires database access needs this database to be imported in the project. In the next section, you will import the TECHBOOK database in the `TechLibEJB` project.

Importing the TECHBOOK Database into the TechLibEJB Project

To import the TECHBOOK database, switch to the Data Perspective. Right-click the `Con1` connection in the DB Servers View and select `Reconnect`. Expand the `Con1` connection so that you can see the TECHBOOK database and its tables.

In the DB Servers View, highlight two tables: `LIB.BOOK_ACTIVITY` and `LIB.BOOK_CATALOG` (keep the Control key pressed during selection). Right-click the selection and select `Import to Folder`. On the next screen, click `Browse` and navigate to the `TechLibEJB` project. Click `OK`. Now you are back to the original screen. Click `Finish`. You will be prompted to confirm the creation of the new folders. Click `Yes`. The TECHBOOK database will be imported to your project along with the schema (`LIB`) and the selected tables.

NOTE *You have several ways to do this importing operation. You can import the entire database and then delete the tables that are not needed. Another way is to import one table first. Then, drag each of the remaining tables you need from the DB Servers View to the Data Definition View and drop them in the* `Tables` *entry.*

You should now see the TECHBOOK database and two tables in your project.

WSAD provides three methods of developing CMP entity beans: Bottom Up, Top Down, and Meet in the Middle.

You use the Bottom Up method when the database and database tables are available; thus, you build the entity beans based on the structure of the corresponding database tables. This is typically the way in which development happens in large organizations where the database design is the responsibility of the database administration. The Top Down approach is the opposite—you already have the entity beans, and you generate the database tables based on the corresponding entity beans. You use the Meet in the Middle approach when both parts are available, and you map fields in the database tables to the corresponding attributes of the entity beans. In this example, you will use the Bottom Up method. The Bottom Up approach provides for a much faster development process. Later, you will see how to use the Top Down and Meet in the Middle methods for CMP entity bean development. In the next section, you will use the Bottom Up method.

Using the Bottom Up Method

To use the Bottom Up method, switch to the J2EE Perspective (J2EE View). Right-click the TechLibEJB project and select Generate ➤ EJB to RDB Mapping. The EJB to RDB Mapping screen will appear with a prefilled option: Use an existing backend folder (that points to the imported database). Click Next. The next screen prompts you to select the type of EJB/RDB mapping. Select Bottom Up and then click Next. On the following screen, select Generate 2.0 enterprise beans. Enter apress.wsad.techlib in the Package for generated EJB classes field and TechLib in the Prefix for generated EJB classes field. Click Finish.

WSAD will generate two entity beans, the TechLib_activityBean.java and TechLib_catalogBean.java implementation classes, along with their Local Home and Local interfaces (TechLib_activityLocal.java, TechLib_activityLocalHome.java, TechLib_catalogLocal.java, and TechLib_catalogLocalHome.java). In addition, WSAD will generate two Primary Key classes: TechLib_activityKey.java and TechLib_catalogKey.java. Notice that the Local Interfaces are generated for both entity beans. WSAD also generates the mapping of the entity bean fields to the corresponding fields of the database tables (see Figure 6-1).

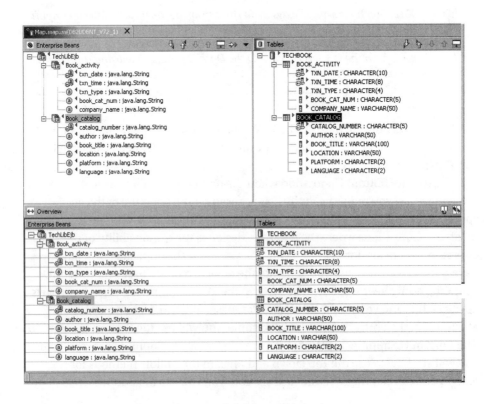

Figure 6-1. Generated entity bean and field mapping

The Content Pane shows the Map.mapxmi file opened in the Map Editor View. The upper part of the screen shows the bean module attributes and the corresponding table fields. The lower part shows the actual field mapping. The lower part shows that all bean attributes for both modules have been automatically mapped to the corresponding table fields. You do not need to change any mapping, so close the Map Editor View.

Building the Entity Bean's Business Methods

Double-click the TechLib_activityBean.java implementation class to open it in the Java Editor View. Notice that the CMP implementation class is an abstract class. The EJB container will generate the actual implementation class by inheriting this abstract class. Figure 6-2 shows the Outline View.

Figure 6-2. The Outline View

Notice also that EJB 2.0 entity beans no longer have attributes defined as fields. Only getter/setter methods are generated for attributes; maintenance of the attribute fields is now the responsibility of the EJB container. You should see that the getter/setter attribute methods are marked with the decorated icon A, which stands for *Attribute*. In addition, all getter/setter methods for all nonkey attributes are marked by the decorated icon L, which stands for *Local Interface* (these methods are promoted to the Local Interface). To verify this, double-click the Local Interface class `TechLib_activityLocal.java`. All getter/setter methods promoted to the Local Interface appear there. Promote the getter/setter methods for the key attribute to the Local Interface. Open `TechLibBook_catalogBean.java`. In the Outline View, right-click the `getCatalog_number` method and select `Enterprise Bean` ➤ `Promote to Local Interface`. Do the same for the `setCatalog_number` method.

WSAD generates only the skeleton of the entity bean Java files. You need to modify the generated Java classes to include the necessary processing logic. This is where you use a new feature of the WSAD 5.0 new release. In the previous releases, WSAD generated only a single `create` method per entity bean with the argument or arguments that are part of the Primary Key. Therefore, developers had to manually build a second `create` method with a full list of attribute fields as arguments for each entity bean so that when this method is called and the new entity bean instance is built, the corresponding database record will be created with all the proper fields.

In addition, whenever you build an additional `create` method in the Home Interface, you have to build the corresponding `ejbCreate` and `ejbPostCreate` methods in the bean implementation class. That is quite a job. Well, IBM listened to developers' suggestions, and in release 5.0, you can see that WSAD has automatically generated the second `create` method with a full list of parameters (and the corresponding `create`-supporting methods). This is very helpful.

Next, you want to build two additional `finder` methods. These `finder` methods are called `findByBook` and `findByCompany`. Each of these method searches the BOOK_ACTIVITY table and selects all transactions for a given `BookCatalogNumber` or `CompanyName`. The following are the signatures of these two `finder` methods:

```
public Collection findByBook(java.lang.String workBookCatNum)
    throws javax.ejb.FinderException;

public java.util.Collection findByCompany(java.lang.String workCompanyName)
    throws javax.ejb.FinderException;
```

Perform the following steps to add these `finder` methods: In the Hierarchical pane, double-click the `TechLibBook_activityLocalHome` module to open it in the Java Editor View. Add your two `finder` method declarations to the Home Interface class `TechLibBook_activityLocalHome`. Next, define each `finder` method's processing logic by executing the following steps: In the J2EE Hierarchical View, right-click the `TechLibEJB` project and select `Open With` ➤ `Deployment Descriptor Editor`. In the screen that appears, click the `Beans` tab, select the `Book_activity` bean, and then scroll down until you see the "Queries" section. Click the `Add` button. The screen that appears already lists the two `finder` methods that you just entered (`findByBook` and `findByCompany`) as the existing methods. The method type of these methods is already correctly preselected as `find method` (see Figure 6-3).

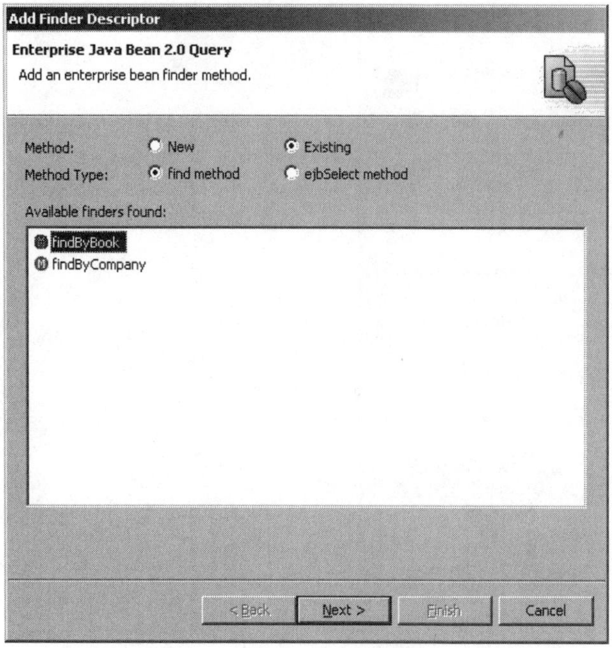

Figure 6-3. Add Finder Descriptor *dialog*

After selecting the findByBook method, click Next. On the next screen, expand the Select a sample query list and select a sample of a query that is close enough to the type of query you need to create. You must write all queries in the Enterprise JavaBean Query Language (EJB QL) language, which is the standard for EJB 2.0. For example, you can select the Single not equal predicate sample and then modify the EJB QL query that was placed in the field (see Figure 6-4).

The EJB QL statement entered for the findByBook() method looks like this:

```
select object(o) from Book_activity o where o.book_cat_num = ?1
```

The meaning of the statement in a plain English is this: "Select all Book_activity records with the book_cat_num field equal to the value of the first parameter passed to the method—in this case, the bookCatalogNumber." If you are not familiar with EJB QL (and who is?), you can refer to the excellent book *Enterprise JavaBeans* (O'Reilly, 2001). Click Finish. You are now back to the original screen, and your query becomes visible in the list of queries. Click the Add button again and select the findByCompany method. Click Next. Enter the following EJB QL statement:

```
select object(o) from Book_activity o where o.company_name = ?1
```

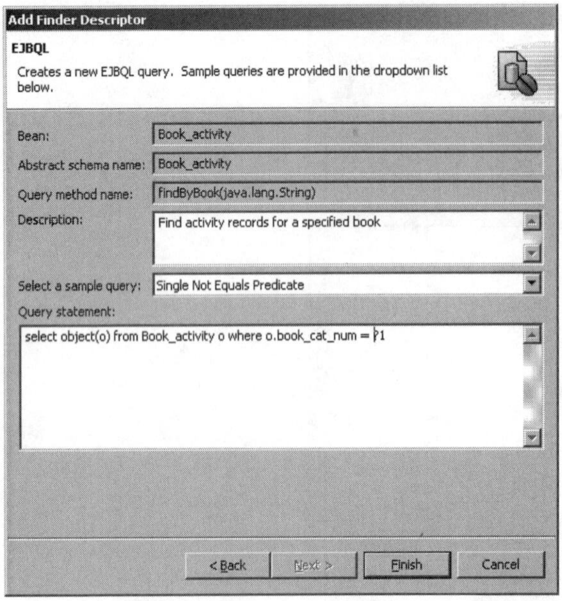

Figure 6-4. EJB QL query statement for the findByBook *method*

In this EJB QL statement, you are selecting all Book_activity bean instances with the company_name field equal to the value of the first parameter passed to the method—in this case, the companyName (see Figure 6-5).

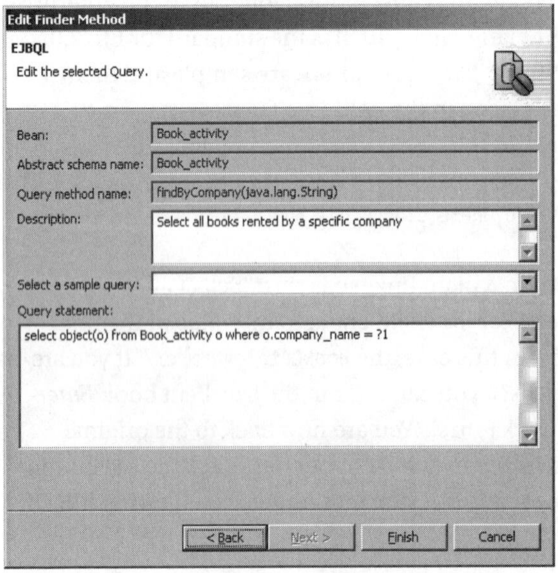

Figure 6-5. EJB QL query statement for the findByCompany *method*

Click Next. You are returned to the original screen where you should see both EJB QL queries in the list (see Figure 6-6).

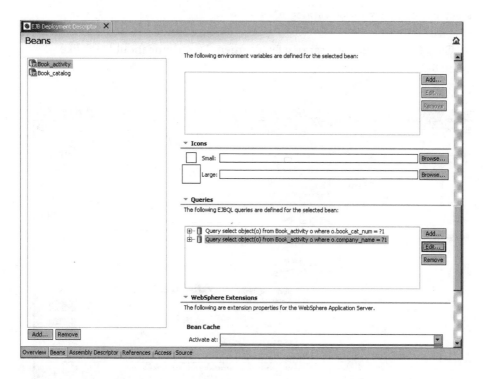

Figure 6-6. Section of the EJB Deployment Descriptor with entered EJB QL statements

Save the results and make sure there are no errors in the Tasks View.

Double-click the TechLibBook_catalogLocalHome Local Home Interface class to open it in the Java Editor View and add following two finder method declarations:

```
public java.util.Collection findByPlatform(java.lang.String workPlatform)
    throws javax.ejb.FinderException;
public Collection findAll()
    throws javax.ejb.FinderException;
```

Next, define each finder method's processing logic by executing the following steps: With the Deployment Descriptor still open, click the Beans tab and scroll down until you see the "Queries" section. Click the Add button. Select the FindByPlatform method and click Next. Enter the following EJB QL query on the next screen:

```
select object(o) from Book_catalog o where o.platform = ?1
```

Click Finish. Click the Add button again. Select the findAll method and click Next. Enter the following EJB QL query on the next screen:

```
select object(o) from Book_catalog o
```

Click Finish. Your Book_catalog Deployment Descriptor should look like Figure 6-7.

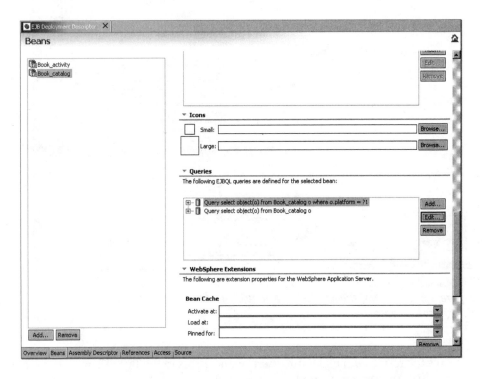

Figure 6-7. Section of the Deployment Descriptor with entered EJB QL statements

Save the results and make sure there are no errors. Close the Deployment Descriptor. You will use the getter/setter methods for the attribute(s) that form the Primary Key for the bean. With TechLibBook_catalogBean still open in the Java Editor View, right-click the getCatalog_number method and select Enterprise Bean ► Promote to the Local Interface. Do the same for the setCatalogNumber method. Use the same steps to promote the getter/setter methods for the key attributes (txnDate and txnTime) for TechLibBook_activityBean.

Listing 6-1 shows the source code for the TechLibBook_catalog entity bean.

Listing 6-1. `TechLibBook_catalogBean.java`*: Implementation Class*

```java
package apress.wsad.techlib;

/**
 * Bean implementation class for Enterprise Bean: Book_catalog
 */
public abstract class TechLibBook_catalogBean implements javax.ejb.EntityBean
{
private javax.ejb.EntityContext myEntityCtx;

    public void setEntityContext(javax.ejb.EntityContext ctx)
{
 myEntityCtx = ctx;
}

  public javax.ejb.EntityContext getEntityContext()
{
return myEntityCtx;
}

public void unsetEntityContext()
{
 myEntityCtx = null;
}

public apress.wsad.techlib.TechLibBook_catalogKey ejbCreate(
    java.lang.String catalog_number)
    throws javax.ejb.CreateException
{
setCatalog_number(catalog_number);
return null;
}

public voidejbPostCreate(java.lang.String catalog_number)
throws javax.ejb.CreateException
{
}

public void ejbActivate()
{
}
```

```java
public void ejbLoad()
{
}

public void ejbPassivate()
{
}

public void ejbRemove() throws javax.ejb.RemoveException
{
}

public void ejbStore()
{
}

public apress.wsad.techlib.TechLibBook_catalogKey ejbCreate(
String catalog_number,
String author,
String book_title,
String location,
String platform,
String language)
throws javax.ejb.CreateException
{
setCatalog_number(catalog_number);
setAuthor(author);
setBook_title(book_title);
setLocation(location);
setPlatform(platform);
setLanguage(language);
return null;
}

public void ejbPostCreate(
String catalog_number,
String author,
String book_title,
String location,
String platform,
String language)
throws javax.ejb.CreateException
{
}
```

```
public abstract java.lang.String getCatalog_number();
public abstract void setCatalog_number(java.lang.String newCatalog_number);
public abstract java.lang.String getAuthor();
public abstract void setAuthor(java.lang.String newAuthor);
public abstract java.lang.String getBook_title();
public abstract void setBook_title(java.lang.String newBook_title);
public abstract java.lang.String getLocation();
public abstract void setLocation(java.lang.String newLocation);
public abstract java.lang.String getPlatform();
public abstract void setPlatform(java.lang.String newPlatform);
public abstract java.lang.String getLanguage();
public abstract void setLanguage(java.lang.String newLanguage);
}
```

Listing 6-2 shows the source code for the TechLibBook_activity entity bean.

Listing 6-2. TechLibBook_catalogLocal.java: *Local Interface*

```
package apress.wsad.techlib;
public interface TechLibBook_catalogLocal extends javax.ejb.EJBLocalObject
{
public java.lang.String getCatalog_number();
public void setCatalog_number(String newCatalog_number);
public java.lang.String getAuthor();
public void setAuthor(java.lang.String newAuthor);
public java.lang.String getBook_title();
public void setBook_title(java.lang.String newBook_title);
public java.lang.String getLocation();
public void setLocation(java.lang.String newLocation);
public java.lang.String getPlatform();
public void setPlatform(java.lang.String newPlatform);
public java.lang.String getLanguage();
public void setLanguage(java.lang.String newLanguage);
}
```

Listing 6-3 shows the source code for the TechLibBook_catalogKey Primary Key class.

Listing 6-3. Primary Key Class TechLibBook_catalogKey.java

```java
package apress.wsad.techlib;
public class TechLibBook_catalogKey implements java.io.Serializable
{
static final long serialVersionUID = 3206093459760846163L;
public java.lang.String catalog_number;

public TechLibBook_catalogKey()
{
}

public TechLibBook_catalogKey(java.lang.String catalog_number)
{
this.catalog_number = catalog_number;
}
public boolean equals(java.lang.Object otherKey)
{
if (otherKey instanceof
                    apress.wsad.techlib.TechLibBook_catalogKey)
{
apress.wsad.techlib.TechLibBook_catalogKey o =
(apress.wsad.techlib.TechLibBook_catalogKey) otherKey;
return ((this.catalog_number.equals(o.catalog_number)));

return false;
}

public int hashCode()
{
return (catalog_number.hashCode());
}

    public java.lang.String getCatalog_number()
{
return catalog_number;
}
public void setCatalog_number(java.lang.String newCatalog_number)
{
catalog_number = newCatalog_number;
}
}
```

Listing 6-4 shows the source code for the TechLibBook_activityBean entity bean.

Listing 6-4. TechLibBook_activityBean.java*: Implementation Class*

```
package apress.wsad.techlib;

public abstract class TechLibBook_activityBean implements javax.ejb.EntityBean
{
private javax.ejb.EntityContext myEntityCtx;
public void setEntityContext(javax.ejb.EntityContext ctx)
{
myEntityCtx = ctx;
}

public javax.ejb.EntityContext getEntityContext()
{
return myEntityCtx;
}

public void unsetEntityContext()
{
myEntityCtx = null;
}

public apress.wsad.techlib.TechLibBook_activityKey ejbCreate(
java.lang.String txn_date,
java.lang.String txn_time)
throws javax.ejb.CreateException
{
setTxn_date(txn_date);
setTxn_time(txn_time);
return null;
}

public void ejbPostCreate(
java.lang.String txn_date,
java.lang.String txn_time)
throws javax.ejb.CreateException
{
}
```

```java
public void ejbActivate()
{
}
public void ejbLoad()
{
}

public void ejbPassivate()
{
}
public void ejbRemove() throws javax.ejb.RemoveException
{
}

public void ejbStore()
{
}

public apress.wsad.techlib.TechLibBook_activityKey ejbCreate(
java.lang.String txn_date,
java.lang.String txn_time,
java.lang.String txn_type,
java.lang.String book_cat_num,
java.lang.String company_name)
throws javax.ejb.CreateException
{
setTxn_date(txn_date);
setTxn_time(txn_time);
setTxn_type(txn_type);
setBook_cat_num(book_cat_num);
setCompany_name(company_name);
return null;
}
public void ejbPostCreate(
java.lang.String txn_date,
java.lang.String txn_time,
java.lang.String txn_type,
java.lang.String book_cat_num,
java.lang.String company_name)
throws javax.ejb.CreateException
{
}
```

```
public abstract java.lang.String getTxn_date();
public abstract void setTxn_date(java.lang.String newTxn_date);
public abstract java.lang.String getTxn_time();
public abstract void setTxn_time(java.lang.String newTxn_time);
public abstract java.lang.String getTxn_type();
public abstract void setTxn_type(java.lang.String newTxn_type);
public abstract java.lang.String getBook_cat_num();
public abstract void setBook_cat_num(java.lang.String newBook_cat_num);
public abstract java.lang.String getCompany_name();
public abstract void setCompany_name(java.lang.String newCompany_name);
}
```

Listing 6-5 shows the source code for the TechLibBook_activityLocalHome interface.

Listing 6-5. TechLibBook_activityLocalHome.java: *Local Home Interface*

```
package apress.wsad.techlib;
import java.util.*;
public interface TechLibBook_activityLocalHome extends javax.ejb.EJBLocalHome
{
public apress.wsad.techlib.TechLibBook_activityLocal
  create(java.lang.String txn_date,
              java.lang.String txn_time)
    throws javax.ejb.CreateException;
public apress.wsad.techlib.TechLibBook_activityLocal findByPrimaryKey(
                                  apress.wsad.techlib.TechLibBook_activityKey
                                  primaryKey)
throws javax.ejb.FinderException;
public apress.wsad.techlib.TechLibBook_activityLocal create(
java.lang.String txn_date,
java.lang.String txn_time,
java.lang.String txn_type,
java.lang.String book_cat_num,
                          java.lang.String company_name)
throws javax.ejb.CreateException;


public Collection findByBook(java.lang.String workBookCatNum)
    throws javax.ejb.FinderException;


public java.util.Collection findByCompany(java.lang.String workCompanyName)
throws javax.ejb.FinderException;
}
```

Listing 6-6 shows the source code for the TechLibBook_activityLocal **interface.**

Listing 6-6. TechLibBook_activityLocal.java: *Local Interface*

```
package apress.wsad.techlib;

public interface TechLibBook_activityLocal extends
            javax.ejb.EJBLocalObject
{
public java.lang.String getTxn_date();
public void setTxn_date(java.lang.String newTxn_date);
     public java.lang.String getTxn_time();
     public void setTxn_time(java.lang.String newTxn_time);
public java.lang.String getTxn_type();
public void setTxn_type(java.lang.String newTxn_type);
public java.lang.String getBook_cat_num();
public void setBook_cat_num(java.lang.String newBook_cat_num);
public java.lang.String getCompany_name();
public void setCompany_name(java.lang.String newCompany_name);
}
```

Listing 6-7 shows the source code for the TechLibBook_activityKey **Primary Key** class.

Listing 6-7. Primary Key Class TechLibBook_activityKey.java

```
package apress.wsad.techlib;

public class TechLibBook_activityKey implements java.io.Serializable
{
static final long serialVersionUID = 3206093459760846163L;
public java.lang.String txn_date;
public java.lang.String txn_time;

public TechLibBook_activityKey()
{
}


public TechLibBook_activityKey(
java.lang.String txn_date,
java.lang.String txn_time)
```

```
{
this.txn_date = txn_date;
this.txn_time = txn_time;
}


public boolean equals(java.lang.Object otherKey)
{
  if (otherKey instanceof apress.wsad.techlib.TechLibBook_activityKey)
    {
apress.wsad.techlib.TechLibBook_activityKey o =
(apress.wsad.techlib.TechLibBook_activityKey) otherKey;
return (
(this.txn_date.equals(o.txn_date)) &&
(this.txn_time.equals(o.txn_time)));
}
return false;
}


public int hashCode()
{
 return (txn_date.hashCode() + txn_time.hashCode());
}


public java.lang.String getTxn_date()
{
  return txn_date;
}


public void setTxn_date(java.lang.String newTxn_date)
{
  txn_date = newTxn_date;
}


public java.lang.String getTxn_time()
{
        return txn_time;
}
public void setTxn_time(java.lang.String newTxn_time)
{
txn_time = newTxn_time;
}
}
```

Binding the Datasource

You can bind the Datasource on the project level. Alternatively, each CMP entity bean can be bound to a Datasource individually. You will do Datasource binding on the project level. In addition, for each EJB module, a Java Naming and Directory Interface (JNDI) name must be assigned and set in the JNDI data space, so each module can be remotely or locally located. Right-click the TechLibEJB project in J2EE Hierarchy Perspective and select Open With ➤ Deployment Descriptor Editor.

Scroll down to the "WebSphere Bindings" section of the Deployment Descriptor. Select the backend ID (which determines the persistent classes to be loaded). Currently, there is only one entry available for selection: DB2UDBNT_V72_1. In the "JNDI–CMP Factory Connection Binding" section, enter jdbc/TECHBOOK in the JNDI name field and select Per_Connection_Factory in the Container authorization field (see Figure 6-8).

Figure 6-8. Binding the CMP entity bean to the Datasource

You need to specify JNDI names for your entity beans so the EJB clients can locate them. With the Deployment Descriptor open to the Beans page, scroll up to the top. Highlight the Book_activity bean and find the "WebSphere Bindings" section. Enter ejb/Book_activity in the JNDI name field (see Figure 6-9).

Next, highlight the Book_catalog bean, and in the same "WebSphere Bindings" section, enter ejb/Book_catalog in the JNDI name field (see Figure 6-10).

The next step is to generate the deployment code for the entity beans. Right-click TechLibEJB and select Generate ➤ Deploy and RMIC code. On the screen that appears, select both modules: Book_activity and Book_catalog.

Click Finish. You can see the generated code by switching to the J2EE Navigator View and expanding the apress.wsad.techlib package.

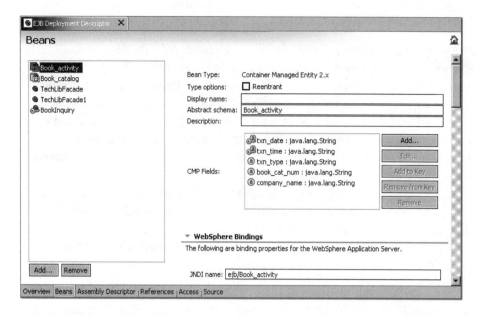

Figure 6-9. Setting the JNDI name for the Book_activity *CMP entity bean*

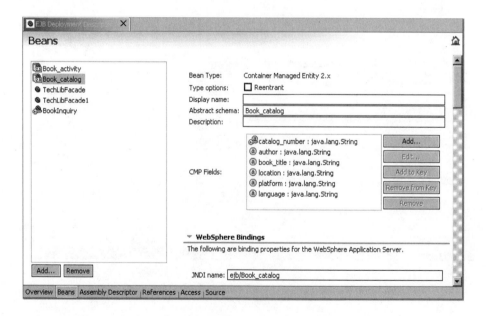

Figure 6-10. Setting the JNDI name for the Book_catalog *CMP entity bean*

Configuring the Test Server

To test the entity beans you have just built, you need to create a test server and add a `Datasource` to its configuration. Switch to the Server Perspective and select `File ➤ New ➤ Server Project`. On the screen that appears, name the project `TechLibTestServerProject` and click `Finish`. The `TechLibTestServerProject` will appear in the Navigator View. Next, right-click `TechLibTestServerProject` and select `New ➤ Server and Server Configuration`. On the screen that appears, name the server `TechLibTestServer`. Also, select `WebSphere version 5.0 Test Environment` as the server instance type.

Click `Finish`. Next, you need to add the `TechLibApp` enterprise project to the server configuration. In the Server Configuration View, right-click `TechLibTestServer` and select `Add ➤ TechLibApp`. You also need to add JDBC `Datasource` to the server configuration. Double-click `TechLibTestServer` to open its configuration in the Editor View. Click the `Data source` tab (see Figure 6-11).

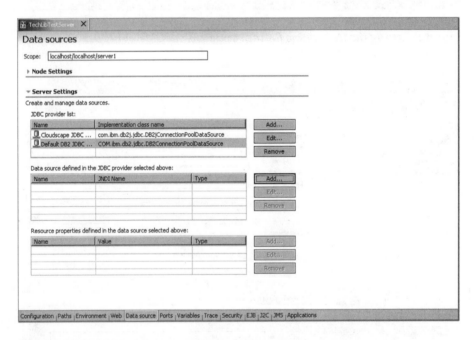

Figure 6-11. Adding a Datasource *to the server configuration*

In the "JDBC provider list" section, select Default JDBC DB2 Provider. Click the Add button attached to the "Datasource defined in the JDBC provider selected above" section. Click Next on the following screen to confirm that you are selecting the version 5.0 Datasource. Set the Datasource parameters on the next screen (see Figure 6-12).

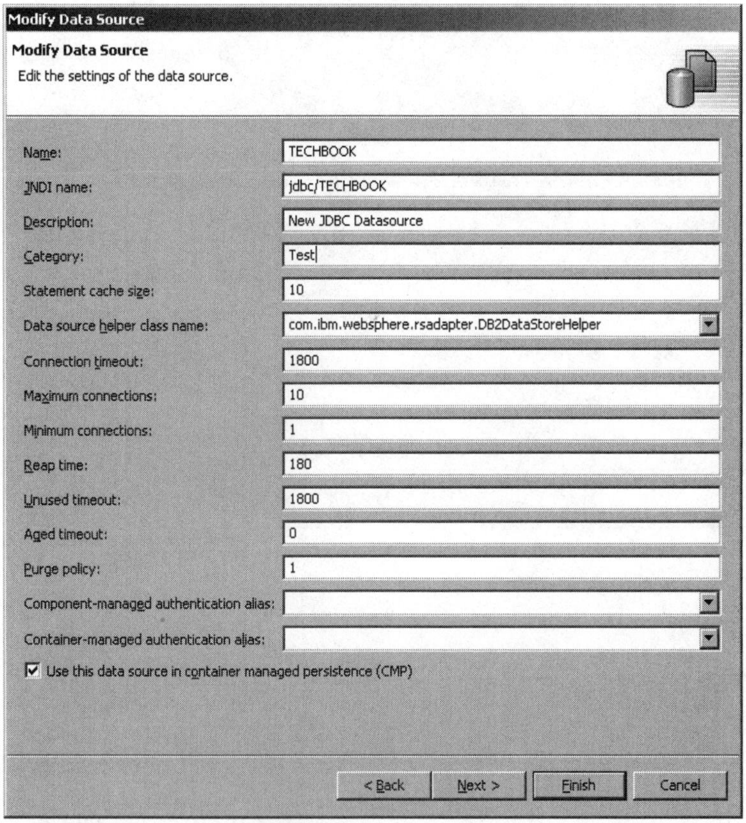

Figure 6-12. Datasource *configuration*

Enter TECHBOOK in the Name field. It is just a display name. Enter jdbc/TECHBOOK in the JNDI name field. This is the same JNDI reference to the Datasource that you used in the entity beans that you just built. Make sure that the Use this data source in container managed persistence (CMP) box is checked (this creates several internal reference names on the server that are necessary for a proper Datasource connection). Click Next. On the following screen, highlight the databaseName field and enter TECHBOOK as the value (see Figure 6-13).

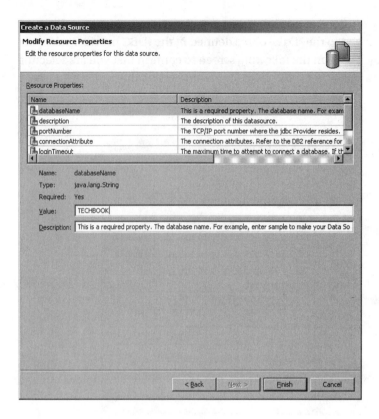

Figure 6-13. Setting the database name

Click Finish. You should see the following section of the server configuration (see Figure 6-14).

Click the Applications tab. You will see the following section of the server configuration (see Figure 6-15).

The classloader setting controls the isolation level of applications and its different parts. If you set the Web Archive (WAR) classloader to APPLICATION, then all parts of the WAR module will be loaded by the application loader that also loads EJB module classes. Selecting the MODULE policy will assign a separate classloader for all classes of the WAR module; therefore, the WAR module will be isolated from the rest of the application classes.

The classloader mode PARENT_FIRST causes the classloader to first delegate the loading of classes to its parent classloader before attempting to load the class from its local CLASSPATH. This is the default setting. PARENT_LAST, on the other hand, causes the classloader to attempt to load classes from its local CLASSPATH before delegating it to the parent classloader. This policy allows an application classloader to override and provide its own version of classes that exist in the parent classloader. Accept the default here and click the Configuration tab.

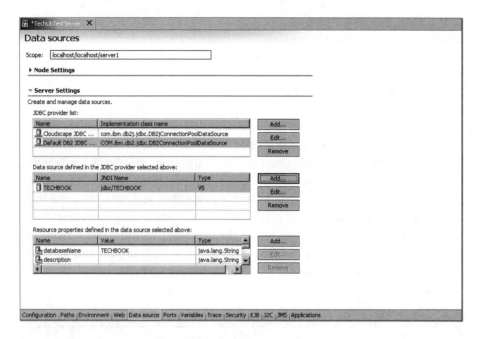

Figure 6-14. Fragment of the server configuration

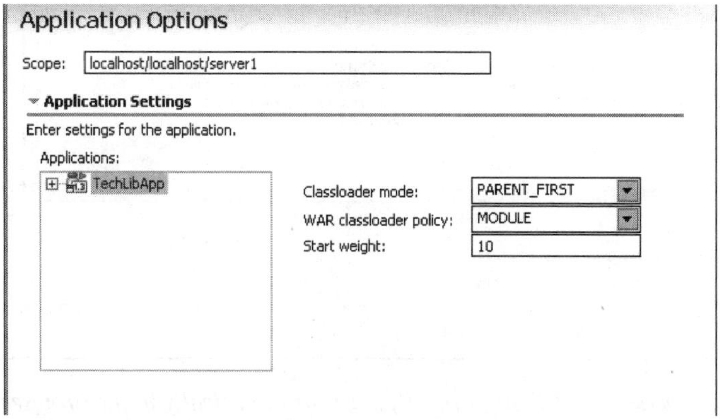

Figure 6-15. Classloader setting

Make sure the `Enable universal test client` box is checked. This allows testing of EJB modules without developing an EJB client. You also see the application classloader policy here. This policy controls the isolation level between applications. `MULTIPLE` means that each application will be assigned its own classloader and will be isolated from the rest of applications. `SINGLE` means that a single classloader will be loading all applications (applications are not isolated from each other). Accept the default here (MULTIPLE). Save and close the **Configuration Editor**. You are ready to test your entity beans.

Using the IBM EJB Test Client

To test EJB modules, you need an EJB client that calls the EJB components you have just developed. Because you do not have the EJB client (it is not developed yet), you will use a standard IBM Universal Test Client tool specifically designed for such situations. To be able to use the Universal Test Client, you must activate it in the server configuration. As you probably remember, you have just done this.

Switch to the Servers View, right-click TechLibTestServer and select Start. Wait until the server starts (you should see the message that the server is ready for e-business). In the Navigator View, right-click the TechLibEJB project and select Run on Server. The Universal Test Client will appear (see Figure 6-16).

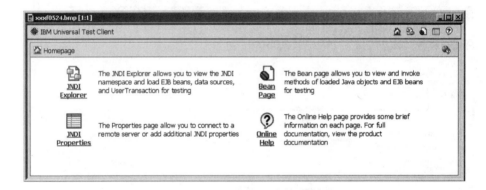

Figure 6-16. The Universal Test Client

 NOTE *The Universal Test Client normally starts automatically in the Browser View of the Server Perspective. If this not the case, just open the Browser View and enter the following URL:* http://localhost:8080/UTC.

Click JNDI Explorer. The JNDI Explorer screen will appear (see Figure 6-17).

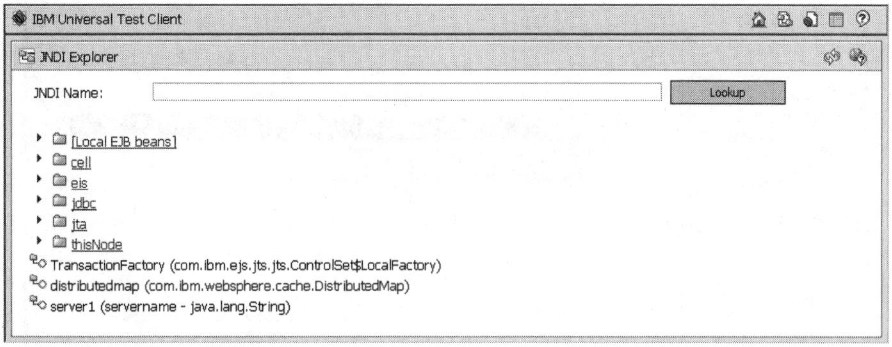

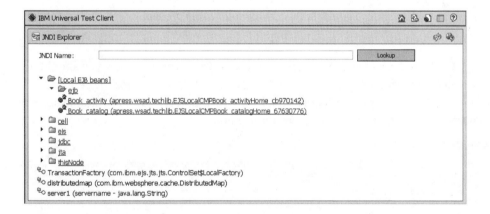

Figure 6-17. JNDI Explorer

Click the Local EJB Beans link, and then click the ejb link. You should see two Local Home interfaces of the Book_activity and Book_catalog entity beans (see Figure 6-18).

Figure 6-18. Local Home Interfaces of the entity beans

Click the Book_catalog link. The EJB References screen will appear. Expand TecLibBook_catalog all the way down until you will see the Local Home Interface methods.

At that point, you should see two create methods and three finder methods. Click the findByPrimaryKey method (you will test it first). On the Parameters pane, select the Constructor drop-down icon and click TechLibBook_catalogKey(String). Click the Expand link and enter 00002 as a BookCatalogNumber key (see Figure 6-19).

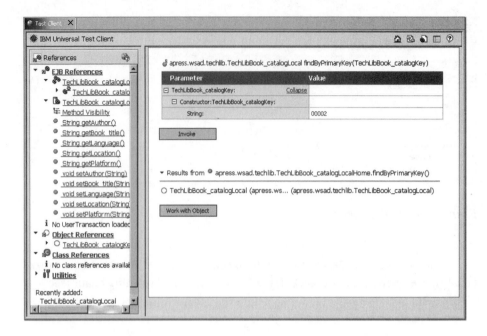

Figure 6-19. Request to find a Book_catalog *with a key of* 00002

Click the Invoke button. Click the Work with Object button. Now you should see all the object's methods promoted to the Local Interface. Click the getAuthor method. Click Invoke to execute it. Click Work with Object again. You should see "Developer Journal" displayed (see Figure 6-20).

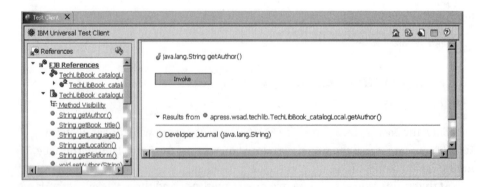

Figure 6-20. Displaying the author of the book

Click the GetBook_title method. Click Invoke to execute it. Click Work with Object. Now you should see "Windows NT Programming in Practice"—the title of the book (see Figure 6-21).

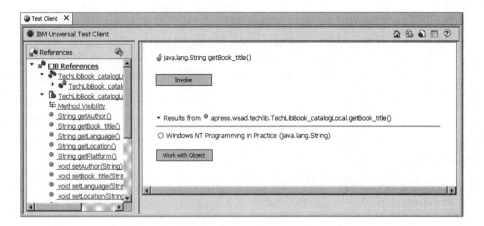

Figure 6-21. Displaying the book title

Let's test another method. Click TechLibBook_catalogLocalHome to get back to the list of available methods. This time, click the findByPlatform method. Again, you are prompted to enter the platform value. Enter 04. Click Invoke. Now, because multiple objects (records) are expected to be returned, a new button is displayed: Work with Contained Objects. Click this button. In the References section, you see three objects returned. Expand the first one and click the getBookTitle method. Next, click Invoke. The "Windows NT Programming in Practice" title is displayed (see Figure 6-22).

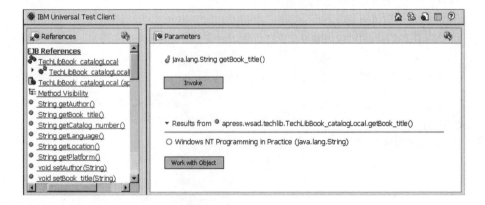

Figure 6-22. Displaying the first book title

Now, repeat the same for the second returned object. The result is "MCSE Windows 2000 Professional" (see Figure 6-23).

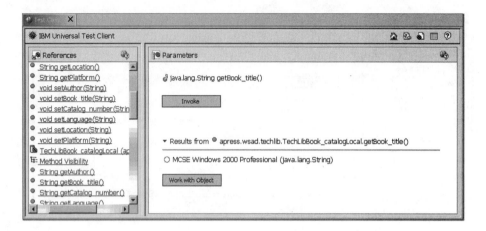

Figure 6-23. Displaying the second book title

Let's create a new record in the BOOK_CATALOG table. Click TechLibBook_catalogLocalHome to get back to the list of available methods. This time, click the create method with a full list of parameters. The screen on the left pane prompts you to enter the value for the six method's arguments. Enter the following values:

- Enter 00008 for Catalog Number.

- Enter Vanderburg and a team for Author.

- Enter Maximum Java 1.1 for Book Title.

- Enter Library for Location.

- Enter 00 for Platform.

- Enter 01 for Language.

Your screen should now look like Figure 6-24.

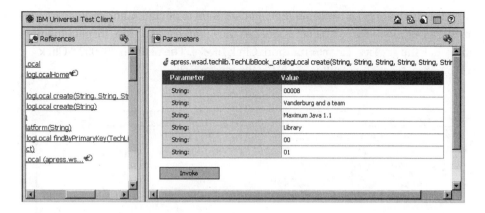

Figure 6-24. Creating a new database record

Click Invoke and then click Work with Object. A new object appears in the References section. You should see a list of available remote methods. Click the getBookTitle method, click Invoke, and then click Work with Object. The book title is displayed: "Maximum Java 1.1." This is the title of the new book that you have just added to the database. Now, let's test the Book_activity entity bean. Click the JNDI Explorer icon on the toolbar. This time, click the Book_activity link. Click Book_activityLocalHome. A list of available methods will be displayed. Click the findByCompany method. You are prompted for the value of the COMPANY_NAME field. Enter AAA_Company (see Figure 6-25).

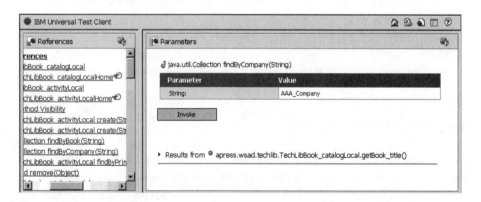

Figure 6-25. Finding records with the AAA_Company *field value*

Click Invoke. Again, multiple return objects are expected. Click Work with Contained Objects. Three objects appear in the References section. Inspect the first one. Click the getBook_cat_num method. Click Invoke. The result is "00002." Click getBook_txn_type. The result is "RENT" (see Figure 6-26).

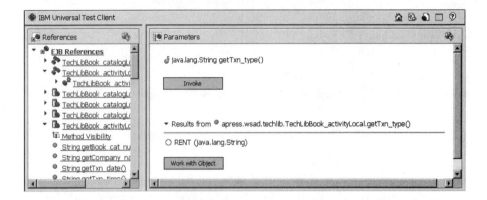

Figure 6-26. The processing results

Close the Universal Test Client and stop the server.

NOTE *If the nature of your database processing is of type Read Only, create only getter methods. The container will be able to recognize this and eliminate unnecessary reading of the database record in memory at the beginning of each transaction, which improves performance.*

This concludes the CMP entity bean Bottom Up development example.

Using the Top Down Method

The next example demonstrates the Top Down method—an alternative way of developing CMP entity beans. In this example, you will develop only a skeleton (not a fully functional) application to introduce you to this alternative method of developing entity beans. After the skeleton is built, the remainder of the development process is identical to the Bottom Up approach described in the previous example. You will do this development in a separate project, outside of your main development work. You will call this new EJB project AltCMPDevEJB (which stands for *alternative method of CMP development*). AltCMPDevApp is the corresponding J2EE application project.

Switch to the J2EE Perspective and create a new EJB project. From the main menu, select File ➤ New ➤ EJB Project. Confirm that this is the EJB 2.0 project type. On the EJB project creation screen, enter AltCMPDevEJB as the project name. Select New and enter AltCMPDevApp as the new J2EE application project name. Click Finish.

WSAD will generate two new projects: AltCMPDevEJB and AltCMPDevApp. Import the TECHBOOK database into the AltCMPDevEJB project. Switch to the Data Perspective. In the DB Servers View, right-click Con1 and select Reconnect. Expand the Con1 connection until you will see all the database tables. Right-click TECHBOOK and select Import to Folder. On the next screen, click Browse and select the AltCMPDevEJB project. Click OK and then click Finish. Finally, confirm the creation of the new folder.

The Top Down method assumes that the CMP entity bean is present. Because you do not have it, you need to build it first to simulate the situation. Right-click the AltCMPDevEJB project and select File ➤ New ➤ Enterprise Bean. On the next screen, select AltCMPDevEJB as the project name and click Next. On the subsequent screen, select CMP 2.0 as the bean type you are developing. Specifically, select Entity bean with container-managed persistence (CMP) fields and select CMP 2.0 Bean. Enter Book_details as the bean name and apress.wsad.sample as the default package. Ensure that AltCMPDevEJB is displayed in the Project name field.

Click Next. On the EJB Details screen, accept the default names of all classes that WSAD generates. Select Local client view (you still use the Local Interface here), and enter the CMP attributes (fields corresponding to the new database table BOOK_DETAILS that will be generated later based on this bean). Of course, I simulated a citation that the database table does not exist. To add the CMP attributes, click the Add button. On the dialog that appears, enter catalogNumber in the Name field. Select java.lang.String as the Type field. Mark the field as the Key field (see Figure 6-27).

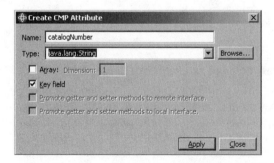

Figure 6-27. Creating CMP attributes

Click Apply. Enter the rest of the fields: publishingCompany and bookPrice. For each field, select String as the field type. Ensure that the Key field box is unselected and that Promote getter and setter methods to local interface is selected. When you have finished entering attributes, click Close. You should see the screen shown in Figure 6-28.

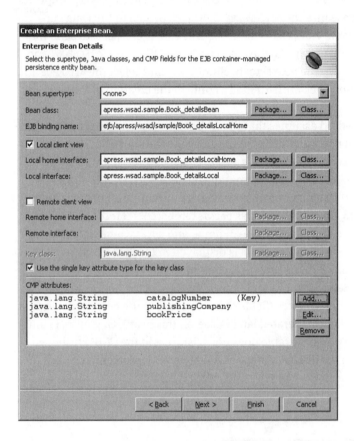

Figure 6-28. Enterprise Bean Details *screen*

What is strange here is that you are forced to generate both the getter and the setter methods, even if you are developing a CMP bean for Read Only database access. Click Next. The subsequent screen allows a new bean to inherit from an existing bean in the same EJB project. You do not need this; click Finish. The Book_detailsBean class will be generated along with its Local Home (Book_detailsLocalHome) and Local (Book_detailsLocal) classes.

At this point, you could edit the classes generated for the Book_details entity bean. You could even add several finder methods. However, this section will not cover those steps because this part of the development is identical to the previous example (the Bottom Up approach). Instead, you will concentrate on what is unique for the Top Down method of development.

Considering that your bean is done, you will define a new database table based on the existing Book_details CMP entity bean. The way to do this is to generate a Data Definition Language (DDL) file that you can use for building a new database table. Switch to the J2EE Hierarchy View of the J2EE Perspective. Expand the Databases folder and then expand the AltCMPDevEJB project all the way down until you see the Tables entry. Right-click the Tables entry and select New ➤ Table Definition. On the New dialog, enter BOOK_DETAILS in the Table name field (see Figure 6-29).

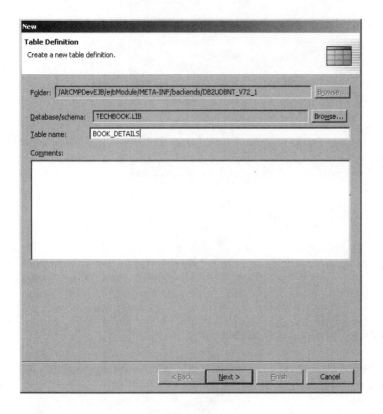

Figure 6-29. Table Definition *screen*

Click Next. On the Table Columns page, click Add Another to add a new column to the table. Enter CATALOG_NUMBER in the Column name field. Select VARCHAR as the column type, set the String length field to 5, uncheck the Nullable and the For bit data fields, and check the Key column box (see Figure 6-30).

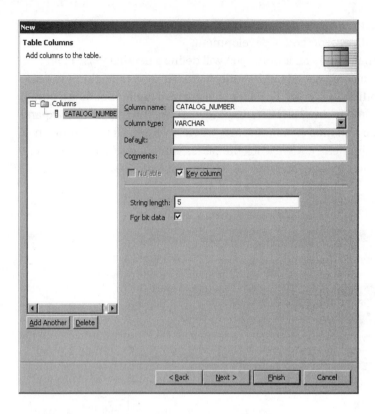

Figure 6-30. The Table Columns *screen*

Click Add Another again. Use the same procedure to enter the rest of the table columns:

- PUBLISHING_COMPANY: Select VARCHAR, uncheck Nullable, set the String length field to 100, and uncheck For bit data.

- BOOK_PRICE: Select VARCHAR, uncheck Nullable, set the String length to 10, and uncheck For bit data.

When you are done entering all the columns, click Next. On the next screen, enter CATALOG_NUMBER in the Primary Key's name field.

NOTE *If you leave this field blank, the name will be autogenerated. Select the* CATALOG_NUMBER *column in the left pane and click the >> button to move it to the right pane if it is not there yet (see Figure 6-31).*

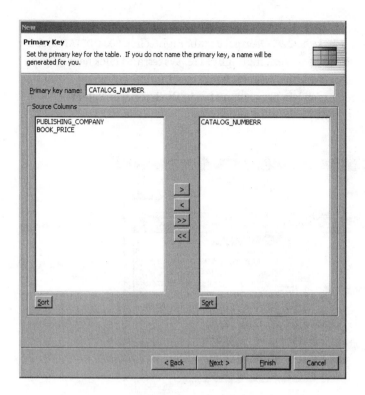

Figure 6-31. Primary Key screen

Click Finish. You should see a new BOOK_DETAILS table appear under the TECHBOOK database. Now, you will generate the DDL file necessary for a new database table creation. Right-click the BOOK_DETAILS table and select Generate DDL. On the next screen, check the following boxes: Generate SQL DDL with fully qualified names, Generate associated Drop statements, and Open SQL DDL file for editing when done. Click Finish. The generated BOOK_DETAILS.sql DDL file will be displayed for editing (see Figure 6-32).

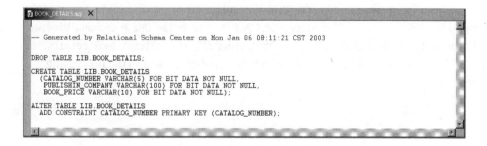

Figure 6-32. Generated DDL file

You do not need to modify it, so close the Editor View. Export the generated DDL to the file system. Click the J2EE Navigator tab. Right-click BOOK_DETAILS.sql and select Export. On the next screen, highlight File system and click Next. On the next screen, specify the destination c:\temp as the destination directory. Expand the AltCMPDevEJB project and select DB2UDBNT_V72_1 in the left pane. Select BOOK_DETAILS.sql in the right pane (see Figure 6-33).

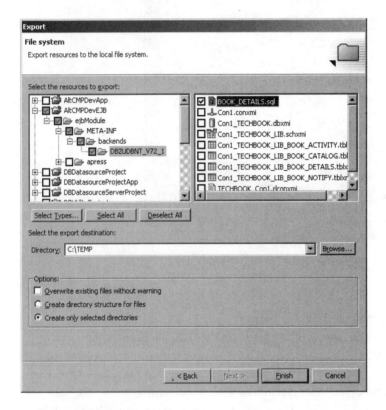

Figure 6-33. Exporting a DDL file

Click Finish. The BOOK_DETAILS.sql file will be exported. To build a new table, open the DB2 Command Window (Start ➤ Programs ➤ IBM DB2 ➤ Command Window). Enter db2 to connect to TECHBOOK. Then, enter db2 -tf c:\temp\ book_details.sql.

This will build the BOOK_DETAILS table. Listing 6-8 shows the processing results.

Listing 6-8. BOOK_DETAILS Processing Results

```
E:\PROGRA~1\SQLLIB\BIN>db2 connect to TECHBOOK
    Database Connection Information
 Database server       = DB2/NT 7.2.0
 SQL autorization ID   = ADMINIST...
 Local database alias  = TECHBOOK


 E:\PROGRA~1\SQLLIB\BIN>db2 -tf c:\temp\book_details.sql
 DB21034E The command was processed as an SQL statement because it was a
 valid Command Line Processor command. During SQL processing it returned:
 SQL0204N "LIB.BOOK_DETAILS" is an undefined name. SQLSTATE=42704
 DB20000I  The SQL command completed successfully.
 DB20000I  The SQL command completed successfully.
```

Mapping Entity Bean Attributes to the Database Tables

Next, you will map the Book_details entity bean to the BOOK_DETAILS database
table. In the J2EE Perspective, right-click the AltCMPDevEJB project and select
Generate EJB to RDB Mapping. On the next screen, you are prompted to create a
new backend folder or to use the existing one. The backend folder keeps the
database imported in the project. You already have the backend folder, so select
Use an existing backend folder and click Next.

The next screen should prompt you to choose the type of the EJB/RDB mapping
(Bottom Up, Top Down, or Meet In The Middle). However, the next screen displays the
preselected choice: Meet In The Middle. The reason for this is that you already built
the BOOK_DETAILS database table, so WSAD sees both the Book_details entity bean
and the BOOK_DETAILS database table. When both artifacts are present, all you
need is a Meet in the Middle method of mapping corresponding fields. Click Next.

The next screen prompts you to match the corresponding database and entity
bean fields. Three choices are available: None, Match by Name, and Match by Name and
Type. The None option assumes you want to manually map fields. The Match by Name
option will simply match fields by name. If identically named fields are present,
you choose Match by Name and Type. Select Match by Name and click Finish. Now you
are presented with the Map.map.xmi file in the Editor View. The Book_details bean is
in the upper-left pane and BOOK_DETAILS table is in the right pane. Expand them
both. The lower pane shows that the BOOK_DETAILS bean fields have not been
mapped yet.

Because the mapping field names are constructed differently (catalogNumber vs. CATALOG_NUMBER), you will do manual mapping here. In the upper part of the screen, select `catalogNumber` in the left pane and `CATALOG_NUMBER` in the right pane. Right-click `CATALOG_NUMBER` and select `Create Mapping`. You should see that both fields are mapped in the lower section of the screen. Do the same for the two remaining fields. You should see all fields that are mapped in the lower section of the screen (see Figure 6-34).

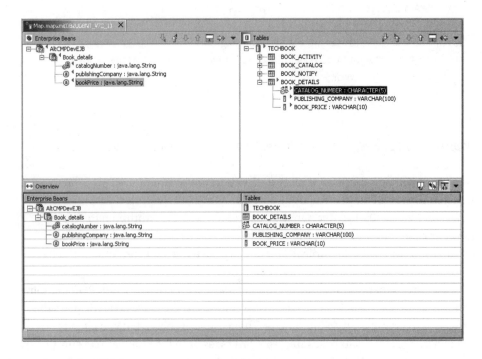

Figure 6-34. Mapping attributes to database fields

Save the results and close the Editor View. Starting from this point, the remainder part of the development is similar to the Bottom Up method.

Using the Meet in the Middle Method

You use the Meet in the Middle method of entity bean development when both the entity bean and the database table are available at the beginning of the project.

The first step is to map the entity bean attributes to the corresponding fields of the database table. To do this, right-click the AltCMPDevProject project and select Generate ➤ EJB to RDB Mapping. On the Create EJB/RDB Mapping dialog, check the Meet In The Middle mode. You will be presented with a similar mapping screen that maps bean attributes to the fields of the corresponding database table. The remainder part of the development is the same.

Developing BMP Entity Beans

In this section, you will develop a BMP entity bean with a Remote Interface. That means that all communication with the EJB client will be over the network. In this example, you will develop a BMP bean called BookInquiry. Typically, development of BMP entity beans requires more effort because the persistence database-related logic and synchronization between bean attributes and the corresponding database record fields must be coded by the developer (instead of simply relying on the EJB container to automatically manage this process as is the case for the CMP entity beans).

On the other hand, BMP entity beans give developers more flexibility in controlling the bean interaction with databases. The BMP entity beans are typically used for beans that need to perform more complex database processing; this frequently includes processing of legacy databases. Your BMP entity bean will have one business method called bookActivityByCompany. For a specified book, the method will return a list of the book-related transactions. The database query you will use in this section is not more complex than the one you used in the CMP examples. However, you will develop this entity bean as a BMP type just to illustrate the BMP development process. With this quick introduction, let's start the development.

You will develop the BookInquiry BMP bean under the same TechLibEJB project. Right-click the TechLibEJB project and select New ➤ Enterprise Bean. The next screen prompts you to select the project. It is already prefilled to TechLibEJB, so click Next. On the next screen, select the BMP entity bean and enter BookInquiry as the bean name. Make sure that apress.wsad.techlib is displayed in the Default package field. If this is not the case, click Browse and navigate to this package (see Figure 6-35).

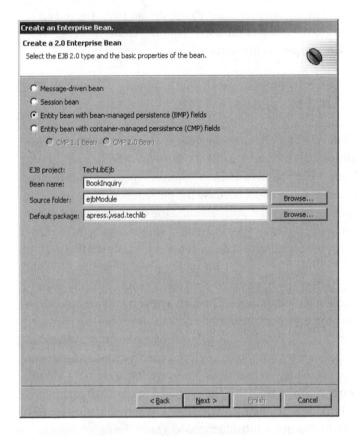

Figure 6-35. Building a BMP entity bean

Click Next. On the next screen, select Remote Client View and unselect Local Client View. In addition, enter ejb/BookInquiry in the EJB binding name field (see Figure 6-36).

Click Finish. WSAD will generate the skeleton of the BMP entity bean. You should see the BookInquiry files generated by WSAD: BookInquiryBean (the Implementation class), BookInquiry (the Remote Interface), BookInquiryHome (the Home Interface), and BookInquiryKey (the Primary Key class).

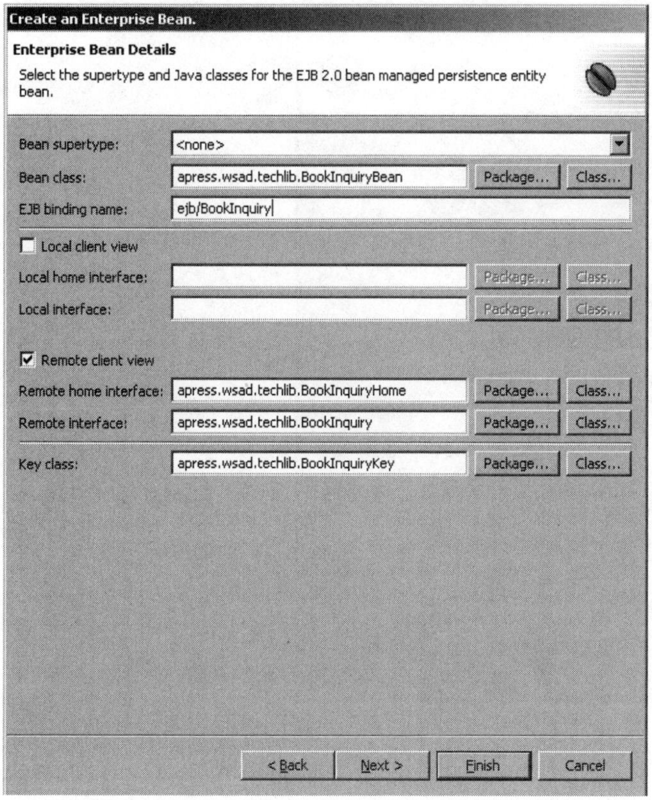

Figure 6-36. BMP details screen

Building the Transport Object

You will now temporarily stop developing the BMP entity bean and build a helper JavaBean class that will serve as a transport object to deliver the database processing results from the entity bean back to the EJB client that called them. The transport object allows you to deliver all SQL processing results as one network data transfer object (eliminating a need for multiple calls over the network).

You will name this transport JavaBean class as TransportBean.java. To create this JavaBean class, right-click the apress.wsad.techlib folder under the TechLibEJB project and select New ➤ Other ➤ Java ➤ Java Class. Make sure that the correct project is selected in the Folder field. If not, click Browse and select the TechLibEJB project. Enter TransportBean in the Name field. Click Browse and enter java.io.Serializable in the Extended interface field. Finally, check Constructors from superclass (see Figure 6-37).

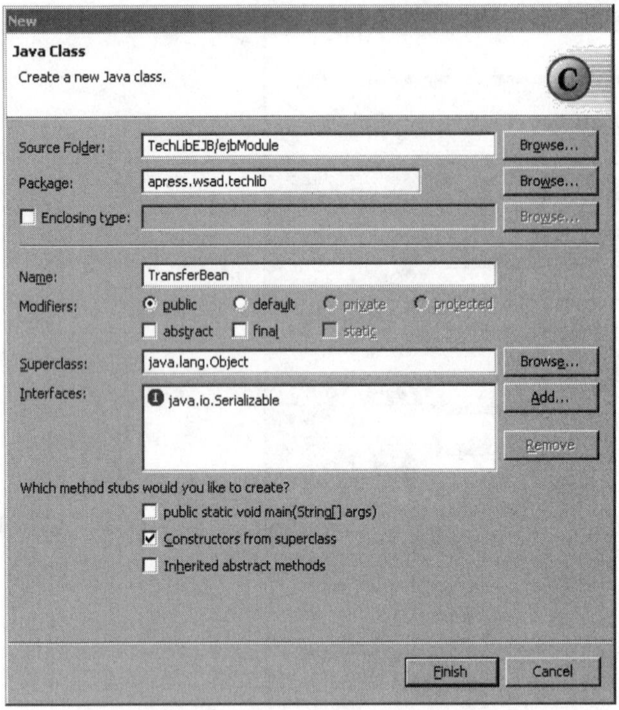

Figure 6-37. Creating a Java class

Click Finish. WSAD will generate the skeleton of the Java class. The generated skeleton of the TransportBean class will open in the Java Editor View for modifications. Enter attributes that correspond to the field of both database tables: BOOK_CATALOG and BOOK_ACTIVITY. Modify the code skeleton as shown in Listing 6-9. Save the results and close the Editor View.

Listing 6-9. TransportBean.java

```
package apress.wsad.techlib;
import java.io.Serializable;
import java.lang.*;
import java.util.*;

public class TransportObjectBean implements Serializable
{
  protected String catalogNumber;
  protected String author;
  protected String bookTitle;
```

```
    protected String location;
    protected String platform;

    protected String txnDate;
    protected String txnTime;
    protected String txnType;
    protected String bookCatNum;
    protected String companyName;

public TransportObjectBean()
 {
  super();
     // Init all fields
  catalogNumber = "";
  author = "";
  bookTitle = "";
  location = "";
  platform = "";
  txnDate = "";
  txnTime = "";
  txnType = "";
  bookCatNum = "";
  companyName = "";


 }
}
```

Next, you need to create the getter/setter methods for this JavaBean attribute. Right-click elsewhere in the Outline View and select Generate Getters/Setters. On the dialog that appears, mark all attributes and click OK (see Figure 6-38). WSAD will generate all getter/setter methods.

Save the results and close the Editor View. There are several important differences between coding CMP and BMP entity beans.

Within the ejbCreate method of BMP entity bean, you need to code the SQL insert statement because the ejbCreate method is responsible for adding a new entity record to the database. The ejbCreate method functions here as a pseudo-constructor. The BMP entity bean can have multiple ejbCreate methods. In this case, the corresponding ejbPostCreate methods must be coded in the implementation class, and the corresponding create methods must be included in the bean's Home or Local Home Interface. Because you coded an additional ejbCreate and corresponding ejbPostCreate methods in your bean implementation class, you also need to add an additional create method in the bean's Home Interface

(BookInquiryHome). All ejbCreate, ejbPostCreate, and FindByPrimeryKey methods must return the Primary Key object to the container (in contrast, CMP entity beans return null in these methods).

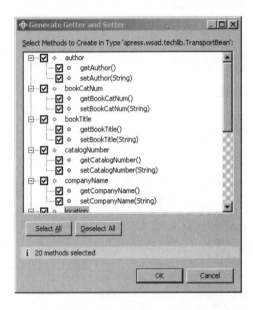

Figure 6-38. Building getter/setter methods

Two other methods require SQL coding: ejbStore and ejbLoad. Both of these methods are callback methods that are called by the EJB container to notify the BMP entity bean that the synchronization of state variables with the corresponding database record(s) needs to be performed. When an EJB client calls some of the setter methods, the state of the bean is changed and needs to be synchronized with the database. In this case, the container calls the ejbStore method, which has to execute the SQL update statement.

The EJB container calls the ejbLoad method in the opposite situation—to reflect a database change in the value of the bean's state variables. Typically, the EJB container calls the ejbLoad method at the start of a new transaction or a new business method. This ensures that the bean's state variables always represent the current data in the database (which could potentially be changed by other beans or other even non-EJB applications).

Therefore, the ejbLoad method needs to execute the SQL Select statement and update the values of the bean's state variables. The database record key that is used by this SQL select statement should be obtained from the bean's EntityContext and not directly from the state variable or variables that represent the Primary Key. The reason is that the container can call the ejbLoad method during the bean activation process (for the bean that has been previously passivated). In this case, the value of the state variable(s) that holds the key is undefined. It is also undefined when the ejbLoad method is executed for the first time. The bookActivityByCompany business method needs to execute the following SQL statement:

```
select BOOK_TITLE, TXN_DATE, TXN_TYPE, COMPANY_NAME form LIB.BOOK_CATALOG,
LIB.BOOK_ACTIVITY where CATALOG_NUMBER=? and CATALOG_NUMBER = BOOK_CAT_NUM
```

The SQL statement simply performs a search for all activity records related to the selected book's catalog number. The connection to the Datasource is encapsulated in the getDBConnection method. To connect to a Datasource (as to any other resource), the bean needs to use the JNDI to locate the resource factory and then use the lookup method to get a reference to the Datasource object. Having the Datasource object, the bean calls its connect method to get the database connection. Notice that the lookup JNDI name originally assigned to your Datasource as jdbc/TECHBOOK is coded in the lookup statement relative to the JNDI ECN Environment Naming Context (ECN) java:comp/env.

You also modified the Primary Key class (BookInquiryKey). You added the second constructor with one String parameter bookCatalogNumber, which saves the value of this parameter in the class variable catalogNumber. You also added a new method getPrimaryKey that returns the catalogNumber string.

Listing 6-10 shows the source code of all BookInquiry modules. You need to reflect all code changes in the BookInquiry modules generated by WSAD.

Listing 6-10. BookInquiryBean.java: *Implementation Class*

```java
package apress.wsad.techlib;
import javax.ejb.*;
import java.rmi.*;
import java.sql.*;
import java.lang.*;
import java.util.*;
import javax.naming.*;
import java.sql.Connection;
import javax.sql.DataSource;

/**
 * Bean implementation class for Enterprise Bean: BookInquiry
 */
public class BookInquiryBean implements javax.ejb.EntityBean
{
  private javax.ejb.EntityContext myEntityCtx;
```

```java
    public String catalogNumber;
    public String author;
    public String bookTitle;
    public String location;
    public String platform;
    public String language;
    private ResultSet result = null;

    public BookInquiryKey ejbCreate()
        throws javax.ejb.CreateException
    {
      return null;
    }


    public BookInquiryKey ejbCreate(String catalogNumber,
                                    String author,
                                    String bookTitle,
                                    String location,
                                    String platform,
                                    String language
                                    )
    throws javax.ejb.CreateException
  {
    Connection dbCon = null;
    PreparedStatement prepStm = null;
    if (catalogNumber == null)
     {
       throw new javax.ejb.CreateException ("Invalid catalogNumber parameter");
     }

    this.catalogNumber = catalogNumber;
    this.author = author;
    this.bookTitle = bookTitle;
    this.location = location;
    this.platform = platform;
    this.language = language;

    try
      {
        dbCon = this.getDBConnection();

          prepStm = dbCon.prepareStatement("insert into LIB.BOOK_CATALOG " +
            "(CATALOG_NUMBER, AUTHOR, BOOK_TITLE, LOCATION, PLATFORM, LANGUAGE) "
```

```
                          "values (?,?,?,?,?,?)");
  prepStm.setString(1, catalogNumber);
  prepStm.setString(2, author);
  prepStm.setString(3, bookTitle);
  prepStm.setString(4, location);
  prepStm.setString(5, platform);
  prepStm.setString(6, language);

  if (prepStm.executeUpdate() != 1)
   {
     throw new EJBException ("Faild to add Catalog record to database -
           Create method");
   }

  }                                // End of the try statement
catch(SQLException sq)
 {
   System.out.println("SQL Error. " + sq);
   throw new EJBException("SQL call failed " + sq);

 }

finally
 {
   try
   {
     if (result != null)
       result.close();

     if (prepStm != null)
       prepStm.close();

     if (dbCon != null)
       dbCon.close();
       }
   catch (SQLException se)
    {
    se.printStackTrace();
    }

 } // End of the finally statement
```

```java
      return new BookInquiryKey(catalogNumber);
   }

   public void ejbPostCreate() throws javax.ejb.CreateException
    {
    }

   public void ejbPostCreate(String catalogNumber,
                             String author,
                             String bookTitle,
                             String location,
                             String platform,
                             String language
                            )
    throws javax.ejb.CreateException
   {

   }

   public BookInquiryKey ejbFindByPrimaryKey(BookInquiryKey primaryKey)
     throws javax.ejb.FinderException
   {
      Connection dbCon = null;

      PreparedStatement prepStm = null;

     catalogNumber = primaryKey.getPrimeKey();

      try
       {
         dbCon = this.getDBConnection();

            prepStm = dbCon.prepareStatement("select
                  CATALOG_NUMBER,AUTHOR,BOOK_TITLE,LOCATION,PLATFORM,LANGUAGE " +
                                            "from LIB.BOOK_CATALOG " +
                                            "where CATALOG_NUMBER=?");
         prepStm.setString(1, catalogNumber);

         result = prepStm.executeQuery();

            // Does the book exists
            if (result.next())
             {
```

```
        author = result.getString("AUTHOR");
        bookTitle = result.getString("BOOK_TITLE");
        location = result.getString("LOCATION");
        platform = result.getString("PLATFORM");
            language = result.getString("LANGUAGE");
    }


}
catch(SQLException sql)
  {
    System.out.println("SQL Error. " + sql);

    try
     {
      if (prepStm != null)
        prepStm.close();

      if (dbCon != null)
        dbCon.close();
      }
     catch (SQLException se)
      {
      // Ignore this exceptin
    }

    throw new EJBException("SQL call failed " + sql);

  }

  finally
   {
     try
     {
       if (result != null)
         result.close();

       if (prepStm != null)
         prepStm.close();

       if (dbCon != null)
         dbCon.close();
       }
     catch (SQLException se)
```

```
          {
            se.printStackTrace();
             }


      } // End of the finally statement


      return primaryKey;
   }


   public Vector bookActivityByCompany(String companyName)
     {
       Connection dbCon = null;

       PreparedStatement prepStm = null;
       Vector vector = new Vector();
       try
       {
       dbCon = this.getDBConnection();

           prepStm = dbCon.prepareStatement("select BOOK_TITLE, TXN_DATE, TXN_TYPE,
                                   COMPANY_NAME " +
                             "from LIB.BOOK_CATALOG, LIB.BOOK_ACTIVITY " +
                                "where CATALOG_NUMBER=? and
                                   CATALOG_NUMBER=BOOK_CAT_NUM");

       prepStm.setString(1, companyName);
       result = prepStm.executeQuery();
       while (result.next())
         {
           TransportBean transObject = new TransportBean();
           transObject.bookTitle =  result.getString("BOOK_TITLE");
           transObject.txnDate =     result.getString("TXN_DATE");
           transObject.txnType =    result.getString("TXN_TYPE");
           transObject.companyName =  result.getString("COMPANY_NAME");

           vector.addElement(transObject);
         }

       return vector;

       }                              // End of the try statement
     catch(SQLException sql)
       {
```

```
        System.out.println("SQL Error. " + sql);
        throw new EJBException("SQL call failed " + sql);


    }


    finally
    {
        try
        {
            if (result != null)
                result.close();

            if (prepStm != null)
                prepStm.close();

            if (dbCon != null)
                dbCon.close();
        }
        catch (SQLException se)
        {
            se.printStackTrace();
        }

    } // End of the finally statement

} // End of the method


public void ejbStore()
{

    Connection dbCon = null;
    PreparedStatement prepStm = null;


    try
    {

        dbCon = this.getDBConnection();

        prepStm = dbCon.prepareStatement("update LIB.BOOK_CATALOG set AUTHOR = ?,
                    BOOK_TITLE = ?, LOCATION = ?, PLATFORM = ?, LANGUAGE = ?" +
                        "where CATALOG_NUMBER = ?");
```

```
            prepStm.setString(1, author);
            prepStm.setString(2, bookTitle);
            prepStm.setString(3, location);
            prepStm.setString(4, platform);
            prepStm.setString(5, language);
            prepStm.setString(6, catalogNumber);

            if (prepStm.executeUpdate() != 1)
             {
               throw new EJBException ("Faild ejbStore processing");
             }

         }                              // End of the try statement
      catch(SQLException sq)
       {
          System.out.println("SQL Error. " + sq);
          throw new EJBException("SQL call failed " + sq);
       }

      finally
       {
         try
         {
           if (result != null)
             result.close();

           if (prepStm != null)
             prepStm.close();

           if (dbCon != null)
             dbCon.close();
           }
         catch (SQLException se)
          {
           se.printStackTrace();
          }

        } // End of the finally statement

     } // End of the method

   public void ejbLoad()
   {
```

```
Connection dbCon = null;
PreparedStatement prepStm = null;
String catalogNumber = (String)myEntityCtx.getPrimaryKey();
try
{
 dbCon = this.getDBConnection();
 prepStm = dbCon.prepareStatement("select AUTHOR, BOOK_TITLE, LOCATION,
                           PLATFORM, LANGUAGE " +
                           "from LIB.BOOK_CATALOG " +
                           "where CATALOG_NUMBER = ?");

 prepStm.setString(1, catalogNumber);
 result = prepStm.executeQuery();

 if (result.next())
  {
    author    = result.getString("AUTHOR");
    bookTitle = result.getString("BOOK_TITLE");
    location  = result.getString("LOCATION");
    platform  = result.getString("PLATFORM");
    language  = result.getString("LANGUAGE");
  }
 else
  {
   throw new EJBException ("Faild ejbLoad processing");
  }

}                               // End of the try statement
catch(SQLException sq)
{
   System.out.println("SQL Error. " + sq);
   throw new EJBException("SQL call failed " + sq);

}

finally
 {
   try
   {
     if (result != null)
       result.close();

     if (prepStm != null)
```

```
        prepStm.close();

     if (dbCon != null)
       dbCon.close();
     }
    catch (SQLException se)
     {
      se.printStackTrace();


      } // End of the finally statement


}

public javax.ejb.EntityContext getEntityContext()
 {
  return myEntityCtx;
 }

public void setEntityContext(javax.ejb.EntityContext ctx)
 {
  myEntityCtx = ctx;
 }

public void unsetEntityContext()
 {
  myEntityCtx = null;
 }

public void ejbActivate()
 {
 }

public void ejbPassivate()
 {
 }

public void ejbRemove() throws javax.ejb.RemoveException
 {
    Connection dbCon = null;
    PreparedStatement prepStm = null;
    String catalogNumber = (String)myEntityCtx.getPrimaryKey();

    try
```

```
  {

    dbCon = this.getDBConnection();

    prepStm = dbCon.prepareStatement("delete from LIB.BOOK_CATALOG where
                            CATALOG_NUMBER = ?");

    prepStm.setString(1, catalogNumber);

    if (prepStm.executeUpdate() != 1)
     {

       throw new EJBException ("Faild ejbRemove processing");
     }


  }                // End of the try statement
catch(SQLException sq)
 {
    System.out.println("SQL Error. " + sq);
    throw new EJBException("SQL call failed " + sq);
 }

 finally
  {
    try
    {
      if (result != null)
        result.close();

      if (prepStm != null)
        prepStm.close();

      if (dbCon != null)
        dbCon.close();
      }
    catch (SQLException se)
     {
      se.printStackTrace();
      }

  } // End of the finally statement


}
```

```
private Connection getDBConnection() throws SQLException
  {
   try
    {
     InitialContext jndiContext = new InitialContext();
     DataSource dataSource =
       (DataSource)jndiContext.lookup("java:comp/env/jdbc/TECHBOOK");
     //DataSource dataSource = (DataSource)jndiContext.lookup("jdbc/TECHBOOK");

     return dataSource.getConnection();
    }
   catch(NamingException ne)
    {
      System.out.println("Error locating jdbc/TECHBOOK: " +  ne.getMessage());

      throw new EJBException(ne);
    }

  }

 }
```

Listing 6-11 shows the source code for the BookInquiryHome interface.

Listing 6-11. BookInquiryHome.java: *Home Interface Class*

```
package apress.wsad.techlib;

public interface BookInquiryHome extends javax.ejb.EJBHome
{

  public BookInquiry create()
    throws javax.ejb.CreateException, java.rmi.RemoteException;


  public BookInquiry create(String catalogNumber,
                            String author,
                            String bookTitle,
                            String location,
                            String platform,
                            String language
```

```
                )
  throws javax.ejb.CreateException,  java.rmi.RemoteException;

public BookInquiry findByPrimaryKey(BookInquiryKey primaryKey)
  throws javax.ejb.FinderException, java.rmi.RemoteException;
}
```

Listing 6-12 shows the source code for the BookInquiry Remote Interface.

Listing 6-12. BookInquiry.java: *Remote Interface Class*

```
package apress.wsad.techlib;

import java.util.Vector;
public interface BookInquiry extends javax.ejb.EJBObject
{
 public Vector bookActivityByCompany(String companyName)
  throws java.rmi.RemoteException;
}
```

Listing 6-13 shows the source code for the BookInquiryKey Primary Key class.

Listing 6-13. BookInquiryKey.java: *Primary Key Class*

```
package apress.wsad.techlib;
public class BookInquiryKey implements java.io.Serializable
{
 static final long serialVersionUID = 3206093459760846163L;

     // Primary key
 public String catalogNumber;
 public BookInquiryKey()
  {
  }

    public BookInquiryKey(String catalogNumber)
     {
      this.catalogNumber = catalogNumber;
     }

    public String getPrimeKey()
     {
```

```
            return catalogNumber;
        }

public boolean equals(java.lang.Object otherKey)
 {
  if (otherKey instanceof apress.wsad.techlib.BookInquiryKey)
  {
   apress.wsad.techlib.BookInquiryKey o =
   (apress.wsad.techlib.BookInquiryKey) otherKey;
   return (super.equals(otherKey));
  }
   return false;
 }

 public int hashCode()
 {
   return (super.hashCode());
 }
}
```

Notice that within a BMP entity bean you do not save the database connection for subsequent reuse; instead, you close it after each method execution. The reason is that a Datasource maintains a pool of connections and a closed connection is simply returned to the pool. Another reason for this is that you never know when the next call to the entity bean will be made, so keeping the database connection open would waste valuable resources.

Now you need to promote the getBookActivity method to the Remote Interface. With BookInquiryBean.java open in the Java Editor View, right-click the getBookActivity method in the Outline View and select EnterpriseBean ➤ Promote to Remote Interface. Validate the bean. Right-click the TechLibEJB project and select Run Validation. There should be no errors. Finally, generate the deployment code. Right-click the TechLibEJB project and select Generate ➤ Deploy and RMIC code. On the dialog that appears, select the BookInquiry module. Click Finish. There should be no errors.

Next, check that the JNDI name for your bean is assigned correctly (ejb/BookInquiry) and that the BMP bean is correctly mapped to the Datasource. In the J2EE Hierarchy View, right-click the TechLibEJB project and select Open With ➤ Deployment Descriptor Editor. Select the Overview tab, click the BookInquiry bean and make sure that the JNDI name in the "WebSphere Bindings" section is set to ejb/BookInquiry. If it is not there, enter ejb/BookInquery in the JNDI name field (see Figure 6-39).

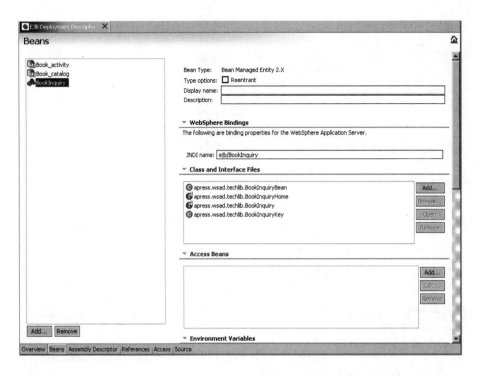

Figure 6-39. The Deployment Descriptor "WebSphere Bindings" section

Next, click the References tab. Select BookInquiry and click the Add button. On the next screen, select EJB resource reference as a reference type and click Next. On the following screen, enter TechbookDS in the Name field, select javax.sql.DataSource for the Type field, select Application for the Authentication field, and select Sharable as the Sharing scope field (see Figure 6-40).

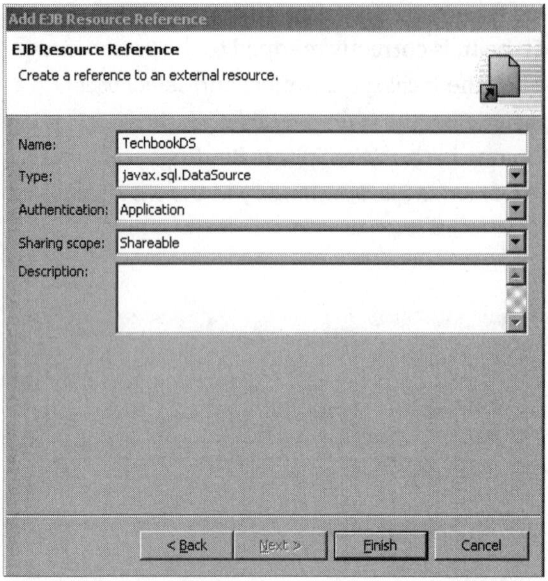

Figure 6-40. Setting the Datasource *reference*

Expand BookInquiry and click ResourceRef TechbookDS. You should see that a new ResourceReference entry has been added below BookInquiry. Enter jdbc/TECHBOOK in the JNDI name field (see Figure 6-41).

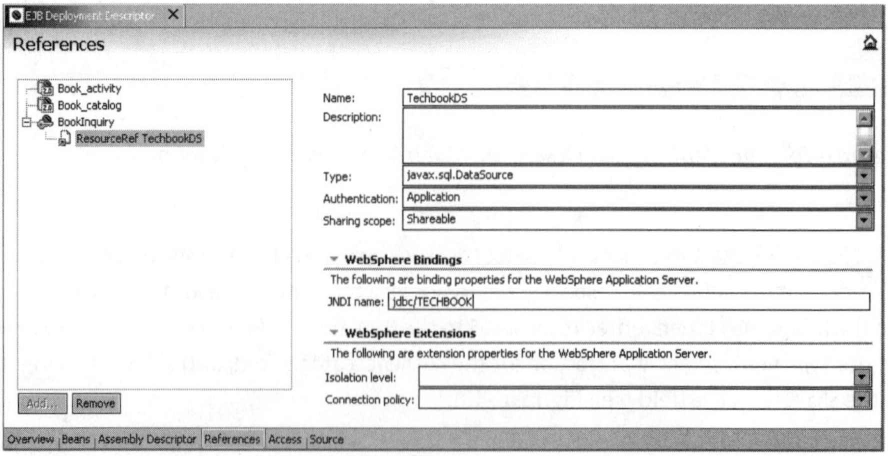

Figure 6-41. Setting the JNDI name for the Datasource *resource*

Finally, save the results and close the Editor View.

Testing BMP Entity Beans

To test the BMP entity beans, switch to the Server Perspective. In the Servers View, right-click TectLibTestServer and select Start. Alternatively, you can highlight the server and click the Start button located on the Servers View toolbar. You should see a set of messages informing you that the server is starting. Wait until you see a message that the server is open for e-business. In the Navigator View of the Server Perspective, right-click the TechLibEJB project and select Run on Server. The IBM Universal Test Client will appear.

Click JNDI Explorer. The JNDI Explorer screen will appear. Expand the ejb entry (which is the naming subcontext for EJB beans that exposes the Remote Interface) and click the BookInquiry link. In the References pane, expand BookInquiry and then expand BookInquiryHome. At that point, you should see the create and FindByPrimaryKey Home Interface methods. Click the create method with the full set of parameters. You are prompted to enter six parameters. Enter 00031 as the bookCatalogNumber, Bob Quinn as the author, Windows Sockets Network Programming as the bookTitle, Library as the location, 04 as the platform, and 00 as the language (see Figure 6-42).

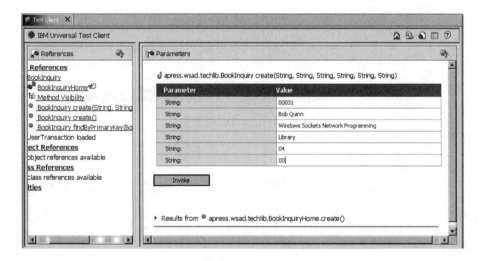

Figure 6-42. Executing the create *method*

Figure 6-43 shows the processing result of the DB2 command that displays all records in the Book_CATALOG table. You should see that the record with the catalogNumber = 00031 has been inserted.

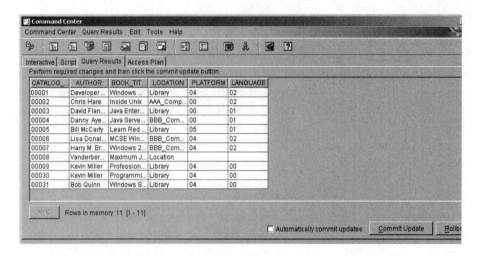

Figure 6-43. The result of the DB2 command execution

Next, click the findByPrimaryKey method. You are prompted to enter the catalog number parameter. Enter 00001 (see Figure 6-44).

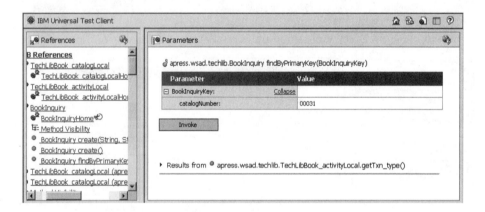

Figure 6-44. Testing a BMP entity bean

Click Invoke. Click Work with Object. A second object will appear under References. Expand it all the way down. You should see the bookActivityByCompany method. Click it. You will be prompted for the value of a single argument—the book's Catalog_Number. Enter 00001. Click Invoke. Click Work with Objects. Two TransferBean objects will appear under References. Expand the first one. You will see all available Remote Interface methods. Click the getCompanyName method. Click Invoke. Click Work with Object. The "AAA_Company" company will be displayed (see Figure 6-45).

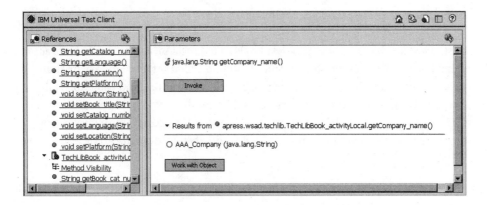

Figure 6-45. The result of executing the `getCompanyName` *method*

Close the Browser View and stop the server. This concludes the BMP entity bean development example.

Developing Session Beans

In this section, you will develop both types of session beans: stateless and stateful session beans. The development of both types of session beans is similar in regards to the tools used and steps that need to be performed. Even the generated code looks similar. However, their life cycle is different, and the way they perform at runtime is substantially different. Stateless beans are selected from a pool to serve a client for the duration of one method execution. After that, they are returned to the pool that is waiting to serve another client request (again to execute one method only). They do not remember any state between method invocations. In comparison with other beans, stateless beans consume the smallest amount of system resources and are the best performers.

On the other hand, stateful session beans are attached to a specific client for the duration of the client session (conversation), which typically involves multiple screens and multiple invocations of the stateful bean's methods. Stateful beans can be temporarily swapped out of memory (passivation) and subsequently brought back in (activation) by the container, but they always maintain the state between multiple method invocations. You will start with the session bean development example from the stateless session bean section.

Developing Stateless Session Beans

The stateless session bean you will develop is called `TechLibFacade`. The `TechLibFacade` session bean will implement one business method called `getBookForPlatform` that should be accessible via Remote and Local Interfaces. This method will return all books written for the platform requested by the user. To perform this processing, it will call local methods of the previously developed entity beans. This technique of wrapping entity beans by a session bean substantially improves the application performance.

NOTE *Using this technique is especially important for working with entity beans that expose a Remote Interface for the EJB clients; therefore, each call is a network call. For entity beans that expose the Local Interface for the EJB client, this method is less useful for improving application performance, but it is still a good development pattern because it provides a more structural organization of the developed application.*

With this quick introduction, let's start developing this project.

You will do the `TechLibFacade` session bean development under the same `TechLibEJB` project. Switch to the J2EE View of the J2EE Perspective. Right-click the `TechLibEJB` project and select New ➤ Enterprise Bean. On the next screen, confirm the project selection and click Next. On the following screen, select the Session bean type. Enter `TechLibFacade` as the bean name. Leave the Source folder field as `ejbModule`, and set the default package name to `apress.wsad.techlib` (see Figure 6-46).

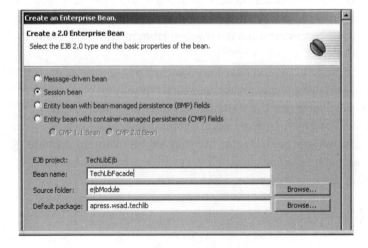

Figure 6-46. The Create an Enterprise Bean *screen*

Click Next. On the subsequent screen, make sure the stateless bean type and the Remote Client Views are selected. Click Finish. WSAD will generate the TechLibFacade stateless session bean classes. In the J2EE View, you should see the generated classes for the TechLibFacade session bean:

- TechLibFacadeBean: The session bean implementation class

- TechLibFacadeHome: The session bean Remote Home Interfaces

- TechLibFacade: The session bean Remote Interfaces

Make sure you are in the J2EE Hierarchy View of the J2EE Perspective. Right-click the TechLibEJB project and select Open With ➤ Deployment Descriptor Editor. On the next screen, find the "WebSphere Bindings" section. Make sure that TechLibFacade is highlighted and enter ejb/TechLibFacade in the JNDI name field (see Figure 6-47).

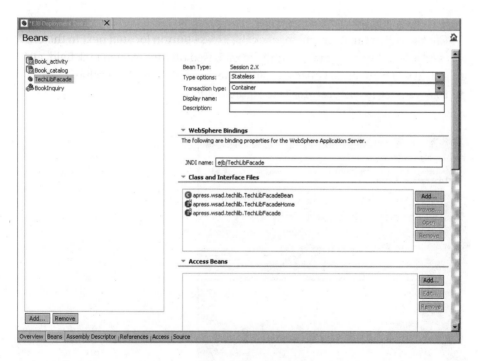

Figure 6-47. Setting the JNDI name for TechLibFacade

Next, click the References tab. On the screen that appears, click the Add button. On the next dialog, select the EJB local reference option because this session bean will be calling the Book_catalog entity bean (see Figure 6-48).

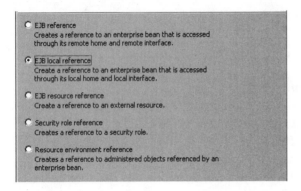

Figure 6-48. The Enterprise Bean Details *screen*

Click Next. On the next screen, click the Browse button located next to the Link field and select the Book_catalog entity bean. Based on the selected Link field, all other field will be filled in already. Change the Name field's prefilled value ejb/Book_catalog to Book_catalog (see Figure 6-49).

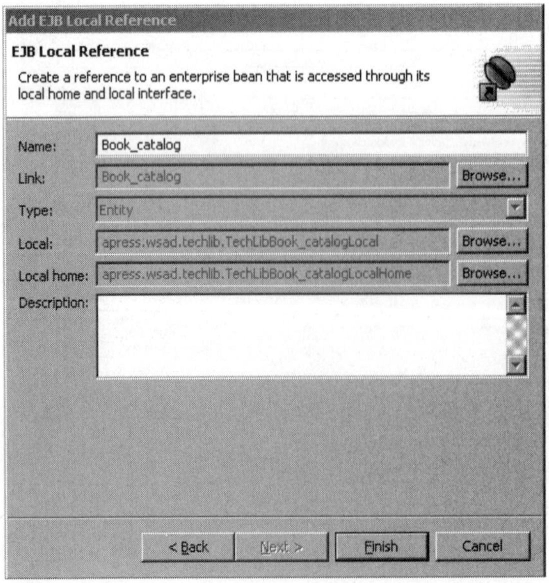

Figure 6-49. The Add EJB Local Reference *screen*

NOTE *You can always use the* Link *field for the EJB reference to the beans located within the same project.*

Click Finish. Expand TechLibFacade and click EJB local ref EJB Book_catalog. You should see all corresponding fields filled with values. Change the Name field by replacing the ejb/Book_catalog value with Book_catalog (see Figure 6-50).

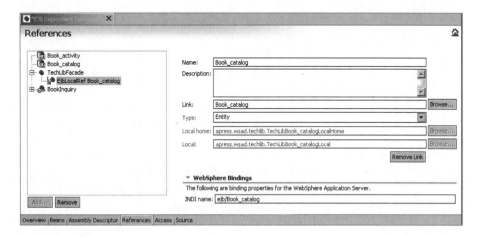

Figure 6-50. Setting EJB references

Save the results and close the EJB Deployment Descriptor Editor. WSAD has generated only the skeletons of the TechLibFacade classes. Now, you need to add the necessary business methods. The session bean is the EJB module where the business logic should be implemented. Open the TechLibFacadeBean implementation class in the Java Editor. You will add one helper method called getCatalogLocalHome, which returns the local reference to the TechLibBook_catalog entity bean object, and a business method called getBookByPlatform (in addition to several variables and import statements to support these methods). Listing 6-14 shows the source code for the TechLibFacadeBean session bean.

Listing 6-14. TechLibFacadeBean.java: *Implementation Class*

```
package apress.wsad.techlib;
import javax.ejb.*;
import javax.naming.*;
import javax.rmi.*;
import java.rmi.*;
import java.lang.*;
import java.util.*;
```

```
public class TechLibFacadeBean implements javax.ejb.SessionBean
{
    private javax.ejb.SessionContext mySessionCtx;

    // Variable to keep the Home Local refernce to TechLibBook_catalog object
    private TechLibBook_catalogLocalHome catalogLocalHome = null;

    // Method to get the Home Interface of the Book_catalog entity bean.
  private TechLibBook_catalogLocalHome getCatalogLocalHome()
   throws RemoteException
   {
        try
         {
           if (catalogLocalHome == null)
            {

              InitialContext initContext = new InitialContext();

              Object objRef =
                 initContext.lookup("java:comp/env/Book_catalog");
              catalogLocalHome = (TechLibBook_catalogLocalHome) objRef;
              return (TechLibBook_catalogLocalHome) objRef;
             }
           else
            {
              return catalogLocalHome;
            }
         }
        catch (NamingException ne)
         {
           System.out.println("Error locating TechLibBook_catalogLocalHome: " +
                                             ne.getMessage());
           throw
             new RemoteException("Error locating TechLibBook_catalogLocalHome: " +
                                             ne.getMessage());
         }
    }

    // This business method must be promoted to the remote interface
    public Vector getBookForPlatform(String workPlatform)
       throws FinderException
     {
     Vector bookVector = new Vector();
     TransportBean transObject;
     TechLibBook_catalogLocal bookCatalogLocal = null;
```

```
  Collection          collBookRecords;
try
  {
   collBookRecords =
         getCatalogLocalHome().findByPlatform(workPlatform);

   Iterator iterator = collBookRecords.iterator();

   while (iterator.hasNext())
    {
     bookCatalogLocal =
         (TechLibBook_catalogLocal) iterator.next();

     transObject = new TransportBean();

     transObject.catalogNumber    = bookCatalogLocal.getCatalog_number();
     transObject.author           = bookCatalogLocal.getAuthor();
     transObject.bookTitle        = bookCatalogLocal.getBook_title();
     transObject.location         = bookCatalogLocal.getLocation();
     transObject.platform         = bookCatalogLocal.getPlatform();
     transObject.txnDate          = bookCatalogLocal.getLanguage();

     bookVector.addElement(transObject);
    } // End of while

  } // End of try
catch(FinderException fe)
  {
     System.out.println("Error executing findByPlatform method: " +
                                           fe.getMessage());

     throw
       new EJBException("Error executing findByPlatform method: " +
                                           fe.getMessage());

  }

catch(Exception e)
  {
     System.out.println("Error getting TechLibBook_catalogLocalHome from
         findByPlatform method:" + e.getMessage());
     throw
       new EJBException("Error getting TechLibBook_catalogLocalHome from
         findByPlatform method:" + e.getMessage());
  }
return bookVector;
```

```
    }

      public javax.ejb.SessionContext getSessionContext()
{
  return mySessionCtx;
}

public void setSessionContext(javax.ejb.SessionContext ctx)
{
  mySessionCtx = ctx;
}

/**
 * ejbCreate
 */
public void ejbCreate() throws javax.ejb.CreateException
{
}
      public void ejbActivate()
{
}

      public void ejbPassivate()
{
}
      public void ejbRemove()
{
}
}
```

Listing 6-15 shows the source code for the TechLibFacade Home interface.

Listing 6-15. TechLibFacadeHome.java: *Home Interface Class*

```
package apress.wsad.techlib;
public interface TechLibFacadeHome extends javax.ejb.EJBHome
{
  public apress.wsad.techlib.TechLibFacade create()
throws javax.ejb.CreateException, java.rmi.RemoteException;
}
```

Listing 6-16 shows the source code for the TechLibFacade Remote Interface.

Listing 6-16. `TechLibFacade.java`: *Remote Interface Class*

```
package apress.wsad.techlib;
import javax.ejb.FinderException;
import java.util.Vector;
/**
 * Remote interface for Enterprise Bean: TechLibFacade
 */
public interface TechLibFacade extends javax.ejb.EJBObject
{
// This business method must be promoted to the remote interface
public Vector getBookForPlatform(String workPlatform)
throws FinderException, java.rmi.RemoteException;
}
```

Listing 6-17 shows the source code for the `TechLibFacadeLocalHome` Local Home Interface.

Listing 6-17. `TechLibFacadeLocalHome.java`: *Local Home Interface*

```
package apress.wsad.techlib;
/**
 * Local Home interface for Enterprise Bean: TechLibFacade
 */
public interface TechLibFacadeLocalHome extends javax.ejb.EJBLocalHome
{
  /**
   * Creates a default instance of Session Bean: TechLibFacade
   */
    public apress.wsad.techlib.TechLibFacadeLocal create()
throws javax.ejb.CreateException;
}
```

Listing 6-18 shows the source code for the `TechLibFacadeLocal` Local Interface.

Listing 6-18. `TechLibFacadeLocal.java`: *Local Interface*

```
package apress.wsad.techlib;
import javax.ejb.FinderException;
import java.util.Vector;

/**
 * Local interface for Enterprise Bean: TechLibFacade
```

```
*/
public interface TechLibFacadeLocal extends javax.ejb.EJBLocalObject
{
  // This business method must be promoted to the remote interface
  public Vector getBookForPlatform(String workPlatform)
        throws FinderException;
}
```

After making all the necessary source code modifications, you need to promote
the getBookForPlatform method to the Remote and Local Interfaces. This will allow
EJB clients to call the method locally and remotely. With the TechLibFacadeBean
implementation class still open in the Java Editor, right-click the getBookForPlatform
method and select Enterprise Bean ➤ Promote to Remote Interface. Repeat the
same step and promote the same method to the Local Interface.

If you get an error message after promotion, all you need to is to include the
following import statement in the TechLibFacade Remote Interface class:

```
import java.util.*;
```

Save the change and the error message will disappear. Next, validate the project.
Right-click the TechLibEJB project and select Run Validation. There should be no
errors. Next, generate the deployment code. Right-click the TechLibEJB project, and
select Generate ➤ Deploy and RMIC code. On the dialog that appears, select the
TechLibFacade module (see Figure 6-51).

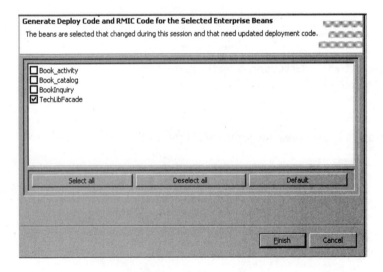

Figure 6-51. Generating deployment code

Click Finish. There should be no errors after the end of the generation process.

Testing the Stateless Session Bean

You are ready to test the TechLibFacade session bean. Switch to the Server Perspective and start TechLibTestServer. Wait until it is ready. Switch to the J2EE Perspective. Right-click the TechLibEJB project and select Run on server. The IBM Universal Test Client's main screen will appear. Click JNDI Explorer. Expand Local EJB beans all the way down. You should see the TechLibFacade module in the list. Now, expand another ejb entry located below Local EJB beans. This entry keeps components with the Remote Client View. Expand ejb. You will see the TechLibFacade module here also. That's because the TechLibFacade module exposes both the Remote and the Local Client View. Therefore, in real-life development, you should remember to test both interfaces. In this section, you will test the Remote Client View. Click the TechLibFacade entry under Local EJB beans. The screen shown in Figure 6-52 will appear.

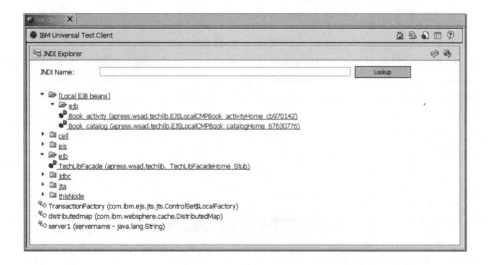

Figure 6-52. The Universal Test Client

Expand the Local EJB beans naming context all the way down. You should see Book_activity and Book_catalog entity beans because they are developed with the Local Client Views. Expand the ejb naming context for modules with the Remote Client Interface. Here you will see the TechLibFacade session bean. Click it. TechLibFacade will appear in the References section. Expand TechLibFacade in the References section all the way down until you see available the Home Interface methods. Notice that you have only one default (with no parameters) create method. Click the create method to create an instance of the session bean object. On the next screen, click the Invoke button. Then click the Work with Object button. The TechLibFacade reference object (named TechLibFacade 1) will appear (see Figure 6-53).

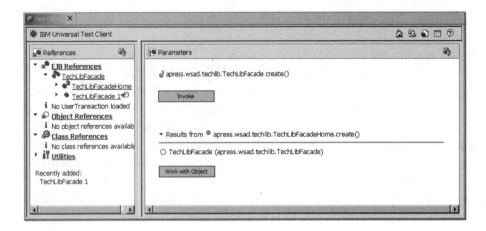

Figure 6-53. Home Interface of the session bean

Expand the TechLibFacade 1 object to see all the Interface methods and click getBookByPlatform. You are prompted to enter the value for the Platform parameter. Enter 04, which means the Windows NT/2000 platform. Click Invoke. Because getBookByPlatform returns a vector of TransferBean objects, a new button appears on the screen called Work with Ojects. Click this button to get all returned object references in the References area of the screen. You will see five object references appear under References (see Figure 6-54).

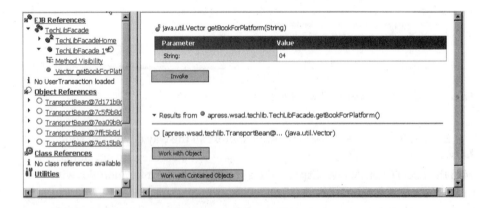

Figure 6-54. A collection of object references is returned

Expand the first one. You will see all available getter/setter methods of the TransferBean object. Click the getAuthor method. Click Invoke. Click Work with Object. You will see the author "Developer Journal" appear in the Parameters section (see Figure 6-55).

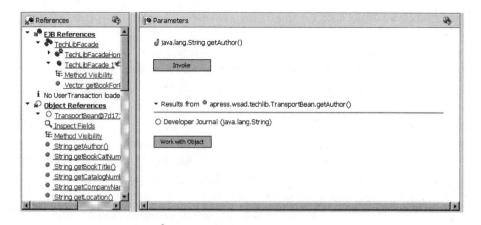

Figure 6-55. The result of executing the getAuthor *method*

Click the getBookTitle method. Click Invoke. Click Work with Object. You will see the "Windows NT Programming" title appear next (see Figure 6-56).

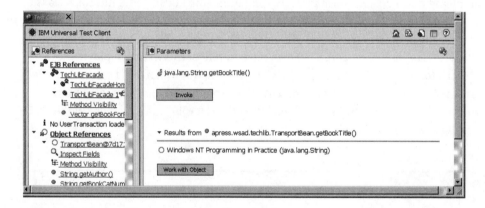

Figure 6-56. The result of executing the getTitle *method*

Expand the last object and click the getAuthor method. Click Invoke. Click Work with Object. The name "Kevin Miller" is displayed. You can check the rest of the return objects. Close the Browser View and stop the server. This concludes development of the TechLibFacade session bean EJB module.

Developing Stateful Session Beans

In this section, you will develop a stateful session bean called TechLibFacade1. The TechLibFacade1 stateful session bean will have two business methods: getBookByPlatform and getBookActivity. Both methods will be promoted to the Local Interface to expose the methods to EJB clients. The main idea is to show that the state of the stateful session bean is maintained between different method invocations. With this quick introduction, let's start development.

You will do the TechLibFacade1 session bean development under the same TechLibEJB project. Switch to the J2EE View of the J2EE Perspective. Right-click the TechLibEJB project and select New ➤ Enterprise Bean. Alternatively, you can click the Create an Enterprise Bean icon on the toolbar. Confirm the TechLibEJB project, and on the next screen, select the session bean as the bean type. Enter TechLibFacade1 as the bean name. Leave the Source folder as ejbModule, and set the default package name to apress.wsad.testlib. Click Next.

On the next screen, select Stateful as a session bean type, check Local client view and uncheck Remote client view. Click Finish. WSAD will generate the necessary classes for the TechLibFacade1 stateful session bean: TechLibFacade1Bean (the implementation class), TechLibFacade1LocalHome (the Local Home Interface class), and TechLibFacade1Local (the Local Interface class).

Because the TechLibFacade1 stateful session bean calls both entity beans (Book_catalog and Book_activity), you need to reflect this in the Deployment Descriptor. In the J2EE Navigator View, right-click the TechLibEJB project and select Open With ➤ Deployment Descriptor Editor. Highlight the TechLibFacade1 module, locate the "WebSphere Bindings" section and enter ejb/TechLibFacade1 in the JNDI name field (see Figure 6-57).

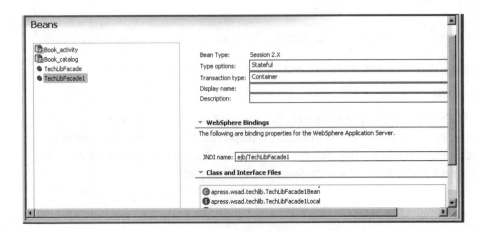

Figure 6-57. Setting the JNDI name for TechLibFacade1

Click the References tab. Highlight TechLibFacade1 and click the Add button. On the dialog that appears, select the EJB local reference and click Next. On the next screen, click the Browse button that is attached to the Link field and select Book_Catalog. Click OK, which sends you back to the original screen. The rest of the fields will be prefilled. Change ejb/Book_catalog to Book_catalog in the Name field.

Repeat the same steps for the Book_activity entity bean. When you are done, your Deployment Descriptor screen should look like Figure 6-58.

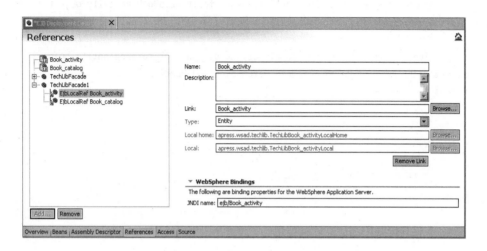

Figure 6-58. Setting the second EJB references for TechLibFacade1

Save the results and close the editor. Double-click the TechLibFacade1Bean implementation class to open it in the Java Editor View. You will now borrow some code from the previously developed stateless session bean TechLibFacade. Open the TechLibFacadeBean implementation class in the Java Editor. Switching between them (by clicking their titles on the editor bar), copy the existing code from TechLibFacadeBean and paste it into the new TechLibFacade1Bean class. Copy and paste the following code fragments: all import statements and code located between the class statement and the first getter method called getSessionContext. Paste this code right after the class statement. Create a new activityLocalHome variable (similar to the catalogLocalHome variable) to keep the Home Local reference to the TechLibBook_activity object. Next, create a new getActivityLocalHome method (similar to the getCatalogLocalHome method) to get the value for the activityLocalHome variable. Create a new method called initStateVariables. This method calls the getCatalogLocalHome and getActivityLocalHome methods to obtain the Local Home Interfaces for both the Book_catalog and Book_activity entity beans. Create a new getBookActivity method (similar to the getBookByPlatform method but for processing the findByBook method).

Listing 6-19 depicts a fragment of the TechLibFacade1Bean file that shows the two variables and four methods discussed previously.

Listing 6-19. Fragments of New Methods

```
// Variable to keep the Home Local refernce to TechLibBook_catalog object
private TechLibBook_catalogLocalHome catalogLocalHome = null;
// Variable to keep the Home Local refernce to TechLibBook_activity object
private TechLibBook_activityLocalHome activityLocalHome = null;

// Helper method to get the LocalInterface of the Book_catalog entity bean.
private TechLibBook_catalogLocalHome getCatalogLocalHome()
 throws RemoteException
 {

     try
      {
        if (catalogLocalHome == null)
         {

           InitialContext initContext = new InitialContext();

           Object objRef =
              initContext.lookup("java:comp/env/Book_catalog");

           catalogLocalHome = (TechLibBook_catalogLocalHome) objRef;

           return (TechLibBook_catalogLocalHome) objRef;

         }
        else
         {
           return catalogLocalHome;
         }

      }

     catch (NamingException ne)
      {
        System.out.println("Error locating TechLibBook_catalogLocalHome: " +
```

```
        throw
          new RemoteException("Error locating TechLibBook_catalogLocalHome: " +

        }

    }


// Helper method to get the LocalInterface of the Book_activity entity bean.
private TechLibBook_activityLocalHome getActivityLocalHome()
throws RemoteException
{
        try
        {
          if (activityLocalHome == null)
           {
            InitialContext initContext = new InitialContext();

            Object objRef =
               initContext.lookup("java:comp/env/Book_activity");

            activityLocalHome = (TechLibBook_activityLocalHome) objRef;

            return (TechLibBook_activityLocalHome) objRef;

           }
          else
           {
            return activityLocalHome;
           }

        }

        catch (NamingException ne)
         {
          System.out.println("Error locating TechLibBook_activityLocalHome: " +
                                          ne.getMessage());
            throw new
              RemoteException("Error locating  TechLibBook_activityLocalHome: " +
                                          ne.getMessage());
         }
    }

// Business helper method. Must be promoted to the local interface
```

```java
public void initStateVariables()
  throws FinderException
{
 try
  {
    // Calculate catalogLocalHome and activityLocalHome variables
    getCatalogLocalHome();
    getActivityLocalHome();


    } // End of try

  catch(Exception e)
   {
     System.out.println("Error executing findByPlatform WITHIN
       getBookByPlatform:" + e.getMessage());

     throw
       new EJBException("Error executing findByPlatform WITHIN
         getBookByPlatform:" + e.getMessage());
   }

}


// Business method
public Vector getBookForPlatform(String workPlatform)
  throws FinderException
 {
  Vector bookVector = new Vector();

  TransportBean transObject;
  TechLibBook_catalogLocal bookCatalogLocal = null;
  Collection          collBookRecords;
  try
   {
     collBookRecords =
          catalogLocalHome.findByPlatform(workPlatform);

     Iterator iterator = collBookRecords.iterator();

     while (iterator.hasNext())
      {
```

```
        bookCatalogLocal =
            (TechLibBook_catalogLocal) iterator.next();

        transObject = new TransportBean();

        transObject.catalogNumber  = bookCatalogLocal.getCatalog_number();
        transObject.author         = bookCatalogLocal.getAuthor();
        transObject.bookTitle      = bookCatalogLocal.getBook_title();
        transObject.location       = bookCatalogLocal.getLocation();
        transObject.platform       = bookCatalogLocal.getPlatform();
        transObject.txnDate        = bookCatalogLocal.getLanguage();

        bookVector.addElement(transObject);
       } // End of while

      } // End of try

    catch(Exception e)
     {
       System.out.println("Error executing findByPlatform WITHIN
          getBookByPlatform:" + e.getMessage());

       throw
         new EJBException("Error executing findByPlatform WITHIN
             getBookByPlatform:" + e.getMessage());
     }

    return bookVector;

  }


// Business method
public Vector getBookActivity(String workCatalogNumber)
   throws FinderException
 {
   Vector activityVector = new Vector();

   TransportBean transObject; // Receiving object from Book_activity method
   TechLibBook_activityLocal bookActivityLocal = null;
   Collection         collActivityRecords;
   try
    {
```

```
      collActivityRecords =
            activityLocalHome.findByBook(workCatalogNumber);

   Iterator iterator = collActivityRecords.iterator();

   while (iterator.hasNext())
    {
      bookActivityLocal =
         (TechLibBook_activityLocal) iterator.next();

      transObject = new TransportBean();

      transObject.txnDate       = bookActivityLocal.getTxn_date();
      transObject.txnType       = bookActivityLocal.getTxn_type();
      transObject.companyName   = bookActivityLocal.getCompany_name();
      activityVector.addElement(transObject);
     } // End of while

    } // End of try

 catch(Exception e)
  {
   System.out.println("Error executing findByPlatform WITHIN
       getBookByPlatform:" + e.getMessage());
   throw
     new EJBException("Error executing findByPlatform WITHIN
       getBookByPlatform:" + e.getMessage());
  }
  return activityVector;
}
```

Notice the following twist. Instead of the methods calling their corresponding getCatalogHome or getActivityHome methods, you added a new initStateVariables method that calls both of them. In addition, you promote this method to the Local Interface so it can be called by the EJB clients. Because this is the stateful session bean and the state of the variables is persistent, your business methods (getBookByPlatform and getBookActivity) no longer need to call the getCatalogHome and getActivityHome methods respectively but instead simply use the catalogLocalHome and activityLocalHome variables calculated during the initStateVariables method call. That demonstrates how the stateful session bean works.

With the TechLibFacade1Bean class open in the Java Editor, right-click the getBookForPlatform method in the Outline View and select Enterprise Bean ➤ Promote to Local Interface. Do the same for the second business method getBookActivity. Save the results and close the Java Editor. Listing 6-20 shows the source code for the TechLibFacade1Bean implementation class.

Listing 6-20. TechLibFacade1Bean.java: *Implementation Class*

```java
package apress.wsad.techlib;
import javax.ejb.*;
import javax.naming.*;
import javax.rmi.*;
import java.rmi.*;
import java.lang.*;
import java.util.*;
import apress.wsad.techlib.TransportBean;

public class TechLibFacade1Bean implements javax.ejb.SessionBean
{
    private javax.ejb.SessionContext mySessionCtx;

    // Variable to keep the Home Local refernce to TechLibBook_catalog object
    private TechLibBook_catalogLocalHome catalogLocalHome = null;

    // Variable to keep the Home Local refernce to TechLibBook_activity object
    private TechLibBook_activityLocalHome activityLocalHome = null;

    // Helper method to get the LocalInterface of the Book_catalog entity bean.
    private TechLibBook_catalogLocalHome getCatalogLocalHome()
     throws RemoteException
      {
       try
          {
             if (catalogLocalHome == null)
              {

                InitialContext initContext = new InitialContext();

                Object objRef =
                    initContext.lookup("java:comp/env/Book_catalog");

                catalogLocalHome = (TechLibBook_catalogLocalHome) objRef;

                return (TechLibBook_catalogLocalHome) objRef;
```

```
        }
      else
       {
        return catalogLocalHome;
       }


      }


    catch (NamingException ne)
      {
       System.out.println("Error locating TechLibBook_catalogLocalHome: " +


       throw
         new RemoteException("Error locating TechLibBook_catalogLocalHome: " +


      }


   }

// Helper method to get the LocalInterface of the Book_activity entity bean.
private TechLibBook_activityLocalHome getActivityLocalHome()
throws RemoteException
{
    try
     {
       if (activityLocalHome == null)
        {

         InitialContext initContext = new InitialContext();

         Object objRef =
            initContext.lookup("java:comp/env/Book_activity");

         activityLocalHome = (TechLibBook_activityLocalHome) objRef;

         return (TechLibBook_activityLocalHome) objRef;


        }
       else
        {
         return activityLocalHome;
        }
```

```
        }

    catch (NamingException ne)
    {
      System.out.println("Error locating TechLibBook_activityLocalHome: " +

        throw new
          RemoteException("Error locating  TechLibBook_activityLocalHome: "
                                              + ne.getMessage());
    }
  }


// Business helper method. Must be promoted to the local interface
public void initStateVariables()
   throws FinderException
 {
  try
  {
          // Calculate catalogLocalHome and activityLocalHome variables
     getCatalogLocalHome();
    getActivityLocalHome();
    } // End of try

    catch(Exception e)
    {
      System.out.println("Error executing findByPlatform WITHIN
          getBookByPlatform:" + e.getMessage());

      throw
        new EJBException("Error executing findByPlatform WITHIN
          getBookByPlatform:" + e.getMessage());
    }

}

// Business method
public Vector getBookForPlatform(String workPlatform)
   throws FinderException
 {
  Vector bookVector = new Vector();

  TransportBean transObject;
```

```
TechLibBook_catalogLocal bookCatalogLocal = null;
Collection          collBookRecords;
try
 {
  // Calculate catalogLocalHome and activityLocalHome variables

  collBookRecords =
       catalogLocalHome.findByPlatform(workPlatform);


  Iterator iterator = collBookRecords.iterator();

  while (iterator.hasNext())
   {
    bookCatalogLocal =
       (TechLibBook_catalogLocal) iterator.next();

    transObject = new TransportBean();

    transObject.catalogNumber  = bookCatalogLocal.getCatalog_number();
    transObject.author         = bookCatalogLocal.getAuthor();
    transObject.bookTitle      = bookCatalogLocal.getBook_title();
    transObject.location       = bookCatalogLocal.getLocation();
    transObject.platform       = bookCatalogLocal.getPlatform();
    transObject.txnDate        = bookCatalogLocal.getLanguage();

    bookVector.addElement(transObject);
   } // End of while

 } // End of try

catch(Exception e)
 {
   System.out.println("Error executing findByPlatform WITHIN
      getBookByPlatform:" + e.getMessage());

   throw
     new EJBException("Error executing findByPlatform WITHIN
        getBookByPlatform:" + e.getMessage());
 }

return bookVector;


}
```

```
// Business method
public Vector getBookActivity(String workCatalogNumber)
   throws FinderException
{
   Vector activityVector = new Vector();
   TransportBean transObject; // Receiving object from Book_activity method
   TechLibBook_activityLocal bookActivityLocal = null;
   Collection         collActivityRecords;
   try
    {
      collActivityRecords =
               activityLocalHome.findByBook(workCatalogNumber);

     Iterator iterator = collActivityRecords.iterator();

     while (iterator.hasNext())
      {
       bookActivityLocal =
           (TechLibBook_activityLocal) iterator.next();

       transObject = new TransportBean();

       transObject.txnDate     = bookActivityLocal.getTxn_date();
       transObject.txnType     = bookActivityLocal.getTxn_type();
       transObject.companyName = bookActivityLocal.getCompany_name();
       activityVector.addElement(transObject);
      } // End of while

     } // End of try

   catch(Exception e)
    {
     System.out.println("Error executing findByPlatform WITHIN
       getBookByPlatform:" + e.getMessage());
     throw
       new EJBException("Error executing findByPlatform WITHIN
         getBookByPlatform:" + e.getMessage());
    }
   return activityVector;
}

public javax.ejb.SessionContext getSessionContext()
 {
```

```
        return mySessionCtx;
    }
    public void setSessionContext(javax.ejb.SessionContext ctx)
{
  mySessionCtx = ctx;
}


    public void ejbCreate() throws javax.ejb.CreateException
{
}

    public void ejbActivate()
{
}

    public void ejbPassivate()
{
}

    public void ejbRemove()
{
}
}
```

Listing 6-21 shows the source code for TechLibFacade1LocalHome Local Home Interface class.

Listing 6-21. TechLibFacade1LocalHome: *Local Home Interface Class*

```
package apress.wsad.techlib;

/**
 * Local Home interface for Enterprise Bean: TechLibFacade1
 */
public interface TechLibFacade1LocalHome extends javax.ejb.EJBLocalHome
{
  /**
   * Creates a default instance of Session Bean: TechLibFacade1
   */
  public apress.wsad.techlib.TechLibFacade1Local create()
throws javax.ejb.CreateException;
}
```

Listing 6-22 shows the source code for the TechLibFacade1Local Local Interface class.

Listing 6-22. TechLibFacade1Local: *Local Interface Class*

```
package apress.wsad.techlib;

import javax.ejb.FinderException;
import java.util.Vector;

/**
 * Local interface for Enterprise Bean: TechLibFacade1
 */
public interface TechLibFacade1Local extends javax.ejb.EJBLocalObject
{
// Business method
public Vector getBookForPlatform(String workPlatform)
 throws FinderException;

// Business method
public Vector getBookActivity(String workCatalogNumber)
     throws FinderException;

// Business helper method. Must be promoted to the local interface
public void initStateVariables() throws FinderException;
}
```

Next, validate the project. Right-click the TechLibEJB project and select Run Validation. There should be no errors. Next, generate the deployment code for all EJB modules by right-clicking the TechLibEJB project and selecting Generate ➤ Deploy and RMIC code. On the dialog that appears, select only the TechLibFacade1 method.

Finally, click Finish. There should be no errors after the end of the generation process. You are now ready to test the TechLibFacade1 session bean.

Testing the Stateful Session Bean

Switch to the Server Perspective and start TechLibTestServer. Wait until it is ready, and then right-click the TechLibEJB project and select Run on Server. The Universal Test Client main screen will appear. Click JNDI Explorer (see Figure 6-59).

> **NOTE** *If you are testing a component that is developed with both Local and Remote Client Views, you need to test both interfaces (by opening both* Local EJB beans *and* ejb *naming contexts and selecting the same module for testing).*

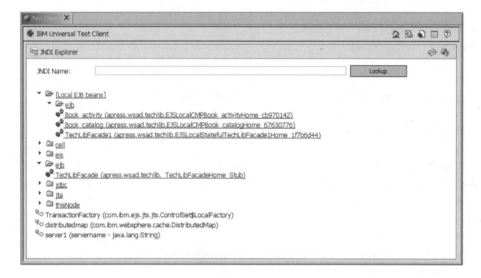

Figure 6-59. Testing the stateful session bean in the Universal Test Client

Click the TechLibFacade1 link (from the Local EJB beans name context. Its Local Interface will appear in the References section. Expand it all the way down. You should see the create method without parameters. Click it and then click Invoke. Next, click Work with Object. Now, the TechLibFacade1Local 1 entry (the Local Home Interface of this stateful session bean) will appear in the References section; it displays three methods: initStateParameters, getBookActivity, and getBookForPlatform.

Click initStateParameters. You will get the message that the method completed successfully. Now, when the state variables are set, you can call your business methods. Click getBookForPlatform. You will be prompted to enter the value of the platform attribute. Enter 04 (which means the Windows NT/2000 platform). Click Invoke. Again, because multiple objects are expected to be returned in a vector, you have the two buttons in the Parameters pane: Work with Object and Work with Contained Objects. Click Work with Contained Objects (see Figure 6-60).

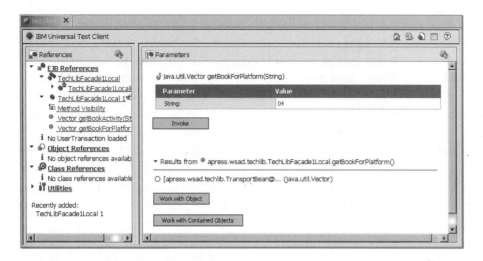

Figure 6-60. Returning multiple objects

Five objects appear in the References section. Expand the last object. Click the getBookTitle method. Click Invoke. The following book title is displayed: "Programming NT Services" (see Figure 6-61).

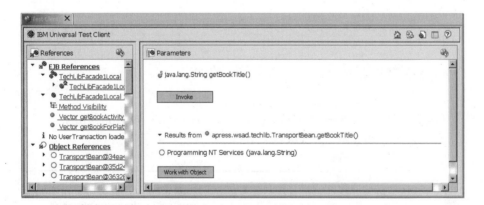

Figure 6-61. Getting the title of the last object

Now, let's test the second method. Click the getBookActivity method. You will be prompted for the value of one parameter—the book CATALOG_NUMBER. Enter 00001 and click Invoke. Because the expected result could include multiple objects, the Work with Object button is displayed. Click it. Several objects are displayed in the References section. Click the last one. You will see all available local methods of the TransferBean object. If you look at the getBookActivity method, you will see that you are returning only three fields within the TransferObject: TxnDate, TxnType, and CompanyName. Click the getTxnDate method. Next, click Invoke. Click Work with Object. The displayed result is "02/11/2002." Click the getTxnType method. Click Invoke. The displayed result is "RENT." Click the getCompanyName method. Click Invoke. The displayed result is "BBB_Company" (see Figure 6-62).

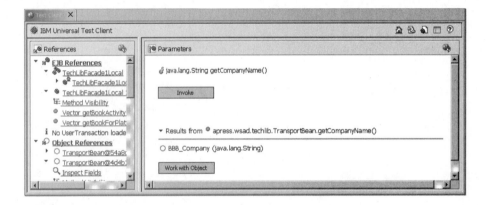

Figure 6-62. Getting the company name of the object

Close the Universal Test Client and stop the server. This concludes this example and the EJB development examples.

TIP *The stateless bean is bound to a client only for a period of one method execution. The second time this method is invoked by the same client, it will most likely be served by another instance of the stateless session bean available from the pool. So, the Local Home Interface to entity beans will be recalculated with every method invocation.*

Multiscreen Considerations

For the sake of simplicity, you did not develop a multiscreen client conversation in this chapter, but the processing logic is the same. Notice that although the code for the stateless and stateful beans are similar, they behave differently during execution. For instance, look at the `initStateVariables` method. It calls the `getCatalogHome` and `getActivityHome` methods to get the Local Home Interfaces for both the entity beans (`TechLibBook_activity` and `TechLibBook_catalog`) and saves it in the state variables: `activityLocalHome` and `catalogLocalHome`. The Local Home Interface is created only if the value of the corresponding variable is equal to `null`. For the stateful beans, these variables are part of the state and are saved and restored during the bean swapping out and in of memory (passivation/activation). So, once calculated as the result of the `initStateVariables` method call, these variables can simply be reused when both business methods (`getBookForPlatform` and `getBookActivity`) are subsequently called by the client.

For the same reason, you developed the TransferBean class that includes all fields from both database tables (regardless of how many fields are actually used in transmission). This is not an efficient way to communicate (especially across the network) where the amount of transmitted data must be reduced to a minimum. Therefore, in real programming, it is recommended you develop several TransferBean-like classes, each specifically designed to carry only the necessary fields.

Summary

In this chapter, you developed a working EJB tier of a J2EE 1.3 application. This example included the development of CMP and BMP entity beans and stateless and stateful session beans. You also learned how to use IBM Universal Test Client tool for testing EJB components. In addition, the chapter discussed the EJB project structure and using EJB QL for developing `finder` methods.

In the next chapter, you will develop the Web part of the J2EE 1.3 application.

CHAPTER 7

J2EE Web Development

THIS CHAPTER CONTINUES the development of the J2EE 1.3 technical library application you started in Chapter 6. You have developed the entire Enterprise JavaBean (EJB) tier of the application. Now, you will concentrate on developing the Web tier of this application. You will build the Web tier of the technical library application by following the industry best-practice Model-View-Controller (MVC) pattern. This will consist of Hypertext Markup Language (HTML), servlets, JavaServer Pages (JSP), and JavaBean files.

This chapter also discusses how the Web projects are organized and developed with WebSphere Studio Application Developer (WSAD) 5.0 by following the industry-standard MVC pattern for the presentation part of the J2EE application. You will also learn how to use the WSAD Web Page Designer tool and how to develop sophisticated dynamic Web pages. You will also learn how to develop stateless and stateful conversation sessions for Web application debugging. Finally, you will learn how the Web application components can function as EJB clients to communicate with the EJB part of the technical library application developed in Chapter 6. The chapter also discusses the Local and Remote Client Views.

The chapter starts by discussing how WSAD 5.0 organizes Web projects.

Understanding the Web Project Organization

The J2EE 1.3 specification requires that any Web application must be built as a Web Archive (WAR) file, which is actually a Java Archive (JAR) file specially structured for Web applications (also called *Web modules*). The structure of a Web module consists of several directories:

Java Source: This is the folder where WSAD stores Java source code for JavaBeans and servlets. When exporting Web applications, the context of this directory is not packaged in the WAR file (unless you check a special option that instructs WSAD to include source files in the WAR file). When files in this directory are saved, they are automatically compiled and added to the Web Content/WEB-INF/classes directory.

Web Content: This folder contains the content of the WAR file that will be deployed on the server. Files that are not placed in this directory or its subdirectories are considered development resources and will not be found during execution. Links to these files will be marked as broken. Files in this directory are deployed to the application server at the time of application deployment.

Web Content/theme: This folder contains Cascading Style Sheet (CSS) files and other style-related objects.

Web Content/WEB-INF: This directory contains supporting Web resources, including web.xml (the standard Deployment Descriptor) and two IBM-extended Deployment Descriptors (ibm-web-bnd.xml and ibm-web-ext.xmi). It also includes the classes and lib directories. All Web resource files (HTML, servlets, JSP, graphics, JavaScript, and so on) reside in this directory.

Web Content/WEB-INF/classes: Java source modules added to the source directory are automatically compiled, and the generated code is placed in this directory. This directory is for storing servlets and utility classes. In addition, any loose classes (classes outside the JAR files) can be stored in this folder. The classes in this directory are used by the application classloader. Folders in this directory map Java class package statements with the corresponding Java classes. Classes are placed in this directory by WSAD only as a result of the compilation of Java source files.

Web Content/WEB-INF/lib: This folder stores supporting JAR libraries files that the Web module references. Any JAR file placed in this directory is included in the project's Build Path and is available for the Web module.

Web Content/WEB-INF/Library: This folder helps to reference and locate JAR files that exist elsewhere in a Java project. If they are in the Web project's Build Path, this allows you to avoid the need to explicitly copy these JAR files into the project's lib folder.

Understanding Web Application Development

WSAD 5.0 contains a new Page Designer (implemented in Java). The Page Designer used in WSAD 4.0x is also available and is now the Page Designer Classic. The new Page Designer tool is capable of processing Extensible HTML (XHTML) and has some other enhancements, but it is not fully complete yet and therefore lacks many features. It does not support dynamic elements, dynamic table extensions, event controls, rollover effects, or many other features available in the Page Designer Classic. The features of the Page Designer Classic that the new Page Designer does not support are so important for these development examples that this book uses the Page Designer Classic in its examples.

If you installed WSAD 5.0 with the new Page Designer, you need to install the additional Page Designer Classic. Fortunately, they can coexist in the same Workbench. First, if you have WSAD running, close it. Second, go to the <WSAD-install-directory>\bin directory and run pdclassic.exe. When you restart WSAD 5.0, the Updates dialog will display. Click Yes. The Configuration Changes dialog will appear next. Check the box within the Detected Changes field and click Finish. Finally, the Install/Update dialog will appear. Click Yes. The WSAD Workbench will restart to make the changes effective.

Now, the new Page Designer is still marked as the default designer on your Workbench. You can go to Windows ➤ Preferences ➤ Workbench ➤ File Associations and assign the Page Designer Classic as the default tool that will automatically invoke for processing HTML or JSP files. Alternatively, you can right-click any HTML or JSP file and select Open With ➤ Page Designer Classic. Whichever method you prefer to use, make sure you use the Page Designer Classic when following this book's examples. With this setting under control, you can start the development.

Creating the Web Project

The first step in developing a Web module is to create the Web project. Switch to the Web Perspective and select New ➤ Web Project. On the screen that follows, enter TechLibWEB as the name and indicate that this is a J2EE project by selecting J2EE Web Project (meaning that it can include servlets and JSPs for generating the dynamic content). The alternative is the Static Web Project option, which means it can be deployed on any standard Web server and does not require the application server for runtime support.

You can also select two files (a .css file and a .cvsignore file) and a variety of libraries to be included in the project. The standard JSP tag library and several custom JSP tag libraries are available for selection, as well as the library that supports Struts development. For this example, deselect the creation of the CSS file (because it is more appropriate for the black-and-white illustrations used for book publishing). Also, select to include the JSP standard tag library (see Figure 7-1).

Click Next. The J2EE Settings Page will appear. Indicate that you will use the existing enterprise application project and select TechLibApp. Make sure that the J2EE level is set to 1.3. Click Next. The Module Dependencies screen will appear. It allows you to indicate other projects on which this project depends. From this Web project, you need to be able to call EJB components located in the TechLibEJB project. Check this project, so it will be included in the Manifest CLASSPATH (see Figure 7-2).

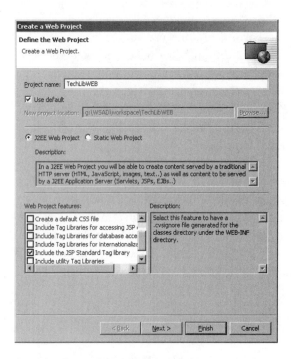

Figure 7-1. Creating a Web project

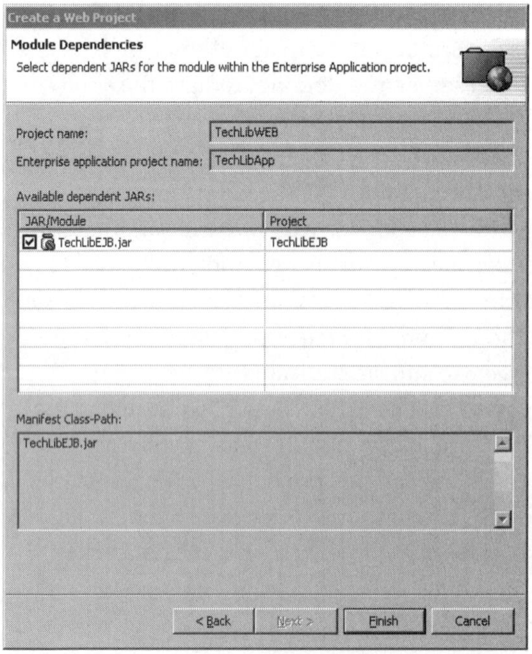

Figure 7-2. Module Dependences *screen*

Click Finish. WSAD will notify you that adding this Web project to the enterprise application project TechLibApp will affect the test server project that TechLibApp uses. Click OK. WSAD will generate the TechLibWEB project.

Understanding Stateless Web Session Development

Because the user interaction with the system consists of a single request and reply screen, you can use stateless processing. Within the TechLibWEB project, you will develop an input screen that allows a user to add a new book to the library catalog and an output screen that confirms the processing results. You will also build a JavaBean class called BookRegisterHelper that will pass information between modules.

Let's build the BookRegisterHelper JavaBean class first. Right-click the TechLibWEB project and select File ➤ New ➤ Other ➤ Java ➤ Class. Click Next. On the next screen, enter apress.wsad.techlib as the package and BookRegisterHelper as the class name. Click the Add button attached to the Interfaces field and type Serializable. Select the Constructors from superclass field and deselect Inherited abstract methods (see Figure 7-3).

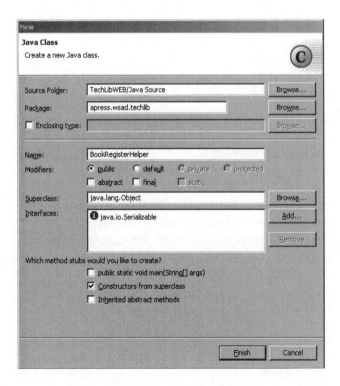

Figure 7-3. Building the BookRegisterHelper *class*

Click Finish. WSAD will generate the BookRegisterHelper class and open it in the Java Editor View. To add a new book to the library catalog, the user needs to provide the following data: catalogNumber, author, bookTitle, location, platform, and language.

Enter these fields (that will be used on the input/output screens) as attributes of the BookRegisterHelper.java class and as private attributes of the type String. In Outline View, right-click anywhere and select Generate Getter and Setter. On the next screen, mark all attributes so the corresponding getter/setter methods will be generated (see Figure 7-4).

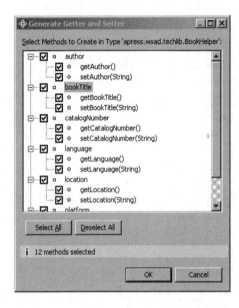

Figure 7-4. Generating the getter/setter methods

Click OK. You should see the generated getter/setter methods. Right-click any empty space within the Java Editor View and select Format. This makes the source file friendlier to read. Save the results and close the editor. See Listing 7-1 for the BookRegisterHelper source code.

Listing 7-1. BookRegisterHelper.java

```
package apress.wsad.techlib;
import java.io.Serializable;
```

```java
public class BookRegisterHelper implements Serializable
{
 // Attributes
 private String catalogNumber;
 private String author;
 private String bookTitle;
 private String location;
 private String platform;
 private String language;

public BookHelper()
 {
   super();
 }
 public String getAuthor()
 {
   return author;
 }
 public String getBookTitle()
 {
   return bookTitle;
 }
 public String getCatalogNumber()
 {
   return catalogNumber;
 }
 public String getLanguage()
 {
   return language;
 }
 public String getLocation()
 {
  return location;
 }
 public String getPlatform()
 {
   return platform;
 }
 public void setAuthor(String author)
 {
   this.author = author;
 }
 public void setBookTitle(String bookTitle)
```

```
{
 this.bookTitle = bookTitle;
}
public void setCatalogNumber(String catalogNumber)
{
 this.catalogNumber = catalogNumber;
}
public void setLanguage(String language)
{
 this.language = language;
}
public void setLocation(String location)
{
 this.location = location;
}
public void setPlatform(String platform)
{
 this.platform = platform;
}
}
```

You will use the BookRegisterHelper JavaBean class to automatically generate your Web pages. Right-click the TechLibWEB project and select File ➤ New ➤ Other. On the screen that appears, select Web on the left pane and Java Bean Web Pages on the right pane (see Figure 7-5).

Figure 7-5. Generating JavaBean Web pages

Click Next. You should see the screen shown in Figure 7-6. Next, click the Browse button attached to the Java package field and then navigate to and select apress.wsad.techlib.

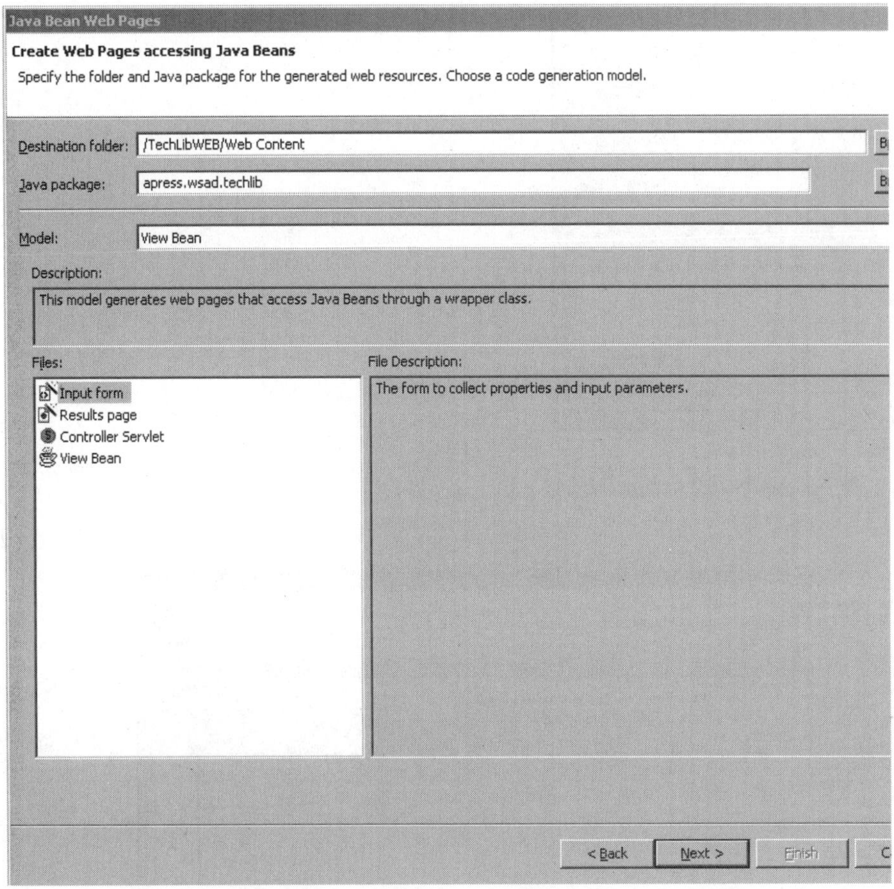

Figure 7-6. Creating Web pages that access JavaBeans

Click Next to continue the building process. On the subsequent screen, click the Browse button attached to the Bean field. Enter Book to ease the navigation process. Next, select BookHelper from the list (see Figure 7-7).

When you click OK, you see the screen shown in Figure 7-8. Here, you can select the fields for building input and output pages. Mark all the BookHelper attributes.

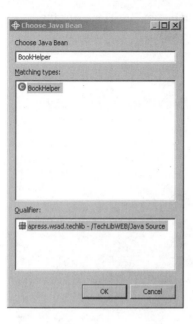

Figure 7-7. Selecting the JavaBean

Figure 7-8. Selecting attributes for building Web pages

Click Next. On the next screen, select Request (you do not need Session here because this is one-screen processing). Leave the rest of the fields as they are and click Next. You will see the input page design form shown in Figure 7-9.

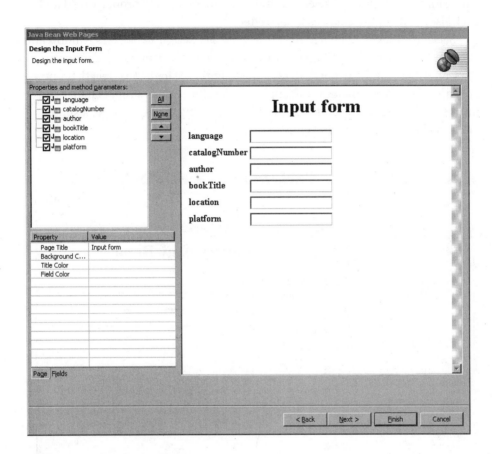

Figure 7-9. Input page design screen

Improving the Form Design

You should probably make some changes to improve how the form looks. First, change the page title. Click the Page tab. Place the cursor in the Value field and enter a different title in the Page Title field: Register a New Book. Click any other field for the new page title to be displayed on the form.

Click the Fields tab. Now, rearrange the screen fields by putting them in the following order: catalogNumber, bookTitle, author, location, platform, and language. In the Properties and method parameters window, click the catalogNumber field. Click the up arrow button to move the catalogNumber field to the first position.

Use similar steps to adjust the position of other fields. Select the catalogNumber field in the Properties and method parameters window and click the Label value field. Change it to Catalog number. Next, enter 5 in the Size property. Click elsewhere for the changes to take effect. Enter 5 in the Max length property field and click elsewhere for the changes to take effect.

Select the bookTitle field in the Properties and method parameters window and click the Label value field. Change it to Book title. Enter 50 in the Size property. Click elsewhere for the changes to take effect. Enter 100 in the Max length property field and click elsewhere for the changes to take effect. Make similar changes for the rest of the fields. When you have finished updating the input page, it should look like the screen shown in Figure 7-10.

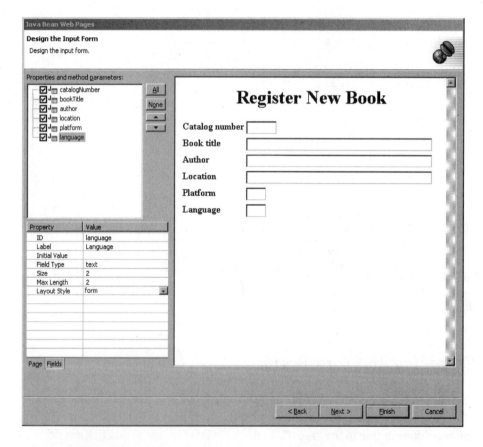

Figure 7-10. Modifying the input page

Click Next. The results form will display. Change the form's title to Registration Status. Select only one field—catalogNumber—and unselect the rest of the fields. Change the catalogNumber label to Catalog number. Change both the Size and the Max Length properties to 5. When you have finished, your screen should look like the one in Figure 7-11.

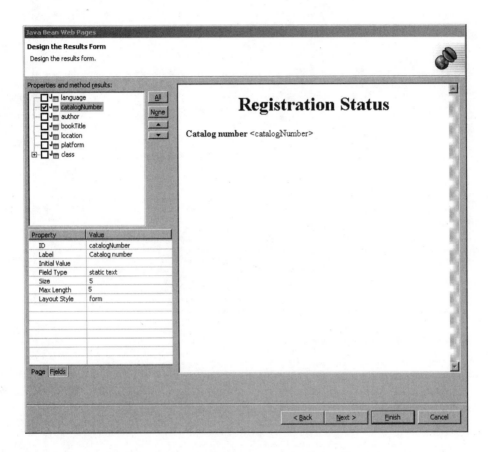

Figure 7-11. Modifying the results form

The final screen prompts you for the prefix that will be used to form the names of the generated files. Change the prefix name to BookRegister (see Figure 7-12).

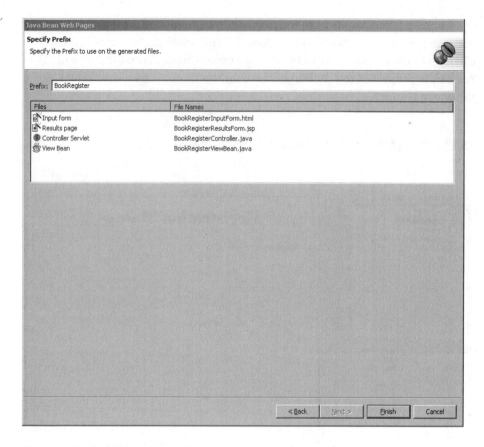

Figure 7-12. Specifying the prefix

Click Finish. WSAD will generate a set of files that maintain the MVC pattern for developing the presentation part of the J2EE application.

Working with WSAD-Generated Files

Files generated by WSAD display in the Navigator View. Two Java-based files (BookRegisterController.java and BookRegisterViewBean.java) reside in the Java Source directory, according to the package name.

As you already know, Java files placed in the Java Source directory (and its sub-directories) are automatically compiled, and the results (class files) are placed in the Web Control\META-INF\classes directory. Two other files (BookRegisterInputForm.html and BookRegisterResultsForm.jsp) are placed in the Web Content directory, according to the package structure. You can see them in Figure 7-13.

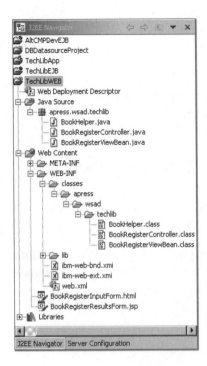

Figure 7-13. The Web project structure

These five classes implement the MVC pattern with the main goal of separating the presentation from the data and processing logic. Let's walk through all the modules and see how it works. The user invokes the `BookRegisterInputForm.html` file, enters all necessary data, and clicks the `Submit` link. See Listing 7-2 for a fragment of the code from `BookRegisterInputForm.html` that handles this `Submit` click logic.

Listing 7-2. Fragment of the `BookRegisterInputForm.html` *file*

```
<BODY>
<!--JavaScript-->
<SCRIPT language="JavaScript" type="text/javascript">
<!--
function submitForm()
  {
    document.myForm.submit()
  }
//-->
</SCRIPT>
```

```
<!--Banner-->
<H1>Register New Book</H1>

<!--Form-->
<FORM name="myForm" method="POST" action="BookRegisterController">
<INPUT type="hidden" name="command" value="BookRegisterResults">
<A href="javascript:submitForm()">Submit</A> <BR>
```

You should see the JavaScript function called `submitForm` at the top of the code fragment. The last line of the code fragment is this:

```
<A href="javascript:submitForm()">Submit</A>
```

This code reacts to the user clicking the `Submit` link and triggers the execution of the JavaScript function called `submitForm`. The `submitForm` function does not have any extra logic, so it simply submits the form data. The action attribute of the `<FORM>` tag indicates the module to be invoked:

```
action="BookRegisterController"
```

Right-click the `web.xmi` file and select `Open With` ➤ `Deployment Descriptor Editor`. On the `Overview` page, click the `BookRegisterController` servlet. The "URL Mappings" section shows you the way this servlet should be invoked under the Web Browser View, relative to the project root directory `TechLibWEB` (see Figure 7-14).

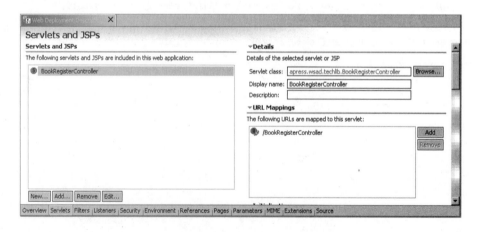

Figure 7-14. The Web project Deployment Descriptor

BookRegisterController is coded under the action keyword (therefore, the BookRegisterController servlet will be invoked).

Now let's look at the code snippet of BookRegisterController. Both the doPost and doGet methods delegate control to the performTask method. The performTask method invokes the performServices method (which is currently empty, but you will put some processing logic here later) and then it calculates the nextPage variable:

```
//Perform any specialized sevices
performServices(request, response);
//Get the Web page associated with the command in the request
nextPage = getInitParameter(request.getParameter("command"));
```

On the BookRegisterInputForm, there is a hidden field called command with a value equal to BookRegisterResults. Therefore, the request.getParameter("command") statement evaluates to BookRegisterResults. To see the final value of this calculation, right-click the web.xmi file and select Open With ➤ Deployment Descriptor Editor. On the Overview page, click BookRegisterController. In the "Initialization" section, you should see that the BookRegisterResults variable has the value /BookRegisterResultsForm.jsp, which is the value to be coded in the Web browser command for the invocation of the BookRegisterResults JSP module (see Figure 7-15).

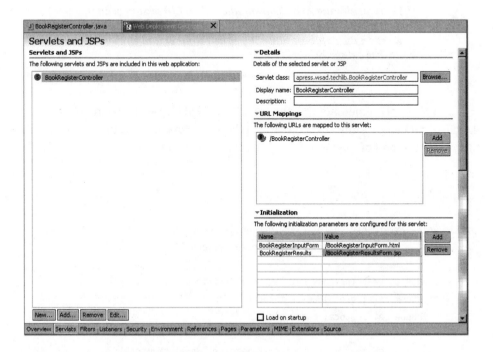

Figure 7-15. The Web project Deployment Descriptor

You can see that the request.getParameter("BookRegisterResults") statement will return the value /BookRegisterResults.jsp, which will be assigned as a value of the nextPage variable. The nextPage variable is later used in the dispatch method:

```
RequestDispatcher dispatch = request.getRequestDispatcher(nextPage);
dispatch.forward(request,response);
```

This effectively forwards control to the BookRegisterResults.jsp module, which will display the results on the user screen. The BookRegisterViewBean class creates an instance of the BookRegisterHelper JavaBean object. It has several methods that wrap around the corresponding methods of the BookRegisterHelper JavaBean class.

Adding the Business Logic

Now that the functionality of the MVC pattern is clear to you, let's add some business code. There is a performServices method in the BookRegisterController class where you are going to put a local call to the Book_catalog entity bean's create method to add a new book in the catalog.

 NOTE *Typically, the Web client should call an EJB session bean that wraps multiple calls to entity beans, but here you deal with a single call that creates a record in the database table. It is much simpler and efficient to call the entity bean directly here.*

You probably remember that the TechLibBook_catalog entity bean provides a Local Client View. Listing 7-3 shows the updated performServices method that calls the create method of the TechLibBook_catalog entity bean.

Listing 7-3. The performServices *Method*

```
public void performServices(HttpServletRequest request,
                            HttpServletResponse response)
{
   // Variable to keep the Book_catalog Home Interface
    TechLibBook_catalogLocalHome catalogLocalHome;
    TechLibBook_catalogLocal catalogLocal;

    String catalogNumber = request.getParameter("catalogNumber");
```

```java
String author        =  request.getParameter("author");
String bookTitle     =  request.getParameter("bookTitle");
String location      =  request.getParameter("location");
String platform      =  request.getParameter("platform");
String language      =  request.getParameter("language");

    try
  {
     InitialContext initContext = new InitialContext();

     catalogLocalHome =
            (TechLibBook_catalogLocalHome)
                initContext.lookup("java:comp/env/Book_catalog");

     catalogLocal =
         catalogLocalHome.create(catalogNumber,
                          author,
                          bookTitle,
                          location,
                          platform,
                          language);

// If we are here, successful result

   }
    catch(Exception e)
     {
     System.out.println("Error locating ejb/Book_catalog Home
                                   interface" + e.getMessage());

        throw new EJBException("Error registering a new book");
     }
   }
```

The method retrieves all parameters passed from the user form. Next, it creates an InitialContext and lookup for the ejb/Book_catalog JNDI entity name. After obtaining the Local Home Interface reference, it calls the create method of the TechLibBook_catalog entity bean to put a new book into the BOOK_CATALOG database table. If any exception happens, the method handles it and throws it as EJBException.

The performTask method calls the performService method. If no exception is thrown, it will form the nextPage field used in the dispatch command to pass control to the BookRegisterResults.jsp module; otherwise, the error_page module will be called. This means that the BookRegisterResults.jsp module will display its page only in the case of successful registration; otherwise, the generic error_page will display. See Listing 7-4 for the BookRegisterController servlet source code.

Listing 7-4. BookRegisterController.java *Servlet*

```java
package apress.wsad.techlib;
import java.rmi.*;
import javax.ejb.*;
import javax.naming.*;
import javax.rmi.*;
import java.rmi.*;
import java.util.*;
import java.io.*;
import javax.servlet.*;
import javax.servlet.http.*;

public class BookRegisterController extends HttpServlet implements Serializable
{
/**************************************************************
* Initializes the servlet
* @param config The servlet's configuration information
*/
public void init(ServletConfig config) throws ServletException
{
  super.init(config);
  //Place code here to be done when the servlet is initialized
}


/**************************************************************
* Destroy the Servlet
*/
public void destroy()
{
  //Place code here to be done when the servlet is shut down
}


/**************************************************************
* This method is run once for each request.
* @param request The incoming request information
* @param response The outgoing response information
*/
```

```java
public void performServices(HttpServletRequest request,
                            HttpServletResponse response)
{
//Place any code here that you would like to run on every request
//Logging, Authentication, Debugging...

 // Variable to keep the Book_catalog Home Interface
  TechLibBook_catalogLocalHome catalogLocalHome;
  TechLibBook_catalogLocal catalogLocal;

  String catalogNumber =  request.getParameter("catalogNumber");
  String author        =  request.getParameter("author");
  String bookTitle      =  request.getParameter("bookTitle");
  String location      =  request.getParameter("location");
  String platform      =  request.getParameter("platform");
  String language      =  request.getParameter("language");

  try
    {
     InitialContext initContext = new InitialContext();

     catalogLocalHome =
                (TechLibBook_catalogLocalHome)
                  initContext.lookup("java:comp/env/Book_catalog");

    catalogLocal =
                catalogLocalHome.create(catalogNumber,
                         author,
                             bookTitle,
                             location,
                             platform,
                             language);

   // If we are here, successful result
    }
  catch(Exception e)
   {
     System.out.println("Error locating ejb/Book_catalog Home
                                      interface" + e.getMessage());

              throw new EJBException("Error registering a new book");   }

  }
```

```
/****************************************************************
* Process both HTTP GET and HTTP POST methods
* @param request The incoming request information
* @param response The outgoing response information
*/
public void performTask(
HttpServletRequest request,
HttpServletResponse response)
throws ServletException, IOException
{
String nextPage;
try
{
   //Perform any specialized sevices
   performServices(request, response);

   //Get the web page associated with the command in the request
   nextPage = getInitParameter(request.getParameter("command"));
}
catch (Exception ex)
{
  //If an exception is thrown serve the error page
  nextPage = getInitParameter("error_page");
}

//Forward the request to the next page
dispatch(request, response, nextPage);
}


/****************************************************************
* Process incoming requests for a HTTP GET method
* @param request The incoming request information
* @param response The outgoing response information
*/
public void doGet(HttpServletRequest request, HttpServletResponse response)
throws ServletException, IOException
{
  performTask(request, response);
}


/****************************************************************
* Process incoming requests for a HTTP POST method
* @param request The incoming request information
```

```
* @param response The outgoing response information
*/
public void doPost(HttpServletRequest request, HttpServletResponse
                                                        response)
          throws ServletException, IOException
{
  performTask(request, response);
}


/****************************************************************
* Dispatches to the next page
* @param request The incoming request information
* @param response The outgoing response information
* @param nextPage The page to dispatch to
*/
public void dispatch(
HttpServletRequest request,
HttpServletResponse response,
String nextPage)
throws ServletException, IOException
{
    RequestDispatcher dispatch = request.getRequestDispatcher(nextPage);
    dispatch.forward(request, response);
}
}
```

Designing the Output User Interface

In this section, you will work on the output user screen. Again, WSAD has already built a skeleton that you can use as a starting point. Open the BookRegisterResults.jsp module in the Editor View. Click the Design tab. Highlight the Catalog number table row. On the main menu, click Table ➤ Add Row ➤ Add below. Type in the text Successful Registration. Save the changes. Click the Preview tab to see the page (see Figure 7-16).

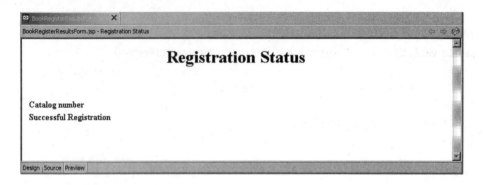

Figure 7-16. Output screen design

Save changes and close the editor. There is one last step before you can test the module. You need to set the EJB reference for the BookRegisterController servlet that points to the TechLibBook_catalog entity bean. Right-click the web.xmi file and select Open With ➤ Deployment Descriptor Editor. On the next screen, click the References tab. On the page that appears, click the EJB Local tab located near the top of the page. Highlight the EJB Local reference and click the Add button. Change the reference name from EJB Local Ref to TechLibBook_catalog. On the right side of the screen, click the Browse button attached to the Link field. On the dialog that appears, select the Book_catalog entry (see Figure 7-17).

Figure 7-17. Setting a local reference to the Book_catalog *entity bean*

Click OK. The rest of the fields will be filled in already (see Figure 7-18).

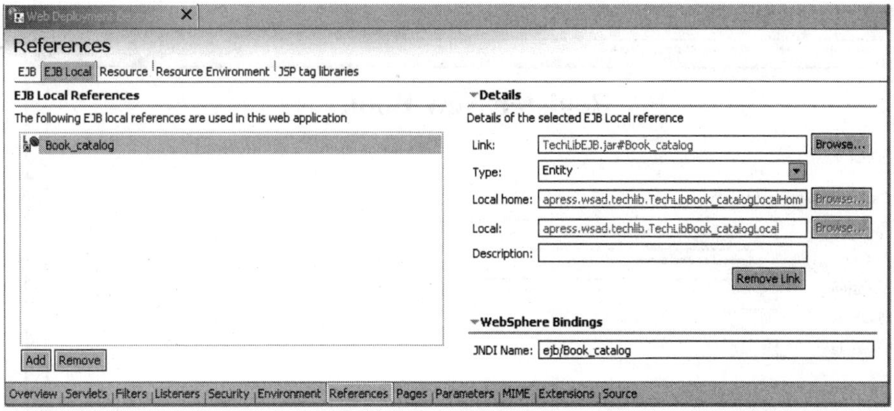

Figure 7-18. Checking the local reference to the Book_catalog *entity bean*

Save the results and close the editor. You are now ready to test the application.

Testing the Application

Switch to the Server Perspective and start the server TechLibTestServer. Wait for the message indicating that the server is ready. Next, switch to the Web Perspective. Right-click BookRegisterInputForm and select Run on Server. You should see the input screen. For the first run, it takes longer for the screen to appear because of the translation of JSP modules. After that, it works much faster. Enter the following data:

- Enter 00016 for Catalog number.

- Enter Java 1.2 Developer's Handbook for Book title.

- Enter Philip Heller and team for Author.

- Enter Library for Location.

- Enter 00 for Platform.

- Enter 01 for Language.

Your input screen should look like the one shown in Figure 7-19.

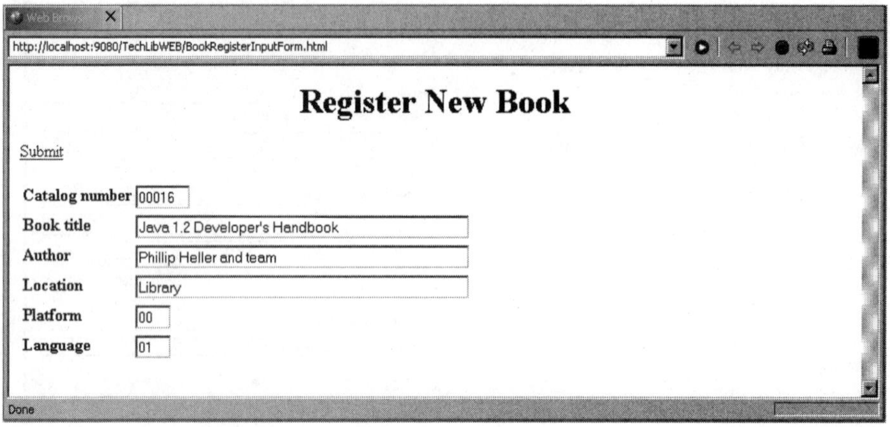

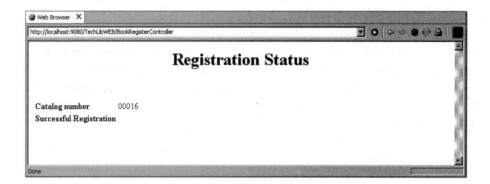

Figure 7-19. Filling the input screen

Click the Submit link. The results screen will display confirming the successful book registration (see Figure 7-20).

Figure 7-20. A successful registration status

Using the WSAD Page Designer

Let's improve the user input screen by replacing the Submit link with a Submit button. You also want the Submit button to be located below the screen elements and not above them. In addition, you probably would like to add a second button called Reset. When the user clicks this button, all form fields are cleared out. This exercise will show you how to use the WSAD Page Designer. (Remember to use the Page Designer Classic for these examples.)

Open the `BookRegisterInputForm.html` file in the Editor View and click the `Design` tab. From the main menu, select `Toolbar`. When the next menu level expands, check the following on the menu list so that the selected items will be included as icons on the Workbench toolbar: `Forms and Input Fields`, `JSP`, `Tables`, `Frames`, `Font`, and `Styles`. There is also a toolbar button that allows you to invoke the Netscape or Microsoft browser from WSAD. As a result of your selection, many controls will appear on the toolbar.

Now, let's get back to the screen design. Click inside the screen where you want to insert a button. Ensure that it is below the form elements already present but still above the end of the form (because the button belongs to the form). Move the cursor along the toolbar slowly (stopping at each toolbar icon). When you place a cursor above any toolbar button, a message displays the description of the button. Locate the button that says `Insert Submit Button` and click it. A dialog will appear; enter `Submit` in the `Label` field and `Submit` in the `Name` field. Click `OK`. Repeat the same steps to insert the `Reset` button. Give it the name `Reset`. Finally, delete the `Submit` link (see Figure 7-21).

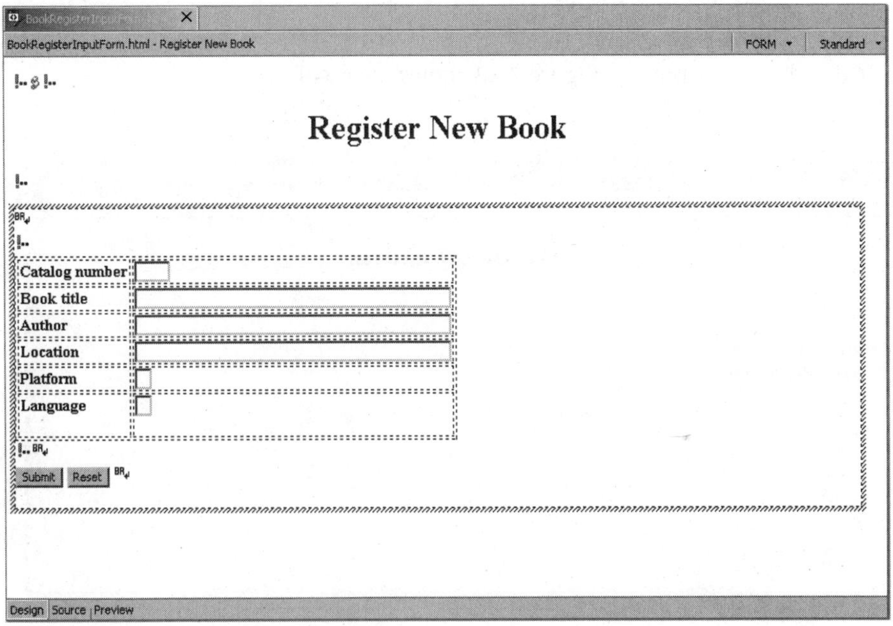

Figure 7-21. Inserting the button controls

Let's run the application. Switch to the Server Perspective and start
TechLibTestServer. Right-click the BookRegisterInputForm.html file and select
Run on Server. Fill in the input screen (see Figure 7-22).

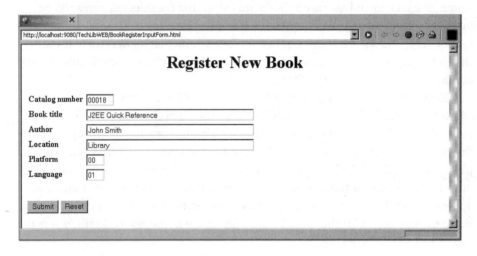

Figure 7-22. Running the application

Click the Submit button. Figure 7-23 shows the result.

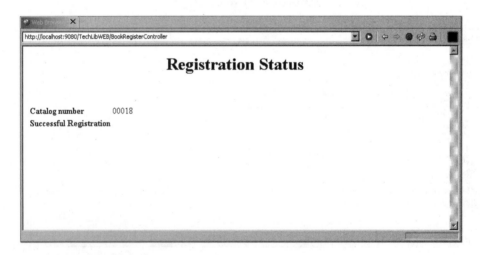

Figure 7-23. The processing results

Clicking the Reset button clears all the fields. Close the Web Browser View and stop the server. Now, you want to develop the local data validating logic. You want to make sure that users enter all the data correctly before submitting their request to the server. You can code the validating logic in several different ways. Open BookRegisterInputForm.html under the Page Designer Classic and click the Source tab. You will manually code a new JavaScript procedure. This way of coding the JavaScript code is much more convenient than using the Page Designer Classic. First, find the JavaScript section where the submitForm procedure is coded:

```
function submitForm()
 {
  document.myForm.submit()
 }
```

Add the code shown in Listing 7-5. It consists of several functions (one function per each input field to be validated). For each field, the corresponding function validates the data entered by the user.

Listing 7-5. JavaScript Validating Functions

```
function checkCatalogNumber()
 {
  if(document.myForm.catalogNumber.value.length < 5)
   {
    alert("Catalog number is a 5-character field")
    return(false)
   }
  else
   {
    return(true)
   }
 }

function checkBookTitle()
 {
  if(document.myForm.bookTitle.value.length < 1)
   {
    alert("Enter Book title data")
    return(false)
   }
  else
   {
```

```
   return(true)
   }
  }

function checkAuthor()
 {
  if(document.myForm.author.value.length < 1)
   {
    alert("Enter Book author data")
    return(false)
   }
  else
   {
    return(true)
   }
  }


function checkLocation()
 {
  if(document.myForm.location.value.length < 1)
   {
    alert("Enter Book location data")
    return(false)
   }
  else
   {
    return(true)
   }
  }

function checkPlatform()
 {
  if(document.myForm.platform.value.length < 2)
   {
    alert("Enter Development platform data (two-character field)")
    return(false)
   }
  else
   {
    return(true)
   }
  }
```

```
function checkLanguage()
{
  if(document.myForm.language.value.length < 2)
  {
    alert("Enter Programming language data (two-character field)")
    return(false)
  }
  else
  {
    return(true)
  }
}
```

Now, click the Design tab. Right-click the Book title input field and select Edit Events. On the next dialog, select OnFocus from the Event list and enter checkCatalogNumber() in the Script field (see Figure 7-24).

Figure 7-24. Event processing

Click OK. The line of the selected event and the corresponding script to be executed appear in the Event/Action box (see Figure 7-25).

Figure 7-25. Event/action assignment

Click OK. Here is how the code works: When the next field in sequence gets the focus (the user moves the cursor to this field), a corresponding procedure is called that validates whether the previous field is coded correctly. Repeat the same steps for the rest of the input fields:

- Enter checkBookTitle() for Author.

- checkAuthor() for Location.

- checkLocation() for Platform.

- checkPlatform() for Language.

To check the last field (Language), you can react on the OnMouseOut event (when the user moves the cursor out of the field and the field loses focus). Right-click the Language input field and select Edit Event. On the next dialog, select the OnMouseOut event and enter checkLanguage() in the Script field. Click the Add button (see Figure 7-26).

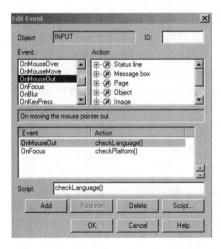

Figure 7-26. Event/action assignment for the last field

As you can see, the last input field (Language) is assigned two events. Click OK. You need to do one last step before testing the logic. You need to assign each field a tab sequence number so that when the user presses the Tab key, the cursor will move to the next field in sequence. On the Design page, right-click the first input field—Catalog number—and select Attributes. Click the Other tab and enter 1 in the Tab display order field (see Figure 7-27).

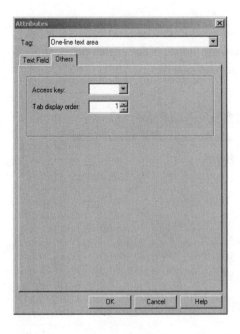

Figure 7-27. Processing attributes for the input field

Repeat the same steps for the rest of the input fields and assign them sequential orders: 2, 3, and so on. Save the updates and close the editor. Now, test the validation logic you just developed. Switch to the Server Perspective and start TechLibTestServer. Next, right-click the BookRegisterInputForm.html and select Run on Server. On the input screen, enter 000 in the Catalog number field (this is wrong because catalog number is a five-character field). Put the cursor in the next field. An error dialog will pop up indicating the coding problem with the Catalog number field (see Figure 7-28).

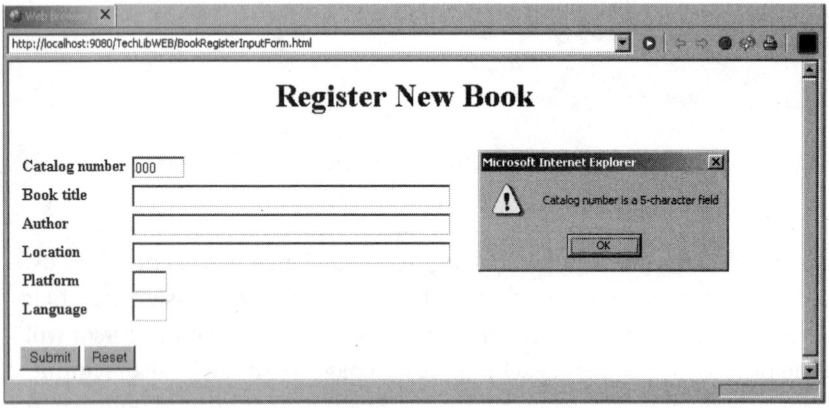

Figure 7-28. Testing data validation

Click OK and enter the correct catalog number. Enter the rest of the fields but leave the Language field empty. When you attempt to leave the cursor out of the Language field, another error message will pop up (see Figure 7-29).

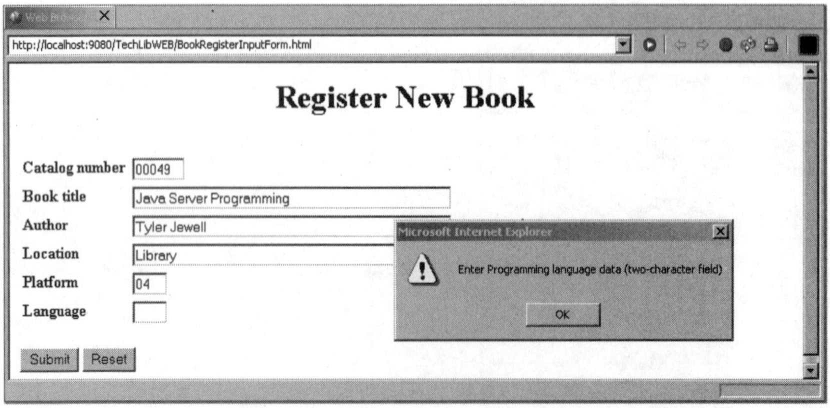

Figure 7-29. Testing data validation of the last field

Click OK. Listings 7-6, 7-7, 7-8, and 7-9 show the final source code for the modified application.

Listing 7-6. The BookHelper *Class*

```java
package apress.wsad.techlib;
import java.io.Serializable;

public class BookHelper implements Serializable
 {
// Attributes
private String catalogNumber;
private String author;
private String bookTitle;
private String location;
private String platform;
private String language;

/**
 * Constructor for BookHelper.
 */
public BookHelper()
{
super();
}

/**
 * Returns the author.
 * @return String
 */
public String getAuthor()
{
return author;
}

/**
 * Returns the bookTitle.
 * @return String
 */
public String getBookTitle()
{
return bookTitle;
```

```
        }

        /**
         * Returns the catalogNumber.
         * @return String
         */
        public String getCatalogNumber()
        {
        return catalogNumber;
        }

        /**
         * Returns the language.
         * @return String
         */
        public String getLanguage()
        {
        return language;
        }

        /**
         * Returns the location.
         * @return String
         */
        public String getLocation()
        {
        return location;
        }

        /**
         * Returns the platform.
         * @return String
         */
        public String getPlatform()
        {
        return platform;
        }

        /**
         * Sets the author.
         * @param author The author to set
         */
        public void setAuthor(String author)
```

```java
{
this.author = author;
}


/**
 * Sets the bookTitle.
 * @param bookTitle The bookTitle to set
 */
public void setBookTitle(String bookTitle)
{
this.bookTitle = bookTitle;
}


/**
 * Sets the catalogNumber.
 * @param catalogNumber The catalogNumber to set
 */
public void setCatalogNumber(String catalogNumber)
{
this.catalogNumber = catalogNumber;
}


/**
 * Sets the language.
 * @param language The language to set
 */
public void setLanguage(String language)
{
this.language = language;
}


/**
 * Sets the location.
 * @param location The location to set
 */
public void setLocation(String location)
{
this.location = location;
}


/**
 * Sets the platform.
 * @param platform The platform to set
```

```
  */
public void setPlatform(String platform)
{
this.platform = platform;
}


}
```

Listing 7-7. The BookRegisterController *Class,* BookRegisterController.java

```
package apress.wsad.techlib;

import java.rmi.*;
import javax.ejb.*;
import javax.naming.*;
import javax.rmi.*;
import java.rmi.*;
import java.util.*;

import java.io.*;
import javax.servlet.*;
import javax.servlet.http.*;


/**
*Description - BookRegister Front Controller
*
* The Controller is the initial point of contact for handling a request.
* Place in this class any services you would like to do on every request
* (Logging, Debugging, Authentication...)
*/


public class BookRegisterController extends HttpServlet implements Serializable
{
/****************************************************************
* Initializes the servlet
* @param config The servlet's configuration information
*/
public void init(ServletConfig config) throws ServletException
{
```

```java
super.init(config);
//Place code here to be done when the servlet is initialized
}


/******************************************************************
* Destroy the Servlet
*/
public void destroy()
{
//Place code here to be done when the servlet is shut down
}


/******************************************************************
* This method is run once for each request.
* @param request The incoming request information
* @param response The outgoing response information
*/
public void performServices(HttpServletRequest request,
                            HttpServletResponse response)
{
//Place any code here that you would like to run on every request
//Logging, Authentication, Debugging...

 // Variable to keep the Book_catalog Home Interface
 TechLibBook_catalogLocalHome catalogLocalHome;
 TechLibBook_catalogLocal catalogLocal;

 String catalogNumber =  request.getParameter("catalogNumber");
 String author        =  request.getParameter("author");
 String bookTitle      =  request.getParameter("bookTitle");
 String location      =  request.getParameter("location");
 String platform      =  request.getParameter("platform");
 String language      =  request.getParameter("language");


 try
    {
    InitialContext initContext = new InitialContext();

            // calling the local reference of the Book_catalog entity bean
    catalogLocalHome =
              (TechLibBook_catalogLocalHome)
                 initContext.lookup("java:comp/env/Book_catalog");
```

321

```
        catalogLocal =
           catalogLocalHome.create(catalogNumber,
                                    author,
                                    bookTitle,
                                    location,
                                    platform,
                                    language);


        // If we are here, successful result


      }
    catch(Exception e)
     {
        System.out.println("Error locating ejb/Book_catalog Home
                            interface" + e.getMessage());


          throw new EJBException("Error registering a new book");
      }
      }


    /**************************************************************
    * Process both HTTP GET and HTTP POST methods
    * @param request The incoming request information
    * @param response The outgoing response information
    */
    public void performTask(
    HttpServletRequest request,
    HttpServletResponse response)
    throws ServletException, IOException
    {
    String nextPage;
    try
    {
    //Perform any specialized sevices
    performServices(request, response);


    //Get the Web page associated with the command in the request
    nextPage = getInitParameter(request.getParameter("command"));


    }
    catch (Exception ex)
    {
    //If an exception is thrown serve the error page
```

```java
      nextPage = getInitParameter("error_page");
   }


   //Forward the request to the next page
   dispatch(request, response, nextPage);
}


/**************************************************************
* Process incoming requests for a HTTP GET method
* @param request The incoming request information
* @param response The outgoing response information
*/
public void doGet(HttpServletRequest request, HttpServletResponse response)
throws ServletException, IOException
{
   performTask(request, response);
}


/**************************************************************
* Process incoming requests for a HTTP POST method
* @param request The incoming request information
* @param response The outgoing response information
*/
public void doPost(HttpServletRequest request, HttpServletResponse
                                                       response)
throws ServletException, IOException
{
   performTask(request, response);
}


/**************************************************************
* Dispatches to the next page
* @param request The incoming request information
* @param response The outgoing response information
* @param nextPage The page to dispatch to
*/
public void dispatch(
HttpServletRequest request,
HttpServletResponse response,
String nextPage)
throws ServletException, IOException
{
   RequestDispatcher dispatch =
```

```
                    request.getRequestDispatcher(nextPage);
        dispatch.forward(request, response);
    }
}
```

Listing 7-8. The BookRegisterInputForm *Page,* BookRegisterInputForm.html

```html
<!DOCTYPE HTML PUBLIC "-//W3C//DTD HTML 4.01 Transitional//EN">
<HTML>
<HEAD>
<META http-equiv="Content-Type" content="text/html; charset=ISO-8859-1">
<META name="GENERATOR" content="IBM WebSphere Studio">

<TITLE>Register New Book</TITLE>

<!--Styles-->
<!--Styles-->
<STYLE type="text/css">
<!--
H1 {
text-align: center !IMPORTANT;
}

TH {
text-align: left !IMPORTANT;
vertical-align: top !IMPORTANT;
}

TD {
text-align: left !IMPORTANT;
vertical-align: top !IMPORTANT;
}

TH.result {
background-color: #999999 !IMPORTANT;
}

TD.result {
background-color: #cccccc;
vertical-align: top !IMPORTANT;
}
```

```
-->
</STYLE>


</HEAD>

<BODY>
<!--JavaScript-->
<SCRIPT language="JavaScript" type="text/javascript">
<!--

function submitForm()
    {
     document.myForm.submit()
    }


function checkCatalogNumber()
    {
 if(document.myForm.catalogNumber.value.length < 5)
      {
        alert("Catalog number is a 5-character field")

         return(false)
       }
       else
        {
         return(true)
        }
    }


    function checkBookTitle()
     {
      if(document.myForm.bookTitle.value.length < 1)
       {
        alert("Enter Book title data")

        return(false)
       }
      else
       {
         return(true)
```

```
      }
   }

function checkAuthor()
 {
  if(document.myForm.author.value.length < 1)
   {
    alert("Enter Book author data")

    return(false)
   }
  else
   {
    return(true)
   }
 }


function checkLocation()
 {
  if(document.myForm.location.value.length < 1)
   {
    alert("Enter Book location data")

    return(false)
   }
  else
   {
    return(true)
   }
 }

function checkPlatform()
 {
  if(document.myForm.platform.value.length < 2)
   {
    alert("Enter Development platform data (two-character field)")

    return(false)
   }
  else
   {
    return(true)
```

```
      }
    }

   function checkLanguage()
    {
     if(document.myForm.language.value.length < 2)
      {
       alert("Enter Programming language data (two-character field)")

       return(false)
      }
     else
      {
       return(true)
      }
    }

//-->
</SCRIPT>

<!--Banner-->
<H1>Register New Book</H1>

<!--Form-->
<FORM name="myForm" method="POST" action="BookRegisterController">

<INPUT type="hidden" name="command" value="BookRegisterResults"> <BR>

<!--Input Fields-->
<TABLE border="0">
<TBODY>
<TR>
<TH width="109">Catalog number</TH>
<TD width="307"><INPUT name='catalogNumber' type='text'
                        size='5' maxlength='5' tabindex="1" ></TD>
</TR>
<TR>
<TH width="109">Book title</TH>
        <TD width="307"><INPUT name='bookTitle' type='text'
                    size='50' maxlength='100' tabindex="2"
                    onMousein="checkBookCatalog()"
                    onfocus="checkCatalogNumber()"></TD>
</TR>
```

```
<TR>
<TH width="109">Author</TH>
<TD width="307"><INPUT name='author' type='text' size='50'
                             maxlength='100'
tabindex="3" onfocus="checkBookTitle()"></TD>
</TR>
<TR>
<TH width="109">Location</TH>
<TD width="307"><INPUT name='location' type='text'
                             size='50' maxlength='50'
tabindex="4" onfocus="checkAuthor()"></TD>
</TR>
<TR>
<TH width="109">Platform</TH>
<TD width="307"><INPUT name='platform' type='text'
                             size='2' maxlength='2'
tabindex="5" onfocus="checkLocation()"></TD>
</TR>
<TR>
<TH width="109" height="22">Language</TH>
<TD width="307" height="22"><INPUT name='language'
                                type='text' size='2' maxlength='2'
tabindex="6" onmouseout="checkLanguage()"
                              onfocus="checkPlatform()"></TD>
</TR>
</TBODY>
</TABLE>

<!--Hidden Fields--><BR>
<INPUT type="submit" name="Submit" value="Submit">
<INPUT type="reset" value="Reset"> <BR>
</FORM>
</BODY>
</HTML>
```

Listing 7-9. The `BookRegisterResultsForm` *Page,* `BookRegisterResultsForm.jsp`

```
<!DOCTYPE HTML PUBLIC "-//W3C//DTD HTML 4.01 Transitional//EN">
<%@ page
import="apress.wsad.techlib.BookRegisterViewBean"
contentType="text/html; charset=ISO-8859-1" pageEncoding="ISO-8859-1"
```

```
%>
<HTML>
<HEAD>
<META http-equiv="Content-Type" content="text/html; charset=ISO-8859-1">
<META name="GENERATOR" content="IBM WebSphere Studio">
<TITLE>Registration Status</TITLE>

<!--Styles-->
<STYLE type="text/css">
<!--
H1 {
text-align: center !IMPORTANT;
}

TH {
text-align: left !IMPORTANT;
vertical-align: top !IMPORTANT;
}

TD {
text-align: left !IMPORTANT;
vertical-align: top !IMPORTANT;
}

TH.result {
background-color: #999999 !IMPORTANT;
}

TD.result {
background-color: #cccccc;
vertical-align: top !IMPORTANT;
}
-->
</STYLE>


</HEAD>
<BODY>

<jsp:useBean id="bookRegisterBean" scope="session"
class="apress.wsad.techlib.BookRegisterViewBean"
type="apress.wsad.techlib.BookRegisterViewBean" />
<%
```

```
%>
<jsp:setProperty name="bookRegisterBean" property="catalogNumber"
  value='<%=new java.lang.String(request.getParameter("catalogNumber"))%>' />
<jsp:setProperty name="bookRegisterBean" property="bookTitle"
  value='<%=new java.lang.String(request.getParameter("bookTitle"))%>' />
<jsp:setProperty name="bookRegisterBean" property="author"
  value='<%=new java.lang.String(request.getParameter("author"))%>' />
<jsp:setProperty name="bookRegisterBean" property="location"
  value='<%=new java.lang.String(request.getParameter("location"))%>' />
<jsp:setProperty name="bookRegisterBean" property="platform"
  value='<%=new java.lang.String(request.getParameter("platform"))%>' />
<jsp:setProperty name="bookRegisterBean" property="language"
  value='<%=new java.lang.String(request.getParameter("language"))%>' />
<%
//Execute Bean Methods whose return type is void

//Execute Other Bean Methods

%>

<!--Banner-->
<H1>Registration Status</H1>

<BR>
<BR>

<!-- Result Table -->
<TABLE border="0">
<TBODY>
<TR>
<TH>Catalog number</TH>
<TD><%=bookRegisterBean.getCatalogNumber()%></TD>
/TR>
<TR>
<TH>Successful Registration</TH>
<TD></TD>
</TR>
</TBODY>
</TABLE>
</BODY>
</HTML>
```

NOTE *WSAD generates the* `BookRegisterViewBean.java` *module; it has not been changed.*

As mentioned, there are many ways to validate the data entered by the user. An alternative way of the data validation is to attach the `OnSubmit` event to the form and call a single procedure that validates all fields. That completes this example. Close the browser and stop the server.

Developing the Stateful Web Session

The next Web example will be developed under the same project, `TechLibWEB`. You will develop a Web function that allows a user to search all the library books for a particular development platform. Upon this Web application activation, the input screen will display that lets the user to enter a platform. The output screen will display the list of book for the specified platform. Although this is a one-screen interaction, the processing logic will call multiple methods from the `TeclLibFacade1` stateful servlet, demonstrating that the state variables are saved between multiple method invocations.

Following the MVC Pattern

Technically, you will implement this functionality by using the MVC pattern. WSAD automatically builds the MVC pattern generating the following modules (all have the same prefix, `BookByPlatform`, which you will specify during the development of this example):

- `BookByPlatformInputForm.html`: The input screen

- `BookByPlatformController.java`: Servlet controlling the flow of data

- `BookByPlatformOutputForm.jsp`: Output result form

- `BookByPlatformHelper1.java`: Helper JavaBean class

The `BookByPlatformController.java` controller servlet coordinates the flow of information for the Web tier of the application. The controller servlet is invoked when the user clicks the `Submit` button. It passes control to the `BookByPlatformOutputForm.jsp` module to display the output screen to the user.

Coding for the Local Client View

You probably remember that you have already developed a stateful session bean called TechLibFacade1 that provides the type of database search required by this example. The TechLibFacade1 stateful session bean has a method called initStateVariables that builds the Local Home references to both entity beans (TechLibBook_catalog and TechLibBook_activity) and saves them in the state variables (catalogLocalHome and activityLocalHome), respectively. Because the stateful session bean keeps the state, you can call the business method getBookForPlatform, which simply reuses the Local Home reference saved in the catalogLocalHome state variable.

When calling the stateful session bean, it is important to ensure that the same instance of the stateful bean is used for the same user. This example shows you how you can do that. For now, all that is needed (in order to find a book written for a selected platform) is to call two methods of the TechLibFacade1 stateful session bean (the initStateVariables method following by the getBookForPlatform method):

```
public void initStateVariables();
public Vector getBookForPlatform(String Platform_Name);
```

The BookByPlatformHelper1.java JavaBean class will provide a method called populateIndexedAttribute that calls the TechLibFacade1 session bean's method getBookForPlatform, gets the results, and populates its indexed property (transObjList). The BookByPlatformOutputForm.jsp module will then call the JavaBean's populateIndexedAttribute method and use the accumulated data to display the dynamic table content on the output screen. With this quick introduction, switch to the Web Perspective to start developing the example.

First, you will build the input user screen (the HTML file called BookByPlatformInputForm.html). Right-click the Web Content subdirectory of the TechLibWEB project and select New ➤ HTML/XHTML File. On the next screen, enter BookByPlatformInputForm in the File Name field (see Figure 7-30).

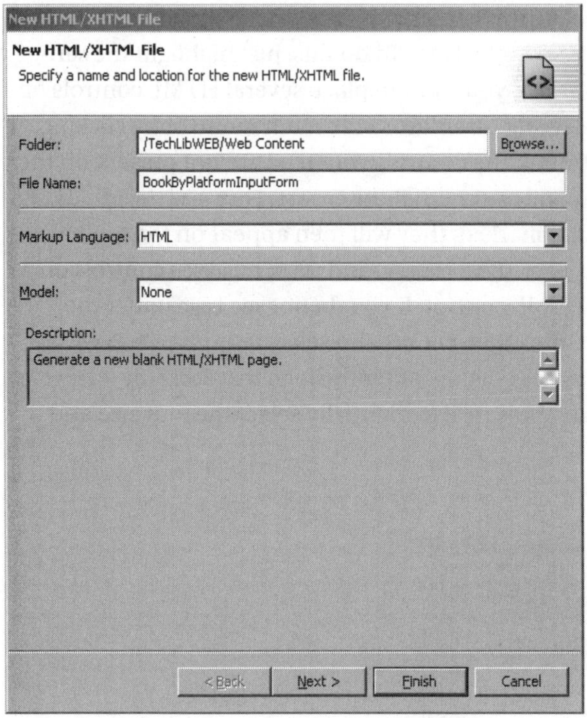

Figure 7-30. Creating the HTML input form

Click Finish. WSAD generates the BookByPlatformInputForm.html file and opens it in the Editor View (see Figure 7-31).

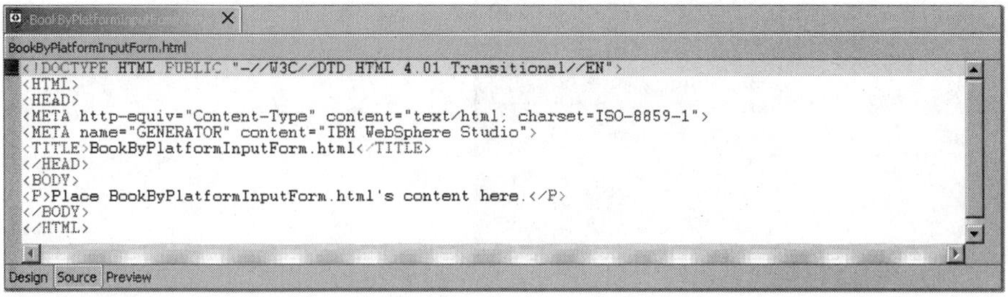

Figure 7-31. Creating the HTML input form

Click the `Design` tab and delete this sentence: `Place BookByPlatformInputForm.html`'s content here. To do this, just highlight the sentence and press the Delete key. Next, you want to place several HTML controls on the page. You can do this by selecting `Insert` from the main menu or by clicking the corresponding toolbar button (if the controls you need are not present on the toolbar, click the `Toolbar` menu and ensure that the `Insert`, `Form and Input Fields`, `Format`, `Table`, and `Frame` items are marked; they will then appear on the toolbar).

You want to place the `Logo`, `Form`, `Option menu`, and `Submit button` controls on the page. First, insert the `Logo` HTML control. If you do not see `Logo` under the `Insert` menu, close your HTML file, right-click it and select `Open With` ➤ `Page Designer Classic`. On the `Create Logo` dialog, enter the logo text `Books by Platform`, scroll down, and select the style. You can also manually select the font size and other attributes (see Figure 7-32).

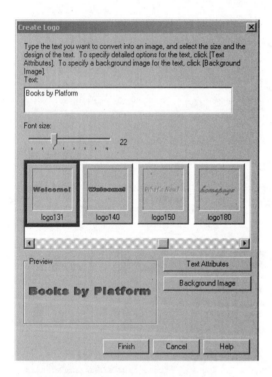

Figure 7-32. Setting the page logo style

Click `Finish`. Below the logo, enter the plain text: `Select the platform and click Submit`. Right-click the text and select `Edit Style`. On the dialog that appears, click `Font` ➤ `Style` and select `Bold` in the `Weight` field (see Figure 7-33).

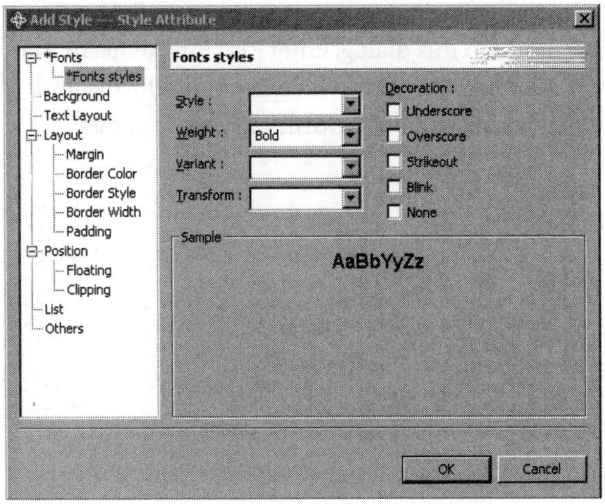

Figure 7-33. Setting the page logo attributes

Click OK twice. Next, enter the Form, Option, and Submit button HTML controls. From the main menu, select Insert ➤ Form and Input Fields ➤ Form. On the dialog that appears, right-click the Form tag and select Attributes. Enter myForm in the Name field. Enter BookByPlatformController in the Action field. Select the Post method (see Figure 7-34).

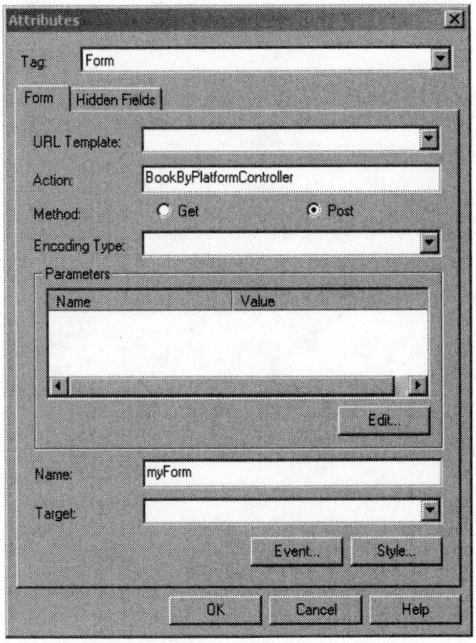

Figure 7-34. Creating the Form HTML tag

Click OK. The outline of the Form control will appear on the screen. Select Insert ➤ Form and Input Fields ➤ Option menu. On this dialog, enter PlatformOption in the Name field. Next, you need to populate the Choice box with a list of platforms and their corresponding code. Table 7-1 describes the platforms and their codes.

Table 7-1. Platforms and Their Codes

PLATFORM	PLATFORM CODE
Cross-platform	00
Unix (AIX)	01
Unix (Solaris)	02
Unix (HP-UX)	03
Windows NT/2000	02
Linux	05

Enter each platform-code pair in the Item and Value fields. Click the Add button. The entered platform-code pair will appear as a line in the Choice list (see Figure 7-35).

Figure 7-35. Entering the item-value pairs in the Choice list

When you are done, click OK. Place the cursor after the Option control and press the Enter key three times. Figure 7-36 shows how the screen looks at this point.

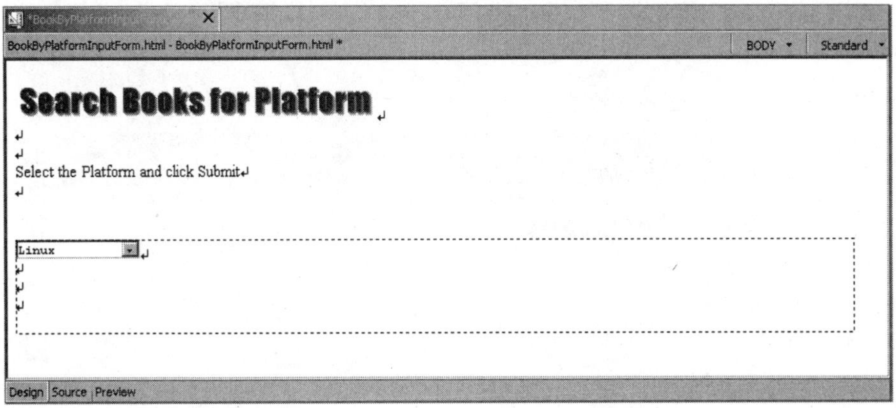

Figure 7-36. Creating the form page

Insert the Submit button. On the Attributes dialog for the push button, enter Submit in both the Name and Label fields (see Figure 7-37).

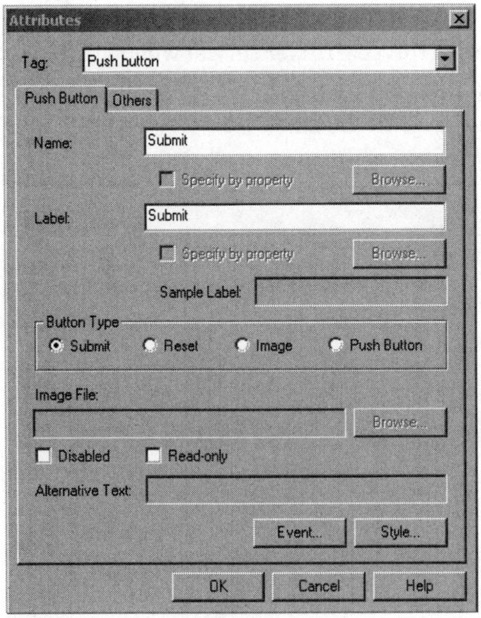

Figure 7-37. Inserting the Submit *button*

Click OK. Next, click the Preview tab. Your page should look like the one shown in Figure 7-38.

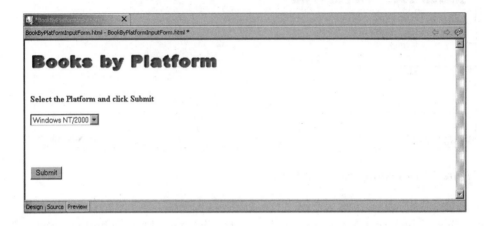

Figure 7-38. The designed input screen

Save the file and close the editor. The action of the form indicates that when a user clicks the Submit button, the BookByPlatformController servlet will be invoked. That is the module that you will develop next, and because it is not available yet, WSAD shows a "broken link" warning message in the Links View (see Figure 7-39).

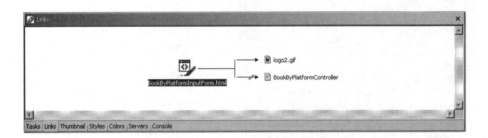

Figure 7-39. The Links View

Just ignore the broken link in the Links View for now. Because the BookByPlatformControllet servlet uses the JavaBean helper class called BookByPlatformHelper1, you will first develop this JavaBean class.

Right-click the `Java Class` folder under the `TechLibWEB` project and select
`New ➤ Class`. On the dialog that appears, click the `Browse` button that is attached to
the `Package` field and select `apress.wsad.techlib`. Enter `BookByPlatformHelper1` in
the `Name` field. Check `Constructors from superclass`. Click the `Add` button and select
`Serializable`. You want this JavaBean class to implement the `Serializable`
interface so that it can be placed in the session object (see Figure 7-40).

Figure 7-40. Building the JavaBean class

Click `Finish`. WSAD will generate the skeleton of the JavaBean class.

Adding the Processing Logic

Add the processing logic for the `BookByPlatformHelper1` class. Listing 7-10 shows
the source code of the `BookByPlatformHelper1` class. It is also included on the
Apress Web site (`http://www.apress.com`) in the Downloads section.

Listing 7-10. BookByPlatformHelper1.java

```java
package apress.wsad.techlib;
import java.io.Serializable;
import java.lang.*;
import java.util.*;
import javax.ejb.*;
import javax.naming.*;
import java.rmi.*;
import javax.ejb.Handle.*;
import apress.wsad.techlib.TransportBean;

public class BookByPlatformHelper1 implements Serializable
{
 // Attributes
 TransportBean[] transObjList;

 // Instance variables
 String selectedPlatform;
 Vector bookVector = null;

 // Variables to keep LocalHome and Local interfaces for
 the TechLibFacade1 stateful session bean
 TechLibFacade1LocalHome facade1LocalHome = null;
 TechLibFacade1Local facade1Local  = null;

 /**
  * Default Constructor
  */
 public BookByPlatformHelper1()
 {
  super();

 }

 // Method to get the LocalHome Interface of the TechLibFacade1 session bean.
 private TechLibFacade1LocalHome getFacade1LocalHome()
  {

  try
   {
     if (facade1LocalHome == null)
       {
```

```java
        InitialContext initContext = new InitialContext();

            Object objRef =
                initContext.lookup("java:comp/env/TechLibFacade1");

            facade1LocalHome = (TechLibFacade1LocalHome) objRef;
            return facade1LocalHome;
            }
          else
            {
            return facade1LocalHome;
            }
        }
    catch (NamingException e)
        {
        System.out.println("Error locating TechLibBook_catalogLocalHome: " +
                                            e.getMessage());
        throw
            new EJBException("Error locating TechLibBook_catalogLocalHome: " +
                                            e.getMessage());
        }


    }


// Method to get the Local Interface of the TechLibFacade1 stateful session
// bean.
private TechLibFacade1Local getFacade1Local()
        throws RemoteException, CreateException
    {
    try
        {
        // Create remote handle for the first time and
        facade1Local = facade1LocalHome.create();

        return facade1Local;

        } // End of the try block

    catch(Exception e)
        {
        System.out.println("Exception in getFacade1Local method: " +
```

```
                                                       e.getMessage());
     throw
        new EJBException("Exception in getFacade1Local method: " +
                                          e.getMessage());

     }

  } // End of getFacade1Remote method


  // Common processing logic
  public void populateIndexedAttribute()
   {

   try
    {
      facade1LocalHome = getFacade1LocalHome();

      facade1Local = getFacade1Local();

      // First call the initSataeVariables
      facade1Local.initStateVariables();

      // Now, we can call the getBookForPlatform business method
      bookVector = facade1Local.getBookForPlatform(selectedPlatform);

      if (bookVector == null)
       {
        transObjList = new TransportBean[1];

        transObjList[0] = new TransportBean();

        transObjList[0].setCatalogNumber("");
        transObjList[0].setBookTitle("");
        transObjList[0].setAuthor("");
        transObjList[0].setLocation("");
       }
      else
        {
        // Convert bookVector to an array of TransportBean objects
        int workSize = bookVector.size();
        transObjList = new TransportBean[bookVector.size()];
        bookVector.copyInto(transObjList);
        }
```

```java
  }
  catch (Exception re)
  {
    System.out.println("RemoteException in the populateIndexedAttribute method:
        + re.getMessage());
    throw
      new EJBException("RemoteException in the populateIndexedAttribute
        method: " + re.getMessage());
  }

} // End of the populateIndexedAttribute method

public TransportBean[] getTransObjList()
  {
    return transObjList;
  }


public void setTransObjList(TransportBean[] transObjList)
 {
  this.transObjList = transObjList;
 }


public String getSelectedPlatform()
  {
    return selectedPlatform;
  }


 public void setSelectedPlatform(String selectedPlatform)
 {
  this.selectedPlatform = selectedPlatform;
 }


}
```

Examining the BookByPlatformHelper1 Code

Let's examine the BookByPlatformHelper1 JavaBean's processing logic. The main processing happens within the populateIndexedAttribute method. This method calls two private methods (getFacade1LocalHome and getFacade1Local) to obtain the Local Home and Local references of the TechLibFacade1 stateful session bean and saves the results in the facade1LocalHome *and* Facade1Local state variables. The populateIndexedAttribute method uses the facade1Local variable to create an instance of the TechLibFacade1 object (by calling the create method). Next, the business method getBookForPlatform is called like this:

```
bookVector = facade1Local. getBookForPlatform(selectedPlatform);
```

This call returns a vector of objects of type TransferBean. Finally, you convert the vector object to an array called transObjList that is an indexed attribute. Later, you will use the values accumulated in this indexed attribute to dynamically build the content of the table on the output page. Now, you are ready to build the BookByPlatformController servlet. Right-click the apress.wsad.techlib folder and select New ➤ Servlet.

TIP *Right-clicking the* apress.wsad.techlib *folder (instead of the* TechLibWEB *project) fills in the* apress.wsad.techlib *package on the next screen.*

On the dialog that appears, shown in Figure 7-41, enter BookByPlatformController in the Class Name field.

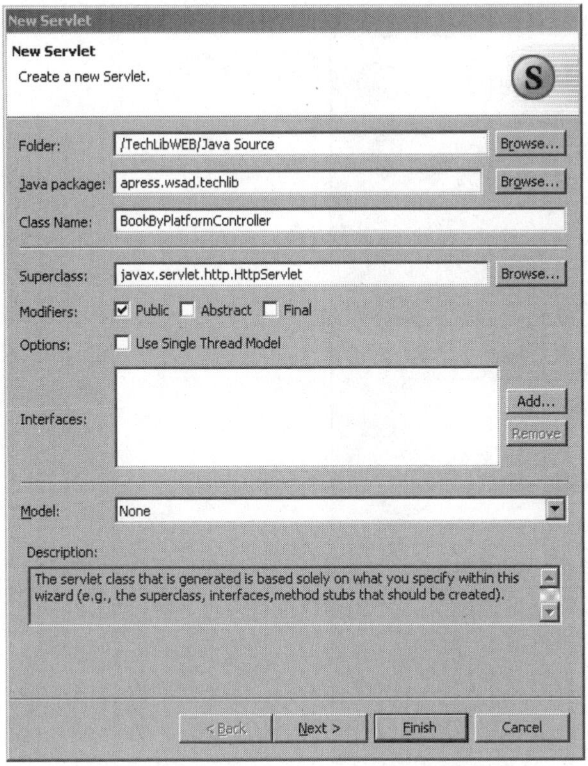

Figure 7-41. Creating a new servlet component

Click Next. On the next screen, select the doPost(), doGet(), doDelete(), and init() methods (see Figure 7-42).

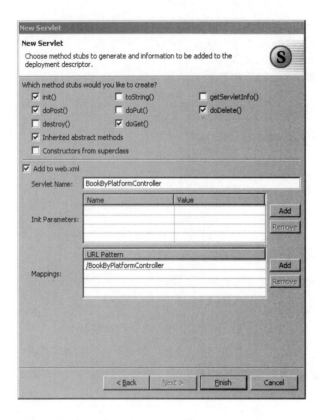

Figure 7-42. Setting servlet attributes

Click Finish. WSAD will generate the skeleton of the BookByPlatformController servlet. Modify the servlet to add the necessary processing logic. See Listing 7-11 for the source code of the BookByPlatformController servlet. (It is also available on the Apress Web site (http://www.apress.com) in the Downloads section.)

Listing 7-11. BookByPlatformController.java

```java
package apress.wsad.techlib;
import java.io.IOException;
import javax.servlet.ServletException;
import javax.servlet.*;
import javax.servlet.http.*;
import javax.servlet.http.HttpServlet;
import javax.servlet.http.HttpServletRequest;
import javax.servlet.http.HttpServletResponse;
```

```java
public class BookByPlatformController extends HttpServlet
{
 public void doDelete(HttpServletRequest req, HttpServletResponse resp)
throws ServletException, IOException
{

}


public void doGet(HttpServletRequest req, HttpServletResponse resp)
throws ServletException, IOException
{
    performTask(req, resp);
}


public void doPost(HttpServletRequest req, HttpServletResponse resp)
 throws ServletException, IOException
{
    performTask(req, resp);
}


public void init() throws ServletException
{
  super.init();
}



public void performTask(HttpServletRequest request,
                    HttpServletResponse response)
            throws ServletException, IOException
 {
  String nextPage;

  try
   {
     HttpSession session = request.getSession(true);

     // Prepare invocation of the jsp module BookByPlatformOutputForm.jsp
     nextPage = "/BookByPlatformOutputForm.jsp";
   }
  catch (Exception ex)
   {
    //If an exception is thrown, serve the error page
    nextPage = getInitParameter("error_page");
```

```
        }

    //Forward the request to the next page
    dispatch(request, response, nextPage);

}

    public void dispatch(HttpServletRequest request,
                    HttpServletResponse response,
                    String nextPage)
        throws ServletException, IOException
    {
     RequestDispatcher dispatch = request.getRequestDispatcher(nextPage);
     dispatch.forward(request, response);
     }
}
```

Notice that the warning message about the broken link has disappeared.

Discussing the BookByPlatformController Servlet

Let's examine the servlet code. You added two new methods called performTask and dispatch. Both methods perform the single task of invoking the BookByPlatformOutputForm.jsp module. The real processing happens in the BookByPlatformHelper1 JavaBean class that is invoked by the BookByPlatformOutputForm JSP module.

Developing the BookByPlatformOutputForm Output Form

Next, you need to develop the BookByPlatformOutputForm.jsp module responsible for displaying the dynamic content on the output screen. Ensure that you are in the Web Perspective. Right-click the TechLibWEB project and select New ➤ Other ➤ Web ➤ JSP File. On the dialog that appears, enter BookByPlatformOutputForm in the File Name field (see Figure 7-43).

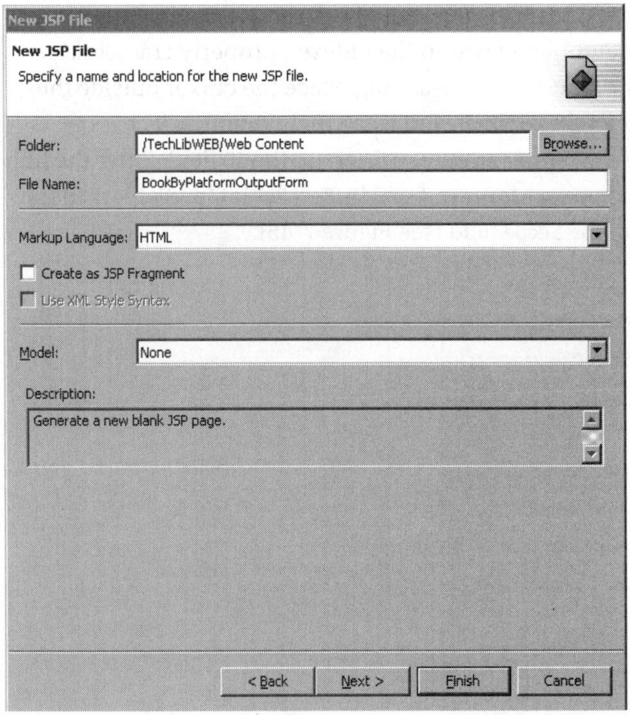

New JSP File

New JSP File
Specify a name and location for the new JSP file.

| Folder: | /TechLibWEB/Web Content | Browse... |

| File Name: | BookByPlatformOutputForm | |

Markup Language: HTML ▼

☐ Create as JSP Fragment

☐ Use XML Style Syntax

Model: None ▼

Description:

Generate a new blank JSP page. ▲ ▼

< Back   Next >   Finish   Cancel

Figure 7-43. Building the JSP component

Click Finish. WSAD will generate the BookByPlatformOutputForm.jsp file. Switch to the Design View by clicking the Design tab. Remove the text saying: Place BookByPlatformOutputForm.jsp's content here. Insert the logo Books by Platform (Search Results). Select the style you like and click OK. The logo will be inserted. Click the Preview tab to see the picture (see Figure 7-44).

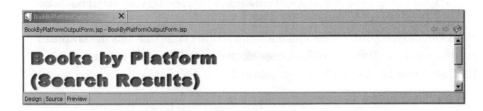

BookByPlatformOutputForm.jsp - BookByPlatformOutputForm.jsp

Books by Platform (Search Results)

Design | Source | Preview

Figure 7-44. Previewing the logo

Now, click the Design tab. This JSP code should call the BookByPlatformHelper1 JavaBean to get the data accumulated within the indexed property transObjList. Therefore, you need to insert the <jsp:useBean> tag. Place the cursor outside the logo and press the Enter key several times. From the main menu, select JSP ➤ Insert Bean. On the dialog that appears, enter Helper1 in the ID field. Enter the fully qualified JavaBean class name: apress.wsad.techlib.BookByPlatformHelper1 in the Class field. Select session in the Scope field (see Figure 7-45).

Figure 7-45. Inserting the JavaBean class in the JSP module

Click OK. WSAD will generate the following <jsp:useBean..> tag:

```
<jsp:useBean id="Helper1"
class="apress.wsad.techlib.BookByPlatformHelper1" scope="session"></jsp:useBean>
```

Switch to the Source View and enter the scriptlet code that sets the JavaBean attribute SelectedPlatform to the value selected by the user and execute the JavaBean's populateIndexedAttribute method:

```
<% String selectedProperty = request.getParameter("PlatformOption");
   Helper1.setSelectedPlatform(selectedProperty);
   Helper1.populateIndexedAttribute();
%>
```

NOTE *On the user input screen maintained by the* BookByPlatformInputForm.html *module, the* Option menu *control has the name* PlatformOption. *You can check it by opening the* BookByPlatformInputForm *in the Editor View, switching to the Source page, and locating the* <FORM> *HTML tag.*

The previous scriptlet code retrieves the platform selected by the user and uses it to set the value of the selectedPlatform property of the BookByPlatformHelper1 JavaBean. After that, the scriptlet calls the populateIndexedAttribute method of the BookByPlatformHelper1 JavaBean class.

Generating a Dynamic Table

Now is the interesting part. You need to dynamically generate a table that displays a list of books found by the search for the selected platform. Switch to the Design View and insert the Table control. On the Insert Table dialog, indicate the table size (2_5). Click OK. The Table control will be inserted in the page. Type the column headings into each cell within the table's first row in the Design View: Catalog number, Book title, Author, Location, Platform. You will not show the Language field on this page (see Figure 7-46).

Figure 7-46. Inserting the Table *control*

NOTE *Of course, the* Platform *value will be the same in each row and should not be included here. You included the* Platform *column here to prove that all selected rows do indeed belong to the requested platform.*

Select the first row (drag over it) and click the Bold icon on the toolbar. Right-click the table in the Design View and select Attributes. On the Attributes dialog, click the Table tab. For the Caption radio button group, select Top of table to indicate that the table headings are located on the top row (see Figure 7-47).

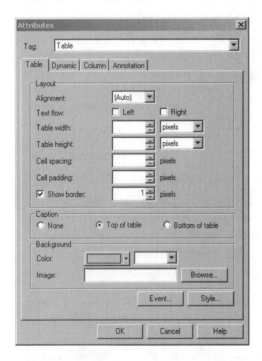

Figure 7-47. Setting the Table *control's attributes*

Next, click the Dynamic tab. First, check the Loop radio button. Leave the Direction field as Vertical (how the table will be processed). Second, for the Loop property field, click the Browse button. Navigate to the Helper1 JavaBean and expand it. Select the transObjList[] indexed attribute of the BookByPlatformHelper1 JavaBean class and click OK. Click OK again to close the Attributes dialog and return to the original screen. Finally, set the Row/Column range Start field to 2 and the Row/Column Range End field to 2 (see Figure 7-48).

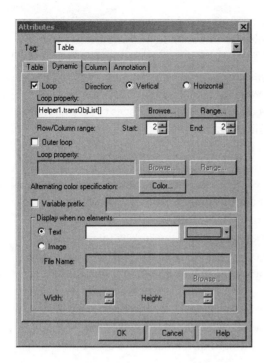

Figure 7-48. Setting dynamic attributes

Now, you need to map the table's columns to the corresponding elements of the transObjList[] indexed property. Click the first cell within the second row. From the main menu, select Insert ➤ Dynamic Elements ➤ Property Display. On the Property Display dialog box, click the Browse button. Expand transObjList[] and select the catalogNumber field. In the Sample Text field, enter 12345 as a string pattern (see Figure 7-49).

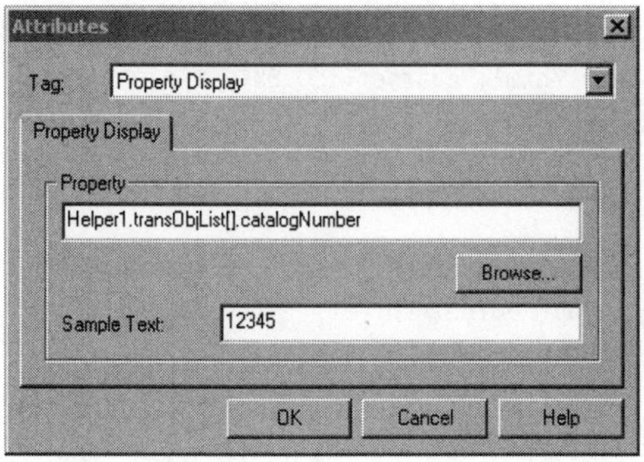

Figure 7-49. Property display settings

Click OK. Repeat the same steps to map the rest of the second row's fields. Save the changes and close the editor. You need to understand one important concept of a Web application. As already mentioned, the stateful session bean represents a client on the remote environment. In addition, the stateful session bean maintains the state (instance variable values) between multiple method invocations. With multiple concurrent user requests processing, multiple instances of the stateful session bean will be activated within the EJB container.

You need to ensure that each subsequent request produced by the same user calls the instance of the session bean that was originally created for the client at his/her first request. Specifically, the instance variables that keep references to the Local Home and Local Interfaces must continue pointing to the same instance of the stateful session bean. The way to ensure this requirement is to set the session attribute of the `<jsp:useBean>` tag to true. In this case, the `BookByPlatformHelper1` JavaBean module will be activated once per user session and will be saved in the session object. For all subsequent invocations, this JavaBean module will be retrieved from the session object.

Listing 7-12 shows the source code of the `BookByPlatformOutputForm.jsp` module that demonstrates the main idea: The JSP module invokes the `BookByPlatformHelper1` JavaBean module that in turn locates and calls the `TechLibFacade1` stateful session bean.

Listing 7-12. `BookByPlatformOutputForm.jsp`

```
<!DOCTYPE HTML PUBLIC "-//W3C//DTD HTML 4.01 Transitional//EN">
<HTML>
<HEAD>
<%@ page
language="java"
contentType="text/html; charset=ISO-8859-1"
pageEncoding="ISO-8859-1"
%>
<META http-equiv="Content-Type" content="text/html; charset=ISO-8859-1">
<META name="GENERATOR" content="IBM WebSphere Studio">
<TITLE>BookByPlatformOutputForm.jsp</TITLE>
</HEAD>
<BODY>
<P><IMG src="logo4.gif" width="697" height="47" border="0"
      alt="Book for Platform (Search Results)"></P>
<P></P>
<P><BR>
<jsp:useBean id="Helper1"
   class="apress.wsad.techlib.BookByPlatformHelper1" scope="session">
```

```
</jsp:useBean>
</P>

<% String selectedProperty = request.getParameter("PlatformOption");
   Helper1.setSelectedPlatform(selectedProperty);
   Helper1.populateIndexedAttribute();
%>

<%--METADATA type="DynamicData" startspan
<TABLE border="1" innerloopproperty=
     "Helper1.transObjList[]"
     innerloopdirection="vertical"
     innerloopstartindex="1" innerloopendindex="1"
     dynamicelement>
<CAPTION></CAPTION>
<TBODY>
<TR>
<TD><B>Catalog number</B></TD>
<TD><B>Book title</B></TD>
<TD><B>Author</B></TD>
<TD><B>Location</B></TD>
<TD><B>Platform</B></TD>
</TR>
<TR>
<TD><WSPX:PROPERTY property="Helper1.transObjList[].catalogNumber"
          authortimetext="12345"></TD>
<TD><WSPX:PROPERTY property="Helper1.transObjList[].bookTitle"
authortimetext="wwwwwwwwwwwwwwwwwww"></TD>
<TD><WSPX:PROPERTY property="Helper1.transObjList[].author"
authortimetext="AAAAAAAAAAAAAAAA"></TD>
<TD><WSPX:PROPERTY property="Helper1.transObjList[].location"
                authortimetext="Library"></TD>
<TD><WSPX:PROPERTY property="Helper1.transObjList[].platform"
     authortimetext="00"></TD>
</TR>
</TBODY>
</TABLE>
--%><%
try {
  apress.wsad.techlib.TransportBean[] _a0 =
   Helper1.getTransObjList();
  apress.wsad.techlib.TransportBean
 _p0 = _a0[0];
```

```
    // throws an exception if empty. %>
     <TABLE border="1">
       <CAPTION></CAPTION>
       <TBODY>
         <TR>
           <TD><B>Catalog number</B></TD>
           <TD><B>Book title</B></TD>
           <TD><B>Author</B></TD>
           <TD><B>Location</B></TD>
           <TD><B>Platform</B></TD>
         </TR><%
         for (int _i0 = 0; ; ) { %>
           <TR>
             <TD><%= _p0.getCatalogNumber() %></TD>
             <TD><%= _p0.getBookTitle() %></TD>
             <TD><%= _p0.getAuthor() %></TD>
             <TD><%= _p0.getLocation() %></TD>
             <TD><%= _p0.getPlatform() %></TD>
           </TR><%
           _i0++;
           try {
             _p0 = _a0[_i0];
           }
           catch
(java.lang.ArrayIndexOutOfBoundsException _e0)
           {
             break;
           }
         } %>
       </TBODY>
     </TABLE><%
}
catch
(java.lang.ArrayIndexOutOfBoundsException _e0)
{
} %><%--METADATA type="DynamicData" endspan--%>
</BODY>
</HTML>
```

Notice the `scope="session"` attribute for the `<jsp:useBean>` tag. The `BookByPlatformHelper1` JavaBean (the source code of this module has been already shown previously) includes two methods (`getFacadeLocalHome` and `getFacadeLocal`) that calculate the Local Home and Local Interfaces to the `TechLibFacade1` stateful session bean, respectively. The JavaBean is a serializeable object, and it is serialized when it is saved in the session object. The important point is that for the Local Client View, the Local Home and Local references are special objects that are correctly serialized by the container. Therefore, they can be properly saved and recovered in the session object. No additional effort is required to use the Handle object (as would be necessary to do with the Remote Client Interface, as shown later).

In this case, you calculate the value of the Local Home and Local Interfaces only once when the JavaBean is created and save them in the state variables (facade1LocalHome and facade1Local). Whenever the JavaBean instance is recovered from the session object, the facade1LocalHome and facade1Local variables will have the correct value, pointing to the same TechLibFacade1 stateful session bean instance. If you run this example in the debug mode and set a breakpoint at the following statement:

```
if (facade1LocalHome == null)
and
if (facade1Local == null)
```

you should see that both variables have the null value only at first invocation. All subsequent invocations by the same user will retrieve the JavaBean from the session object; because both variables are not equal to null, they never recalculate again.

Coding for the Remote Client View

This section interrupts the example for a moment to show how this module would look if the TechLibFacade1 stateful session bean exposed the Remote Interface (see Listing 7-13).

Listing 7-13. BookByPlatformHelperX.java

```
package sams.wsad.techlib;
import java.io.Serializable;
import java.lang.*;
import java.util.*;
import javax.ejb.*;
import javax.naming.*;
import javax.rmi.*;
import java.rmi.*;
import javax.ejb.Handle.*;
```

```
import apress.wsad.techlib.TransportBean;

public class BookByPlatformHelperX implements Serializable
{
 // Attributes
 TransportBean[] transObjList;
 String selectedPlatform;
 Vector bookVector = null;

 // Variable that keeps the Home Interface
 // reference to Facade1 session bean
 transient TechLibFacade1Home facade1Home = null;
 transient TechLibFacade1 facade1Remote  = null;
 private   Handle remoteHandle = null;
 public BookByPlatformHelper1()
 {
  super();
 }

 // Method to get the Home Interface of the
 // TechLibFacade1 session bean.
 private TechLibFacade1Home getFacade1Home()
  {

    if (facade1Home == null)
     {

       try
        {
         InitialContext ic = new InitialContext();

         Object objRef =
             ic.lookup("ejb/TechLibFacade1");

         facade1Home =
            (TechLibFacade1Home)
                  javax.rmi.PortableRemoteObject.narrow
                   (objRef, TechLibFacade1Home.class);
        }
      catch (NamingException ne)
       {
        System.out.println
          ("Error locating TechLibFacade1Home: " +
```

```
                ne.getMessage());

          throw
            new EJBException
            ("Error locating TechLibFacade1Home: " +
                    ne.getMessage());
        }

    } // End of IF

  return facade1Home;
}

// Method to get the Remote Interface of
// the TechLibFacade1 session bean.
private TechLibFacade1 getFacade1Remote()
      throws RemoteException, CreateException
  {
    try
     {
      if (remoteHandle == null)
       {
        // Create remote handle for the first time and
        facade1Remote = facade1Home.create();
        remoteHandle = facade1Remote.getHandle();
       }
      else
       {
         // Re-create remote reference from handle
         facade1Remote = (TechLibFacade1)
          remoteHandle.getEJBObject();
       }

        return facade1Remote;

      } // End of the try block

     catch(RemoteException re)
      {
       System.out.println
         ("Error executing facade1.create() method: " +
                    re.getMessage());
       throw
```

```
            new RemoteException
              ("Error executing facade1.create() method: " +
                        re.getMessage());
        }


      catch(CreateException cr)
       {
          System.out.println
             ("Error executing facade1.create() method: " +
                        cr.getMessage());
        throw
           new CreateException
            ("Error executing facade1.create() method: " +
                cr.getMessage());
        }



  } // End of getFacade1Remote method

// Common processing logic
public void populateIndexedAttribute()
 {
 try
  {
    facade1Home = getFacade1Home();
    facade1Remote = getFacade1Remote();

    // First call the initSataeVariables
    facade1Remote.initStateVariables();

    // Now, we can call the getBookForPlatform
    // business method
    bookVector = facade1Remote.
       getBookForPlatform(selectedPlatform);

    if (bookVector == null)
     {
      transObjList = new TransportBean[1];

      transObjList[0] = new TransportBean();

      transObjList[0].setCatalogNumber("");
      transObjList[0].setBookTitle("");
```

```
          transObjList[0].setAuthor("");
          transObjList[0].setLocation("");
        }
    else
        {
          // Convert bookVector to an array of
          // TransportBean objects
          int workSize = bookVector.size();
          transObjList = new
              TransportBean[bookVector.size()];
          bookVector.copyInto(transObjList);
        }


    }
    catch (RemoteException re)
     {
        System.out.println
         ("Error within populateIndexedAttribute() method: " +
                                re.getMessage());
        throw
           new EJBException
            ("Error within populateIndexedAttribute() metho: " +
                           re.getMessage());
     }

    catch (CreateException ce)
     {
        System.out.println
         ("Error executing getFacade1Remote() method: " +
                             ce.getMessage());
        throw
         new EJBException
         ("Error executing getFacade1Remote() method: " +
                     ce.getMessage());
     }

    } // End of the populateIndexedAttribute method

public TransportBean[] getTransObjList()
  {
    return transObjList;
  }
```

```
public void
  setTransObjList(TransportBean[] transObjList)
 {
  this.transObjList = transObjList;
 }

public String getSelectedPlatform()
  {
   return selectedPlatform;
  }

public void
 setSelectedPlatform(String selectedPlatform)
 {
  this.selectedPlatform = selectedPlatform;
 }

}
```

Examining the Processing Logic

This JavaBean includes two methods (getFacadeHome and getFacadeRemote) that
calculate the Home and Remote Interfaces, respectively. The JavaBean is a serializeable object, and it is serialized when it is saved in the session object. The
problem is that the Home and Remote references are not serializable objects, and
they cannot be properly saved in the session object. Fortunately, you can use the
remoteHandle, which is a serializable object.

In this case, you calculate the value of the Home and Remote Interfaces only
once when the JavaBean is created. Next, you calculate the remoteHandle based on
the remote reference. Because the remoteHandle is a serializable object, it is correctly saved within the session object. Whenever the JavaBean instance is
recovered from the session object, the remoteHandle will have the correct value,
and the remote reference will be recalculated based on that remoteHandle value.

For this logic to work, it is important to define both the facade1Home and
facade1Remote variables as *transient variables*, so the container will not save them
when the JavaBean module is saved in the session object between method invocations. If you run this example in the debug mode and set a breakpoint at the
following statement:

```
if (remoteHandle == null)
```

you should see that the remote handle is null only at first invocation. All subsequent invocations by the same user will retrieve the JavaBean from the session object; the remoteHandle is never null, so it is never recalculated.

Now, let's get back to the example (which uses the Local Client View of the TechLibFacade1 stateful session bean). You need to indicate that this Web module uses the TechLibFacade1 module. Right-click the web.xmi file and select Open With ➤ Deployment Descriptor Editor. On the next screen, click the References tab. Highlight EJB Local at the top of the screen and click the Add button. Replace the reference name with TechLibFacade1. Select TechLibFacade1. In the "Details" section, click the Browse button attached to the Link field. Select TechLibFacade1 and click OK (see Figure 7-50).

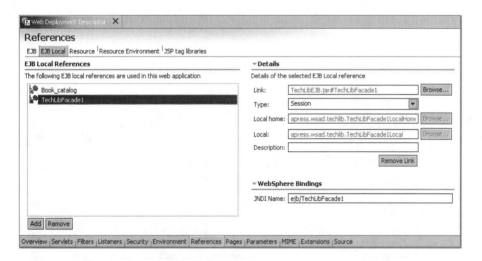

Figure 7-50. TechLibFacade *bean setting*

Testing the Stateful Web Application

You are now ready to test your application. Switch to the Server Perspective. You already have a server instance called TestTechLibServer that includes the TechLibApp project (which, in turn, includes the TechLibWEB project). Start this server instance, and wait until the server is ready. Right-click BookByPlatformInputForm.html and select Run on Server. On the user input screen that appears, extend the Option menu control and select Cross platform (see Figure 7-51).

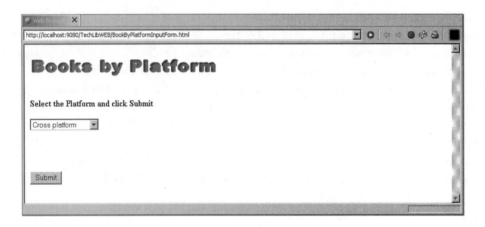

Figure 7-51. Starting the application and filling the input screen

Click the Submit button. Figure 7-52 shows the result.

Catalog number	Book title	Author	Location	Platform
00002	Inside Unix	Chris Hare	AAA_Company	00
00003	Java Enterprise in a Nutshell	David Flanagan and a team	Library	00
00004	Java Server Programming	Danny Ayers and a team	BBB_Company	00
00008	Maximum Java 1.1	Vanderberg and a team	BBB_Company	00
00010	Java Server Programming	John Davies	Library	00
00013	Advanced Techniques for Java Development	Daniel Berg	Library	00
00032	Examples of using MQSeries	IBM	Library	00
00016	Java 1.2 Developer's Handbook	Phillip Heller	Library	00
00018	J2EE Quick Reference	John Smith	Library	00

Figure 7-52. The processing results

Close the Web Browser View, and stop the server.

Debugging the TechLibWEB Project

Open the BookByPlatformHelper1 module in the Java Editor View (just double-click
the BookByPlatformHelper1 module). Set the breakpoint inside the
getFacade1LocalHome method on the following statement:

if (facade1LocalHome == **null**)

To set the breakpoint, double-click the left vertical bar for the line. You should
see a blue icon appear on the vertical bar (see Figure 7-53).

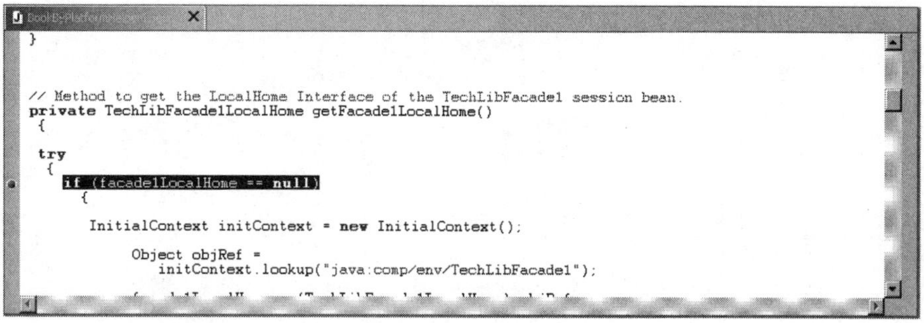

```
}

    // Method to get the LocalHome Interface of the TechLibFacade1 session bean.
    private TechLibFacade1LocalHome getFacade1LocalHome()
    {

    try
    {
        if (facade1LocalHome == null)
        {

            InitialContext initContext = new InitialContext();

            Object objRef =
                initContext.lookup("java:comp/env/TechLibFacade1");
```

Figure 7-53. Setting a breakpoint

NOTE *To remove the breakpoint, just double-click on the breakpoint.*

Switch to the Server Perspective and start the server in the debug mode (right-
click TechLibTestServer and select Debug). Wait until the server is ready. The Servers
View will indicate that the server TechLibTestServer has started in the debug mode
(see Figure 7-54).

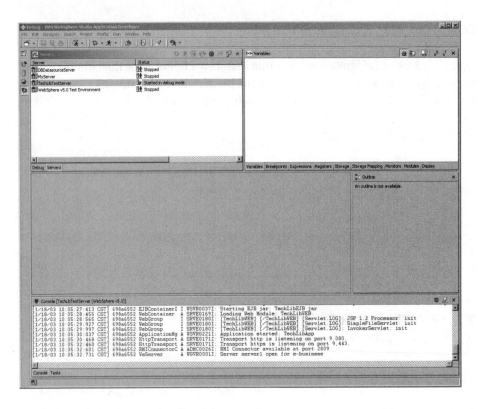

Figure 7-54. Server started in the debug mode

Switch to the Web Perspective, right-click BookByPlatformInputForm.html and select Debug on Server. The user input screen will display. Select Cross platform as the platform of choice and click the Submit button. You should see the screen shown in Figure 7-55.

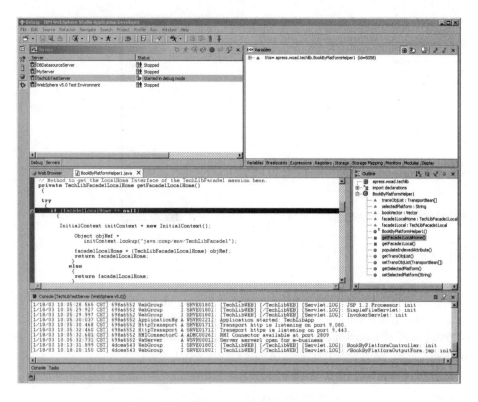

Figure 7-55. Stopping the debugging program at the breakpoint

The next section discusses how to use breakpoints during debugging.

Using Breakpoints

In the center of the screen, you should see the BookByPlatformHelper1 program stopped at the breakpoint. In the Variables View, expand this=apress.wsad.techlib.BookByPlatformHelper1. You should see the value of the selectedPlatform variable that is equal to "OO"—the cross-platform code— and the value of the facade1LocalHome variable that is equal to null (see Figure 7-56).

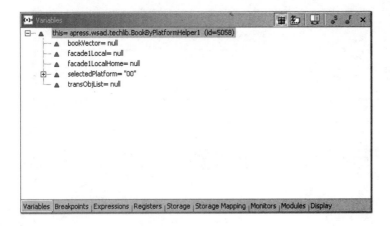

Figure 7-56. The Variables View

Click the Debug tab in the Servers View. The Debug View will display. Three icons (buttons) in the form of curved arrows will appear on the Debug View's toolbar. Locating a cursor over each of them displays their descriptions: Step Into, Step Over, and Step Return (see Figure 7-57).

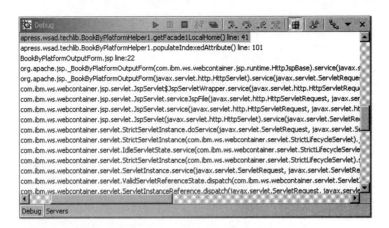

Figure 7-57. The Debug View

Click the Step Over button. One command (Step) will be executed and the program will stop on the next line (see Figure 7-58).

```
Web Browser     BookByPlatformHelper1.java   X
// Method to get the LocalHome Interface of the TechLibFacade1 session bean.
private TechLibFacade1LocalHome getFacade1LocalHome()
{

  try
  {
    if (facade1LocalHome == null)
    {
      InitialContext initContext = new InitialContext();

      Object objRef =
        initContext.lookup("java:comp/env/TechLibFacade1");

      facade1LocalHome = (TechLibFacade1LocalHome) objRef;
      return facade1LocalHome;
    }
    else
    {
      return facade1LocalHome;
    }
```

Figure 7-58. Stepping through the program

On the Debug View bar, click the button that looks like a triangle (the `Resume` button). The application will run to the end. The debug-related buttons will disappear from the Debug View toolbar. Click the Web Browser View in the middle of the screen. You should see the user output screen (see Figure 7-59).

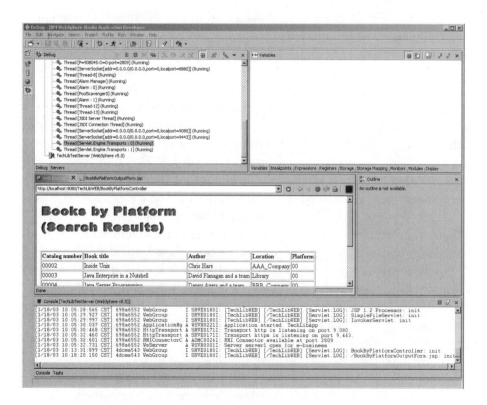

Figure 7-59. End of the program debugging

Run this application again in the debug mode. When it stops at the break-point, examine the value of the `facade1LocalHome` variable. Now, it is not equal to `null` (because the instance of the `BookByPlatformHelper1` JavaBean has been retrieved from the session object); therefore, it will not be recalculated and will continue to point to the same instance of the `TechLibFacade1` stateful session bean. Stop the server.

TIP *Starting from version 4.0, WebSphere Application Server (WAS) auto-matically detects and reloads servlets and JSPs, so there is no need to restart the server each time you change your servlets or JSPs. Just restart the Web application again.*

The next section discusses the development of the conversational session.

Understanding Multiscreen Conversational Sessions

The next example involves a stateful session bean in a multiscreen conversation. Readers who have reached this point should be quite comfortable with J2EE development. Therefore, this section presents a scenario for developing an application that uses a stateful session bean, and the reader is expected to develop this example by using the explanations that follow. The main benefit of the stateful session bean is its ability to maintain the state of the conversation, which means that the content of the instance variables are saved between multiple stateful bean methods invocations. This typically happens when a user conversation session consists of multiple user screens that are necessary to perform a business function. You will develop a stateful session bean called `TechLibFacade2`.

Follow the same procedure as described previously to create the `TechLibFacade2` stateful session bean. Now, copy all import statements, instance variables, and methods from `TechLibFacade1` class and paste them inside the `TechLibFacade2` class. Modify the business logic of the `TechLibFacade2` class. Instead of having two business methods (`getBookForPlatform` and `getBookActivity`), develop a new business method called `getBooksAndActivityForPlatform` that combines the processing logic of both methods.

You could copy the first part of this method code from the original `getBookForPlatform` method. Then, develop new code that is similar to but not the same as the `getBookActivity` method. You should iterate through the objects in `bookVector`. For each object in `bookVector`, obtain the `catalogNumber` field and then locate all objects that represent the transaction activity for this book. Use the code logic of the `getBookActivity` method as an example of how to do this.

Accumulate the transaction activity objects for each catalogNumber in a new vector called transactionVector. Create a separate two-dimensional array called catalogArray that will function as a catalog of transaction objects accumulated within transactionVector. Each row in the catalogArray will consist of three fields: the catalogNumber field, the starting position of the first object that belongs to this catalogNumber, and the number of transaction objects for this catalogNumber located in the transactionVector object. The idea is that you use the catalogArray to quickly locate all transaction objects within transactionVector for a selected catalogNumber.

Next, develop a second method called getActivityForBook(Character workCatalogNumber), which locates all transaction objects that belong to the book in question and forms the result as a resultVector object. However, the resultVector object will not be returned to the caller. It is simply another instance variable. The idea is that you do not know in advance which book (displayed on the list of book for a selected platform) for which the user will request to display the transaction activity data.

This technique demonstrates that for stateful session beans the state variables are saved between method invocations. So, when a user selects a book and clicks Submit, the JavaBean helper module will call the getActivityForBook method, which will select all the transaction objects for the selected book from transactionVector (without calling the corresponding database table again).

Next, develop the Web part similar to the previous example. The user will enter the Platform number on the first HTML input form and click the Submit button. The control is passed to a servlet controller that you need to develop in the way similar to the one in the previous example. You also need to develop a JavaBean helper class similar to the BookByPlatformHelper1.java class.

This helper class will have two indexed attributes. One is identical to the TransportBean[] transObjList attribute, which will be populated by calling getBooksAndActivityForPlatform. The second indexed attribute will be populated by calling the getActivityForBook method. For each indexed attribute, you will develop a corresponding JSP that will be dynamically populated and displayed to a user. Good luck with your development.

That concludes the Web application development. See the appendix for the deployment of the J2EE application.

Summary

In this chapter, you developed a working Web tier of the J2EE 1.3 application. This example included the development of servlets and JSP modules, the use of the MVC pattern, and the use of the Page Designer tool. You also learned how to use indexed attributes of the JavaBean class for developing dynamic content and how to use transfer objects for exchanging data between two tiers. You also learned how the Web project is organized and how to debug the complete J2EE application. See the appendix to learn how to deploy this application on WAS 5.0.

The next three chapters cover J2EE 1.3 Java Message Service (JMS).

CHAPTER 8

J2EE XML Development

THIS CHAPTER EXPLORES Extensible Markup Language (XML) and the XML-related tools that WebSphere Studio Application Developer (WSAD) 5.0 provides. Although you should be familiar with Java 2 Enterprise Edition (J2EE) technology (and with XML in particular), this chapter introduces some important concepts of XML. Specifically, it dedicates several sections to the XML namespace.

Introducing XML

XML is primarily used for sharing information between different systems (typically running on heterogeneous environments). These applications can belong to different companies or even different departments inside the same company. The main idea is that XML should be used when the programs involved in exchanging data are not aware of the data structure and need to figure it out programmatically. For instance, you can use XML when your company is collecting data from the Internet that was published by another company in a different format.

XML is actually a meta-language for describing the data in a highly structured and widely adopted, standard way. Listing 8-1 shows an example of a simple XML document.

Listing 8-1. A Simple XML Document

```
<?xml version="1.0"? encoding="UTF-8"?>
<Library>
 <Book year="1997">
   <BookTitle>The Java 1.1 Programmer's Reference</BookTitle>
   <Author>
      <FirstName>Daniel</FirstName>
      <MiddleName>I</MiddleName>
      <LastName>Joshi</LastName>
   </Author>
   <Author>
      <FirstName>Pavel</FirstName>
      <MiddleName>A</MiddleName>
```

```
            <LastName>Vorobiev</LastName>
        </Author>
      </book>
    <book year="1999">
      <BookTitle>Java in a Nutshell</title>
      <Author>
          <FirstName>David</FirstName>
          <LastName>Flanagan</LastName>
      </Author>
    </Book>
</Library>
```

As you can see from this example, XML documents are composed of markups and content. *Markups* are elements, attributes, entities, references, comments, processing instructions, marked sections, and corresponding Document Type Definition (DTD) files. *Elements* are markups delimited by angle brackets, such as `<BookTitle>The Java 1.1 Programmer's Reference</BookTitle>`. In XML, you can use a shortcut for coding empty elements: `<title/>`. Attributes are name-value pairs coded inside the element's start tag, such as `<Book year="1997">`.

Whether an XML document is correct is based on two criteria: The XML document must be a *well-formed* document, and it must be a *valid* document. To be more specific, these terms mean the following:

- An XML document is well-formed if all constructs used in the document meet the set of constraints defined in the XML specification.

- Validation is the process of checking an XML document against the coding rules (vocabulary) specified in the corresponding DTD or XML Schema file. A well-formed document is not necessarily a valid document.

A DTD is a language that specifies rules to be applied against a particular XML file to validate it. Validation checks the structure and semantics of the XML file. The DTD document also determines how an XML file can be generated. Unfortunately, the DTD language was created in the early stages of XML and has several serious limitations. One DTD problem is its limited ability to deal with complex data types.

Another serious problem is its inability to support namespaces (covered in the next section). On top of that, DTD is not based on XML. To rectify these problems, XML Schema files provide for a richer constraint mechanism (the ability to specify complex types and a wider variety of simple types such as `booleans`, `strings`, and `integers`). Another advantage is that XML Schema uses the same XML-based markup language. Finally, XML Schema supports XML namespaces. DTD files are still maintained for backward compatibility.

Understanding XML Schema Support for Namespaces

An XML *document* is a collection of elements and attributes names. However, an XML *namespace* is collection of names (not elements and attributes). In addition, the XML namespace concept is only applicable to element types (no entity names, notation names, and processing instructions can be namespace qualified).

An XML namespace is identified by a universally unique name—the Universal Resource Identifier (URI). A URI guarantees the uniqueness of an XML namespace and does not necessarily point to any XML Schema document on the Internet. URIs are just unique identifiers because the domain names they represent are uniquely assigned to each company. Any element type or attribute in an XML namespace can be uniquely identified by a two-part name: the name of its XML namespace and its local name.

Why is XML namespace support important for XML Schema and XML files? You can use XML namespaces to avoid element and attribute naming conflicts for multiple XML Schemas or XML files that come from different vocabularies and need to be combined for processing. To some extent, an XML namespace is analogous to a package. Listing 8-2 shows an example of two separate XML documents. If these two XML documents need to be combined or processed together, the <Address> element, defined within each file, would present a naming conflict. Each <Address> element belongs to a different vocabulary and has a different meaning. Programs that process such combined documents need to be able to distinguish these two <Address> elements.

Listing 8-2. Two XML Documents With a Potential Naming Conflict

```
<?xml version="1.0" ?>
<Book-Author>
   <First Name>Washington</First Name>
   <Last Name>Washington</Last Name>
   <Address>
     <Street>Washington</Street>
     <City>Chicago</City>
     <State>IL</State>
     <Postal Code>60686</Postal Code>
   </Address>
</Book-Author>

<?xml version="1.0" ?>
<WebShere-Server>
```

```
    <Name>MyWebSphereServer</Name>
    <Address>124.10.10/7</Address>
</WebShere-Server>
```

This is where an XML namespace comes into play. By assigning a different XML namespace to each document, you eliminate the conflict. You will learn about XML namespaces in more detail shortly after learning about XML Schema. Listing 8-3 shows an example of an XML Schema file (`books.xsd`).

Listing 8-3. The XML Schema File `books.xsd`

```
<? xml version="1.0"?>
<xsi:schema xmlns:xsi="http://www.w3.org/2001/XMLSchema"
            targetNamespace="http://www.apress.wsad.techlib"
                xmlns="http://www.apress.wsad.techlib"
                elementFormDefault="qualified">

<! -- Simple type elements definition -- >
<xsi:element name="title" type="xsi:string"/>
<xsi:element name="firstName" type="xsi:string"/>
<xsi:element name="meddleName" type="xsi:string"/>
<xsi:element name="lastName" type="xsi:string"/>

<! -- Complex type elements definition -- >
<xsi:element name="author">
  <xsi:complexType>
    <xsi:sequence>
      <xsi:element ref="firstName"/>
      <! -- Cordinality is defined when the element is referenced -- >
      <xsi:element ref="middleName" minOccurs="0"/>
      <xsi:element ref="lastName"/>
    </xsi:sequence>
  <xsi:complexType>
  </xsi:element>

<! -- Attributes definition -- >
<xsi:attribute name="publishYear" type="xsi:string" use="required"/>

<xsi:element name="book">
  <xsi:complexType>
    <xsi:sequence>
      <xsi:element ref="title"/>
```

```
        <! -- Cordinality is defined when the element is referenced -- >
        <xsi:element ref="author"> minOccurs="1" maxOccurs="unbounded"/>
      </xsi:sequence>
      </xsi:attribute ref="publishYear"/>
     </xsi:complexType>
   </xsi:element>

 <xsi:element names="books">
   <xsi:complexType>
     <xsi:sequence>
       <! -- Cordinality is defined when the element is referenced -- >
       <xsi:element ref="book" minOccurs="0" maxOccurs="unbounded"/>
     </xsi:sequence>
   </xsi:complexType>
 </xsi:element>
</xsi:schema>
```

All XML Schema documents have the schema tag in the root element. The xmlns attribute of the schema tag (xmlns:xsi = http://www.w3.org/2001/XMLSchema) determines if the XML Schema is namespace qualified. If the xmlns attribute contains a prefix, the schema is namespace qualified, and all schema elements and data types that are defined in the XML Schema language (schema, element, complexType, sequence, string, integer, and boolean) come from this namespace and must be namespace qualified by the prefix coded within the xmlns attribute of the schema tag. Listing 8-4 shows a fragment of an XML Schema file.

Listing 8-4. Fragment of an XML Schema File

```
<xsi:schema xmlns:xsi ="http://www.w3.org/2001/XMLSchema"
               targetNamespace="http://www.apress.wsad.techlib"
               xmlns="http://www.apress.wsad.techlib"
               elementFormDefault="qualified">
</xsi:schema>
```

Understanding XML Namespace Declarations

The xmlns attributes inside the schema tag are XML namespace declarations. In addition to being used inside the schema tag (with the scope of the entire XML Schema file), they can be declared on any element (with the scope of that element and its dependents).

NOTE *The XML Schema shown in Listing 8-3 has the* xmlns *attribute namespace qualified by the prefix* xsi; *therefore, all schema elements and type definitions should be namespace qualified by the prefix* xsi *and separated with a colon (:) from the local name. The namespace-qualified local name is called the* universal name. *For example,* xsi:element *is the proper format of the namespace-qualified universal name.*

Let's return for a moment to the name conflict shown in Listing 8-2. Let's combine both documents into a single document and use XML namespaces to avoid the naming conflict (see Listing 8-5).

Listing 8-5. Using XML Namespaces to Avoid a Naming Conflict

```
<?xml version="1.0" ?>
<Library>
 <author:Book-Author xmlns:author="http://www.apress.wsad.techlib/authors">
   <author:First Name>Washington</author:First Name>
   <author:Last Name>Washington</author:Last Name>
   <author:Address>
     <author:Street>Washington</author:Street>
     <author:City>Chicago</author:City>
     <author:State>IL</author:State>
     <author:Postal Code>60686</author:Postal Code>
   </author: Address>
 </Book-Author>

 <server:WebShere-Server xmlns:server="http://www.apress.wsad.techlib/servers">
   <server:Name>MyWebSphereServer</server:Name>
   <server:Address>124.10.10/7</server:Address>
 </server:WebShere-Server>
</Library>
```

Using the Default Namespace

Let's continue exploring the XML namespace concept. If the xmlns attribute within the schema tag does not contain a prefix, the namespace is the default XML namespace and all elements in that namespace are coded without a prefix (see Listing 8-6).

Listing 8-6. XML Schema with a Default Namespace (books2.xsd)

```xml
<? xml version="1.0"?>
<schema xmlns= http://www.w3.org/2001/XMLSchema
            targetNamespace="http://www.apress.wsad.techlib"
              xmlns="http://www.apress.wsad.techlib"
              elementFormDefault="qualified">


<! -- Simple type elements definition -- >
<element name="title" type="string"/>
<element name="firstName" type="string"/>
<element name="middleName" type="string"/>
<element name="lastName" type="string"/>


<! -- Attributes definition -- >
<attribute name="publishYear" type="string" use="required"/>


<! -- Complex type elements definition -- >
<element name="author">
  <complexType>
    <sequence>
      <element ref="firstName"/>
      <! -- Cordinality is defined when the element is referenced -- >
      <element ref="middleName" minOccurs="0"/>
      <element ref="lastName"/>
    </sequence>
  <complexType>
  </element>


  <element name="book">
    <complexType>
      <sequence>
        <element ref="title"/>
        <! -- Cordinality is defined when the element is referenced -- >
        <element ref="author" minOccurs="1" maxOccurs="unbounded"/>
      </sequence>
    </attribute ref="publishYear"/>
   </complexType>
  </element>

<element name="books">
  <complexType>
    <sequence>
```

```
    <! -- Cordinality is defined when the element is referenced -- >
    <element ref="book" minOccurs="0" maxOccurs="unbounded"/>
  </sequence>
 </complexType>
 </element>
</schema>
```

 NOTE *XML elements (even those that are not namespace prefixed) still belong to an XML namespace—specifically, they belong to the default XML namespace (*http://www.apress.wsad.techlib*). It is important to understand that only elements belong to the default XML namespace (attributes are indirectly qualified by being inside of the elements).*

When should you use the default XML namespace instead of the prefixed namespace? For the documents that belong to a single namespace, using a default XML namespace makes the document more readable. For documents whose names are in multiple namespaces, using default XML namespaces makes a document more difficult to read. Multiple namespaces can be declared on the XML Schema document, but they all must use different prefixes. Listing 8-7 shows the schema tag of the XML Schema file.

Listing 8-7. XML Schema Root Element

```
<xsi:schema xmlns:xsi="http://www.w3.org/2001/XMLSchema"
            targetNamespace="http://www.apress.wsad.techlib"
            xmlns:x="http://www.apress.wsad.techlib"
            elementFormDefault="unqualified">
<xsi:element name="Book"></xsi:element>
</xsi:schema>
```

Using XML Namespace Attributes

As mentioned, the xmlns attribute defines the XML namespace. The first xmlns attribute in Listing 8-7 (xmlns:xsi="http://www.w3.org/2001/SMLSchema") defines the standard XML Schema namespace. It controls all elements of the XML Schema language. Therefore, if it is coded with the prefix, all standard XML Schema–building elements must be qualified with this prefix. If no prefix is coded, the standard XML Schema namespace is the default namespace, and all standard schema-building elements are coded without a prefix.

The next `schema` tag attribute in Listing 8-7 is `targetNamespace`. The `targetNamespace` attribute defines the XML namespace for all user-defined elements and types in the XML Schema. If the `targetNamespace` element has the `xmlns` keyword with a suffix, it is a qualified namespace; otherwise, it is a default namespace. For a qualified `targetNamespace` attribute in the XML Schema, the XML instance document created from the XML Schema should use the `schemaLocation` attribute that indicates the XML namespace and the XML Schema used in constructing this XML document.

The following is a fragment of the XML file built based on the XML Schema file in Listing 8-6 (with the XML Schema saved on disk as the `Book.xsd` file):

```
<?xml version="1.0" ? >
<x:Book xmlns:x="http://www.apress.wsad.techlib"
        xmlns:xsi="http://www.w3.org/2001/XMLSchema-instance"
        xsi:schemaLocation="http://www.apress.wsad.techlib/Book.xsd">

</x:Book>
```

If the `targetNamespace` attribute is undeclared in the XML Schema, the XML instance document created from such an XML Schema should use the `noNamespaceSchemaLocation` attribute:

```
<xsd:schema xmlns:xsd="http://www.w3.org/2001/XMLSchema">
<xsd:element name="Book"></xsd:element>
```

The following example shows the XML file built based on the XML Schema with the undeclared `targetNamespace`:

```
<?xml version="1.0" ? >
  <Book xmlns:xsi="http://www.w3.org/2001/XMLSMLSchema-instance"
  xsi:noNamespaceSchemaLocation="Book.xsd">
</Book>
```

Understanding Local Elements Qualification

The `targetNamespace` attribute has another keyword (`elementFormDefault`) that has two valid values: `qualified` and `unqualified`. When `elementFormDefault="qualified"` is coded in the XML Schema (see Listing 8-8), all local elements and attributes within the corresponding XML file must be namespace qualified (see Listing 8-9).

Listing 8-8. XML Schema with `elementFormDefault="qualified"`

```
<schema xmlns="http://www.w3.org/2001/XMLSchema"
                targetNamespace="http://www.apress.wsad.techlib"
                xmlns:x="http://www.apress.wsad.techlib"
                elementFormDefault="qualified">
<complexType name="BookType">
  <sequence>
      <element name="BookTitle" type="string"></element>
   </sequence>
</complexType>

<element name="MyBook" type="x:BookType"></element>
</schema>
```

Listing 8-9. XML File Built Based on the XML Schema with
`elementFormDefault="qualified"`

```
<?xml version="1.0" ? >
  <x:MyBook xmlns:x="http://www.apress.wsad.techlib"
           xmlns:xsi="http://www.w3.org/2001/XMLSMLSchema-instance"
           xsi:schemaLocation="http://www.apress.wsad.techlib/Book.xsd">
  <x:BookTitle>Using JavaScripts</x:BookTitle>
</x:MyBook>
```

When `elementFormDefault="unqualified"` is coded in the XML Schema, only global elements within the corresponding XML file must be namespace qualified (see Listing 8-10).

Listing 8-10. XML Schema with `elementFormDefault="unqualified"`

```
<schema xmlns="http://www.w3.org/2001/XMLSchema"
                targetNamespace="http://www.apress.wsad.techlib"
                xmlns:x="http://www.apress.wsad.techlib"
                elementFormDefault="unqualified">
<complexType name="BookType">
  <sequence>
      <element name="BookTitle" type="string"></element>
   </sequence>
</complexType>

</element name="MyBook" type="x:BookType"></element>
</schema>
```

Listing 8-11. XML File Built Based on the XML Schema with
elementFormDefault="unqualified"

```xml
<?xml version="1.0" ? >
  <x:MyBook xmlns:x="http://www.apress.wsad.techlib"
            xmlns:xsi="http://www.w3.org/2001/XMLSMLSchema-instance"
            xsi:schemaLocation="http://www.apress.wsad.techlib/Book.xsd">


  <BookTitle>Using JavaScripts</BookTitle>
</x:MyBook>
```

Additional Considerations for XML Schemas

You should also consider the following when using XML Schemas:

Declaration vs. definition: You declare elements and attributes. XML Schema components that are declared are those that are represented in an XML instance document. Defined schema components (type, attribute group definitions, and model group definitions) are used just within the schema document. The implication is that you should not declare an element simply because you want to reference it from another element (instead, define the type). Declare elements that you need to be present in the XML instance document.

Global element declarations and global type definitions: They are immediate children of the schema. Local element declarations and local type definitions are always nested within other elements/types. Only global elements and types can be referenced (reused). Local elements/types are effectively invisible to the rest of the schema (and to other schemas).

Complex type elements: Use the complexType element when you need to define child elements and/or attributes. Use the simpleType element when you want to create a new type that is a refinement of a built-in type (string, date, gYear, and so on).

Local elements: Local elements are not formally in the targetNamespace. They informally belong to this namespace only by association with the global element with which they are in line.

Attributes: Attributes are not namespace qualified, but they do not belong to the default namespace. Rather, they are associated with the elements, which are in the namespace.

Global element declarations and global type definitions: These must be namespace qualified when they are referenced within the XML Schema.

Elements: Elements must be namespace qualified on the instance document:

- When the `schema` tag has `elementFormDefault="qualified"`

- When the element is declared globally

- When the element is declared with `form="qualified"`

That concludes the XML introduction. The goal of this part of the chapter was to help you better understand the XML namespace and other XML Schema constructs. The rest of this chapter uses XML namespaces in the development examples. You are now ready to explore the many XML-related tools that WSAD 5.0 provides.

Using WSAD's XML Tools

WSAD provides an impressive array of XML-related tools. They allow building, importing, editing, and validating of XML Schema files (the XML Schema Editor), DTD files (the DTD Editor), and XML files (the XML Editor). Additional functionality is provided for many XML cross-file manipulations:

- Generating XML, JavaBean, and DTD files from XML Schema

- Generating XML Schema, DTD, and Hypertext Markup Lanugage (HTML) files from XML files

- Generating XML, DTD, JavaBean, and HTML files from DTD files

- Generating Extensible Stylesheet Language (XSL), XML, and XML Schema from JavaBean files

Tools are also available for developing XSL Transformations (XSLT) and for XML integration with databases. You will build a series of examples that use some of these tools. You will develop all the XML examples under a new project called `XMLSamplesProject`.

To create a new project, select `File ➤ New ➤ Project ➤ Simple Project`. On the screen that appears, enter `XMLSamplesProject` in the `Project Name` field. Click `Finish`. WSAD will create the project `XMLSamplesProject`.

Building an XML Schema

The first example shows how to create a new XML Schema using the XML Schema Editor. You will build the XML Schema shown in Listing 8-12.

Listing 8-12. XML Schema

```
<?xml version="1.0"? encoding="UTF-8"?>
<schema xmlns="http://www.w3.org/2001/XMLSchema"
   targetNamespace="http://www.techlib.com"
               xmlns:bk="http://www.techlib.com">

  <! -- Simple type definitions (declared globally to be referenced) -- >
  <simpleType name="bookTitle">
     <restriction base="string">
        <maxLength value="200"/>
     </restriction>
  </simpleType>

  <simpleType name="firstName">
     <restriction base="string">
        <maxLength value="20"/>
     </restriction>
  </simpleType>

  <simpleType name="middleName">
     <restriction base="string">
        <maxLength value="10"/>
     </restriction>
  </simpleType>

  <simpleType name="lastName">
     <restriction base="string">
        <maxLength value="50"/>
     </restriction>
  </simpleType>

  <! -- Complex type definition (declared globally
                   to be referenced) -- >
  <complexType name=authorType>
    <sequence>
      <element name="FirstName" type="bk:firstName"
```

```
                    minOccurs="1" maxOccurs="1"/>
        <! -- Cordinality is defined when the element is referenced -- >
        <element name="MiddleName" type="bk:middleName"
           minOccurs="0" maxOccurs="1"/>
        <element name="LastName" type="bk:lastName" minOccurs="1"
           maxOccurs="1"/>
      </sequence>
   <complexType>


   <complexType name=bookType>
     <sequence>
        <element type="bk:bookTitle" minOccurs="1" maxOccurs="1"/>
    <! -- Cordinality is defined when the element
            is referenced -- >
        <element name="Author" type="bk:authorType"
           minOccurs="1" maxOccurs="unbounded"/>
      </sequence>
      <attribute name="PublishYear" type="gYear" use="required"/>
   </complexType>


   <complexType name=libraryType>
     <complexType>
       <sequence>
         <! -- Cordinality is defined when the element is referenced -- >
         <element ref="bk:Book" minOccurs="0" maxOccurs="unbounded"/>
       </sequence>
     </complexType>


   <element name="Book" type="bk:bookType"></element>

   <element name="Library" type="bk:libraryType"></element>>


</schema>
```

Switch to the XML Perspective. From the main menu, select File ➤ New ➤ XML Schema. On the screen shown in Figure 8-1, select XML on the left pane and XML Schema on the right.

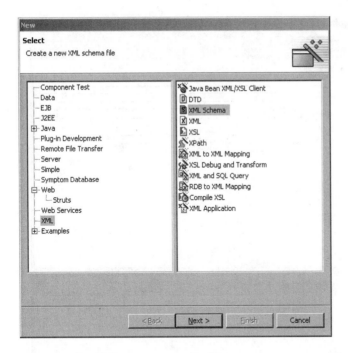

Figure 8-1. Building the XML Schema

Click Next. On the next screen, the project XMLSamplesProject will be filled in already. Just enter Library.xsd in the File name field and click Finish. The Library.xsd XML Schema appears under XMLSamplesProject and automatically opens in the XML Schema Editor (see Figure 8-2).

By default, you are in the Design View, where you can also switch to the Source and Graph Views. The Workbench also presents the Outline View. All the items you will be adding to the XML Schema will appear in the Outline View. You can also edit the XML Schema in the Source View; however, any changes made in the Source View will not be reflected in the Outline View.

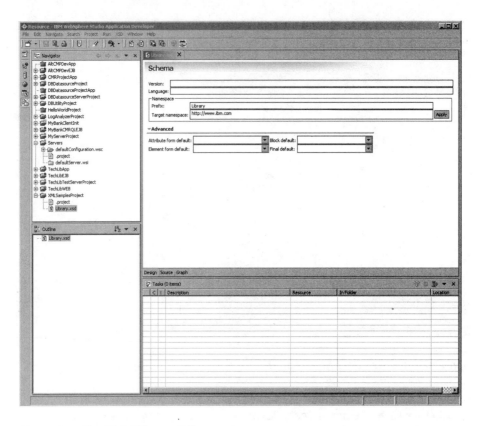

Figure 8-2. The XML Schema Editor

Adding Global Elements

To build your XML Schema, you need to add several global elements (four simple types, three complex types, and two global elements). In the Outline View, right-click `Library.xsd` and select `Add Simple Type`. In the Design View, change the name to `bookTitle`. Repeat the previous steps three times to add three more simple types (`firstName`, `middleName`, and `lastName`). Notice that four simple types appear in the Outline View. In the Outline View, right-click `Library.xsd` and select `Add Complex Type`. In the Design View, change the name to `authorType`. Repeat the same steps to enter two more complex elements: `bookType` and `LibraryType`.

To add the global `Book` elements, right-click `Library` in the Outline View and select `Add Global Element`. In the Design View, change the name to `Book`. Check the `User-defined complex type` box and select `bookType` as a user-defined complex type. Repeat the same steps to add the second global element `Library`; however, select `libraryType` as the user-defined complex type (see Figure 8-3).

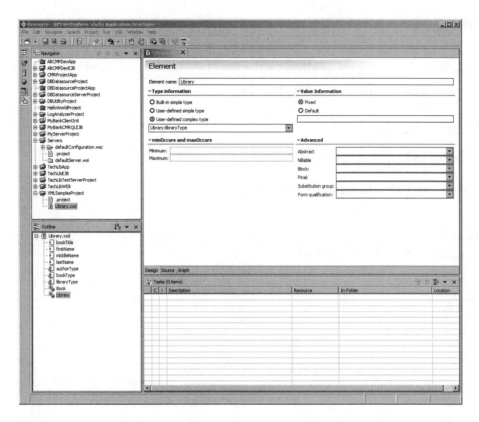

Figure 8-3. XML Schema general outline

Adding Details for Each Objects

You just built the general outline for the XML Schema, so now you will fill in the details for each object. You will start from the simple types. In the Outline View, right-click bookTitle and select Add Restriction. On the screen shown in Figure 8-4, check Built-in simple type and make sure that string is selected. Enter 200 in the maxLength field.

Repeat the same steps for the rest of the simple types, but set a different maxLength value (20 for firstName, 2 for middleName, and 50 for lastName). Next, you will enter details for the complex types. In the Outline View, right-click authorType and select Add Content Model. Check the Sequence box. Right-click the content model in Outline View and select Add Element. On the screen that appears, enter FirstName in the Element name field. Check User-defined simple type and select firstName. Notice that the type is made namespace qualified by the Library prefix. Enter 1 in the Minimum and Maximum fields (see Figure 8-5).

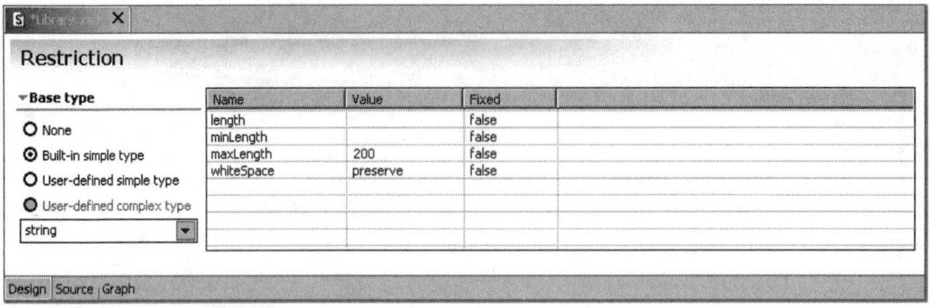

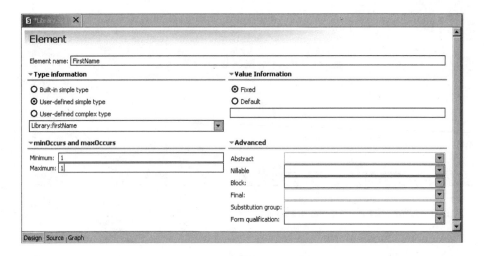

Figure 8-4. *XML Schema simple type details*

Figure 8-5. *Details for the XML Schema complex type* FirstName

Repeat the same steps to add two more elements (MiddleName and LastName). Next, right-click the second complex type bookType and select Add Content Model. Right-click the content model in Outline View and select Add Element. On the screen that appears, enter BookTitle in the Element name field. Enter bookTitle in the User-defined simple type field. Enter 1 in the Minimum and Maximum fields. Repeat the same steps to add the second element called Author (see Figure 8-6).

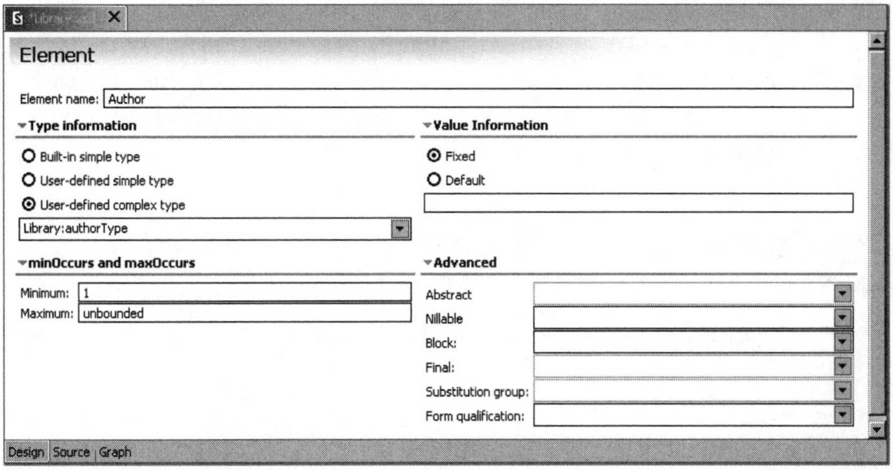

Figure 8-6. Details for the XML Schema complex type Author

You also need to add an attribute field here called PublishYear. In the Outline View, right-click bookType and select Add Attribute. On the next screen, shown in Figure 8-7, enter PublishYear as the Attribute name, select gYear as the simple type, and indicate that the attribute is required.

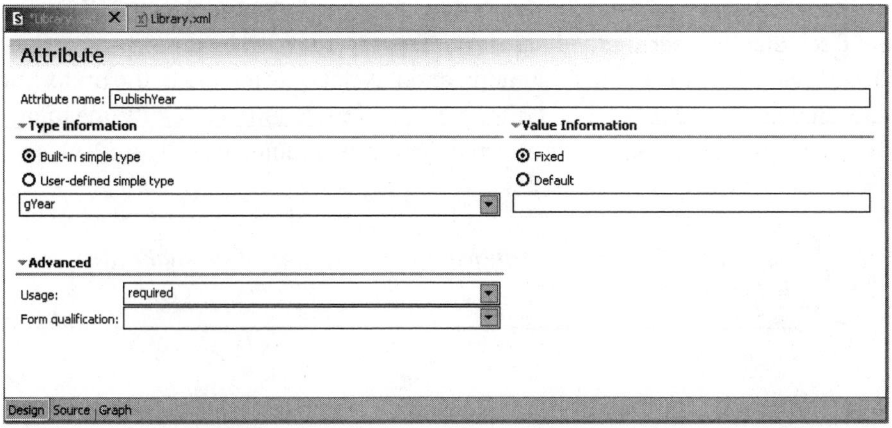

Figure 8-7. Adding a required attribute

Repeat similar steps to enter the last complex type named `libraryType`. The only difference is that you need to add an element reference and not an element, and you select the element from the list of available elements—in this case, `Book` (see Figure 8-8). Make sure `0` is specified as the value for the `Minimum` field and `unbounded` is specified as the value for the `Maximum` field.

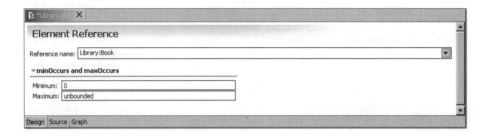

Figure 8-8. Details for the XML Schema complex type `bookType`

You are almost done. You still need to correct the value of `targetNamespace` and the prefix automatically generated by the XML Schema Editor. In the Outline View, click `Library.xsd` and switch to the Design View (if you are not already there). Enter `http://www.techlib.com` in the `Target namespace` field and enter `bk` in the `Prefix` field. Click `Apply`.

Now, click the `FirstName` element inside the `authorType` complex type. You should see that the user-defined type is namespace qualified by the `bk` prefix. The change is global for the entire document, and it is not only related to the prefix but to any change. The XML Schema Editor maintains a referential integrity, meaning that when you make a change, all affected fields are modified (see Figure 8-9).

NOTE *The referential integrity feature does not work if you make changes on the source page.*

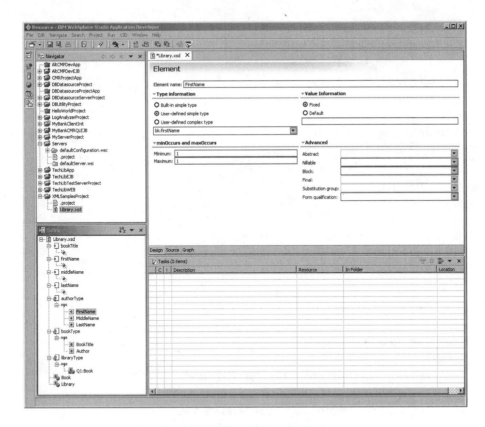

Figure 8-9. Changed namespace prefix

Your XML Schema is ready. Click the Source tab to see the generated code (see Listing 8-13).

Listing 8-13. Generated XML Schema

```
<?xml version="1.0" encoding="UTF-8"?>
<schema xmlns="http://www.w3.org/2001/XMLSchema"
        targetNamespace="http://www.techlib.com"
        xmlns:bk="http://www.techlib.com">

    <simpleType name="bookTitle">
        <restriction base="string">
            <maxLength value="200"></maxLength>
        </restriction>
    </simpleType>
```

```
<simpleType name="firstName">
    <restriction base="string">
        <maxLength value="20"></maxLength>
    </restriction>
</simpleType>

<simpleType name="middleName">
        <restriction base="string">
        <maxLength value="2"></maxLength>
    </restriction>
</simpleType>

<simpleType name="lastName">
    <restriction base="string">
 <maxLength value="50"></maxLength>
    </restriction>
</simpleType>

<complexType name="authorType">
  <sequence>
        <element name="FirstName" type="bk:firstName"
                minOccurs="1" maxOccurs="1"></element>
        <element name="MiddleName" type="bk:middleName"
                minOccurs="0" maxOccurs="1"></element>
        <element name="LastName" type="bk:lastName"
                minOccurs="1" maxOccurs="1"></element>
    </sequence>
  </complexType>

<complexType name="bookType">
    <sequence>
      <element name="BookTitle" type="bk:bookTitle"
                minOccurs="1" maxOccurs="1"></element>
      <element name="Author" type="bk:authorType"
                minOccurs="1" maxOccurs="unbounded"></element>
    </sequence>
  </complexType>

<complexType name="libraryType">
    <sequence>
      <element ref="bk:Book" minOccurs="0"
            maxOccurs="unbounded"></element>
    </sequence>
```

```
    </complexType>

        <element name="Book" type="bk:bookType">
        </element>

        <element name="Library" type="bk:libraryType">
        </element>

</schema>
```

Validating XML Schema

The XML Schema Editor has a useful feature that allows incremental validation. At any point during schema development, you can click the Validate toolbar button. The validation is also automatically performed any time you save the schema document. The Tasks View should show no errors when you save the XML Schema file. Let's validate the XML Schema Library.xsd. In the Navigator View, right-click Library.xsd and select Validate XML Schema. The message shown in Figure 8-10 will confirm that the schema is valid.

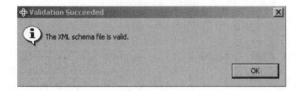

Figure 8-10. Validating the XML Schema

Building XML Documents

There are two ways of creating an XML document. You build it from scratch or you generate a skeleton of the XML document based on a corresponding DTD or XML Schema document. In this section, you will generate the XML document based on the XML Schema you just built.

In the Navigator View, right-click the Library.xsd file and select Generate ➤ XML File. Accept the defaults on the next screen and click Next. On the subsequent screen, select Library as the Root element (see Figure 8-11). Check the Create required and optional content box (otherwise, optional content such as attributes and others will not be included).

Create XML File
Select Root Element
Select the root element of the XML File
Root element:
Library
Content options
Create required content only
Create required and optional content
XML Schema Information
Namespace Name
Prefix
Location Hint
http://www.techlib.com
bk
Library.xsd
New...
Edit...
Delete
< Back
Next >
Finish
Cancel

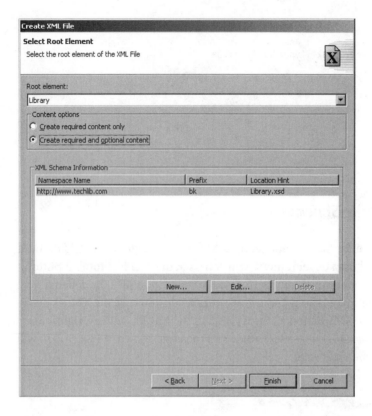

Figure 8-11. Generating the XML file

Click `Finish`. The `Library.xml` skeleton file will be generated and will open in the XML Editor View. Expand the XML document by clicking on the plus (+) signs (see Figure 8-12).

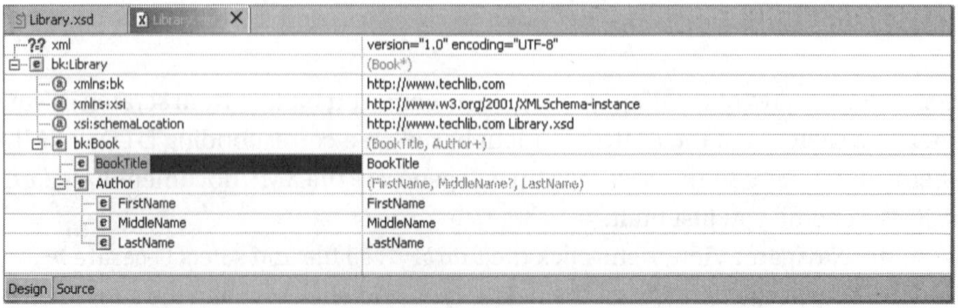

Library.xsd
?:? xml
version="1.0" encoding="UTF-8"
bk:Library
(Book*)
xmlns:bk
http://www.techlib.com
xmlns:xsi
http://www.w3.org/2001/XMLSchema-instance
xsi:schemaLocation
http://www.techlib.com Library.xsd
bk:Book
(BookTitle, Author+)
BookTitle
BookTitle
Author
(FirstName, MiddleName?, LastName)
FirstName
FirstName
MiddleName
MiddleName
LastName
LastName
Design
Source

Figure 8-12. XML Editor View

You should see the content of the generated XML file. Let's validate the generated `Library.xml` file against its XML Schema `Library.xsd`. Right-click `Library.xml` and select `Validate XML File`. The message shows that there is an error. In the Tasks View, the error message indicates that the value of the `MiddleName` element is not valid. Switch to the Source View. Listing 8-14 shows the generated skeleton.

Listing 8-14. The Generated `Library.xml` *Skeleton File*

```xml
<?xml version="1.0" encoding="UTF-8"?>
<bk:Library xmlns:bk="http://www.techlib.com"
            xmlns:xsi="http://www.w3.org/2001/XMLSchema-instance"
            xsi:schemaLocation="http://www.techlib.com Library.xsd">
  <bk:Book PublishYear="2001">
    <BookTitle>BookTitle</BookTitle>
    <Author>
      <FirstName>FirstName</FirstName>
      <MiddleName>MiddleName</MiddleName>
      <LastName>LastName</LastName>
    </Author>
  </bk:Book>
</bk:Library>
```

Indeed, the generated content for the `MiddleName` element is the string `MiddleName`, but the schema code related to the `MiddleName` element restricts the length to two characters:

```xml
<simpleType name="middleName">
   <restriction base="string">
 <maxLength value="2"></maxLength>
   </restriction>
</simpleType>
```

This is wrong, and you will correct it when replacing the skeleton data with the real data.

Refer to the XML file that you planned to build originally (in Listing 8-1). It has two books. The first book published in 1997 (*Java 1.1 Programmer's Reference*) has two authors, Daniel I. Joshi and Pavel A. Vorobiev. The second book published in 1999 (*Java in a Nutshell*) has one author, David Flanagan. Let's enter this data in the `Library.xml` skeleton file.

You can edit the XML file in the Source View and in the Design View. For the Source View, the XML Editor provides the XML-specific Content Assist tool. You can type any tag and then press Control+spacebar. The Content Assist will display a list of valid elements and attributes for selection. In general, editing the XML file in the Source View is similar to editing any text file. In this example, you will use the Design View to edit the XML file. With the Library.xml file open in the XML Editor View, click the Design tab to get to the Design View (see Figure 8-13).

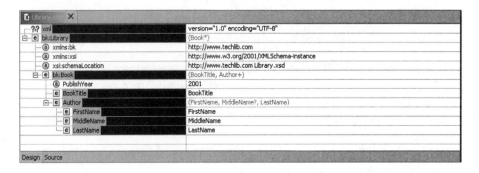

Figure 8-13. Editing the XML file

The screen consists of two panes. Elements are displayed on the left pane and their values are displayed on the right pane. Let's start editing the file. For the first book, click the PublishYear element and enter 1997 as the value. Next, change the value of the BookTitle element to The Java 1.1 Programmer's Reference and the value of the Author element to Daniel I. Joshi.

Next, you need to enter the second author of the first book. Right-click the Book element and select Add Child ➤ Author. The second Author element will be inserted. Next, you want to add the MiddleName element. Right-click the Author element and select Add Child ➤ MiddleName. Enter Pavel A. Vorobiev as the value for the second Author element. Save the XML file. No errors should be displayed on the Tasks View.

Next, you need to add a second book. Right-click the Library element and select Add Child ➤ Book. A new Book element will be inserted (see Figure 8-14). Enter 1999 as the PublishYear, Java in a Nutshell as the BookTitle, and David Flanagan as the Author. Save the XML file. There should be no errors. The Library.xml file is ready.

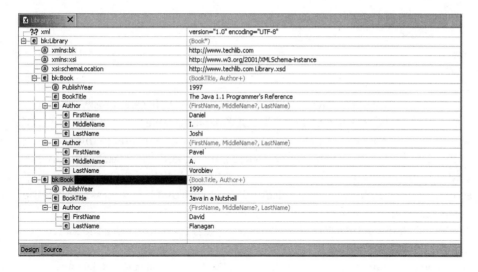

Figure 8-14. Library.xml

You can also switch to the Source View to see the Library.xml source code (see Listing 8-15).

Listing 8-15. Library.xml

```xml
<?xml version="1.0"? encoding="UTF-8"?>
<Library>
   <Book year="1997">
     <BookTitle>The Java 1.1 Programmer's Reference</BookTitle>
     <Author>
        <FirstName>Daniel</FirstName>
        <MiddleName>I</MiddleName>
        <LastName>Joshi</LastName>
     </Author>
     <Author>
        <FirstName>Pavel</FirstName>
        <MiddleName>A</MiddleName>
        <LastName>Vorobiev</LastName>
     </Author>
   </book>
   <book year="1999">
     <BookTitle>Java in a Nutshell</title>
     <Author>
        <FirstName>David</FirstName>
```

```
        <LastName>Flanagan</LastName>
      </Author>
    </Book>
</Library>
```

While you are here, you can quickly build the DTD file called `BookLibrary.dtd` that resembles the structure of the TECHBOOK database table called BOOK_CATALOG. You will use this file in one of the examples you will develop later in this section. In the XML Perspective, right-click `XMLSampleProject` and select `New ➤ DTD`. On the next screen, select `Create DTD file from scratch` and click `Next`. On the following screen, name the file `BookCatalog.dtd` and make sure that `XMLSamplesProject` is the destination folder. Click `Finish`.

The skeleton of the DTD file will open in the DTD Editor. Click the `Source` tab (for the sake of demonstration, you will quickly build the DTD file using the Source View). In the Outline View, right-click `BookCatalog.dtd` and select `Add Element`. Replace the `NewElement` name with `CatalogNumber`. Replace `EMPTY` with `(#PCDATA)`. Repeat the same steps and enter the following elements: `Author`, `BookTitle`, `Location`, `Platform`, and `Language`.

Then, add a new element called `Book` and indicate that it consists of single `CatalogNumber` and `BookTitle` elements, one or more `Author` elements, and single `Location`, `Platform`, `Language` elements:

```
<!ELEMENT Book (CatalogNumber, BookTitle, Author+, Location, Platform, Language)>
```

Finally, add one more element called `BookCatalog` and indicate that it consists of multiple `Book` elements:

```
<!ELEMENT BookCatalog (Book*)>
```

You should see the screen shown in Figure 8-15.

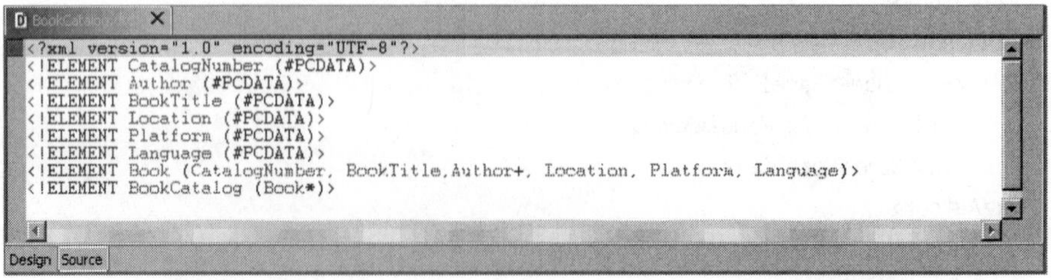

Figure 8-15. Building the DTD file

Parsing XML Documents

Among the many different Application Programming Interfaces (APIs) for parsing XML documents, the Document Object Model (DOM) and Simple API for XML (SAX)—together with their corresponding parsers—are the most popular and widely used. When DOM parses an XML document, the returned result is a tree structure (located in memory) that contains all of the elements of the document. DOM provides various APIs for traversing the DOM tree, making modifications to its structure, and making other tree manipulations.

The advantage of the DOM is that it allows direct access to any node in the memory-based node tree. DOM processing has some limitations because it keeps the entire document tree structure in memory. For large XML documents, the memory requirement could be a prohibitive factor.

SAX is an event-driven methodology. When SAX parses an XML document, the parser generates events at various points in the document, passing control to the program's callback methods that handle the events. SAX also provides a class called DefaultBase that implements all of these callback functions, providing default empty implementations. The SAX developer extends this DefaultBase class and overrides those callback functions that require nondefault processing. SAX events that have no corresponding event handlers are ignored (default processing).

NOTE *SAX APIs were developed by David Meggison and members of the XML-Dev mailing list. The World Wide Web Consortium (*http://www.w3.org*) has not yet standardized SAX.*

The main SAX limitation is its inability to manipulate the XML file as an object in memory. It always requires sequential processing. The main SAX advantage is that it does not need to keep the entire node tree in memory. Another SAX advantage is that it can be instructed to stop the parsing process before reaching the end of the document without losing the data already collected. To stop the parsing process, you throw a new SAXException.

Use DOM in the following circumstances:

- When you need to perform processing that requires the entire document structure (sorting is one example).

- When you can parse the document once and then process the document tree multiple times.

Use SAX in the following circumstances:

- When you need to extract only limited number of elements

- If the document is large and you have a limited memory

- If you need to process the document only once

Many DOM and SAX parsers are available from different vendors (each with its own proprietary features). Again, as with Java Database Connectivity (JDBC), Java Naming and Directory Interface (JNDI), and Java Message Service (JMS), Sun Microsystems developed a set of vendor-independent APIs, classes, and interfaces called Java APIs for XML Processing (JAXP). Using JAXP, developers are able to work with any DOM or SAX JAXP-compatible parser. The latest release is JAXP 2, which supports the latest DOM 2.0 and SAX 2.0 standards.

You will develop the following XML programming examples as Web applications; therefore, you need to create a Web project. Switch to the Web Perspective and select File ➤ New ➤ Web Project. Enter XMLProjectWEB in the Project name field and click Next. On the next screen, indicate that this Web module will belong to a new enterprise application project; name it XMLProjectApp and click Finish. WSAD will generate two new projects.

You now need to update the project's Java Build Path to include three XML supporting tools that you will be using: the XERCER parser, the XALAN transformation engine, and the SQLTOXML tool. When you are in the XML Perspective, these variables are automatically initialized. You can check which variables are initialized by selecting Windows ➤ Preferences ➤ Java ➤ Classpath Variables. You should see that three variables—XERCES, WAS_V5XALAN, and SQLTOXML—are initialized (see Figure 8-16).

Next, you need to update the project's Java Build Path to include these three variables. Right-click XMLProjectWEB and select Properties ➤ Java Build Path. Select the Libraries tab and click the Add Variable button. Scroll down on the dialog that appears, and select the SQLTOXML variable. Then, click OK (see Figure 8-17).

Figure 8-16. List of WSAD environment variables

Figure 8-17. Adding environment variables to the Java Build Path

Repeat the same steps and include two more variables: WAS_V5_XALAN and XERCES. You should see all three variables being added to the Java Build Path. Click OK to save the results.

As mentioned, you use the Java Build Path at development time. The runtime environment has no idea about the Java Build Path, projects, Perspectives, and so on. Therefore, you always have to think about the runtime environment. To make these three XML tools accessible by all Web module classes at runtime, you will add them to the Web-INF/lib directory. If this does not look familiar, refer to the "Understanding Classloaders" section of Chapter 5. To do this, select File ➤ Import ➤ File system. Click Next. On the next screen, click Browse and navigate to the <WSAD-Install-directory>\wstools\eclipse\plugins\com.ibm.etools.sqltoxml_5\jars library (see Figure 8-18).

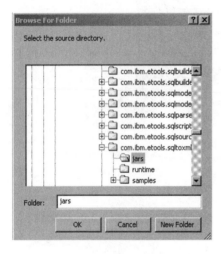

Figure 8-18. Selecting the JAR library

Click OK. Next, check the sqltoxml.jar box and click OK. Use the Browse button attached to the Folder field to set the destination folder to the XMLProjectWEB/ Web Content/WEB-INF/lib folder (see Figure 8-19).

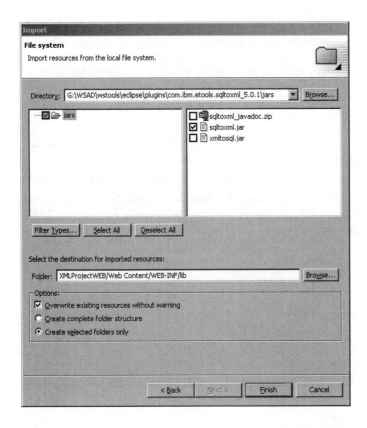

Figure 8-19. Adding the JAR library to the Web-INF/lib *folder*

Click Finish. The sqltoxml.jar will be added to the WEB-INF/lib folder. You do not need to do the same for XERCES.JAR and XALAN.JAR because they are already included in the WAS server runtime environment. Look again at the list of WSAD environment variables. Both are located in the <WSAD-Install-Directory>\runtimes\ base_V5\lib folder. Of course, you always need to consult the WAS administration to make sure that this is the case with your specific WAS instance.

TIP *Right-click the* lib *folder under* WEB-INF *and select* Import ➤ File system. *The next screen will be prefilled with the correct destination folder.*

NOTE *If your application uses a database, you need to do the same with the JDBC drivers. The DB2 JDBC drivers are already included in the WebSphere Application Server (WAS) runtime; however, other databases' JDBC drivers need to be placed in the* WEB-INF/lib *folder.*

The project environment is now ready for XML development. Before you can go on, you need to update the Library.xml file to correctly reflect the location of the XML Schema file Library.xsd. The XML Schema Library.xsd file is located in the WSAD environment at <WSAD-Install-Directory>\workspace\XMLSamplesProject\ Library.xsd. You need to modify the Library.xml file to correctly point to the XML Schema location (see Listing 8-16).

Listing 8-16. Corrected XML Schema Location

```
<?xml version="1.0" encoding="UTF-8"?>
<bk:Library xmlns:bk="http://www.techlib.com"
 xmlns:xsi="http://www.w3.org/2001/XMLSchema-instance"
 xsi:schemaLocation="http://www.techlib.com"
 g:\WSAD\workspace\XMLSamplesProject\Library.xsd">

  <bk:Book PublishYear="1997">
    <BookTitle>The Java 1.1 Programmer's Reference</BookTitle>
    <Author>
      <FirstName>Daniel</FirstName>
      <MiddleName>I.</MiddleName>
      <LastName>Joshi</LastName>
    </Author>
    <Author>
        <FirstName>Pavel</FirstName>
        <MiddleName>A.</MiddleName>
        <LastName>Vorobiev</LastName>
    </Author>
  </bk:Book>
  <bk:Book PublishYear="1999">
      <BookTitle>Java in a Nutshell</BookTitle>
      <Author>
          <FirstName>David</FirstName>
          <LastName>Flanagan</LastName>
      </Author>
  </bk:Book>
</bk:Library>
```

Now, you are ready for development. You will start by developing two XML parsing examples (one for DOM and another for SAX) written in JAXP 2.0.

Using the DOM Parser

In this example, you will parse the previously built Library.xml document using the XERCER parser that comes with WSAD. Let's create a servlet called ParserServlet. Right-click XMLProjectWeb and select New ➤ Other ➤ Web ➤ Servlet. On the next page, enter apress.wsad.techlib in the Package name field, enter ParseServlet in the Class name field, and click Finish. WSAD will generate a skeleton of the ParseServlet class and open it in the Editor View. All you want this program to do is to parse the Library.xml file and print its content. In a real-world application, you would do something useful with the data retrieved. Listing 8-17 shows the ParseServlet source code.

Listing 8-17. ParseServlet.java

```java
package apress.wsad.techlib;
import java.io.File;
import java.io.IOException;
import java.io.OutputStreamWriter;
import java.io.Writer;
import java.util.Enumeration;

import javax.servlet.ServletConfig;
import javax.servlet.ServletException;
import javax.servlet.http.HttpServlet;
import javax.servlet.http.HttpServletRequest;
import javax.servlet.http.HttpServletResponse;

// JAXP
import javax.xml.parsers.*;

// DOM
import org.w3c.dom.*;
import org.xml.sax.ErrorHandler;
import org.xml.sax.helpers.DefaultHandler;

/**
 * @version    1.0
 * @author
```

```
      */
    public class ParseServlet extends HttpServlet
    {

        // Variable to keep the initialization parameter
        protected String parserType;

        public void doDelete(HttpServletRequest req, HttpServletResponse resp)
            throws ServletException, IOException
        {

        }

        public void doGet(HttpServletRequest req, HttpServletResponse resp)
            throws ServletException, IOException
        {
          //ServletConfig config = req.getServletConfig();

          if (parserType.equalsIgnoreCase("DOM"))
           {
            ParseUsingDOM();
           }
          else
           {

           }
        }

        public void doPost(HttpServletRequest req, HttpServletResponse resp)
            throws ServletException, IOException
        {

        }

            public void init(ServletConfig config)  throws ServletException
        {
         super.init(config);

         parserType = config.getInitParameter("Parser");

        }
```

```java
public void ParseUsingDOM()
    throws ServletException, IOException
{
 try
  {
    String filename = "workspace/XMLSamplesProject/Library.xml";

    // Get Document Builder Factory
    DocumentBuilderFactory factory = DocumentBuilderFactory.newInstance();

    // Turn on validation. The file has been already validated
    //factory.setValidating(true);

    // Turn on namespaces
    factory.setNamespaceAware(true);

    // Setting Error Handling as anonymous inner class
    builder.setErrorHandler(
      new org.xml.sax.ErrorHandler()
      {
        // Ignore fatal errors because an exception is guaranteed to be thrown
        public void fatalError(SAXParseException fx)
          throws SAXParseException
          {
          }

        // Treat validation errors as fatal
        public void error(SAXParseException ex)
          throws SAXParseException
          {
           throw ex;
          }

        // Dump warning also
        public void warning(SAXParseException wx)
          throws SAXParseException
          {
            System.out.println("Warning, " + "line " + wx.getLineNumber() +
              ", uri " + wx.getSystemId());

            System.out.println(" " + wx.getMessage());

          }
```

```
        } // End of new

    ); //End of parameters

  DocumentBuilder builder = factory.newDocumentBuilder();
  //Document document = builder.parse(xmlFile);

  Document document = builder.parse(filename);

   System.out.println("Parsed results: ");

domWriter(document.getDocumentElement());

}
 catch(Exception e)
  {
    System.err.println("XML exception has occured:" + e.getMessage());
    e.printStackTrace(System.err);
}


}

public String domWriter(Node node)
{
    String workName = null;

 if ( node == null )
    return "";

 int type = node.getNodeType();

workName = node.getNodeName();

 switch( type )
  {

    case Node.DOCUMENT_NODE:
     {

      domWriter(((org.w3c.dom.Document)node).
            getDocumentElement());
      break;
     }
```

```
case Node.ELEMENT_NODE:
 {
  if (workName.equals("bk:Library"))
   {
     System.out.println(workName + " ");
   }

  if (workName.equals("bk:Book"))
   {
     System.out.println(workName + " ");
   }

  if (workName.equals("BookTitle"))
   {
     System.out.print(workName + " ");
   }

  if (workName.equals("Author"))
   {
     System.out.println(workName + " ");
   }

  if (workName.equals("FirstName"))
   {
     System.out.print(workName + " ");
   }

  if (workName.equals("MiddleName"))
   {
     System.out.print(workName + " ");
   }

  if (workName.equals("LastName"))
   {
    System.out.print(workName + " ");

   }

   NamedNodeMap attrs = node.getAttributes();

     int length = (attrs != null) ? attrs.getLength() : 0;

   for(int i = 0; i < length; i++)
```

```
        {
         Attr attr = (org.w3c.dom.Attr) attrs.item(i);
         System.out.println(attr.getNodeName() + "=" + attr.getNodeValue());
        }

      NodeList children = node.getChildNodes();

      if( children != null)
       {
        int len = children.getLength();

        for( int i = 0; i < len; i++)
         {
domWriter(children.item(i));
         }
       }

    break;

  } // End of case

 case Node.CDATA_SECTION_NODE:
  {
   System.out.println(node.getNodeValue());
   break;
  }

    case Node.TEXT_NODE:
   {
   String nodeValue = node.getNodeValue();
   if (nodeValue.trim().length() > 0)
    {
     System.out.println(nodeValue);
    }

   break;
  }

  } // End of the switch

  return "";


 }
}
```

Before examining the servlet code, you want to set the servlet's initialization parameter, called Parser, to the value DOM. The servlet will read this parameter in the init method and save it in the parserType global variable. The parserType variable is checked in the doGet method; based on its value, the DOM or SAX parser will be called. Initially, the initialization parameter value will be set to DOM; therefore, the DOM parser will be invoked. Later, you will change the value of this parameter to SAX, causing the SAX parser to be invoked.

Let's set the servlet's initialization parameter. In the Web Perspective, double-click the web.xml (Deployment Descriptor) file to open it in the Editor View. Click the Servlets tab. On the next screen, locate the "Initialization" section and click Add. In the dialog that appears, add Parser as the parameter name and DOM as its value. Click OK. You should see the screen shown in Figure 8-20.

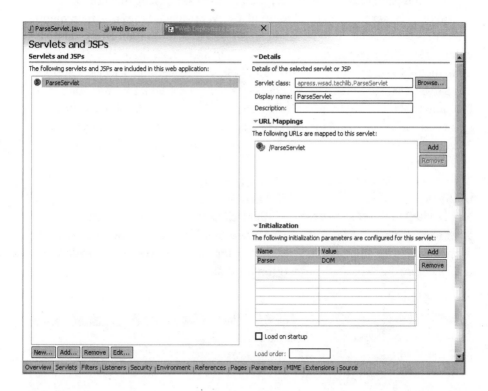

Figure 8-20. Setting the initialization parameter

Now, let's examine the code. First, a DocumentBuilderFactory object is instantiated. Next, you set the factory attributes. You turn validation off (the file has been already validated), and you make the parser namespace aware. By default, JAXP parsers are not namespace aware. The factory object builds the document object (for the Library.xml file passed as a parameter to the parse method). Next, you execute the domWriter, passing it the root element as a parameter. The domWriter method traverses the entire DOM object tree, processing each node. It starts from the root and gets its children; for each child, it recursively calls the domWriter method again.

Depending on the type of the element, specific processing is performed. The DOM produces many insignificant whitespaces as elements. The insignificant whitespaces are carriage returns, set after each element, and spaces to produce a readable print document in its original form (each element on a separate line and the relative embedding of elements are remembered). On the other hand, when an application needs to recover values encoded in the XML document, the insignificant whitespace should be ignored. To achieve this, you truncate each text element and print only those that have characters after the truncation of spaces.

To test this servlet, you need to build a server project. From the main menu, select File ➤ New ➤ Other ➤ Server ➤ Server Project. On the screen that appears, enter XMLServerProject in the Project name field and click Finish. WSAD will generate the new server project. Right-click XMLServerProject and select New ➤ Server and Server Configuration. On the next screen, enter XMLServer in the Server name field and make sure that WebSphere version 5.0 Test Environment is selected. Click Finish. In the Server Configuration View, right-click XMLServer and select Add ➤ XML Server. The new server project (XMLServer) will become the default test server for XMLProjectApp.

You are now ready to run your application. Switch to the Server Perspective. In the Servers View, right-click XMLServer and select Debug. Wait for the server to start. Next, switch to the Web Perspective. Right-click ParseServlet.java and select Run on Server. Because ParseServlet prints the execution results to the standard output, they are visible in the Console View for the server started in the debug mode. Figure 8-21 shows the execution results.

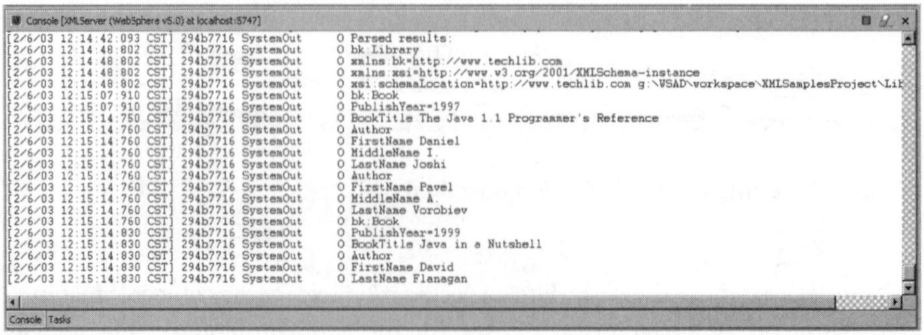

Figure 8-21. The DOM parsing results

The DOM parsing method also provides APIs for manipulating the DOM tree in memory (sorting, rearrangement, changing, deleting elements, and so on).

Stop the server.

Using the SAX Parser

Let's change the value of the servlet's initialization parameter, called Parser, from DOM to SAX. Save the Deployment Descriptor. Next, add a new method to ParserServlet called ParseUsingSAX. This method (as you can probably guess) is responsible for parsing the Library.xml document using the SAX parser. The logic of SAX parsing is event driven. SAX provides several interfaces that can be overwritten. The most important is the ContentHandler interface.

This interface provides a number of methods that the SAX parser invokes in response to different events. The major event handling methods the interface provides are as follows: startDocument, endDocument, startElement, endElement, and characters. To implement the ContentHandler interface, you create a class that extends the DefaultHandler class. For the sake of demonstration, turn the validation on for the SAX parser. Listing 8-18 shows the complete ParserServlet source code that includes both the DOM and SAX parsing methods.

Listing 8-18. ParserServlet.java

```
package apress.wsad.techlib;
import java.io.File;
import java.io.IOException;
import java.io.OutputStreamWriter;
import java.io.Writer;
import java.util.Enumeration;
import javax.servlet.ServletConfig;
import javax.servlet.ServletException;
import javax.servlet.http.HttpServlet;
import javax.servlet.http.HttpServletRequest;
import javax.servlet.http.HttpServletResponse;

// JAXP
import javax.xml.parsers.*;

// DOM
import org.w3c.dom.*;
import org.xml.sax.ErrorHandler;
import org.xml.sax.SAXException;
```

```java
import org.xml.sax.helpers.DefaultHandler;

public class ParseServlet extends HttpServlet
{

    // Variable to keep the initialization parameter
    protected String parserType;

    protected String filename = "workspace/XMLSamplesProject/Library.xml";


    public void doDelete(HttpServletRequest req, HttpServletResponse resp)
        throws ServletException, IOException
    {

    }

    public void doGet(HttpServletRequest req, HttpServletResponse resp)
        throws ServletException, IOException

      //ServletConfig config = req.getServletConfig();

      if (parserType.equalsIgnoreCase("DOM"))
       {
        ParseUsingDOM();
       }
      else
       {
           ParseUsingSAX();
       }
    }

    public void doPost(HttpServletRequest req, HttpServletResponse resp)
        throws ServletException, IOException
    {

    }

    public void init(ServletConfig config)  throws ServletException
    {
     super.init(config);

     parserType = config.getInitParameter("Parser");
```

```
}

public void ParseUsingDOM()
    throws ServletException, IOException
{
 try
  {


    // File xmlFile = new File(filename);

    // Get Document Builder Factory
    DocumentBuilderFactory factory = DocumentBuilderFactory.newInstance();

    // Comment on the validating request because
    //the file has already been validated.
    //factory.setValidating(true);

    // Turn on namespaces
    factory.setNamespaceAware(true);

    DocumentBuilder builder = factory.newDocumentBuilder();

    // Setting Error Handling as anonymous inner class
    builder.setErrorHandler(
      new org.xml.sax.ErrorHandler()
      {
        // Ignore fatal errors because an exeption is guaranteed to be thrown.
        public void fatalError(SAXParseException fx)
          throws SAXParseException
          {

          }

        // Treat validation errors as fatal
        public void error(SAXParseException ex)
          throws SAXParseException
          {
           throw ex;
          }

        // Dump warning also
        public void warning(SAXParseException wx)
          throws SAXParseException
```

```
                    {
                      System.out.println("Warning, " + "line " + wx.getLineNumber() +
                        ", uri " + wx.getSystemId());

                      System.out.println(" " + wx.getMessage());

                    }

                } // End of new

          ); //End of parameters

          Document document = builder.parse(filename);

          System.out.println("Parsed results: ");

          domWriter(document.getDocumentElement());

      }
    catch(Exception e)
      {
        System.err.println("XML exception has occured:" + e.getMessage());
        e.printStackTrace(System.err);
      }

}

public String domWriter(Node node)
{
    String workName = null;

  if ( node == null )
      return "";

  int type = node.getNodeType();

  workName = node.getNodeName();

  switch( type )
    {

      case Node.DOCUMENT_NODE:
        {
```

```java
    domWriter(((org.w3c.dom.Document)node).
        getDocumentElement());
    break;
}


case Node.ELEMENT_NODE:
{
 if (workName.equals("bk:Library"))
  {
    System.out.println(workName + " ");
  }


 if (workName.equals("bk:Book"))
  {
    System.out.println(workName + " ");
  }


 if (workName.equals("BookTitle"))
  {
    System.out.print(workName + " ");
  }


 if (workName.equals("Author"))
  {
    System.out.println(workName + " ");
  }


 if (workName.equals("FirstName"))
  {
    System.out.print(workName + " ");
  }


 if (workName.equals("MiddleName"))
  {
    System.out.print(workName + " ");
  }


 if (workName.equals("LastName"))
  {
   System.out.print(workName + " ");

  }
```

```java
        NamedNodeMap attrs = node.getAttributes();

          int length = (attrs != null) ? attrs.getLength() : 0;

        for(int i = 0; i < length; i++)
          {
           Attr attr = (org.w3c.dom.Attr) attrs.item(i);
           System.out.println(attr.getNodeName() + "=" + attr.getNodeValue());


          }



        NodeList children = node.getChildNodes();

        if( children != null)
          {
           int len = children.getLength();

           for( int i = 0; i < len; i++)
            {
             domWriter(children.item(i));
            }
          }

        break;

    } // End of case

case Node.CDATA_SECTION_NODE:
 {
  System.out.println(node.getNodeValue());
  break;
 }

case Node.TEXT_NODE:
 {
  String nodeValue = node.getNodeValue();
  if (nodeValue.trim().length() > 0)
   {
    System.out.println(nodeValue);
   }

  break;
```

```java
      }

   } // End of the switch

   return "";

}

// === SAX Parser ===

public void ParseUsingSAX()
      throws ServletException, IOException
 {

   try
    {
    // Get SAX Parser Factory
    SAXParserFactory factory = SAXParserFactory.newInstance();

    // Turn on validation, and turn off namespaces
    factory.setValidating(true);
    factory.setNamespaceAware(true);

    SAXParser parser = factory.newSAXParser();
    parser.parse(new File(filename), new eventHandler());
    }
   catch (ParserConfigurationException e)
    {
    System.out.println(
        "Parser error " + e.getMessage());
    }
   catch (FactoryConfigurationError e)
    {
    System.out.println("SAX Factoty Configuration Error " +
                                        e.getMessage());

    }

    catch (SAXException se)
    {
    System.out.println("SAX Execption " +
                                        se.getMessage());
    }
```

```java
      catch (Exception e)
       {
        System.out.println("SAX Paser Error" + e.getMessage());
       }
  }
}


// Content Handler Implementation
class eventHandler extends DefaultHandler
{
 private Writer out;

 public eventHandler() throws SAXException
  {
   try
    {
     out = new OutputStreamWriter(System.out, "UTF8");
    }
   catch (IOException e)
   {
    throw new SAXException("Error getting output handle");
   }
  }


// *** Event handling methods ***

 public void startDocument() throws SAXException
 {
  System.out.println("SAX Parsing Results");
 }

 public void startElement(String namespaceURI, String localName,
                          String qName, org.xml.sax.Attributes attrs)
    throws SAXException
 {

   String workName;

   if (namespaceURI.equals(""))
    {
    workName = qName;
    }
   else
```

```
    {
     workName = localName;
    }

  if (workName.equals("FirstName") ||
      workName.equals("MiddleName") ||
      workName.equals("LastName"))
   {
   System.out.print(workName + " ");
   }   else
   {
    System.out.println(workName);
   }

  if (attrs != null)
   {
    for (int i = 0, len = attrs.getLength(); i < len; i++)
     {
       String workURI = attrs.getURI(i);

       if (workURI == null)
        {
        System.out.println(attrs.getQName(i) + attrs.getValue(i));
        }
       else
        {
         System.out.println(attrs.getLocalName(i) + attrs.getValue(i));
        }

     }
   }

 }

public void endElement(String namespaceURI, String localName,
                    String qName, org.xml.sax.Attributes attrs)
                         throws SAXException
 {

 }

//public void ignorableWhiteSpace(char[] ch, int start, int len)
//                      throws SAXException
```

```
// {
//
// }

    public void characters(char[] ch, int start, int len)
                            throws SAXException
    {
      String workString = new String(ch, start, len);

      if (workString.trim().length() > 0)
        {
          System.out.println(workString);

    }
}
```

You are now ready to run the application. Switch to the Server Perspective. In the Servers View, right-click XMLServer and select Start. Wait for the server to start. Switch to the Web Perspective. Right-click ParseServlet.java and select Run on Server. Figure 8-22 shows the SAX parsing results.

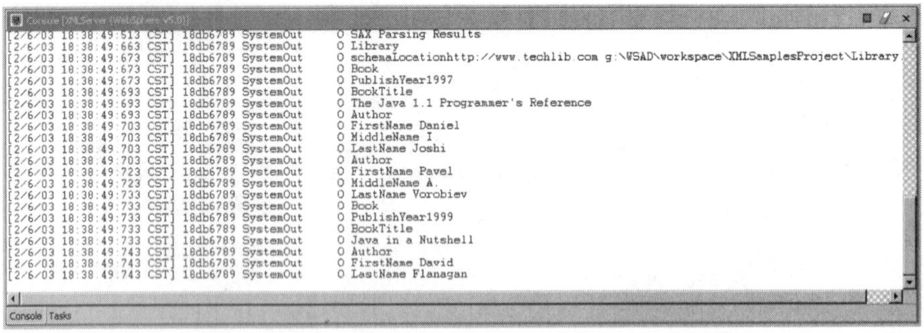

Figure 8-22. The SAX parsing results

Integrating XML and DB2

Starting from DB2 Universal Database (UDB) 7.1 (with Fixpack 6 or higher), the DB2 database supports the DB2 XML Extender that facilitates XML and database integration. It allows *data shredding* from an XML document and also allows storing it in a database table. Alternatively, it can store the entire XML document directly in a table. It also supports generating XML documents from existing relational data.

The RDB to XML Mapping Editor uses the DB2 XML Extender and allows mapping of any SQL query or multiple tables to an XML document. For non-DB2 databases, WSAD provides another tool, SQL to XML, which is restricted to one table per XML document. In this example, you will use the RDB to XML Mapping Editor.

Installing the DB2 XML Extender

You need to download and install the DB2 XML Extender. Go to the following IBM page to download the DB2 XML Extender:
`http://www.ibm.com/software/data/db2/extenders/xmlext/`.

On this Web page, find the "Product Bundles" section and click the Getting DB2 XML Extender link. Download the XML Extender, unzip it, and execute setup.exe. The DB2 XML Extender will be installed, and you will need to reboot your machine.

You will use the same Web project, XMLProjectWEB, for developing this example. First, you need to import the TECHBOOK database into the XMLProjectWEB project. Switch to the Data Perspective. In the DB Servers View, right-click Con1 and select Reconnect. Con1 will point to the TECHBOOK database.

Expand Con1, right-click the TECHBOOK database and select Import to Folder. On the screen that appears, click Browse, navigate to XMLProjectWEB/Web Content, and click OK. The wizard will enter the following standard directory for the database: XMLProjectWEB/Web Content/WEB-INF/databases. Click Finish. Click Yes to confirm the creation of a new folder. The TECHBOOK database will be imported to XMLProjectWEB.

Switch back to the Web Perspective. Next, you will create two folders (dtd and testharness) to keep the Library.dtd and the generated testharness files, respectively. Right-click the XMLProjectWEB project and select New ➤ Folder. On the next screen, enter dtd as the name and click Finish. Repeat the same steps to build the second folder, testharness. Now, import the BookTitle.dtd file, which you built during the development of the XMLSamplesProject project. Right-click the dtd folder and select Import. Select FileSystem and click Next. On the next screen, click Browse and navigate to the <WSAD installation directory>\workspace\XMLSamplesProject. Click OK. On the next screen, check the BookCatalog.dtd box and click Finish.

With all this under control, you are ready to create the RDB-to-XML mapping session. Perform the following steps. Right-click the Web Content folder under the XMLProjectWEB project and select File ➤ New ➤ Other. On the next screen, select XML on the left side and RDB to XML Mapping on the right side. Click Next. On the next screen, enter BookCatalog.rmx in the File name field (this is the name of the RDB-to-XML mapping session file to be created).

The Location field should already be correctly filled (XMLProjectWEB/Web Content). Click Next. The next screen allows you to choose between two methods: RDB table to XML mapping or SQL query to XML mapping. The RDB table to XML mapping option allows you to map RDB columns to XML data and to store them in the database or retrieve them from the database. During this process, the Document Access Definition (DAD) file is created that is used for decomposing an XML file and storing it as relational data or for doing the opposite (composing relational data into an XML file).

The SQL query to XML mapping option allows you to map the SQL processing result columns to XML attributes and elements. This option is useful for converting complex SQL queries into XML files. This option works only in one direction (executing SQL queries and getting the result as an XML file). The opposite process is not available.

Select RDB table to XML mapping and click Next. On the subsequent screen, select the database tables and columns you want to map to the XML data. Expand XMLProjectWEB all the way until you see the imported TECHBOOK database and its tables. In this example, you will use one table: BOOK_CATALOG. Select this table (see Figure 8-23).

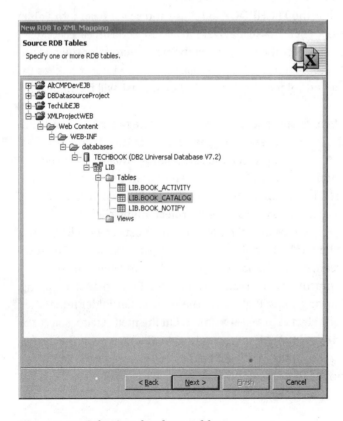

Figure 8-23. Selecting database tables

NOTE *Press the Control key if you want to select multiple tables.*

Click Next. On the next screen, specify the DTD file. Expand the dtd folder under XMLProjectWEB and select the BookCatalog.dtd file. Click Next. On the following screen, select the root element of the DTD file where the mapping will start. Select BookLibrary and click Finish. On the next screen, the RDB-to-XML session will open in the RDB to XML Mapping Editor (see Figure 8-24).

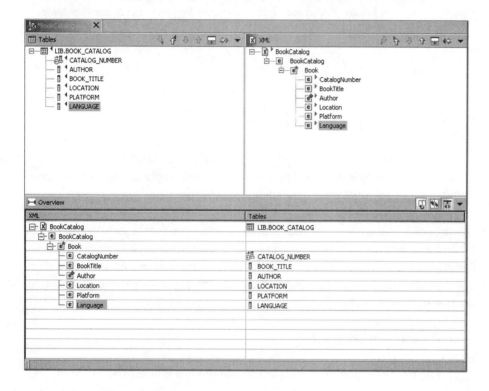

Figure 8-24. RDB to XML Mapping Editor

Here, you will map the BOOK_CATALOG table's columns to the appropriate attributes and elements of the XML file. On the left pane, you see the BOOK_CATALOG table and its columns. On the right pane, you see the XML representation of the BookCatalog DTD file (expand its structure). The pane at the bottom of the screen presents the Overview View that shows the summary of mapping to the XML document. In addition, on the left part of the screen, the Outline View shows elements/attributes that have been mapped already.

Follow these steps to map a table's column to the corresponding XML element/attribute: First, select CatalogNumber on the left pane, select CatalogNumber on the right pane, and right-click it. Second, from the menu that appears, select Create mapping. Repeat the same steps to map the rest of the identically named (in this case) fields. Notice that every mapped pair of fields is marked by an icon (which looks like an arrow). In addition, the corresponding mapped fields appear in the lower section of the screen.

 NOTE *If multiple tables are participating in this mapping, you need to perform one more step (*Join Condition*) where you specify the columns of one table that should match the corresponding columns of another table.*

Save the results and close the editor.

Generating the DAD file

The DAD file is an XML-formatted file that associates the XML document structure to a DB2 database. The DB2 XML Extender uses it to compose XML data into relational data or decompose relational data into XML data.

Right-click the BookCatalog.rmx file and select Generate DAD to launch the Generate DAD file wizard. The next screen prompts you for the location and name of the DAD file to be generated. Select or enter the XMLProjectWEB/testharness folder as the location and BookCatalog.dad as the name of the DAD file. Click Next. The next screen allows you to specify the enclosing tag, which encloses the entire document. This is useful in situations where the following is true:

- You are composing an XML file.

- The top element of the XML document contains PCDATA or an attribute.

- The value of this PCDATA or attribute can have multiple values.

In this case, multiple XML files may be generated as output because you have multiple top elements. The enclosing tag option allows a convenient way to specify a single tag to enclose the results. Consequently, only one XML document will be generated. In this scenario, there is no need to specify an enclosing tag; therefore, click Next. The next screen prompts you for information to generate the test harness.

Generating the Test Harness

The test harness provides the operating system–specific command line that will activate the DB2 for the XML Extender and process the specified DAD file in order to generate the XML file from relational data or decompose XML data into relational data.

To generate the test harness, mark the Generating a test harness check box and complete the following steps:

1. Make sure that the Folder field contains the correct folder (\XMLProjectWEB\ testharness).

2. Provide the environment variable values. These environment variables contain specific path information on the destination machine where the test harness will actually be executed. It does not necessarily need to be on the same machine (but in this case, the task will execute on this machine).

3. Populate the SQLLIB environment variable with the location of DB2's SQLLIB directory.

4. Populate the DB2EXTENDER environment variable with the location of the DB2 XML Extender directory. In this environment, it is located at g:\dxx.

5. Populate the XMLDIR environment variable with the location of where you want to generate XML files (in this environment, g:\Temp). This directory must exist (see Figure 8-25).

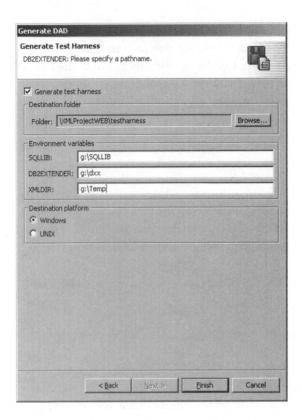

Figure 8-25. Generating the test harness

Click Finish. The BookCatalog.dad file is generated, and it opens in the Editor View. You do not need to make any changes, so close it.

Enabling DB2 for the XML Extender

Before you can store an XML document in DB2 or retrieve it from DB2, you need to first enable the DB2 database for XML. Enabling the database for XML is done for you in the test harness files retrieveXML and storeXML. Open the DB2 command window and switch to the directory <WSAD-Install-Directory>\workbench\XMLProjectWEB\testharness. Next, run the following command: setup.bat. When this procedure runs, it sets the environment variables necessary to run other procedures. It also opens a new shell window where this environment setting is done; so you must run all other procedures from this new shell.

You will run the retrieveXML procedure to enable the DB2 database for the DB2 XML Extender, as well as retrieve relational data and store it in an XML file following the mapping defined in the DAD file. Run the `retrieveXML.bat` procedure from the newly displayed shell command. Listing 8-19 shows the generated `BookCatalog.xml` file.

Listing 8-19. Generated `BookCatalog.xml` *File*

```
<?xml version="1.0"?>
<!DOCTYPE BookCatalog PUBLIC "BookCatalogId" "BookCatalog.dtd">
<BookCatalog>
  <Book>
    <CatalogNumber>00001</CatalogNumber>
    <BookTitle>Windows NT Programming in Practice</BookTitle>
    <Author>Developer Journal</Author>
    <Location>Library</Location>
    <Platform>04</Platform>
    <Language>02</Language>
  </Book>
  <Book>
    <CatalogNumber>00002</CatalogNumber>
    <BookTitle>Inside Unix</BookTitle>
    <Author>Chris Hare</Author>
    <Location>AAA_Company</Location>
    <Platform>00</Platform>
    <Language>02</Language>
  </Book>
  <Book>
    <CatalogNumber>00003</CatalogNumber>
    <BookTitle>Java Enterprise in a Nutshell</BookTitle>
    <Author>David Flanagan and a team</Author>
    <Location>Library</Location>
    <Platform>00</Platform>
    <Language>01</Language>
  </Book>
  <Book>
    <CatalogNumber>00004</CatalogNumber>
    <BookTitle>Java Server Programming</BookTitle>
    <Author>Danny Ayers and a team</Author>
    <Location>BBB_Company</Location>
    <Platform>00</Platform>
    <Language>01</Language>
  </Book>
  <Book>
```

```
      <CatalogNumber>00005</CatalogNumber>
      <BookTitle>Learn Red Hat Linux</BookTitle>
      <Author>Bill McCarty</Author>
      <Location>Library</Location>
      <Platform>05</Platform>
      <Language>01</Language>
   </Book>
   <Book>
      <CatalogNumber>00006</CatalogNumber>
      <BookTitle>MCSE Windows 2000 Professional</BookTitle>
      <Author>Lisa Donald and a team</Author>
      <Location>BBB_Company</Location>
      <Platform>04</Platform>
      <Language>02</Language>
   </Book>
   <Book>
      <CatalogNumber>00007</CatalogNumber>
      <BookTitle>Windows 2000 Server Secrets</BookTitle>
      <Author>Harry M. Brelsford</Author>
      <Location>BBB_Company</Location>
      <Platform>04</Platform>
      <Language>02</Language>
   </Book>
   <Book>
      <CatalogNumber>00008</CatalogNumber>
      <BookTitle>Maximum Java 1.1</BookTitle>
      <Author>Vanderberg and a team</Author>
      <Location>BBB_Company</Location>
      <Platform>00</Platform>
      <Language>01</Language>
   </Book>
   <Book>
      <CatalogNumber>00009</CatalogNumber>
      <BookTitle>Professional NT Services</BookTitle>
      <Author>Kevin Miller</Author>
      <Location>Library</Location>
      <Platform>04</Platform>
      <Language>02</Language>
   </Book>
   <Book>
      <CatalogNumber>00031</CatalogNumber>
      <BookTitle>Windows Sockets Network Programming</BookTitle>
      <Author>Bob Quinn</Author>
      <Location>Library</Location>
```

```
      <Platform>04</Platform>
      <Language>00</Language>
    </Book>
    <Book>
      <CatalogNumber>00010</CatalogNumber>
      <BookTitle>Java Server Programming</BookTitle>
      <Author>John Davies</Author>
      <Location>Library</Location>
      <Platform>00</Platform>
      <Language>01</Language>
    </Book>
    <Book>
      <CatalogNumber>00013</CatalogNumber>
      <BookTitle>Advanced Techniques for Java Development</BookTitle>
      <Author>Daniel Berg</Author>
      <Location>Library</Location>
      <Platform>00</Platform>
      <Language>01</Language>
    </Book>
    <Book>
      <CatalogNumber>00032</CatalogNumber>
      <BookTitle>Examples of using MQSeries</BookTitle>
      <Author>IBM</Author>
      <Location>Library</Location>
      <Platform>00</Platform>
      <Language>01</Language>
    </Book>
    <Book>
      <CatalogNumber>00016</CatalogNumber>
      <BookTitle>Java 1.2 Developer&apos;s Handbook</BookTitle>
      <Author>Phillip Heller</Author>
      <Location>Library</Location>
      <Platform>00</Platform>
      <Language>01</Language>
    </Book>
    <Book>
      <CatalogNumber>00018</CatalogNumber>
      <BookTitle>J2EE Quick Reference</BookTitle>
      <Author>John Smith</Author>
      <Location>Library</Location>
      <Platform>00</Platform>
      <Language>01</Language>
    </Book>
  </BookCatalog>
```

Understanding XSL Transformations

XSL includes two independent languages for transforming and formatting documents. For XML-based processing, the XSLT language is used mostly for converting XML to XML, XML to HTML, and XML to text documents.

The transformation is performed by an XSLT processor (such as XALAN), which reads the XML input document and the XSLT stylesheet (which contains the transformation rules applied to the input file) and produces the output document.

An XSLT stylesheet that does not specify any templates simply outputs a text file that includes the value of all elements (dropping off tags and attributes). It happens this way because in the absence of templates in the stylesheet, XSLT provides the default templates that produce such transformation results.

All transformation examples will be developed under the existing XMLProjectWEB. In the first transformation example, you will use the XML file Library.xml as the input XML file (see Listing 8-1). You will also build for this example a simple XSLT stylesheet (Library.xsl) that has no templates:

```
<? Version="1.0" ?>
<xsl:stylesheet version="1.0"
          xmlns:xsl="http://www.w3.org/1999/XSL/Transform">
</xsl:stylesheet>
```

Building an XML Project

Let's build this file using the WSAD XML tools. Switch to the XML Perspective. First, you will import the Library.xml file. Right-click the Web Content folder and select Import. On the next screen, select File system and click Next. On the next screen, click Browse and navigate to <WASD-Install-Directory>\workspace\XMLSamplesProject. Select it and click OK. Then select Library.xml and click OK. You are now back to the original screen. Make sure that XMLProjectWEB/Web Content is shown in the Folder field and click Finish. The Library.xsl file will be imported into XMLProjectWEB.

Creating the XSLT Stylesheet

Right-click XMLProjectWEB and select New ➤ Other ➤ XML ➤ XSL. Click Next. On the next screen, enter XMLProjectWEB/Web Content in the Project folder field and Library.xsl in the File name field. Click Next. You do not want to associate the Library.xml file with Library.xsl file, so click Finish. WSAD will generate the following Library.xsl file:

```xml
<?xml version="1.0" encoding="UTF-8"?>
<xsl:stylesheet xmlns:xsl="http://www.w3.org/1999/XSL/Transform"
    version="1.0"
    xmlns:xalan="http://xml.apache.org/xslt">
</xsl:stylesheet>
```

Close the Library.xsl Editor View.

Debugging the XSL

Let's quickly debug the Library.xsl file before running the transformation. Double-click the Library.xml file to open it in the Editor View. Click the Debug toolbar button (which looks like a bug). The screen that appears will prompt you to select the XML file and associate it with the Library.xsl file. Locate XMLProjectWEB, expand it, and select Library.xml (see Figure 8-26).

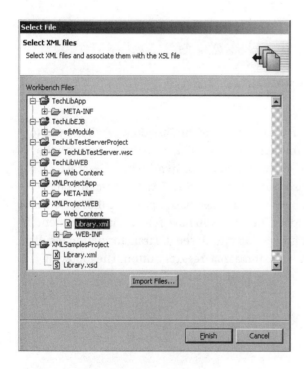

Figure 8-26. Selecting the XSL stylesheet file

NOTE *If the file is not in the project, you can import it by clicking the* Import
Files *button.*

Click Finish. The next screen shows the XML Debug Perspective (see Figure 8-27).

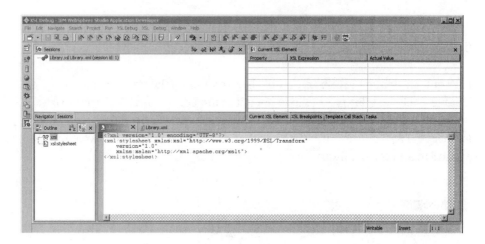

Figure 8-27. XML Debug Perspective

Both Library.xml and Library.xsl files open. The Session View allows you to
debug the session by stepping through both files. There are five buttons on the
Session View toolbar that allow you to Step forward, Step backward, Restart from
the beginning, Run to a breakpoint, and Open a Browser on the transformation
results. Click the Step forward button. A message pops up stating that the current
session has reached the end. Indeed, because you have no template statement in
the stylesheet, only the default processing ran. To see the transformation results,
click the Open a browser on the transformation results button. The following
result displays in the Browser View (see Figure 8-28).

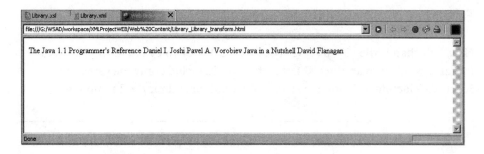

Figure 8-28. Transformation results

As already mentioned, this is the result of the default template work:

- "The Java 1.1 Programmer's Reference" came from the first `BookTitle` element.

- "Daniel I. Joshi" came from the first `Author` element.

- "Pavel A. Vorobiev" came from the second `Author` element.

- "Java in a Nutshell" came from the second `BookTitle` element.

- "David Flanagan" came from the only `Author` element of the second book.

As you can see, the attributes and the XML tags are not included in the result. In the Navigator View, you should see the result file `Library_Library_Transform.html`. The name `Transform.html` is concatenated with two prefixes that come from the name of both input files: `Library.xml` and `Library.xsl`. Instead of clicking the `Debug` button, you can click `Run Transformation` to perform the transformation without debugging.

Editing the Stylesheet

Now, let's change the Library.xsl stylesheet. Let's say you want to transform the Library.xml file into another XML file that would include only the Author and BookTitle elements. Listing 8-20 shows the modified Library.xsl template.

NOTE *If you want to save the original* Library.xsl *stylesheet, save it elsewhere.*

Listing 8-20. Library.xsl *File*

```
<?xml version="1.0" encoding="UTF-8"?>
<xsl:stylesheet xmlns:xsl=
    "http://www.w3.org/1999/XSL/Transform"
    version="1.0"
    xmlns:xalan="http://xml.apache.org/xslt">
  <xsl:template match = "Book"
    <xsl:appy-template match = "Book"/>
    <xsl:value-of select "."/>
  </xsl:template>
  <xsl:template match = "Book/BookTitle"
    <xsl:appy-template match = "Book"
    <xsl:value-of select "."/>
  </xsl:template>
</xsl:stylesheet>
```

Close the Web Browser View and the Library.xml Editor View. Leave only the Library.xsl file opened. You can change the code manually using Content Assist (Control+spacebar) or using XSL wizards. For this example, you will use the XSL wizards to modify a couple of XSLT statements at the beginning of the XSLT stylesheet (just to show you how it works). However, working with the XSL wizards is slow and not very convenient. Therefore, after a couple of statements, you will switch back to the manual mode of modification.

With Library.xsl open in the Editor View, place your cursor on the line where you want to insert the template tag, and click the Template button located on the toolbar. Enter Book in the Match field (see Figure 8-29).

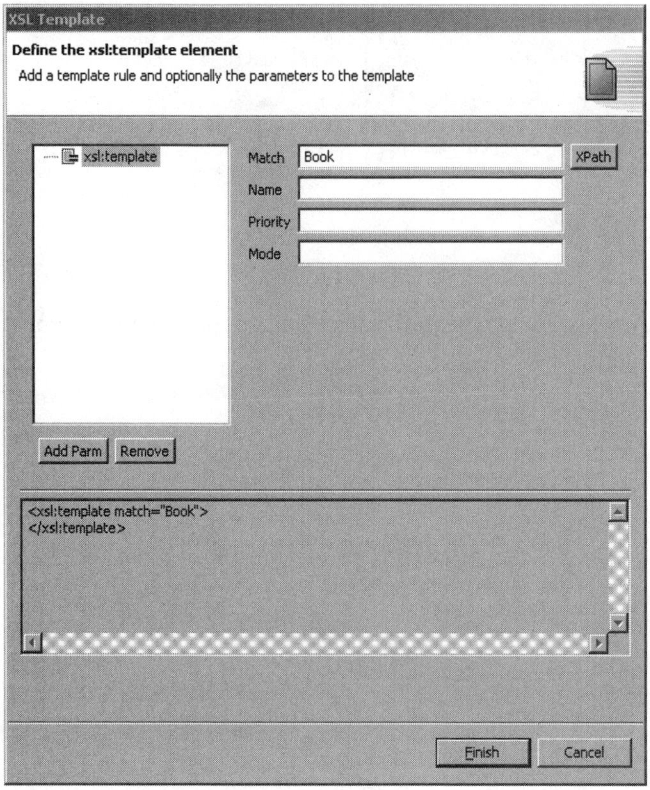

Figure 8-29. Definition of the template *element*

Click Finish. The starting and ending template tags will be inserted at the cursor location. Next, place the cursor inside the template tags and click the apply-template button on the toolbar. The apply-template clause will be inserted. Next, insert another template tag. You see how slow this process is, let's do the rest of the modifications manually. If you prefer, you can continue working with XSL wizards by locating and clicking their buttons on the toolbar.

Now, you want to insert a new template with match="BookTitle". Copy the previous pair of template tags and modify them appropriately. Notice that you can insert three lines inside the template tags. The HTML paragraph tags <P> and </P> are inserted for formatting purposes. The value-of select="." XSLT tag puts the value of the selected element in the output. The HTML break tags <BR> and </BR> are inserted for formatting purposes.

Next, do the same thing to insert the template that matches the Author element. Just insert the value-of select="." XSLT tag inside the template tags. No formatting is necessary here. The stylesheet is ready. Click the Validate button located on the toolbar. A message confirms that XSLT stylesheet is valid (see Figure 8-30).

Figure 8-30. Ready XSLT stylesheet

Click OK. Let's examine how this stylesheet works when applied to transforming the Library.xml file (see Listing 8-21).

Listing 8-21. Library.xsl

```
<?xml version="1.0" encoding="UTF-8"?>
<xsl:stylesheet xmlns:xsl="http://www.w3.org/1999/XSL/Transform"
    version="1.0"
    xmlns:xalan="http://xml.apache.org/xslt">
    <xsl:template match="Book">
      <xsl:apply-templates/>
    </xsl:template>
    <xsl:template match="BookTitle">
        <P></P>
        <xsl:value-of select="."/>
        <BR></BR>
    </xsl:template>
    <xsl:template match="Author">
        <xsl:value-of select="."/>
    </xsl:template>
 </xsl:stylesheet>
```

The XSLT processor (in this case, XANLAN) will enumerate over elements of the document tree, checking for a template that matches each selected element. When it hits the Book element, the template with match="Book" will be triggered. The apply-templates clause within this template instructs the XSLT to process all child elements of the Book parent. During enumeration of Book's child elements, templates that match BookTitle and Author will be triggered in turn. Each of them selects the value of the child element it matches and sends this value to the output. The formatting HTML tags are also included in the output.

To run the transformation, click the Run Transformation button located on the toolbar (next to the Debug button). Figure 8-31 shows the transformation results.

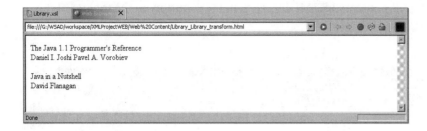

Figure 8-31. Transformation results

Close the `Library.xsl` Editor View. Close the Web Browser View. There is another way to run the transformation, which is covered in the next section.

Creating the XSL Transformation Another Way

In the Navigator View, select the `Library.xml` and `Library.xsl` files (press the Control key during selection). Right-click them and select `Apply XSL` ➤ `As HTML`. The XSL Debugger Perspective will open. Using the Session View, you can step through the two input files (by clicking the `Step forward` button located on the Session View's toolbar (see Figure 8-32).

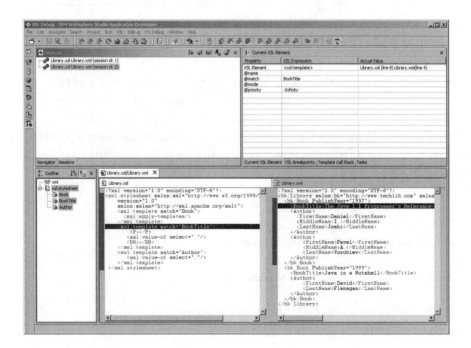

Figure 8-32. Debugging the XSL transformation

To view the generated HTML file, click the Glob button on the toolbar of the Session View (see Figure 8-33).

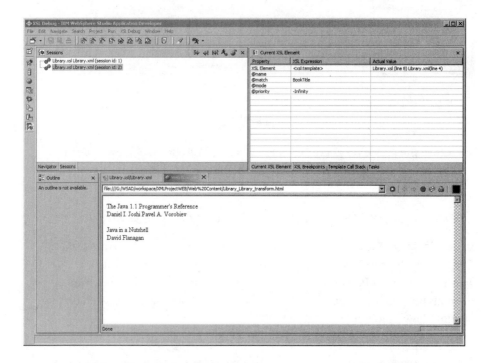

Figure 8-33. Transformation results

WSAD provides the XML to XML Mapping Editor. This is a visual tool for mapping one or more input XML documents to a single target XML document. The tool requires two DTD or XML Schema files that describe the structure of the input XML document and the output of the XML document. You can provide a DTD or XML Schema for each input and output side in the following combinations:

- DTD for input, DTD for output

- DTD for input, XML Schema for output

- XML Schema for input, DTD for output

- XML Schema for input, XML Schema for output

In addition, you should provide an XML input file that validates against its DTD or XML Schema file. You use the Visual Editor to visually indicate the desired transformation. Based on this information, the XSLT stylesheet is generated automatically and is used to transform the input XML file. WSAD provides several examples of this XML to XML transformation. Select File ➤ New ➤ Project ➤ Examples ➤ XML. Next, select the Transforming XML Documents examples and then click Next. Click Finish to complete the wizard and load the example project (see Figure 8-34).

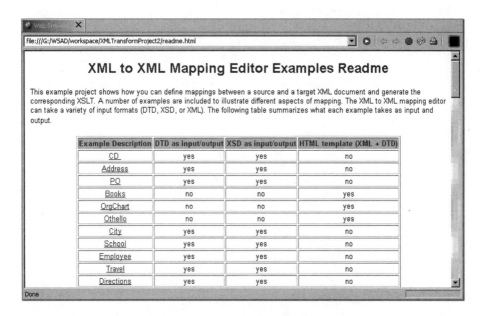

Figure 8-34. XML to XML transformation examples

Summary

This chapter presented the various XML-related tools that WSAD provides. The chapter first discussed the XML namespace, why it is used, and how it impacts the formatting of an XML document. You learned how to build and edit different types of XML files and how to generate one XML file format from another (XML from XML Schema, DTD from XML Schema, and so on). You also discussed the XML transformation process.

The next three chapters cover J2EE JMS and MQSeries as the underlying middleware that supports JMS.

Part Three

Working with Enterprise Messaging

CHAPTER 9

J2EE Enterprise Messaging

THE ENTERPRISE JAVABEAN (EJB) 2.0 and Java 2 Enterprise Edition (J2EE) 1.3 specifications now support Java Message Service (JMS). By including JMS in the J2EE specification, Sun Microsystems added extremely important functionality to the J2EE 1.3 environment—*asynchronous communication*. Before this addition, J2EE was a strictly *synchronous* environment of J2EE components communicating over the RMI-IIOP protocol.

 NOTE *RMI-IIOP is a Common Object Request Broker Architecture (CORBA)–compliant version of the Java Remote Method Invocation (RMI) communication protocol that sends RMI messages via the CORBA platform and language-independent communication protocol.*

To support asynchronous communication, J2EE 1.3 also introduced a new type of EJB bean: the Message Driven Bean (MDB). An MDB is capable of receiving asynchronous messages in an otherwise synchronous J2EE environment. As already mentioned, before JMS, J2EE was a synchronous environment based on the Java RMI-IIOP communication protocol.

Asynchronous communication gives enterprise developers an alternative form of communication with the following important advantages:

- Asynchronously communicating programs do not exchange messages directly with each other. Subsequently, a user on each side of the communication session can continue working (sending messages) even if a program on the opposite (receiving side) is down.

- Asynchronous communication offers reliability. Middleware packages that support asynchronous communication provide guaranteed (assured) message delivery even if the entire environment is down. This is an attractive feature for applications involved in communication over the Internet (which is not a reliable medium).

- Programs sending messages asynchronously are not locked when waiting for a response (which is a substantial performance improvement).

JMS is not communication software but rather a set of standard Application Programming Interfaces (APIs) for vendor-independent asynchronous communication. In that respect, JMS is similar to Java Database Connectivity (JDBC) and Java Naming and Directory Interface (JNDI). As is the case with JDBC, which requires an underlying database provider, JMS requires an underlying asynchronous communication middleware provider that supports the JMS standard. This is typically called Message-Oriented Middleware (MOM).

MOM is a technology that allows programs to asynchronously communicate by exchanging messages. To some extent, this process is similar to people communicating via email. Making the same analogy, synchronously communicating programs are similar to people communicating over the phone. Programs involved in asynchronous communication are loosely coupled. In other words, it means they do not communicate directly but via virtual channels called *queues* or *topics*.

 It also means they maintain a staged *store-and-forward* way of communication, which allows a program on the sending side to send messages even when a program on the opposite side of the communication is not running at that moment. When a program on the receiving side is up and running, the messages will be delivered to it. To some extent, this oversimplifies the real communication process that is subject to certain conditions, but it gives you a general idea of how this type of communication happens.

The main advantage of JMS communication is an environment where programs communicate using standard APIs that shield programmers from the complexities of different operating systems, data representation, and underlying network protocols.

This chapter discusses JMS and two JMS communication methods: Point-to-Point (P2P) and Publish/Subscribe (Pub/Sub). It also covers the structure of a JMS message, the main JMS objects, MDBs, JMS programming, message persistence, and JMS transaction support.

The chapter begins by discussing JMS.

Understanding JMS

Because JMS is a relatively new technology, this chapter discusses JMS programming in detail, followed by a discussion of WSAD 5.0 JMS development. As mentioned, JMS programs do not communicate directly. Messages are sent to destination objects: queues or topics. Both queues and topics are staging media objects capable of accumulating messages; however, queues and topics support different types of message delivery corresponding to two *domains* of communication: P2P and Pub/Sub.

Understanding the P2P Domain of Communication

The P2P domain of communication can operate as a "pull" or "push" type of message delivery. In the P2P pull type of communication, programs communicate using a virtual channel called a *queue*. On the sending side of the communication session, a sender program "puts" a message on a queue. On the receiving side, a receiver program periodically searches this queue looking for a message it expects to receive and process. The pull type is a less efficient message delivery method than the push type because it consumes resources during this repetitive checking for the arrival of the message. It is also important to understand that when the receiver program finds the message, it "gets" it, effectively removing it from the queue.

Therefore, even if multiple receiver programs process the same queue, only one receiver is capable of receiving a particular message. JMS programs can use multiple queues, and each queue can be processed by multiple programs, but only one program receives any specific message.

When the P2P domain of communication operates as the push type of message delivery, a sender program works in the same way, sending a message on a queue. However, the receiver program works differently. The receiver program implements a Listener Interface and includes the implementation of its onMessage callback method. In the J2EE environment, the task of listening on a specific queue for the arrival of messages is delegated to the container. Whenever a new message arrives on the queue, the container calls the onMessage method, passing the message as a parameter.

The most important point of a P2P communication domain (both types of message delivery) is that each message is received by a single program. Typically, P2P programs are more actively involved in the communication. A sender program can indicate to a receiver program the name of the queue to which it expects the reply messages to be sent. It also can request confirmation or report messages.

Understanding the Pub/Sub Domain of Communication

In the Pub/Sub domain of communication, programs communicate via a topic. Topics as a medium of communication require the support of a Pub/Sub *broker*. On the sending side, a producer program sends messages to a topic. On the receiving side, consumer programs subscribe to the topics of interest. When a message arrives at a topic, all consumer programs that are subscribed to the topic receive the message as a parameter of the onMessage method.

This is a push message delivery method. As you can see, multiple programs can receive a copy of the same message. Pub/Sub programs are less actively involved in communication. A producer program that sends messages to a particular topic does not know how many subscribers are receiving published messages (many or even none). Subscribing to a topic is a flexible scheme of communication. The number of subscribers to a topic changes dynamically without any change to the underlying communication infrastructure and is completely transparent to the overall communication process.

The Pub/Sub type of communication requires support from the Pub/Sub broker—a software package that coordinates messages to be delivered to subscribers. In contrast to the P2P domain where programs use a queue as a staging area for communication, programs involved in the Pub/Sub domain communicate directly with the special broker queues. This is why you later install the MA0C package on top of the regular WebSphere MQ installation. (This is necessary only if you are using WebSphere MQ as a JMS provider. MQ 5.3.1 or higher is required.) This package is a broker software package that supports the Pub/Sub domain of communication. (For more information, see the "Understanding JMS Pub/Sub Programming" section.)

The `QueueConnectionFactory` and `TopicConnectionFactory` JMS objects are factory classes that create the corresponding `QueueConnection` and `TopicConnection` objects used by JMS programs to connect to the underlying MOM technology.

Communicating with JMS Messages

JMS-based programs communicate by exchanging JMS messages. The JMS message consists of three parts: a header, the properties (optional), and a message body. The header consists of header fields that contain the delivery information and meta-data.

The properties part contains standard and application-specific fields that message selector can use to filter retrieved messages. JMS defines a standard and optional set of properties that is optional for MOM providers to support (see Table 9-1). The body part contains the application-specific data (the content to be delivered to a target destination).

Table 9-1. JMS Standard Message Properties

PROPERTY	TYPE	DESCRIPTION
JMSXProducerTXID	String	Transaction within which this message was produced
JMSXConsumerTXID	String	Transaction within which this message was consumed

Optional properties include JMSXUserID, JMSXAppID, JMSXProducerTXID, ConsumerTXID, JMSXRcvTimestamp, JMSXDeliveryCount, and JMSXState. The message headers provide information for the JMS messaging middleware that describes such system information as the intended message destination, the creator of the message, how long the message should be kept, and so on (see Table 9-2).

Table 9-2. JMS Header Fields

HEADER	FIELD	TYPE DESCRIPTION
JMSMessageID	String	This uniquely identifies a message and is set by the provider. This is undetermined until after the message is successfully sent.
JMSDeliveryMode	int	DeliveryMode.PERSISTENT or NON_PERSISTENT. This is a tradeoff between reliability and performance.
JMSDestination	Destination	This contains where the message is sent and is set by a message provider. The destination can be a queue or a topic.
JMSTimestamp	long	This is set by the provider during the send process.
JMSExpiration	long	This is the time the message should expire. This value is calculated during the send process. It can take a value of 0, meaning no expiration.
JMSPriority	int	This is the priority of the message. A priority of 0 is the lowest priority, and 9 is the highest priority.
JMSCorrelationID	String	This links a response message with a request message. The responding program typically copies JMSMessageID to this field.
JMSReplyTo	Destination	This is used by a requesting program to indicate a queue where a reply message should be returned.
JMSType	String	This indicates the type of message. The available types are as follows:* MapMessage contains a set of name-value pairs, where the name is a string and the value is a primitive Java type. TextMessage contains a serialized Java object. BytesMessage contains a byte stream in the message body.
JMSRedelivered	boolean	This indicates that the message was delivered, but the program did not acknowledge its receipt.

* Of all these types, TextMessage is the most widely used because of its simplicity and because of its ability to encapsulate Extensible Markup Language (XML) data.

JMS defines several types of body parts depending how this part is coded. You indicate the type of the body in the `JMSType` header field with the following possible values:

`TextMessage`: This contains the `java.lang.String` object. This is the simplest message format. You can set XML documents as `TextMessage`.

`ObjectMessage`: This contains a serializable Java object, which is built based on the serializable Java class.

`MapMessage`: This contains a set of name-value pairs of elements. It is typically used to transfer keyed data. To set the element of the message, you use setter methods such as `setInt`, `setFloat`, `setString`, and so on. On the receiving side, you use the corresponding getter methods such as `getInt`, `getFloat`, `getString`, and so on.

`BytesMessage`: This contains an array of primitive bytes. It is typically used when there is a need to send the message in the application's native format.

`StreamMessage`: This contains a stream of primitive Java types such as `int`, `char`, `double`, and so on. Primitive types are read from the message in the same order they are written. Similar getter and setter methods are provided to manipulate the message elements: `writeInt` and `readInt`, `writeString` and `readString`, and so on.

You create the JMS message object by using a JMS session object (discussed in the "Using the JMS QueueConnection Object" section). The following are examples of creating different message types:

```
TextMessage textMsg = session.createTextMessage();
MapMessage mapMsg = session.createMapMessage();
ObjectMessage objectMsg = session.createObjectMessage();
BytesMessage byteMsg = session.createBytesMessage();
```

The message object provides setter and getter methods for all message header fields. The following are several examples of getting and setting values of the JMS message header fields:

```
String messageID = testMsg.getJMSMessageID();
testMsg.setJMSCorrelationID(messageID);

int messagePriority = mapMsg.getJMSPriority();
mapMsg.setJMSPriority(1);
```

The message object also provides similar setter and getter methods for standard and application-specific property fields. The following are several examples of getting and setting values of the JMS message standard and application-specific property fields:

```
int groupSeq = objectMsg.getIntProperty("JMSGroupSeq");
objectMsg.setStringProperty("FirstName", "Joe");
```

JMS provides a set of APIs for setting and getting the content of the message's body part. Listing 9-1 shows several examples of how to work with different types of message bodies.

Listing 9-1. Working with Different Types of Message Bodies

Text Message
```
TextMessage textMsg = session.createTextMessage();
textMsg.setText("This is the text type message");
```

Map Message
```
MapMessage mapMsg = session.createMapMessage();
mapMsg.setInt(BookCatalogNumber, 100);
mapMsg.setString(BookTitle, "WinSocks 2.0");
mapMsg.setLong(BookCost, 50.00);

String bookTitle = mapMsg.getString("BookTitle");
```

Object Message
```
ObjectMessage objectMsg = session.createObjectMessage();
Book book = new Book("WinSocks 2.0");
objectMsg.setObject(book);
```

BytesMessage

NOTE *The class of the object placed in the* ObjectMessage *type must implement the* Serializable *interface.*

The BytesMessage type contains a stream of uninterrupted bytes. The receiver of the message provides interpretation of the message bytes. You should use this message type for communication that requires the proprietary interpretation of message data.

Understanding JMS P2P Programming

In a JMS P2P domain, a sending application puts a message on a queue. Depending on the nature of communication, the sending application can expect a reply message (a *request-reply* pattern). In other situations, the sending application does not need an immediate reply (a *send-and-forget* pattern). If a reply message is necessary, the sending application indicates to the receiving application (in the message header field called JMSReplyTo) the name of a local queue where it expects to receive the reply message.

In the request-reply pattern, the sending application can function in two ways. In a pseudo-synchronous way, the application is blocked while waiting for the arrival of the reply message. In an asynchronous way, the application is not blocked and can perform other processing. Later, it can check the reply queue for the expected reply message. Listing 9-2 shows a fragment of the JMS code that sends a message.

Listing 9-2. Sending a Message

```
import javax.jms.Message;
import javax.jms.TextMessage;
import javax.jms.QueueConnectionFactory;
import javax.jms.QueueConnection;
import javax.jms.QueueSender;
import javax.jms.QueueSession;
import javax.jms.Queue;
import javax.jms.JMSException;
import javax.naming.InitialContext;
import javax.naming.Context;

public class MyJMSSender
  {
    private String requestMessage;
    private String messageID;
    private int requestRetCode = 1;

    private QueueConnectionFactory queueConnectionFactory = null;
    private Queue requestQueue = null;
    private Queue responseQueue = null;
    private QueueConnection queueConnection = null;
    private QueueSession queueSession = null;
    private QueueSender queueSender = null;
    private TextMessage textMsg = null;
```

```java
// Some code here
// some code here

public int processOutputMessages(String myMessage)
 {
  // Lookup Administered Objects
  try {
      InitialContext initContext = new InitialContext();
      Context env = (Context) initContext.lookup("java:comp/env");
      queueConnectionFactory =
        (QueueConnectionFactory) env.lookup("tlQCF");

      requestQueue = (Queue) env.lookup("tlReqQueue");
      responseQueue = (Queue) env.lookup("tlResQueue");
      queueConnection = queueConnectionFactory.createQueueConnection();
      queueConnection.start();
      queueSession = queueConnection.
            createQueueSession(true, 0);
      queueSender = queueSession.createSender(requestQueue);
      textMsg = queueSession.createTextMessage();
      textMsg.setText(myMessage);
      textMsg.setJMSReplyTo(responseQueue);

      // Some processing here
      // Some processing here

      queueSender.send(textMsg);

      queueConnection.stop();
      queueConnection.close();
      queueConnection = null;
  }
  catch (Exception e)
  {
      // do something
  }
  return requestRetCode = 0;
 }
}
```

Let's examine Listing 9-2. The first thing a JMS program needs to do is find the
location of the JNDI naming context. If the program is developed under WSAD
and is a part of a J2EE project, the location of the JNDI namespace is maintained

by the WSAD test server and is known to the runtime environment. In this case, it is sufficient to instantiate an instance of the InitialContext class by simply calling its default constructor:

```
InitialContext initContext = new InitialContext();
```

A program that runs outside WSAD or a program using a non-WSAD JNDI namespace—Lightweight Directory Access Protocol (LDAP), for example—has to provide some help in locating the JNDI namespace. This is done by specifying the INITIAL_CONTEXT_FACTORY class and PROVIDER_URL as parameters of the Properties or Hashtable object and then using this object as an input parameter to the Initial-Context constructor method. You will now see several examples of creating the InitialContext object. Listing 9-3 is an example of locating the WSAD Initial-Context object with a program running outside WSAD.

Listing 9-3. Locating the WSAD InitialContext *Object with a Program Running Outside WSAD*

```
Properties props = new Properties();
props.put(Context.INITIAL_CONTEXT_FACTORY,
        "com.ibm.websphere.naming.WsnInitialContextFactory");
props.put(Context.PROVIDER_URL, "iiop://localhost/");

InitialContext initialContext = InitialContext(props);
```

 NOTE *Replace* localhost *with the hostname of your server where the JNDI server is located.*

Listing 9-4 shows an example of locating the file-based JNDI InitialContext.

Listing 9-4. Locating the File-Based JNDI Context

```
Hashtable hashTab = new Hashtable ();
hashTab.put(Context.INITIAL_CONTEXT_FACTORY,
        "com.sun.jndi.fscontext.RefFSContextFactory");
hashTab.put(Context.PROVIDER_URL, "file://c:/temp");

InitialContext initialContext = InitialContext(hashTab);
```

Listing 9-5 shows an example of locating the LDAP-based JNDI
InitialContext.

Listing 9-5. Locating the LDAP JNDI Context

```
Hashtable hashTab = new Hashtable ();
hashTab.put(Context.INITIAL_CONTEXT_FACTORY,
        "com.sun.jndi.ldap.LdapCtxFactory");
hashTab.put(Context.PROVIDER_URL,
  "file://server.company.com/o=provider_name, c=us");
InitialContext initialContext = InitialContext(hashTab);
```

The next step is to do a lookup for the subcontext java:comp/env. This is the
J2EE-recommended JNDI naming subcontext where the environment variables
are located. In this subcontext, the JMS program expects to find JMS-administered
objects such as QueueConnectionFactory objects and Queue objects:

```
Context env = (Context) initContext.lookup("java:comp/env");
```

The following code fragment locates the JMS-administered object necessary
for your program to operate:

```
queueConnectionFactory  =
    (QueueConnectionFactory) env.lookup("QCF");
requestQueue = (Queue) env.lookup("requestQueue");
```

Next, you use the QueueConnectionFactory object to build the QueueConnection
object:

```
queueConnection  = queueConnectionFactory.createQueueConnection();
```

Using the JMS QueueConnection Object

The JMS QueueConnection object provides a connection to the underlying MOM (in
this case, to the WebSphere MQ queue manager). A connection created this way
uses the default Java binding transport to connect to the local queue manager.
For an MQ client (an MQ program running on a machine without the local queue
manager), the QueueConnectionFactory object needs to be adjusted to use the client
transport:

```
QueueConn.setTransportType(JMSC.MQJMS_TP_CLIENT_MQ_TCPIP);
```

The QueueConnection object is always created in the stop mode and needs to be started:

```
queueConnection.start();
```

Once a connection is built, you use the createQueueSession method of the QueueConnection object to obtain a session. The QueueSession object has a single-threaded context and is not thread-safe. Therefore, the session object and objects created based on the session are not thread-safe and must be protected in a multi-threaded environment. The method takes two parameters. This is the statement that builds the QueueSession object:

```
queueSession =
      queueConnection.createQueueSession(false, Session.AUTO_ACKNOWLEDGE);
```

The first is a boolean parameter that specifies the JMS transaction type—in other words, whether the queue session is transacted (true) or nontransacted (false). The JMS transaction type is primarily used to regulate the message delivery mechanism and should not be confused with the EJB transaction type (NotSupported, Required, and so on), which determines the transaction context of the EJB module itself. The second parameter is an integer that determines the acknowledge mode. It determines how the message delivery is confirmed to the JMS server.

If the queue session is specified as transacted (true), the second parameter is ignored because the acknowledgment in this case happens automatically when the transaction is committed. If the transaction is rolled back, no acknowledgment will be performed, the message is considered undelivered, and the JMS server will attempt to redeliver the message. If multiple messages participate in the same session context, they are all processed as a group. Acknowledgment of the last message automatically acknowledges all previously unacknowledged messages. Similarly with rollback, the entire message group is considered undelivered with the JMS server attempting to redeliver them again.

This is how it works beneath the surface: When the sender sends a message, the JMS server receives the message. If the message is persistent, it writes the message to a disk first and then it acknowledges the message. Starting from this point, the JMS server is responsible for delivering the message to the destination. It will not remove the message from the staging area until it gets a client acknowledgment. For non-persistent messages, acknowledgment is sent as soon as the message is received and kept in memory.

If the queue session is specified as nontransacted (`false`), then the second parameter defines the acknowledgment mode. The available values are AUTO_ACKNOWLEDGE, DUPS_OK_ACKNOWLEDGE, and CLIENT_ACKNOWLEDGE:

- It is typical to use the AUTO_ACKNOWLEDGE mode for nontransacted sessions. For transacted sessions, AUTO_ACKNOWLEDGE is always assumed.

- The DUPS_OK_ACKNOWLEDGE mode is a "lazy acknowledgment" message delivery. It reduces the network overhead by minimizing work done to prevent message duplicates. You should only use it if duplicate messages are expected and there is logic in place to handle them.

- With the CLIENT_ACKNOWLEDGE mode, message delivery is explicitly acknowledged by calling the acknowledge method on the message object.

With the AUTO_ACKNOWLEDGE mode, acknowledgment is typically done at the end of the transaction. The CLIENT_ACKNOWLEDGE mode allows the application to speed up this process and make an acknowledgment as soon as the processing is done, well before the end of the transaction. This type of acknowledgment is also useful when a program is processing multiple messages. In this case, the program can issue an acknowledgment when all required messages are received.

For a nontransacted session, once a message is successfully put on a queue, it immediately becomes visible to the receiving program and it cannot be rolled back. For a transacted session, the JMS transacted context ensures that messages are sent or received as a group in one unit of work. The transacted context stores all messages produced during the transaction but does not send them to the destination.

Only when the transacted queue session is committed are the stored messages sent to the destination as one block and become visible to the receiving program. If an error occurs during the transacted queue session, messages that have been successfully processed before the error occurred will be undone. A queue session defined as transacted always has a current transaction; no begin statement is explicitly coded. As always, there is a tradeoff—transacted sessions are slower than nontransacted.

NOTE *You should not confuse the transacted and nontransacted JMS* QueueSession *modes with the corresponding property of the Java method that implements the JMS logic. The method property* TX_REQUIRED *indicates that the method runs within a transaction context. This ensures that a database update and a message placement on the queue would be executed as a unit of work (both actions committed or rolled back). By the way, when a container-managed transaction is selected, a global two-phase commit transaction context will be activated. (See the "Understanding Two-Phase Commit Transactions" section for more information.)*

In this case, the Datasource participating in the global transaction should be built based on the XA database driver. You will see an example of this type of processing in Chapter 10.

On the other hand, indicating true as the first parameter of the createQueueSession method establishes the JMS transaction context; multiple messages are treated as a unit of work. On the receiving side, multiple received messages are not confirmed until queueSession.commit() is issued, and when it is issued, it confirms receiving all messages uncommitted up to this point. On the sending side, all messages put on the destination queue are invisible until the sending program issues the session.commit statement.

Handling a Rollback

As already mentioned, for an abended transaction, a received message is sent back to the original queue. The next time the receiving program processes the queue, it will get the same message again, and the most likely scenario is that the transaction will again abend, sending the message back to the input queue. That creates a condition for an infinite loop.

To prevent this, you can set the Max_retry count on the listening port. After exhausting Max-retry, the message will no longer become available for selection by the receiving program or for a delivery in a push mode session. In addition, in a push mode, redelivered transactions will have a JMSRedelivered flag set. A program can check this flag by executing the getJMSRedelivered method on the message object. Messages are sent using a QueueSender JMS object. QueueSender is created by using the createSender method on the QueueSession object. A separate QueueSender is built for each queue:

```
queueSender = queueSession.createSender(requestQueue);
```

Next, you create a message (in this case, a TextMessage type) and set its content based on the string myMessage (passed to the method as an input parameter):

```
textMsg = queueSession.createTextMessage(myMessage);
```

You also specify the receiving queue where the receiving program should send a reply message:

```
textMsg.setJMSReplyTo(responseQueue);
```

Finally, with the Sender object, you send a message and then stop and close the connection:

```
queueSender.send(textMsg);
queueConnection.stop();
queueConnection.close();
```

After the message is sent, you can recover the message ID assigned by JMS to a message (by getting the value of the JMSMessageID header field). Later, you can use this value to find a reply message that matches your request messageID:

```
String messageID = message.getJMSMessageID();
```

With the JMS connection pooling in place, the closed session is not discarded but simply returned to the pool of available connections for reuse.

Closing JMS Objects

Garbage collection does not close a JMS object in a timely manner, which could lead to a problem when a program tries to create many short-lived JMS objects. It also consumes valuable resources. Therefore, it is important to explicitly close all JMS objects when they are no longer needed:

```
if (queueConn != null)
  {
  queueConn.stop();
  queueConn.close();
  queueConn = null;
  }
```

Closing a queue connection should automatically close all dependent objects created based on the connection. If this is not the case with your JMS provider, explicitly close all the open JMS objects in the order shown in Listing 9-6.

Listing 9-6. Closing JMS Objects

```
if (queueReceiver != null)
 {
  queueReceiver.close();
  queueReceiver = null;
 }

if (queueSender != null)
 {
  queueSender.close();
  queueSender = null;
 }

if (queueSession != null)
 {
  queueSession.close();
  queueSession = null;
 }

if (queueConn != null)
 {
  queueConn.stop();
  queueConn.close();
  queueConn = null;
 }
```

Receiving Messages

On the receiving side, the processing logic is similar to the sending side. Messages are received by the JMS QueueReceiver object, which is built based on the QueueSession object created for a specific queue. The important difference is how QueueReceiver receives messages. The QueueReceiver object can receive messages in a pseudo-synchronous or in an asynchronous way. Listing 9-7 shows the code fragment of the pseudo-synchronous way of receiving messages.

Listing 9-7. A Pseudo-Synchronous Way of Receiving Messages

```java
import javax.jms.Message;
import javax.jms.TextMessage;
import javax.jms.QueueConnectionFactory;
import javax.jms.QueueConnection;
import javax.jms.QueueSender;
import javax.jms.Queue;
import javax.jms.Exception;
import javax.naming.InitialContext;

public class MyJMSReceiver
 {
  private String responseMessage;
  private String messageID;
  private int replyRetCode = 1;

  private QueueConnectionFactory queueConnectionFactory = null;
  private Queue inputQueue = null;
  private QueueConnection queueConnection = null;
  private QueueSession queueSession = null;
  private QueueReceiver queueReceiver = null;
  private TextMessage textMsg = null;

  public void processIncomingMessages()
   {
    // Lookup Administered Objects
    InitialContext initContext = new InitialContext();
    Context env = (Context) initContext.lookup("java:comp/env");
    queueConnectionFactory =
      (QueueConnectionFactory) env.lookup("tlQCF");
    inputQueue = (Queue) env.lookup("tlQueue");
    queueConnection = queueConnectionFactory.createQueueConnection();
    queueConnection.start();
    queueSession = queueConnection.createQueueSession(true, 0);
    queueReceiver = queueSession.createReceiver(inputQueue);

    // Wait one second for the arrival of a message
    TextMessage inputMessage = queueReceiver.receive(1000);

    // Some processing here
    // Some processing here
```

```
    queueConnection.stop();
    queueConnection.close();
  }


}
```

Let's examine Listing 9-7. The message is received by the QueueReceiver object executing the receive method. This method has one parameter that indicates the wait interval (in milliseconds). In Listing 9-7, the QueueReceiver object waits for one second before it expires, gets unblocked, and returns control to the program. If the wait-interval parameter is specified, the QueueReceiver object is blocked for the specified interval, waiting for the arrival of a message. If no message arrives during the wait interval, the QueueReceiver object times out without getting a message and returns control to the program.

There is a "no wait" version of this method where the QueueReceiver checks for the message and immediately returns control to the program if no message is available. The following is the example:

```
TextMessage message = queueReceiver.receiveNoWait();
```

If the wait-interval parameter is not specified, the QueueReceiver waits indefinitely for the message. This version of the receive method should be used with great care because the program can be locked indefinitely:

```
TextMessage message = queueReceiver.receive();
```

Regardless of the variations in the wait-interval parameter, this is a pull method of message delivery, which (as mentioned) is quite inefficient. In addition to just being inefficient, it is inappropriate for the J2EE EJB layer and cannot be used inside EJB components for reasons discussed shortly. However, this type of processing is suitable for processing inside servlets, JavaServer Pages (JSP), and stand-alone Java JMS applications.

The second way of receiving messages is asynchronous. To do this, the QueueReceiver object must register a MessageListener class by using the setMessageListener(class_name) method of the QueueReceiver object. The class_name parameter can point to any class that implements the onMessage interface method. In this example, it is the same class (indicated by the this parameter). Listing 9-8 shows a code example where the onMessage method is implemented in the same class (the try/catch blocks are not shown here for simplicity).

NOTE *The upcoming receiving message listings are not suitable for the EJB components. These code fragments are suitable for processing inside servlets, JSPs, and stand-alone Java JMS applications.*

Listing 9-8. Example of the Listener *Class*

```
import javax.jms.Message;
import javax.jms.TextMessage;
import javax.jms.QueueConnectionFactory;
import javax.jms.QueueConnection;
import javax.jms.QueueReceiver;
import javax.jms.Queue;
import javax.jms.Exception;
import javax.naming.InitialContext;

public class MyListenerClass implements javax.jms.MessageListener
  {
  private int responseRetCode = 1;
  private boolean loopFlag = true;

  private QueueConnectionFactory queueConnectionFactory = null;
  private Queue responseQueue = null;
  private QueueConnection queueConnection = null;
  private QueueSession queueSession = null;
  private QueueSender queueSender = null;

  public void prepareEnvironment(String myMessage)
    {
    // Lookup Administered Objects
    InitialContext initContext = new InitialContext();
    Context env = (Context) initContext.lookup("java:comp/env");
    queueConnectionFactory =
      (QueueConnectionFactory) env.lookup("tlQCF");
    responseQueue = (Queue) env.lookup("tlResQueue");
    queueConnection = queueConnectionFactory.createQueueConnection();
    queueSession = queueConnection.createQueueSession(true, 0);
    queueReceiver = queueSession.createReceiver(responseQueue);

    queueReceiver.setMessageListener(this);
    queueConnection.start();
  }
```

```java
public void onMessage(Message message)
 {
  // We expect the text message type
  if (message instanceof TextMessage)
   {
     String responseText = "Confirmed. " +
                          ((TextMessage) message).getText();


    // When a message that starts from the @ character arrives, it stop the loop
    // and the MessageListener terminates.

     if (responseText.charAt(0) == '@')
       {
        loopFlag = 1; // Terminate processing;
       }
     else
      {
        // Continue processing message
        // We know the Reply Queue here and don't need this field.
        // It is used here to show how a queue to send the reply
        // message to can be obtained
        Destination replyToQueue = message.getJMSReplyTo();

        // Set the reply message
       TextMessage  responseMessage =
               responseSession.createTextMessage(responseText);

        // Form a CorrelationID equal to the MessageID, so the client
        // can map the response record to his/her original request.
        messageID = message.getJMSMessageID();
        responseMessage.setJMSCorrelationID(messageID);
       //Set the message destination
       responseMessage.setJMSDestination(replyToQueue)
        queueSender.send(responseMessage);
      }
   }
 }

// Keep the listener alive
 while(loopFlag)
  {
    // Yield control to other tasks (sleep for 2 seconds)
    System.out.println("Inside the listener loop");
    Thread.currentThread().sleep(2000);
  }
```

```
// Terminate processing when the loopFlag field is set to false.
queueConn.stop();
queueConnection.close();
} // End of the MyListenerClass
```

When a `MessageListener` object is registered, a new thread is created that implements the `MessageListener` logic. You need to keep this thread alive, so you run a `while` loop that sleeps for a specified number of seconds (two seconds, in this case) to yield the processor control to other tasks. When it wakes up, it checks the monitored queue and goes back to sleep. Whenever a message arrives on a queue that is monitored by the registered `MessageListener` object, JMS invokes the `MessageListener` object and calls its `onMessage(message)` method, passing the message as a parameter.

This is a push method of message receiving. It is more efficient but still inappropriate inside EJB components. The following section discusses why both methods of receiving messages are inappropriate to use inside the EJB components and then shows the solution. Although this is discussed in the P2P domain, the same considerations apply to the Pub/Sub domain as well.

Using JMS Message Driven Beans (MDBs)

Earlier in this chapter (when discussing the JMS receive processing logic), you learned that the code listings are not suitable for EJBs, but they are suitable for servlets, JSPs, and stand-alone Java applications. This is because there are several technical issues involved with the receiving side of the JMS processing. Typically, JMS programs are developed using two interaction patterns:

Send-and-forget: The JMS client program sends a message but does not need a reply. From a performance point of view, this is the best pattern because the sender does not need to wait for the request to be processed and can continue processing.

Synchronous request-reply: The JMS client program sends a message and waits for a reply. Such interaction under JMS is done by executing a pseudo-synchronous receive method (already discussed). There is an issue here, however. If your EJB module operates under a transaction context (which is typically the case), you cannot perform request-reply processing in one transaction. The reason is that when the sender submits a message, the receiver can get it only when the sender commits the transaction. Therefore, within a single transaction, it is impossible to get a reply because within the uncommitted transaction context the receiver will never get the message and will not be able to reply. The solution is that request-reply must always be performed as two separate transactions.

There is an additional problem on the receiving side of the communication that is specific to EJBs. With asynchronous communication, you never know when to expect the reply. The main idea of asynchronous communication is that you can continue working on the sending side even if the receiving side is not currently active. The request-reply mode presumes that an EJB component (say, a session bean) should wait for a response after sending a message to a particular destination. J2EE is actually a component-based transaction-processing environment designed for processing a large number of short-lived tasks. It is not intended for tasks being blocked for a substantial period waiting for a response.

To solve this problem, Sun Microsystems developed and added to the EJB 2.0 specification a new type of EJB bean, the MDB. The MDB was specifically designed to handle the problems of processing JMS asynchronous messages (on the receiving side) with the EJB components. The solution was to remove the task of listening for a message's arrival from an EJB component and delegate it to a container. Thus, MDB components run under the control of the container. The container works as a listener on a particular queue or topic on behalf of an MDB. When a message arrives on that queue or topic, the container activates this MDB and calls its onMessage method (passing the arrived message as a parameter).

MDBs are asynchronous components, and they work differently than the rest of EJB components (session and entity beans) that are synchronous. MDBs do not have Remote and Home Interfaces because they cannot be activated by clients. MDBs are activated only by the arrival of messages. Another important aspect of MDBs is the way in which they run under the transaction and security contexts. Because MDB components are completely decoupled from their clients, they do not use the client's transaction and security contexts.

Remote clients that send JMS messages can potentially run in different environments that are not J2EE environments (they can be just Java programs). They might not have any security or transaction context. Therefore, the transaction and security contexts of the sender are never propagated to the receiver MDB components. Because MDBs are never activated by clients, they can never execute under the client's transaction context. Therefore, the following transaction attributes have no meaning for MDBs: Supports, RequiresNew, Mandatory, and None. These transactional attributes imply propagation of the client transaction context. Only two transactional attributes, NotSupported and Required, can be used with MDBs. MDB components with the NotSupported attribute process messages without any transaction context.

MDBs (as EJB beans) may participate in two types of transactions: bean-managed or container-managed transactions. Of all the MDB methods, only the onMessage method can participate in the transaction context. If a developer selects an MDB to participate in the bean-managed transaction context, then the MDB is allowed to begin and end a transaction inside the onMessage method. The problem with this assignment is that the received message stays outside of the transaction context that always starts inside the onMessage method (too late for the message to be a part of it). In this case, you should handle messages in a rollback situation manually.

If a developer selects an MDB to participate in the container-managed transaction context, the entire scenario works differently. With the Required transactional attribute selected, the container starts a transaction at the time it receives a message; therefore, the message becomes part of the transaction, and it can be acknowledged whether the transaction is committed or returned to the sending queue if the transaction is rolled back.

Transaction rollback could happen in two situations: The program can explicitly call the setRollBackOnly method or throw a system exception within the onMessage method (remember that throwing the application exception does not trigger the rollback). In the case of transaction rollback, the message will be returned to the original queue, and the listener will send the message for processing again. Typically, this will create an indefinite loop and cripple the application. The Max_retries attribute, set during configuration of the listener port, controls the number of times the listener is allowed to retrieve the re-sent message. After that, the listener will stop processing messages (not a good solution).

WebSphere MQ, when used as the JMS provider, has a better solution. You can configure it to stop delivering the message after the specified number of attempts and send it to a specified error queue or Dead.Letter.Queue. Remember that MDBs are stateless components, meaning they do not maintain any state between different method invocations. They also have no identity of the client because they are never called by clients. MDB execute anonymously. All MDB components must implement the javax.ejb.MessageDrivenBean and javax.jms.MessageListener interfaces.

In addition to the onMessage method, MDBs have several callback methods—methods called by a container:

- The ejbCreate method is called by a container to create the MDB instance. Some initialization logic can happen here.

- The setMessageDrivenContext method is called by the container when the bean is first added to the pool of MDB beans. This is typically used to capture the MessageDrivenContext and save it in a class variable, for example:

```
public void setMessageDrivenContext
    (java.ejb.MessageDrivenContext mdbContext)
{
 messageDrivenContext = mdbContext;
}
```

- The ejbRemove method is called when the container moves the bean from the pool to no state. Typically, cleanup processing happens here.

Typically, it is not recommended to perform the business logic inside the onMessage method. It is a best practice to delegate other EJB components to perform these tasks. You will see an example of this type of delegation in Chapter 10.

The MDB container automatically handles the concurrency of processing multiple messages. Each MDB instance processes one message and is never called for processing another message until the onMessage method returns control to the container. When multiple messages need to be concurrently processed, the container activates multiple instances of the same MDB.

Starting from WebSphere 5.0, full support of MDBs is provided by the development environment (WSAD 5.0) and the runtime environment (WAS 5.0). Listing 9-9 shows a conceptual fragment of the MDB code example.

Listing 9-9. Conceptual Fragment of the MDB Code

```
package some-package
import javax.jms.Message;
import javax.jms.MapMessage;
import javax.naming.InitialContext;
import java.util.*;

public class LibraryNotificationBean implements javax.ejb.MessageDrivenBean,
javax.jms.MessageListener
  {
    MessageDrivenContext messageDrivenContext;
    Context   jndiContext;

    public void setMessageDrivenContext(MessageDrivenContext msgDrivenContext)
      {
        messageDrivenContext = msgDrivenContext;
        try
          {
          jndiContext = new InitialContext();
          }
        catch(NamingException ne )
          {
            throw new EJBException(ne);
          }

      }
```

```
   public void ejbCreate()
    {
    }

   public void onMessage(Message notifyMsg)
    {
     try
     {
       MapMessage notifyMessage = (MapMessage) notifyMsg;
       String bookTitle = (String) notifyMessage.getString("BookTitle");
       String bookAuthor = (String) notifyMessage.getString("BookAuthor");
       String bookCatalogNumber = (String)
        notifyMessage.getString("bookCatalogNumber");

       Integer bookQuantity = (Integer)
                notifyMessage.getInteger("BookQuantity");

       // Do some processing (call EJB components)

     }
    catch (Exception e)
     {
      throw new EJBException(e);
     }
  }

 public void ejbRemove()
  {
   try
    {
     jndiContext.close();
     jndiContext = null;
    }
    catch(NamingException ne)
    {
    // Do nothing
    }
  }
}
```

Regulating Message Persistence

Messages can be persistent and nonpersistent. A single queue can hold both persistent and nonpersistent messages. Persistent messages are written to a disk and are recoverable if the system goes down. As usual, there is a performance cost for persistence. Persistent messages are about seven percent slower. One way of controlling the persistence of messages is to use the queue property when defining a queue: `DEFINE TYPE (name) [property]`. If the persistent property is not set explicitly, the system will use a default. The JMS application can also define persistence:

- `PERSISTENCE(QDEF)`: Persistence is inherited from the queue default.

- `PERSISTENCE(PERS)`: Messages are persistent.

- `PERSISTENCE(NON)`: Messages are nonpersistent.

You can also regulate message persistence by setting the value of the message attribute header `JMSDeliveryMode` to `DeliveryMode.PERSISTENT` or `DeliveryMode.NON_PERSISTENT`. Messages processed under the transacted session must always be persistent.

Using Message Selectors

JMS provides a mechanism for selecting a subset of messages on a queue by filtering out all messages that do not meet the selection condition. The selector can refer to message header fields as well as message property fields. The following are examples of using this facility:

```
QueueReceiver queueReceiver =
 queueSession.createReceiver(requestQueue, "BookTitle = 'Windows 2000'");
QueueBrowser queueBrowser =
 queueSession.createBrowser(requestQueue,
"BookTitle = 'Windows 2000' AND
 BookAuthor = 'Robert Lee'");
```

Notice that the strings (such as `Windows 2000`) are surrounded by single quotes inside double quotes.

Understanding JMS Pub/Sub Programming

Programming for the Pub/Sub domain is similar to the P2P domain. The main difference is in the destination objects. Messages in the Pub/Sub domain are published to (similar to *sent*) and consumed from (similar to *received*) JMS objects called *topics*. Topics function as virtual channels and encapsulate a Pub/Sub destination object.

In the P2P mode, a message (sent to a queue) can be received by only one message consumer. In the Pub/Sub domain, a message producer can publish a single message on a topic that can be distributed and consumed by many message consumers. More than that, a message producer and its message consumer are so loosely coupled that a producer does not need to know anything about the message consumers. Both message producers and message consumers only need to know a common destination (which is a topic of conversation).

A message producer is called a *publisher,* and a message consumer is called a *subscriber*. All messages published by a publisher for a specific topic are distributed to all subscribers of that topic. A subscriber receives all messages for which it has subscribed. Each subscriber receives its copy of the message. Subscriptions can be durable or nondurable. Nondurable subscribers receive only messages that have been published after they have subscribed.

Durable subscribers are able to disconnect and later reconnect and still receive messages that have been published while they were disconnected. Durable subscribers in the Pub/Sub domain (with some level of approximation) are similar to persistent messages/queues in the P2P domain. Publishers and subscribers never communicate directly. The Pub/Sub broker functions as a message cop, delivering all published messages to their subscribers.

 NOTE *Starting from WebSphere MQ 5.2, WebSphere MQ with the MA88 and MA0C extensions can function as JMS Pub/Sub brokers. In addition, WebSphere MQ Integrator can function as a Pub/Sub broker. Starting from MQ 5.3, MA88 became part of the base package, so you need to install only MA0C on top of the MQ 5.3 installation. For MQ JMS, for Pub/Sub to work correctly, you must create a number of system queues on the queue manager that runs the Pub/Sub broker.*

The MQ JMS MA0C extension provides a procedure that builds all the necessary Pub/Sub system queues. This procedure is called `MQJMS_PSQ.mqsc`, and it resides in the `<MQ-Install-Directory>\java\bin` directory. To build the system queues required by the Pub/Sub domain, enter the following command from this directory:

```
runmqsc < MQJMS_PSQ.mqsc
```

and press Enter.

You can arrange topic names in a tree-like hierarchy. Each topic name in the tree is separated by a slash (/)—for example, `Books/UnixBooks/SolarisBooks`. You can use wildcards within topics to facilitate subscribing to more than one topic. This is an example of a wildcard used within the topic hierarchy: `Books/#`.

Listing 9-10 shows a code fragment of JMS Pub/Sub coding (the try/catch blocks are not shown for simplicity). In this example, subscribers of the `Books/UnixBooks/SolarisBooks` topic will receive all messages sent to the `SolarisBooks` topic, and subscribers of the `Books/#` topic will receive all `Books` messages (including messages sent to the `UnixBooks` and `SolarisBooks` topics).

Listing 9-10. Seeing JMS Pub/Sub in Action

```
import javsx.jms.*;
import javax.naming.*;
import javax.ejb.*;

public class PublisherExample implements javax.ejb.SessionBean
{
 private  TopicConnectionFactory topicConnFactory = null;
 private  TopicConnection topicConnection = null;
 private  TopicPublisher topicPublisher = null;
 private  TopicSession topicSession = null;
 private  SessionContext sessionContext = null;

public void setSessionContext(SessionContext ctx)
 {
   sessionContext = cts;
}
public void ejbCreate() throws CreateException
 {
    InitialContext initContext = new InitialContext();

    // Look up the topic connection factory from JNDI
```

```
      topicConnFactory =
          (TopicConnectionFactory)
                initContext.lookup("java:comp/env/TCF");


      // Look up the topics from JNDI
      Topic unixBooksTopic = (Topic)
            initContext.lookup("java:comp/env/UnixBooks");
      Topic javaBooksTopic = (Topic)
            initContext.lookup("java:comp/env/JavaBooks");
      Topic linuxBooksTopic = (Topic)
            initContext.lookup("java:comp/env/LinuxBooks");
      Topic windowsBooksTopic = (Topic)
            initContext.lookup("java:comp/env/WindowsBooks");
      Topic allBooksTopic = (Topic)
            initContext.lookup("java:comp/env/AllBooks");


    // Create a connection
    topicConnection = topicConnFactory.createTopicConnection();
    topicConn.start();


// Create a session
topicSession =
        topicConn.createTopicSession(false, Session.AUTO_ACKNOWLEDGE);
}


public void publishMessage(String workMessage, String topicToPublish)
{

    // Create a message
    TextMessage message = topicSession.createTextMessage(workMessage);

    // Create topic publishers and send messages
    if ((topicToPublish.toLowerCase()).equals("java"))
      {
        TopicPublisher javaBooksPublisher =
                    topicSession.createPublisher(javaBooksTopic);
        javaBooksPublisher.publish(message);
      }

    if ((topicToPublish.toLowerCase()).equals("unix"))
      {
        TopicPublisher unixBooksPublisher =
                    topicSession.createPublisher(unixBooksTopic);
```

```
          unixBooksPublisher.publish(message);
        }

     if ((topicToPublish.toLowerCase()).equals("linux"))
        {
         TopicPublisher linuxBooksPublisher =
                      topicSession.createPublisher(linuxBooksTopic);
         linuxBooksPublisher.publish(message);
        }

     if ((topicToPublish.toLowerCase()).equals("windows"))
        {
         TopicPublisher windowsBooksPublisher =
                      topicSession.createPublisher(windowsBooksTopic);
         windowsBooksPublisher.publish(message);
        }

     TopicPublisher allBooksPublisher =
                      topicSession.createPublisher(allBooksTopic);
     allBooksPublisher.publish(message);
   }

   public void ejbActivate()
   {
   }

   public void ejbPassivate()
   {
   }

   public void ejbRemove()
   {
     // Clean up code fragment

     if (javaBooksPublisher != null)
       {
         javaBooksPublisher.close();
         javaBooksPublisher = null;
       }

     if (unixBooksPublisher != null)
       {
         unixBooksPublisher.close();
```

```
    unixBooksPublisher = null;
   }

  if (linuxBooksPublisher != null)
   {
    linuxBooksPublisher.close();
    linuxBooksPublisher = null;
   }

  if (windowsBooksPublisher != null)
   {
    windowsBooksPublisher.close();
    windowsBooksPublisher = null;
   }

  if (allBooksPublisher != null)
   {
    allBooksPublisher.close();
    allBooksPublisher = null;
   }

  if (topicSession != null)
   {
    topicSession.close();
    topicSession = null;
   }

  if (topicConnection != null)
   {
    topicConnection.stop();
    topicConnection.close();
    topicConnection = null;
    }
 }
```

This code is straightforward and does not need additional explanation. The only original part is how you publish a message for different topics. For each specific topic, you create a corresponding publisher and use it to publish a message on this topic.

If an MDB only receives messages and delegates future message processing to business components (meaning that there is no message sending or publishing logic inside the MDB), the code for the MDB is identical to the P2P domain of processing (see Listing 9-9). The only change for using the same MDB is that you must change the listener port from listening on a queue to listening on a topic. You will see the example of this dual usage in Chapter 10.

Understanding Two-Phase Commit Transactions

For enterprise-level processing, you typically operate under a transaction context to control the integrity of the JMS and non-JMS processing of the business logic (committing or rolling back all steps as a unit of work). The transaction context is especially important when (in addition to placing a message on a queue) you also need to place a record on a database (two-phase commit—all or nothing).

To support two-phase commit, the JMS specification provides an XA version of the following JMS objects: XAConnectionFactory, XAQueueConnectionFactory, XASession, XAQueueSession, XATopicConnectionFactory, XATopicConnection, and XATopicSession. In addition, you must use XA versions of other resources involved in the global transaction. Specifically, for JDBC resource, you must use the JDBC XADatasource. Finally, the JTA TransactionManager coordinates the global transaction. Listing 9-11 shows the steps necessary to establish a global transaction.

Listing 9-11. Setting a Global Transaction

```
// Obtain the JTA TransactionManager from the JNDI namespace.
TransactionManager globalTxnManager =
  jndiContext.lookup("java:comp/env/txt/txnmgr");



// Start the global transaction
globalTxnManager.begin();

// Get the transaction object
Transaction globalTxn = globalTxnManager.getTransaction();

// Obtain the SA Datasource
XADatasource xaDatasource =
  jndiContext.lookup("java:comp/env/jdbc/datasource");
```

```
// Obtain the connection
XAConnection jdbcXAConn = xaDatasource.getConnection();

// Obtain the XAResource from the XA connection
XAResource jdbcXAResource = jdbcXAConn.getXAResource();

// Enlist the XAResource in the global transaction
globalTxn .enlist(jdbcXAResource);

// Obtain XA Queue Connection Factory
XAQueueConnectionFactory xaQueueConnectionFactory =
   JndiContext.lookup("java:comp/env/jms/xaQCF")

// Obtain XA Queue Connection
XAQueueConnection xaQueueConnection =
    XaQueueConnectionFactory.createXAQueueConnection();

// Obtain XA Queue Session
XAQueueSession xaQueueSession = xaQueueConnection.createXAQueueSession();

// Obtain XA Resource from session
XAResource jmsXAResource = xaQueueSession.getXAResource();

// Enlist the XAResource in the global transaction
globalTxn .enlist(jmsXAResource);

// --- some work ---

// Commit global transaction
globalTxn.commit();
```

Summary

This chapter introduced you to JMS, the new J2EE 1.3 asynchronous messaging standard. It discussed the advantages of the asynchronous communication, the two JMS domains (P2P and Pub/Sub), MDBs, JMS transactions, and two-phase commit global transactions. In the next two chapters, you will see examples of JMS programming with WSAD 5.0.

CHAPTER 10

Using the WSAD-Embedded JMS Provider

BEFORE INSTALLING WSAD embedded messaging support, it is important to mention that, starting from Java 2 Enterprise Edition (J2EE) 1.3, Java Message Service (JMS) is an integral part of the Enterprise JavaBean framework, and the J2EE specification requires that J2EE application servers support JMS and function as native JMS providers.

Consequently, the WebSphere Application Server (WAS) 5.0 package has a native JMS server—the embedded JMS provider. It is built based on WebSphere MQ and supports the Point-to-Point (P2P) and Publish/Subscribe (Pub/Sub) JMS modes (*domains* in JMS jargon) with persistent and nonpersistent messages. The embedded JMS provider supports JMS messaging within the WAS environment, so WAS 5.0 no longer needs to depend on external JMS providers. Only one embedded JMS provider is available per node, and it installs during the WSAD 5.0 installation. It is also possible to configure WAS 5.0 to use WebSphere MQ as a JMS provider for enterprise-level application integration.

Why would you need to configure WebSphere MQ as a JMS provider for WAS 5.0 if WAS 5.0 already supports the embedded JMS provider internally? The reason is that although the embedded JMS provider is built on MQ, it is not a full-blown WebSphere MQ package. It does not support MQ channels and therefore is not capable of communicating with other MQ installations. Of course, it does not support WebSphere MQ clustering because MQ channels are not supported. It also does not provide the store-and-forward messaging from one queue manager to another.

The embedded JMS provider also includes a subset of the MQ Event Broker 2.1, providing basic support for the Pub/Sub domain of JMS. It also supports persistent messages and durable subscriptions, but they do not persist across the application server restarts, effectively making persistent messages and durable subscriptions hardly suitable for a production environment. The embedded JMS provider can only be installed during WAS 5.0 installation if MQ is not installed on the same node. It automatically starts with WAS startup and automatically stops with WAS shut down.

The embedded JMS provider supports communication over the network; however, this support is limited to the WAS environment. An example of this type of JMS messaging support would be a WAS cell that consists of WAS 5.0 instances installed on multiple network nodes. J2EE applications deployed in such environment could exchange JMS messages over the networks using the embedded JMS provider subject to the following condition: Two applications must agree on the JMS server (node) that they will use.

Therefore, if you need support for JMS messaging inside the WAS 5.0 environment, the embedded version JMS provider is sufficient. However, to use the full features of MQ (channels, clusters, communication between multiple Queue Managers, and so on), you need to set MQ as the JMS provider. It is important to understand that setting the JMS provider is declarative, so switching from one JMS provider to another does not require any change in the application.

WSAD 5.0 also comes with the embedded JMS provider that is used for the WSAD integrated test server environment. The embedded JMS provider behaves identically under WSAD 5.0 test server and WAS 5.0 runtime environments.

With this explanation, you are well equipped for making an intelligent decision about building your development and runtime environment. In this chapter, you will install the embedded JMS client and server and develop a JMS application that runs under the control of the embedded JMS environment. Next, you will uninstall the embedded JMS server (leaving the embedded JMS client). You will install WebSphere MQ 5.3 on top of this installation and configure it as the WSAD JMS provider. Following the WebSphere MQ 5.3 installation and configuration, you will develop a new JMS application supported by MQ as the JMS provider.

Installing WSAD Embedded Messaging Support

In this section, you will install the WSAD 5.0 embedded JMS client and server. You should remember that in Chapter 2 you downloaded twelve WSAD 5.0 installation files and unzipped them all in the same directory. To start the installation, double-click install.exe located in this directory. The WebSphere Studio Installation Launcher screen, shown in Figure 10-1, appears. Click Install embedded messaging client and server.

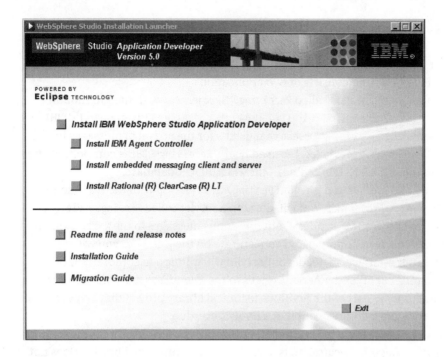

Figure 10-1. Choosing to install the WSAD embedded client and server

Follow the installation instructions. When asked for the destination folder, enter the directory of where to install the embedded JMS server. Again, keep it short (I selected g:\wsmq on my development machine). After clicking the Install button, the embedded JMS client and server will be installed. This installation also creates a queue manager, whose name is important to remember. Activate the Windows command prompt and enter the following command: dspmq. The queue manager name and its status will be displayed in the following form:

```
QMNAME<WAS_localhost_server1>        STATUS<Ended immediately>
```

Developing a Point-to-Point JMS Application

You are ready to develop your first JMS example. The first example demonstrates the JMS P2P mode and consists of two applications.

The first application is called `ReceivingJMSProjectApp` with the EJB module called `ReceivingJMSProjectEJB`. You will develop a Message Driven Bean (MDB) component called `ReceivingMDBBean` that listens for the arrival of messages on the queue called `NotifyQ`. Messages, received by the `ReceivingMDBBean` component, are written to the BOOK_NOTIFY table of the TECHBOOK database.

The second application is called `SendingJMSProjectApp` with the Web module called `SendingJMSProjectWEB`. You will develop a servlet called `SendingServlet`, which functions as a JMS sender client that sends messages to the `NotifyQ` queue.

To keep the project simple and concentrate on the JMS part, you will not develop a user interface. Instead, your servlet will mimic a user (librarian) by sending a number of predefined messages to the queue. You can consider this development to be part of the fictitious technical library project that allows a librarian to notify a library client that a book is overdue.

The example demonstrates the type of business processing that is most suitable for using JMS because of its asynchronous nature. The librarian does not need a response and, therefore, does not need to wait for the processing of the messages received on the opposite side of communication. If the receiving part is down at the time the librarian sends messages, the messages will not be lost. They will be received by the library client later (when its receiving application is up and running).

It is also a best-practice recommendation to develop an MDB to delegate the business processing to another enterprise bean. This design separates the JMS communication from the business logic and allows for the reuse of JMS components. Of course, considering the limitations of the embedded JMS provider used in this example, you should assume that the library client's J2EE receiving application runs on the same WAS 5.0 cell and both applications agree upon the node where they use the JMS provider. This sounds a little artificial, but it is okay for demonstrating the embedded JMS provider example.

Developing the Receiving Part

With this quick introduction, you are ready to start development. You will develop the receiving part of the application first, following by the development of the sending part. With a number of J2EE-developed applications behind you, your WSAD 5.0 environment has probably become crowded and slow. So, you need to do some cleanup work. In this case, close all projects you do not need for the current development (just switch to the server configurations, right-click each of them, and select Close). Each open project consumes resources and slows the startup and shutdown of the WSAD Workbench. However, do not close the DBUtilityProject because it holds the TECHBOOK database that you need for this new development.

In addition, close all opened Perspectives (presented as buttons on the vertical Perspective Bar) that you no longer need. This is good practice. First, it protects the finished project from accidental changes. In addition, it reduces the resources used by WSAD and makes it more responsive. Another alternative is to start this new development under a new Workbench (discussed in Chapter 3).

Once you have cleaned up the Workbench, switch to the J2EE Perspective and create a new EJB project called ReceivingJMSProjectEJB. Make it a part of the new enterprise application called ReceivingJMSProjectApp (see Figure 10-2).

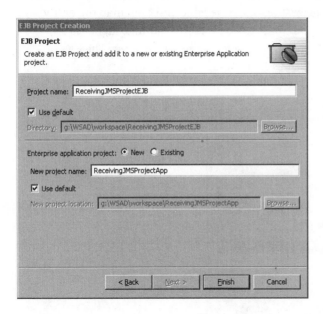

Figure 10-2. Building a new EJB project

Click Finish. Because the MDB (that you will develop next) needs to interact with the database (to save the received messages in the database), you will first develop a Container Managed Persistence (CMP) entity bean. You will generate the CMP entity bean based on the existing BOOK_NOTIFY table of the TECHBOOK database. To do this, you first need to import the TECHBOOK database in your project.

Importing the TECHBOOK Database into the Project

Switch to the Data Perspective, right-click the Con1 connection and select Reconnect. Now, expand Con1 until you see the BOOK_NOTIFY table. Right-click this table and select Import to Folder. Click Browse, navigate to ReceivingJMSProjectEJB, and click OK. Click Finish and confirm the creation of a new folder. The TECHBOOK database, its schema, and the BOOK_NOTIFY table will be imported in your project. Now, you are ready to generate a CMP entity bean based on the BOOK_NOTIFY table.

Developing the Entity Bean Component

Instead of developing the entity bean from scratch, WSAD allows you to automatically generate it based on the existing database table and then map the entity bean's attributes to the corresponding database table columns. Right-click ReceivingJMSProjectEJB and select Generate ➤ EJB to RDB Mapping. The EJB to RDM Mapping screen will appear (see Figure 10-3).

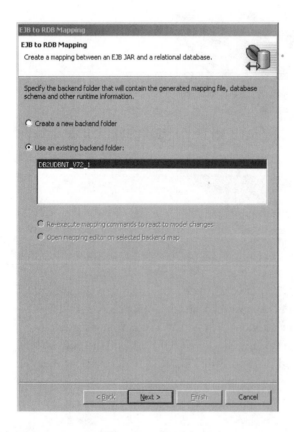

Figure 10-3. Building new CMP bean

Click Next twice. On the next screen, shown in Figure 10-4, select Generate 2.0 enterprise beans, enter apress.wsad.techlib in the Package for generated EJB classes field, and enter SaveMsg in the Prefix for generated EJB classes field.

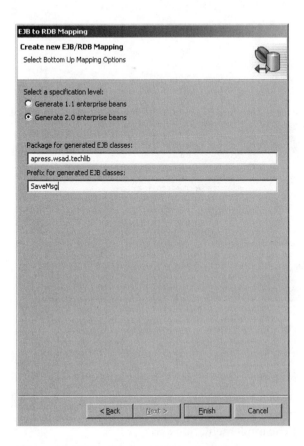

Figure 10-4. The EJB to RDB Mapping *screen*

Click Finish. Figure 10-5 shows the next screen, which maps the columns of the BOOK_NOTIFY database table to the attributes of the entity bean.

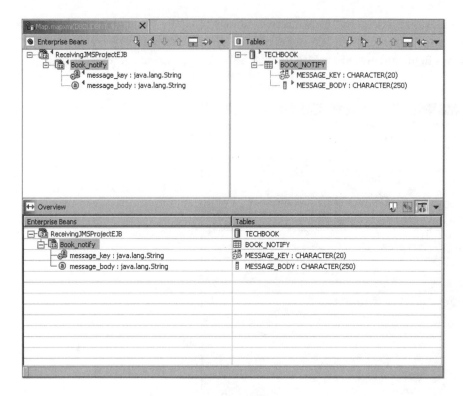

Figure 10-5. Mapping database columns to the attributes of the entity bean

You do not need to make any changes; therefore, close the editor. WSAD will generate the following CMP entity bean files:

* SaveMsgBook_notifyBean: The implementation class

* SaveMsgBook_notifyLocalHome: The Local Home Interface class

* SaveMsgBook_notifyLocal: The Local Interface class

* SaveMsgBook_notifyKey: The Primary Key class

Double-click the SaveMsgBook_notifyBean implementation class to open it in the Editor View. Notice the ejbCreate method and full list of parameters that have been automatically generated along with the corresponding ejbPostCreate and create methods within the Local Home Interface. In the Outline View, you can see that both ejbCreate methods are promoted to the Local Interface. The CMP entity bean is ready without a single line of code written by you. Close the Editor View.

Developing the MDB Component

Next, you will develop an MDB component. In the J2EE Perspective (the J2EE Hierarchy View), right-click ReceivingJMSProjectEJB and select New ➤ Enterprise Bean. Click Next. On the next screen, select Message-driven bean as the bean type, enter ReceivingMDB in the Bean name field, and enter apress.wsad.techlib in the Default Package field. Click Next.

On the subsequent screen, shown in Figure 10-6, select Container as the Transaction type and Queue as the Destination Type. Enter TechLibListenerPort in the ListenerPort name field. You are creating an MDB with the container-controlled transaction that will listen on port TechLibListenerPort. Later you will link this port to the NotifyQ queue, effectively causing the MDB to listen for the arrival of messages on the NotifyQ queue.

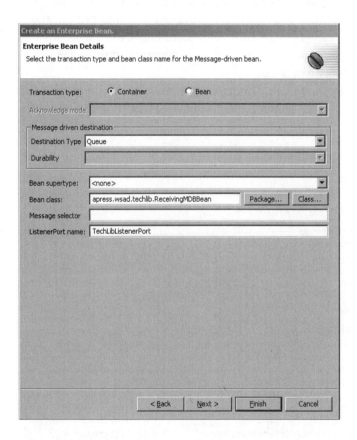

Figure 10-6. Building an MDB

Click `Finish`. WSAD will generate `ReceivingMDBBean`. **Double-click** `Receiving-MDBBean` to open it in the Editor View. The generated skeleton of the MDB contains several methods. The `setMessageDrivenContext` method is a callback method called by the container to set the message context. The message context provides an interface for the MDB component to interact with the container. For MDBs with the `Bean` transaction type, the message context allows the bean to roll back the transaction, which returns the message back to the queue. This method can also be used to perform necessary initialization processing. The corresponding `getMessageDrivenContext` method allows the bean to get the saved message context.

The container uses the `ejbCreate` callback method to create an instance of the MDB. The `ejbRemove` method is a callback method called by the container to notify the MDB before shutting it down. This gives the MDB an opportunity to do necessary cleanup. The main workhorse of the MDB is the `onMessage` method. That is where the main processing happens. The MDB listens on a particular queue, which actually means that the MDB registered its interest to monitor this queue and delegates this responsibility to the container. Accordingly, when a message arrives on this queue, the container calls the `onMessage` method of this MDB, passing the arrived message as a parameter.

Let's add the necessary processing logic to the `setMessageDrivenContext` and `onMessage` methods. Listing 10-1 shows the source code of `ReceivingMDBBean`.

Listing 10-1. The `ReceivingMDBBean` *MDB*

```
package apress.wsad.techlib;
import java.text.SimpleDateFormat;
import java.util.*;
import javax.ejb.CreateException;
import javax.ejb.EJBException;
import javax.jms.*;
import javax.naming.*;
import javax.naming.directory.*;
import javax.rmi.PortableRemoteObject;

/**
 * Bean implementation class for Enterprise Bean: ReceivingMDB
 */
public class ReceivingMDBBean
    implements javax.ejb.MessageDrivenBean, javax.jms.MessageListener
  {
    SaveMsgBook_notifyLocalHome saveMessagesLocalHome = null;
    SaveMsgBook_notifyLocal saveMessagesLocal = null;
    Object objRef= null;
```

```java
    private javax.ejb.MessageDrivenContext fMessageDrivenCtx;

    private String messageKey = "";
    private String messageBody = "";
    private Date today;

    InitialContext initContext = null;

  /**
   * getMessageDrivenContext
   */
  public javax.ejb.MessageDrivenContext getMessageDrivenContext()
   {
    return fMessageDrivenCtx;
   }

/**
 * setMessageDrivenContext
 */
public void setMessageDrivenContext(javax.ejb.MessageDrivenContext ctx)
{
  fMessageDrivenCtx = ctx;

}

/**
 * ejbCreate
 */
public void ejbCreate()
{

}

    /**
     * onMessage
     */
    public void onMessage(javax.jms.Message msg)
    {

    SimpleDateFormat sFormat;

    try
```

```
       {
    if (initContext == null)
     {
       initContext = new InitialContext();
     }

    if (objRef == null)
     {
       objRef = initContext.lookup("java:comp/env/Book_notify");

       saveMessagesLocalHome =
              (SaveMsgBook_notifyLocalHome) objRef;
         }

     TextMessage textMessage = (TextMessage) msg;
     String textBody = textMessage.getText();

     messageBody = "The book " + textBody + " is due to be returned";


     today = new Date();
     sFormat = new SimpleDateFormat("hh:mm:ss");

     messageKey = sFormat.format(today);

     System.out.println("Message: " + messageKey + " " + messageBody);

     //Save the message in the database
     saveMessagesLocal =
     saveMessagesLocalHome.create(messageKey, messageBody);

   } // Enf of try

catch (JMSException e)
 {
  System.out.println ("Error JMS Processing" + e.getMessage());
  e.printStackTrace();
 }

  catch (NamingException e)
  {
   System.out.println ("Error locating SaveMessage Local Home Interface" +
                                           e.getMessage());
```

```
      e.printStackTrace();
    }


    catch (CreateException e)
    {
     System.out.println ("Error creating the SaveMessage Local Interface" +
                                             e.getMessage());
      e.printStackTrace();
    }

  }

  /**
   * ejbRemove
   */
  public void ejbRemove()
  {
  }
}
```

Let's examine Listing 10-1. It uses the setMessageDrivenContext callback method to save the MessageDrivenContext passed here by the container as a parameter. At the beginning of the onMessage method, you do some initialization logic necessary for locating the Local Interface of the SaveMsgBook_notify entity bean. This logic can also be placed in the ejbCreate or setMessageDrivenContext methods (because these methods are called only once by the container). In the onMessage method, you get the message and cast it to the TextMessage type because you know the type of the message you expect to receive.

TIP *In general, it is good practice to first check for the type of arrived message and then cast it.*

Having the TextMessage object, you get the message body. Next, you use the time of the day to create a record key necessary for saving the message in the database. You print both the message key and the message body.

Next, you use the JNDI Local Interface of the SaveMsgBook_notify entity bean and call its create method with a full set of parameters to create the instance of the entity bean. With the creation of the entity bean instance, the received message will be saved in the BOOK_NOTIFY database table.

Right-click the `ReceivingJMSProjectEJB` and select `Generate ➤ Deploy and RMIC Code`. Figure 10-7 shows the next screen. On this screen, check `Book_notify` and make sure that the `ReceivingMDB` is unchecked.

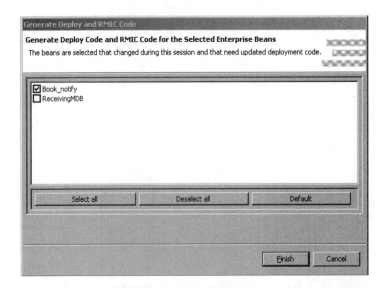

Figure 10-7. Generating the deployment and Remote Method Invocation Code (RMIC)

Click `Finish`. The deployment code and RMIC will be generated. Make sure there are no errors in the Tasks View.

NOTE *Remember that unlike session and entity beans, MDBs do not provide client interfaces (neither Local nor Remote) because they are never directly called by EJB clients. Therefore, you never generate deployment and RMIC code for MDBs.*

Creating the Test Server Project

Now, you need to set the development and runtime environments. You will create a new server project that will be used for testing both of your applications. Select `File ➤ New ➤ Project ➤ Server ➤ Server Project`. On the screen that appears, enter `JMSTestServerProject` in the `Project` name field. Click `Finish`. Next, right-click `JMSTestServerProject` and select `New ➤ Server and Server Configuration`. On the next screen, enter `JMSServer` in the `Server` name field. Select `WebSphere version 5.0 Test Environment` and click `Finish`.

In the Server Configuration View, right-click JMSServer, select Add ➤ ReceivingJMSProjectApp. This makes this server the default server for testing the ReceivingJMSProjectApp project. In the Server Configuration View, double-click JMSServer to open it in the Editor View. Click the Configuration tab. Figure 10-8 shows the JMSServer configuration. Check the Enable administration console and Enable universal test client boxes.

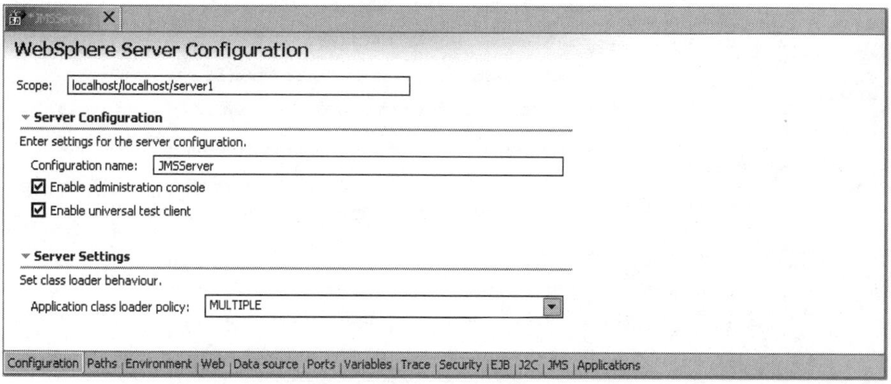

Figure 10-8. Enabling the Administrative Console and Universal Test Client

Configuring the Datasource

To configure the Datasource, click the Data Source tab and select Default DB2 JDBC Provider DB2. Next, click the Add button attached to the "Data source" section of the screen. Figure 10-9 shows the screen you use to set the Datasource. Make sure that the Datasource is called DBDatasource and its JNDI name is jdbc/DBDatasource.

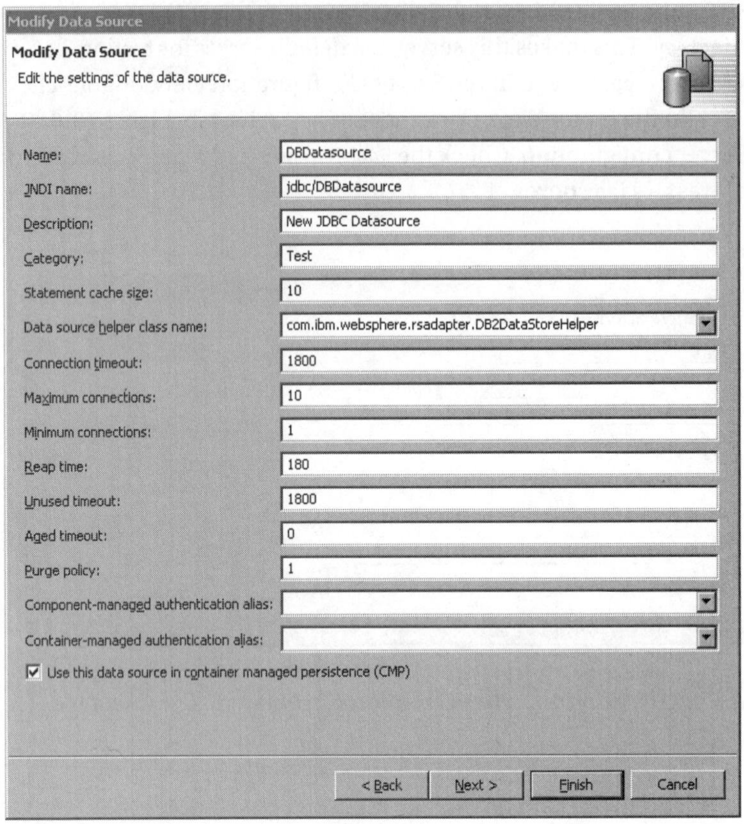

Figure 10-9. Setting DBDatasource

Click Next. On the next screen, shown in Figure 10-10, highlight the databaseName field and enter TECHBOOK in the Value field.

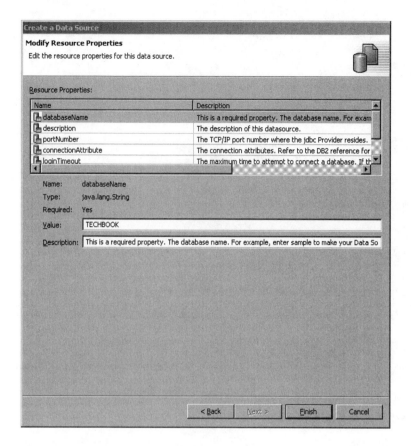

Figure 10-10. Setting the database name

Click Finish. You should see the Data sources page shown in Figure 10-11.

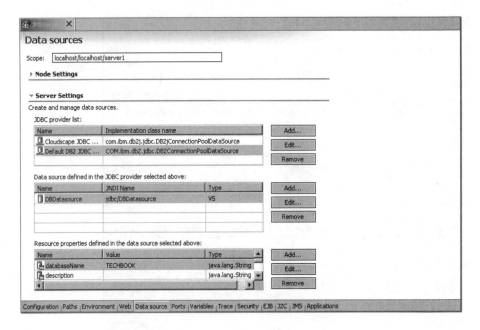

Figure 10-11. The Data sources *page*

In the next section, you will configure the JMS objects (also called *administered objects*) that are necessary for running this example.

Configuring JMS Administered Objects

Any JMS program requires the presence of the corresponding JMS-administered objects (queue connection factories and queues for the P2P domain or topic connection factories and topics for the Pub/Sub domain). You are developing this example to initially run as a JMS P2P application. Later, with minor changes, you will make this example run as a JMS Pub/Sub application. To support both the P2P and Pub/Sub domains for this example, you will set all the necessary administered objects (queue-related and topic-related). Click the JMS tab to configure the embedded JMS server and define the necessary administered objects (queue connection factory, queue, topic connection factory, and topic). You should see that you can do JMS configuration on three different levels:

- **Server**: The individual application server

- **Node**: A set of application servers running on the same machine/node

- **Cell**: A set of nodes that belong to a cell, which determines the scope of the availability of the administered objects

You will configure administered objects on the server level.

For the server-level setting, get to the "JMS Server Properties" section and click the Add button. Enter NotifyQ in the Queue Names field and click OK. The server will maintain this queue. In addition, select START as the server instance's Initial State. Select localhost in the Host field.

Scroll down to the "JMS Connection Factories" section. Click the Add button attached to the "WASQueueConnectionFactory entries" section of the screen. Figure 10-12 shows the next screen. Enter NotifyQCF in the Name field and jms/ NotifyQCF in the JNDI Name field. Select localhost as the Node. Click OK. Scroll to the "JMS Destination" section and click the Add button attached to the "WASQueue entries" section of the screen. Enter NotifyQ in the Name field and jms/NotifyQ in the JNDI Name field. Select localhost in the Node field.

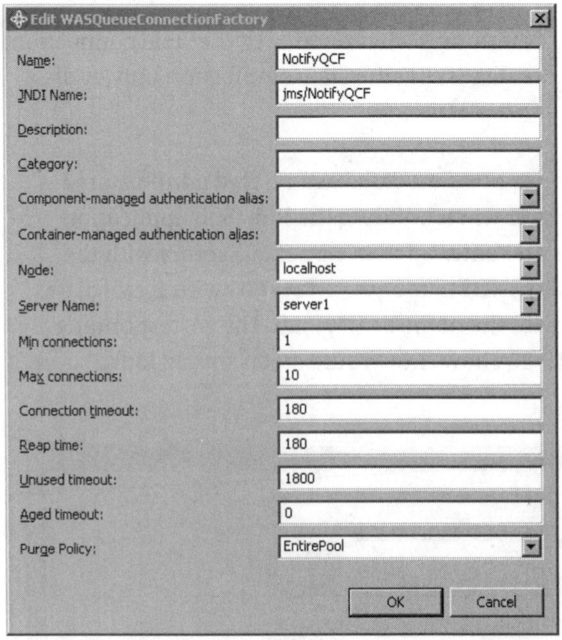

Figure 10-12. Configuring runtime connection factories

The following fields are available on this screen:

- The Min connections property determines the minimum number of physical connections to be maintained for the destination virtual channel (a queue in this case).

- The Max connections property determines the maximum number of physical connections that can be created.

- The Connection timeout property specifies the interval, in seconds, after which the connection request times out and an exception is thrown.

- The Reap time property specifies the interval, in seconds, between runs of the pool maintenance thread.

- The Unused timeout property specifies the interval, in seconds, after which an unused or idle connection is returned to the pool. This value must be higher than the Reap timeout property for optimum performance.

- The Aged timeout property specifies the interval, in seconds, after which the physical connection is discarded. This value must be higher than the Reap timeout property for optimum performance. A value of zero means active physical connections are never discarded from the pool.

- The Purge Policy property determines what to do with the stale connection. The available alternatives are discarding the stale connection only or discarding the entire pool of connections.

Click OK. As mentioned, you also build the Pub/Sub-related administered objects here. (You will use them later when building the Pub/Sub application example.) Repeat the same steps and enter a TopicConnectionFactory with the name NotifyTCF and corresponding JNDI name jms/NotifyTCF, with localhost as the selected node. Enter a topic with the name NotifyT and the corresponding JNDI name jms/NotifyT. Figure 10-13 shows how your screen should look.

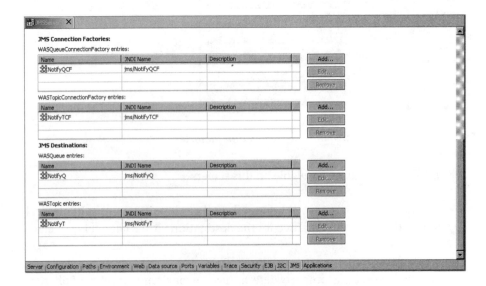

Figure 10-13. Setting queue and queue connection factory names

Configuring the Listener Port

Next, you add a new listener port. Click the EJB tab. Locate the "Listener Ports" section and click the Add button. Figure 10-14 shows the Add Listener Port screen that will appear. Enter TechLibListenerPort in the Name field. Select jms/NotifyQCF as the Connection Factory JNDI name. Select jms/NotifyQ as the Destination JNDI name. Make sure that the Initial State field is set to START, so when the server starts, the listener will also activate.

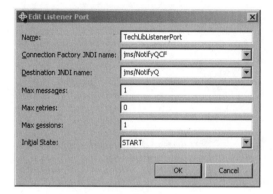

Figure 10-14. Mapping the listener port

The most significant fields on this screen are as follows:

- The Max messages property determines the maximum number of messages the listener can process in one JMS server session.

- The Max retries property of the listener port determines the maximum number of times the listener attempts to read a message from a destination (queue or topic). When the Max retries limit is reached, the listener for that destination stops. When the problem is resolved, the administrator must restart the listener. The zero value means no retries happen.

- The Max sessions property determines the maximum number of concurrent JMS server sessions used by listener to serve the associated MDB.

- The Initial State property determines the state of the listener port the next time the JMS server starts.

Click OK. Figure 10-15 shows the next screen. Notice that you mapped the listener port (TechLibListenerPort) to the destination queue named jms/NotifyQ, making the MDB effectively request the container to listen on the destination queue NotifyQ. You can also set the Datasource on the server level. Select DBDatasource in the Default data source field.

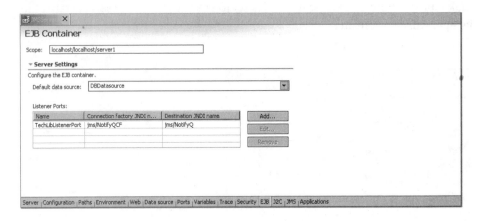

Figure 10-15. Mapping the listener port to a queue

Save the Server Configuration and close the Editor View.

TIP *When using an external JMS provider (such as WebSphere MQ), you need to make this configuration by using the WebSphere Administrative Console.*

Setting JMS Resource References

Make sure you are in the J2EE Perspective and J2EE Hierarchy View. Right-click the ReceivingJMSProjectEJB and select Open With ► Deployment Descriptor Editor. Click the References tab. This is the page for setting resource references. Because the ReceivingMDB MDB calls the create method of the Book_notify entity bean, you need to set the EJB Reference to the Book_notify entity bean. Highlight ReceivingMDB and click the Add button. Figure 10-16 shows the next screen. Check EJB local reference and click Next. On the next screen, click the Browse button attached to the Link field and select the Book_notify link. The rest of the fields will be automatically set. Change the Name field to Book_notify.

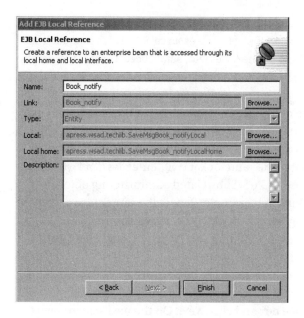

Figure 10-16. Setting a reference to the entity bean component

Click Finish. Click EJBLocalRef. Figure 10-17 shows the next screen. Change the value of the JNDI name field to ejb/Book_notify.

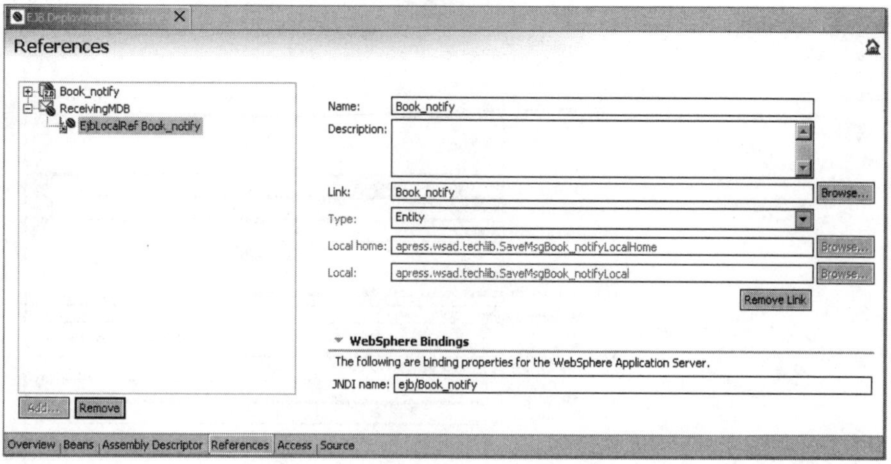

Figure 10-17. Setting the JNDI name for reference

Next, you need to add references to the administered objects. **Highlight** ReceivingMDB and click the Add button. Select EJB Resource Reference and click Next. On the next screen, enter NotifyQCF in the Name field; select QueueConnectionFactory in the Type field and Application in the Authentication field. Click Finish. **Highlight** ReceivingMDB again and click the Add button. Select EJB Resource Environment Reference and click Next. On the next screen, enter NotifyQ in the Name field; select Queue in the Type field. Click Finish. For each entered reference, highlight it and enter the corresponding name with the jms/ suffix in the JNDI Name field. Specifically, for NotifyQCF, enter jms/NotifyQCF, and for NotifyQ, enter jms/NotifyQ.

You will also enter references for Pub/Sub-related administering objects, which you will use later in the Pub/Sub example. Repeat the same steps and enter NotifyTCF and the corresponding jms/ NotifyTCF (select TopicConnectionFactory as the type). Enter NotifyT and the corresponding jms/ NotifyT (select Topic as the type).

For the Book_notify entity bean, you need to build the reference to the Datasource resource. Highlight the Book_notify entity bean and click the Add button. Select the EJB Resource Reference box and click Next. On the next screen, select javax.sql.DataSource as the resource type. Enter DBDatasource in the Name field, and select Application in the Authentication field. Click Finish. The ResourceRef Datasource reference will appear under Book_notify. Highlight this resource reference and enter jdbc/DBDatasource in the JNDI Name field. Your final screen should look like the one shown in Figure 10-18.

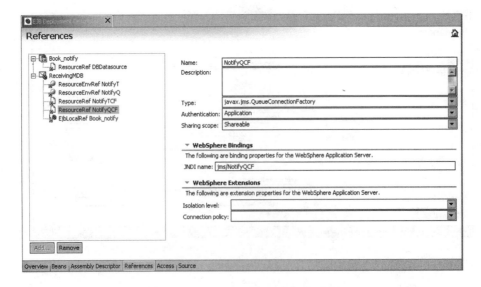

Figure 10-18. Setting the JNDI name reference to the Book_notify *entity bean*

Click the Assembly Descriptor tab, locate the "Container Transaction" section, and click the Add button. On the screen that appears, select both components (Book_notify and ReceivingMDB) and click Next. On the next screen, shown in Figure 10-19, expand the Book_notify entity bean and check the create method with two parameters. Expand ReceivingMDB and check the onMessage method. Finally, select NotSupported in the Container transaction type field.

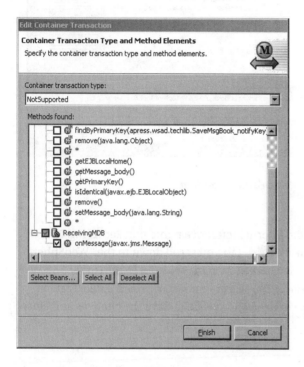

Figure 10-19. Setting a reference to the entity bean component

Click Finish. Figure 10-20 shows the next screen. Here, you will configure the Book_notify entity bean. Click the Beans tab. Highlight Book_notify and enter Book_notify in the Display name field. Enter ejb/Book_notify in the JNDI name field.

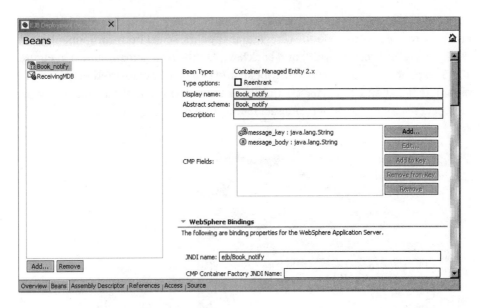

Figure 10-20. Configuring the entity bean component

Notice that Book_notify is the internal reference name that ReceivingMDB uses to call this entity bean. Click the Overview tab and scroll down to the "WebSphere Bindings" section. Make sure that DB2UDBNT_V72_1 is selected in the Current backend ID field. Select Per_Connection_Factory in the Container authorization type field and jdbc/DBDatasource in the JNDI name field. Save the changes and close the Editor View.

Testing the Receiving Side of the Application

You are ready to test this project. Switch to the Server Perspective and start JMSServer. Wait for the server to start, right-click ReceivingJMSProjectEJB, and select Run on Server. The IBM Universal Test Client will appear. Click JNDI Explorer to get to the screen shown in Figure 10-21. Expand the Local EJB beans and ejb entries.

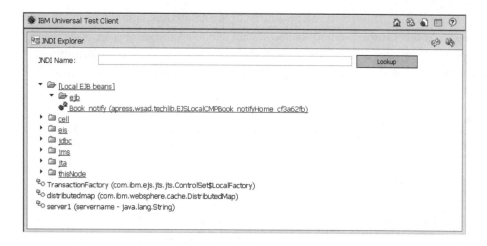

Figure 10-21. The Universal Test Client

Click Book_notify. To test the Book_notify entity bean, expand
SaveMsgBook_notifyLocal and SaveMsgBook_notifyLocalHome. On the next screen,
shown in Figure 10-22, you should see the create method with two String type
parameters. Click it. You are prompted to add two parameters. The first parameter
is messageKey, and the second parameter is messageBody. Enter Message 1 in the first
field and The book you rented is due to be returned in the second field.

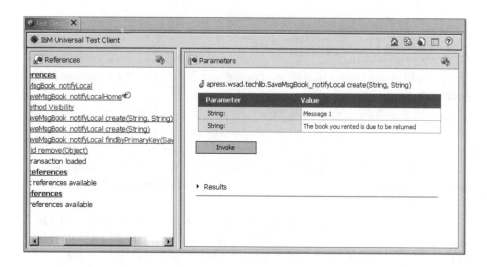

Figure 10-22. Testing the create *method*

Click `Invoke`. The record will be written to the database. Click `Work with Object`. Now, the object's local methods become available. Click the `getMessage_body` method. Next, click `Invoke`. Figure 10-23 shows the subsequent screen. You should see the `messageBody` you just entered: "The book you rented is due to be returned."

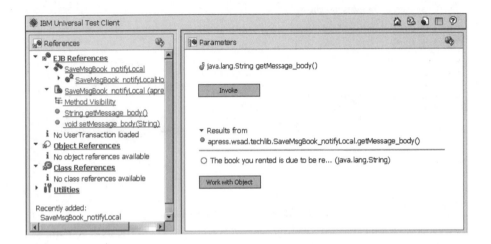

Figure 10-23. Testing the `getMessage` *method*

Close the Test Client Web Browser View and stop the server.

Developing the Sending Part

Now, you will create the second project called `SendingJMSProjectWEB` and the corresponding enterprise application project called `SendingJMSProjectApp`. You will build the servlet called `SendingServlet`, which functions as a JMS client that sends messages to the `NotifyQ` queue. Switch to the Web Perspective and select `File` ➤ `New` ➤ `Web Project`. On the screen that appears, enter `SendingJMSProjectWEB` in the `Project Name` field. Uncheck `Create default CSS file` and click `Next`. On the next screen, select a new enterprise application project and name it `SendingJMSProjectApp`. Click `Finish`.

Right-click `SendingJMSProjectWEB` and select `New` ➤ `Other` ➤ `Web` ➤ `Servlet`. On the next screen, enter `apress.wsad.techlib` in the `Package` field and `SendingServlet` in the `Class Name` field. Click `Finish`. WSAD will generate the skeleton of the `SendingServlet` servlet class and open it in the Editor View. You now need to add the necessary processing logic. Listing 10-2 shows the source code of the `SendingServlet.java` class.

Listing 10-2. SendingServlet.java

```java
package apress.wsad.techlib;
import javax.jms.*;
import javax.naming.*;
import java.util.*;
import java.io.IOException;
import javax.servlet.ServletException;

import javax.servlet.http.HttpServlet;
import javax.servlet.http.HttpServletRequest;
import javax.servlet.http.HttpServletResponse;

public class SendingServlet extends HttpServlet
{
    String queueConnectionFactoryName = "java:comp/env/NotifyQCF";
    String queueName = "java:comp/env/NotifyQ";
    String[] messageList = {"Enterprise Java",
                            "Using HTML",
                            "Java in a Nutshell",
                            "EJB Design Patterns",
                            "Hacking Java"
                           };

    private QueueConnectionFactory queueConnectionFactory = null;
    private Queue requestQueue = null;
    private QueueConnection queueConnection = null;
    private QueueSender queueSender = null;
    private QueueSession queueSession = null;

    public void doDelete(HttpServletRequest req, HttpServletResponse resp)
        throws ServletException, IOException
    {

    }

    public void doGet(HttpServletRequest req, HttpServletResponse resp)
        throws ServletException, IOException
    {
     processRequest();
    }

    public void doPost(HttpServletRequest req, HttpServletResponse resp)
```

```
        throws ServletException, IOException
{
 processRequest();
}

public void init() throws ServletException
{

 super.init();

 // Get Administered object (only once per servlet)
  try
   {
    InitialContext initContext = new InitialContext();
    queueConnectionFactory =
        (QueueConnectionFactory)
          initContext.lookup(queueConnectionFactoryName);

    requestQueue = (Queue) initContext.lookup(queueName);

    queueConnection = queueConnectionFactory.createQueueConnection();
    queueConnection.start();


   }
  catch(NamingException ne)
   {
     System.out.println("Error locating Administrated Objects " +
            ne.getMessage());
   }

  catch(JMSException je)
   {
      System.out.println("JMS Exception " + je.getMessage());
      Exception le = je.getLinkedException();
      if (le != null)
       {
        System.out.println("Linked Exception " + le.getMessage());
       }
   }
 }

public void processRequest()
```

```
{
 try
  {
   queueSession =
     queueConnection.createQueueSession(false, Session.AUTO_ACKNOWLEDGE);

   QueueSender queueSender = queueSession.createSender(requestQueue);

   // Send five message
   for (int i = 0; i < 5; i++)
    {
     TextMessage message = queueSession.createTextMessage(messageList[i]);
     Thread.sleep(10000);
     queueSender.send(message);


    }
  } // End of try

catch(JMSException je)
 {
  System.out.println("Send message failed " + je.getMessage());
 }
catch(InterruptedException se)
 {
   System.out.println("Interrupted exception for sleep" +
                                        se.getMessage());
 }

// Clean up. Make sure that Administered objects are closed
finally
 {
  if (queueSender != null)
    try
     {
      queueSender.close();
     }
   catch (JMSException je) {}

  if (queueSession != null)
   try
    {
     queueSession.close();
```

```
      }
    catch (JMSException je) {}

   if (queueConnection != null)
    try
     {
      queueConnection.close();
     }
    catch (JMSException je) {}

  } // End of finally

 } // End processRequest method

} // End of the class
```

Let's examine the SendingServlet source code. This servlet acts as a JMS client, putting messages on the NotifyQ queue. First, you need to use JNDI and locate two administered objects: QueueConnectionFactory and Queue. A QueueConnection is started. This logic is performed in the init method because it needs to execute only once. Next, the doGet method executes. From this method, you call the processRequest method where JMS processing logic resides. Here, you run a loop producing five messages and put them on the NotifyQ queue. Inside the loop, you use the sleep statement to avoid duplication of the record keys that are built based on the current time. In the finally method, you close all opened objects. Save the results and close the editor.

Next, you need to include this project in the JMSServer configuration. Right-click JMSServer and select Add ➤ SendingJMSProjectApp. Then, you need to set the development and runtime environment. Switch to the J2EE Perspective, right-click SendingJMSProjectWEB and select Open With ➤ Deployment Descriptor Editor. Click the References tab. Figure 10-24 shows the next screen. Highlight the Resource tab at the top of the screen. Click the Add button. Replace Resource Reference with NotifyQCF. Click Browse, navigate to QueueConnectionFactory, select it, and click OK. Select Application in the Authentication field and put jms/NotifyQCF in the JNDI Name field. Set the Isolation level field to TRANSACTION_NONE.

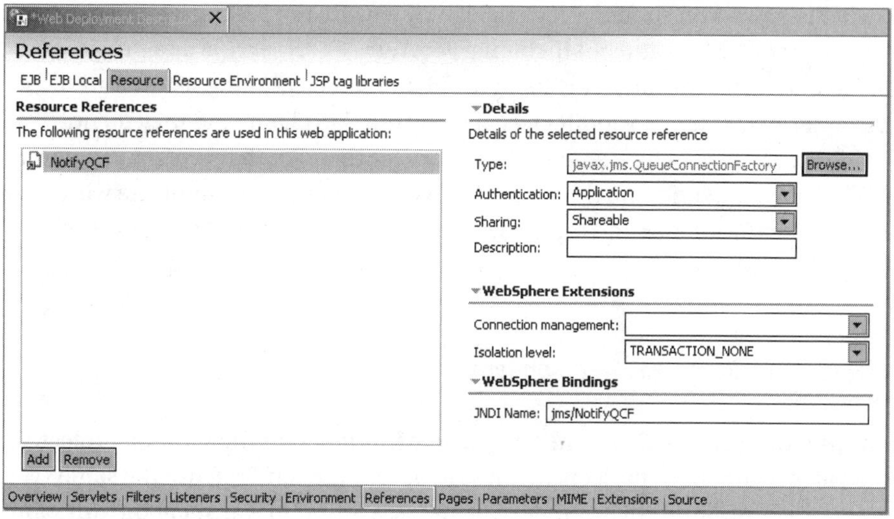

Figure 10-24. Configuring QueueConnectionFactory

On the same page, highlight the Resource Environment tab at the top of the screen. Click the Add button. Replace the Resource Environment Reference name with NotifyQ. Click Browse, navigate to the Queue interface, select it, and click OK. Enter jms/NotifyQ in the JNDI Name field. Figure 10-25 shows how your screen should look.

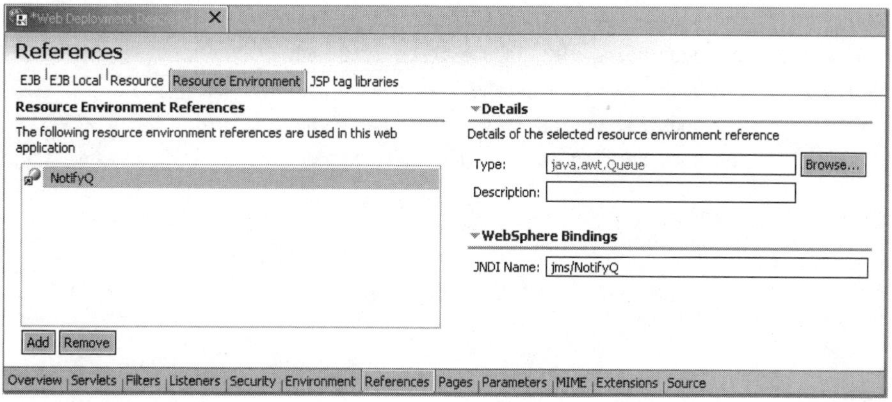

Figure 10-25. Configuring Queue

At this point, you should ask yourself why you are not setting a reference to the `ReceivingMDB` MDB and not including `ReceivingJMSProjectEJB` as a project you need to reference. The answer is that you are not directly calling `ReceivingMDB`. Remember, MDBs are never directly called by the JMS client, and they do not provide (neither Local nor Remote) interfaces for that. For that reason, you never create deployment and RMIC code for MDBs. JMS clients communicate with MDB indirectly via the queues and topics, which means less work for you. Save the results and close the editor.

Setting the Runtime Environment

Next, you would normally set the runtime environment for the sending project. However, because both projects (the receiving and the sending) use the same `JMSServer` as a runtime environment, the necessary option was set at the time you configured the receiving project. You can check that the necessary setting is there. In the server configuration, double-click `JMSServer` to open it in the Editor View. Click the `JMS` and `EJB` tabs to do that. Finally, close the editor.

You are now ready to execute the example. Both enterprise projects, `SendingJMSProjectApp` and `ReceivingJMSProjectApp`, are included in `JMSServer`; therefore, starting this server automatically activates the `ReceivingMDB` MDB because you set the `Initial State` value to `START`.

Right-click `SendingServlet.java` and select `Run on Server`. The five messages should display in the Console View.

```
04:43:11      The book Enterprise Java is due to be returned.
04:46:34      The book Using HTML is due to be returned.
04:58:23      The book Java in a Nutshell is due to be returned.
04:58:27      The book EJB Design Patterns is due to be returned.
04:58:28      The book Hacking Java is due to be returned.
```

When the processing is done, you should see five messages added to the BOOK_NOTIFY table. Activate a DB2 command window and issue the following commands:

```
DB2 connect to TECHBOOK.
DB2 select * from LIB.BOOK_NOTIFY
```

The execution results are as follows:

```
Database Connection Information
Database server       = DB2/NT 7.2.4
SQL authorization ID  = c6023
Local database alias  = TECHBOOK
```

Stop the server and close the DB2 command window. Congratulations on developing your first WSAD P2P JMS application! In the next section, you will develop a similar Pub/Sub application.

Developing a Publish/Subscribe JMS Application

Next, you will use the same projects for developing a Pub/Sub application. On the sending side, you will develop a new servlet called PublishingServlet that publishes messages on a topic. On the receiving side, all you need to do is to make your ReceivingMDB MDB listen on a topic instead of on a queue. You will start your development from the receiving side. The receiving ReceivingMDB MDB listens on the port TechLibListenerPort. In the previous example, you mapped this port to the NotifyQ queue. Now, you will remap it to the topic called NotifyT. With this introduction, let's start developing the example.

Setting Administered Objects

Switch to the Server Perspective. In the Server Configuration View, double-click JMSServer to open its configuration in the Editor View. Here, you need to set the properties of TopicConnectionFactory and Topic. However, you already did this during the development of the P2P example. Figure 10-26 displays this setting.

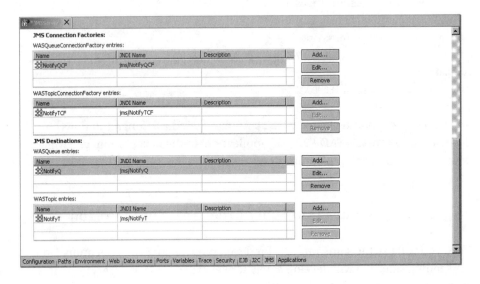

Figure 10-26. Setting TopicConnectionFactory *and* Topic

Next, you want your MDB to listen on the topic and not on the queue. Click the EJB tab. You will see the screen depicted in Figure 10-27. Highlight TechLibListenerPort and click the Edit button. On the pop-up screen, select NotifyTCF in the Connection Factory JNDI name field and jms/NotifyT in the Destination JNDI name field. Make sure that the Initial State is set to START, so when the server starts, the MDB will be activated automatically.

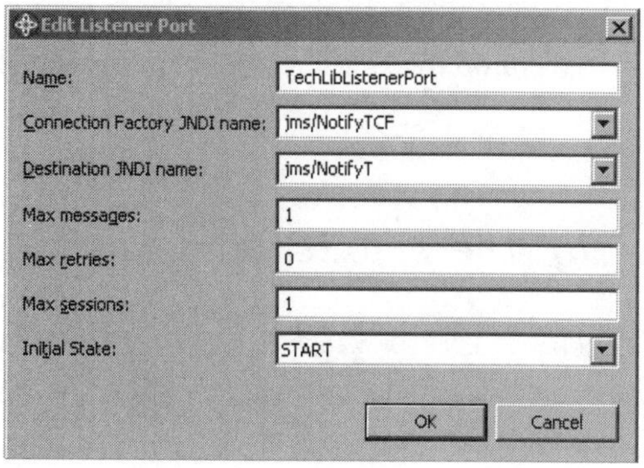

Figure 10-27. The EJB *tab*

Click OK. Save and close the JMSServer configuration. In the J2EE Perspective, expand ReceivingJMSProjectEJB and double-click its EJB Deployment Descriptor.

Click the Beans tab and highlight ReceivingMDB. For the P2P example, the Destination type field was Queue. Now, change it to Topic. Figure 10-28 shows how your screen should look.

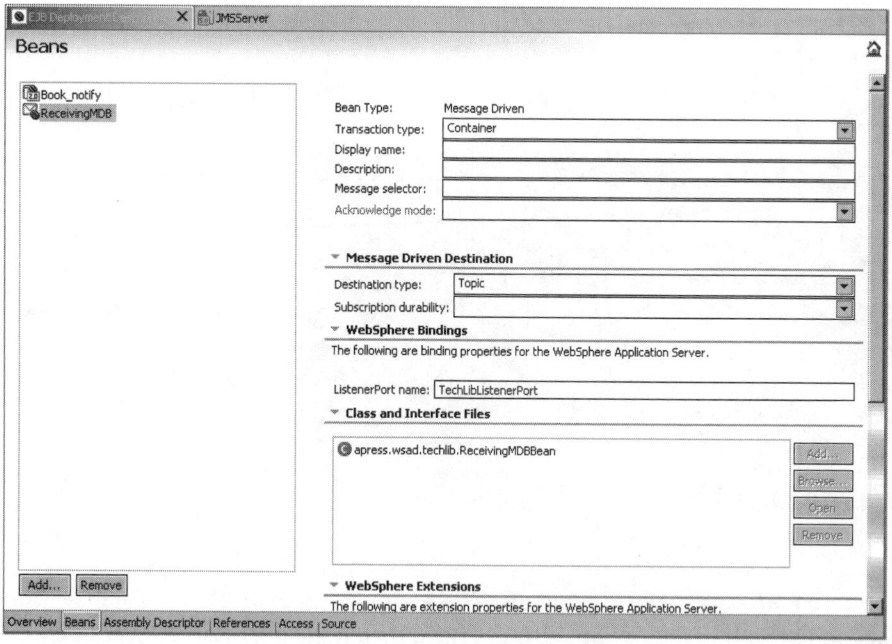

Figure 10-28. Setting the destination type for the ReceivingMDB *component*

Click OK. Save the results and close the editor. After the necessary administered objects are in place, you are ready to develop the sending application. That is
what you will do in the next section.

Building the Sending Part of the Application

Right-click SendingJMSProjectWEB and select New ➤ Other ➤ Web ➤ Servlet. On the next
screen, enter apress.wsad.techlib in the Java Package field and PublishingServlet in
the Class Name field. Figure 10-29 shows how your screen should look.

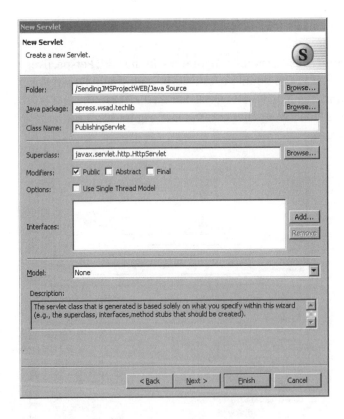

Figure 10-29. Building PublishingServlet

Click Finish. WSAD will generate the skeleton of the PublishingServlet servlet
class and open it in the Editor View. You need to add the necessary processing
logic. Listing 10-3 shows the source code of the PublishingServlet.java class.

Listing 10-3. PublishingServlet

```java
package apress.wsad.techlib;
import javax.jms.*;
import javax.naming.*;
import java.util.*;

import java.io.IOException;
import javax.servlet.ServletException;

import javax.servlet.http.HttpServlet;
import javax.servlet.http.HttpServletRequest;
import javax.servlet.http.HttpServletResponse;

public class PublishingServlet extends HttpServlet
{
    String topicConnectionFactoryName = "java:comp/env/NotifyTCF";
    String topicName = "java:comp/env/NotifyT";
    String[] messageList = {"WinSock 2.0",
                            "NT Services",
                            "Visual C++",
                            "Socket Programming",
                            "Mastering Delphi"
                            };

    private TopicConnectionFactory topicConnectionFactory = null;
 private Topic requestTopic = null;
 private TopicConnection topicConnection = null;
    private TopicPublisher topicPublisher = null;
    private TopicSession topicSession = null;

    public void doDelete(HttpServletRequest req, HttpServletResponse resp)
        throws ServletException, IOException
    {
     processRequest();
    }

    public void doGet(HttpServletRequest req, HttpServletResponse resp)
        throws ServletException, IOException
    {
     processRequest();
    }
```

```java
public void doPost(HttpServletRequest req, HttpServletResponse resp)
    throws ServletException, IOException
{
 processRequest();
 }

public void init() throws ServletException
{

  super.init();

    // Get administered object (only once per servlet)
  try
   {
    InitialContext initContext = new InitialContext();
    topicConnectionFactory =
     (TopicConnectionFactory) initContext.lookup(topicConnectionFactoryName);

    requestTopic = (Topic) initContext.lookup(topicName);

    topicConnection = topicConnectionFactory.createTopicConnection();
    topicConnection.start();


   }
  catch(NamingException ne)
   {
       System.out.println("Error locating Administrated Objects " +
                                   ne.getMessage());

   }

  catch(JMSException je)
   {
       System.out.println("JMS Exception " + je.getMessage());
       Exception le = je.getLinkedException();
       if (le != null)
   {
     System.out.println("Linked Exception " + le.getMessage());
       }
   }


 }
```

```java
public void processRequest()
{
  try
   {


    topicSession =
    topicConnection.createTopicSession(false, Session.AUTO_ACKNOWLEDGE);

    TopicPublisher topicPublisher = topicSession.createPublisher(requestTopic);

    // Send five messages
    for (int i = 0; i < 5; i++)
     {

      TextMessage message = topicSession.createTextMessage(messageList[i]);
      Thread.sleep(10000);
      topicPublisher.publish(message);

     }
   } // End of try

  catch(JMSException je)
   {
    System.out.println("Publish message failed " + je.getMessage());
   }

  catch(InterruptedException se)
   {
    System.out.println("Interrupted exception for sleep" + se.getMessage());
   }

  // Clean up. Make sure that Administered objects are closed
  finally
   {
    if (topicPublisher != null)
     try
      {
       topicPublisher.close();
      }
    catch (JMSException je) {}

    if (topicSession != null)
```

```
    try
     {
      topicSession.close();
     }
    catch (JMSException je) {}

   if (topicConnection != null)
    try
     {
      topicConnection.close();
     }
    catch (JMSException je) {}

  } // End of finally

 } // End processRequest method
}
```

Let's examine the PublishingServlet source code. Again, the servlet acts as a JMS client, publishing messages on the NotifyT topic. Before doing this, you need to use JNDI and locate two administered objects: TopicConnectionFactory and Topic. This logic is performed in the init method because it needs to execute only once. Next, the doGet method executes. From this method, you call the processRequest method where the JMS processing logic resides. Here, you run a loop, produce five messages, and publish them on the NotifyT topic (you set different book titles in this program to distinguish them from messages that came from the queue). Inside the loop, you use the sleep statement to avoid duplication of the record keys that are built based on the current time. In the finally method, you close all opened objects. Save the results and close the editor.

Setting References to the Administered Objects

Next, you need to add the topic-related administered objects to the development environment. Switch to the J2EE Perspective and J2EE Hierarchy View, right-click SendingJMSProjectWEB, and select Open With ➤ Deployment Descriptor Editor. Click the References tab. There are several reference-related tabs located at the top of the page. Two of these tabs are used for setting the JMS-related resources. The Resource tab is used for setting the connection factories (queue or topic related). The Resource Environment tab is used for setting the destination objects (queues and topics).

Highlight the Resource tab at the top of the screen. Click the Add button. Replace the resource reference name with NotifyTCF. Click Browse, navigate to TopicConnectionFactory, select it, and click OK. Select Application in the Authentication field, select TRANSACTION_NONE in the Isolation Level field, and enter jms/NotifyTCF in the JNDI Name field. Figure 10-30 shows the completed screen.

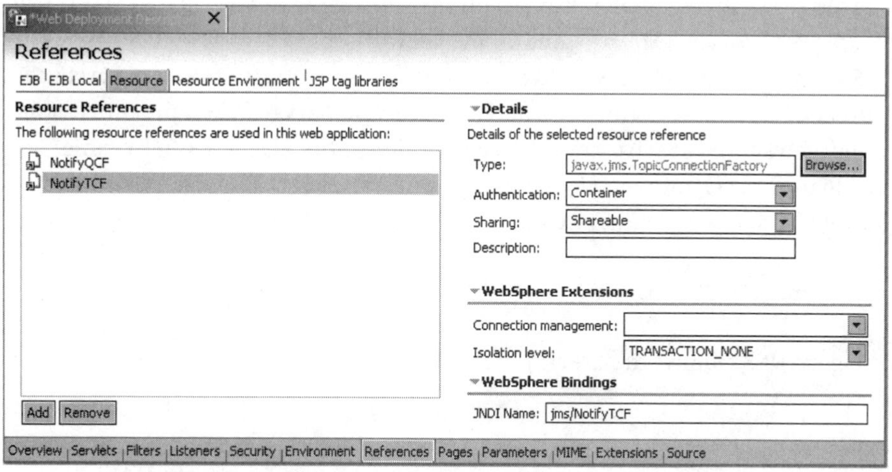

Figure 10-30. Configuring the topic connection factory

On the same page, highlight the Resource Environment tab at the top of the screen. Click the Add button. Replace the resource environment reference name with NotifyT. Click Browse, navigate to javax.jms.Topic, select it, and click OK. Enter jms/NotifyT in the JNDI name field. Figure 10-31 shows how the completed screen should look.

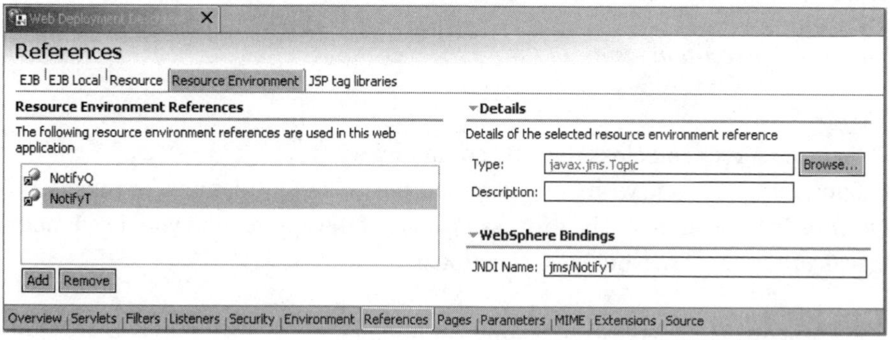

Figure 10-31. Configuring the topic

523

Remember that you already set the runtime environment and mapped the listener port to the NotifyT topic. Save the results and close the editor.

Testing the Pub/Sub Application

You are ready to execute the example. Again, starting JMSServer automatically activates the ReceivingMDB MDB because you set the Initial State value to START. This time, the ReceivingMDB MDB listens on the NotifyT topic.

Switch to the Server Perspective and start JMSServer. When the server is started, right-click PublishingServlet.java and select Run on Server. When the processing is done, you should see five new messages added to the BOOK_NOTIFY table. Activate the DB2 Command Center, click Interactive, and connect to the TECHBOOK database. Next, issue the following statement:

```
select * from LIB.BOOK_NOTIFY
```

Figure 10-32 shows the execution results.

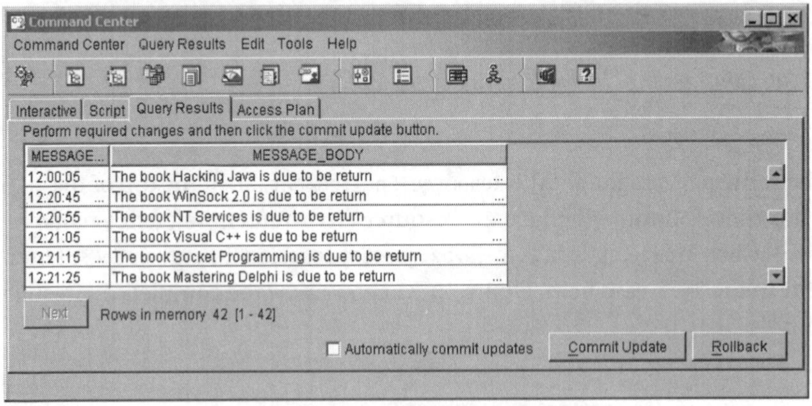

Figure 10-32. Execution results of the Pub/Sub example

Stop the server and close the DB2 command window.

Something is wrong with these two examples. (Congratulations for those who have already noticed this!) The processing logic of the application you developed consists primarily of two business functions:

- Receiving a message from a queue or topic

- Writing this message in a database table

Each of these business functions is performed by an independent sub-system—JMS and Java Database Connectivity (JDBC). Because the entire processing happens outside of the transaction context, these two business functions are uncoordinated and could potentially lead to the data integrity problem. The next section discusses how this application should be developed to maintain data integrity.

Using Two-Phase Commit Transactions

These two examples are fine for the initial demonstration of JMS processing. However, they are hardly suitable for the real application—not just because they are simple but because their designs have a serious flaw. Let's come back to the processing these examples do on the receiving side.

The ReceivingMDB MDB receives messages from the NotifyQ queue or NotifyT topic and calls the SaveMsgBook_notify CMP entity bean to save the messages in the database. For both examples, you selected the NotRequired transaction type, effectively running your receiving-side processing outside of the transaction context.

To run under the transaction context, the receiving side requires support of two-phase commit processing. Indeed, to maintain data integrity, you should receive a message and put it in a database inside a single unit of work (or transaction). Outside of the transaction context, reading a message and writing it in the database can go uncoordinated. Reading a message can be successful but writing it to a database cannot be. This would be the equivalent of missing the message. Therefore, the two-phase commit is necessary to coordinate two independent processing subsystems: JMS and the database.

To support two-phase commit processing, you need to use the XA-compliant database driver and XA-compliant administered objects (queue and topic connection factories, queues, and topics). In this example, the ReceivingMDB MDB does not directly manipulate administered objects (the container does). Therefore, it is sufficient for this example to change only the database driver to the XA-compliant DB2 database driver. Switch to the Server Perspective. Double-click JMSServer in the server configuration and click the Data Sources tab. Then select DB2 JDBC Provider and click the Edit button. On the Create a JDBC Provider dialog shown in Figure 10-33, change the Name and Description fields to DB2 JDBC Provider (XA). Select COM.ibm.db2.jdbc.DB2XADataSource as the Implementation class name.

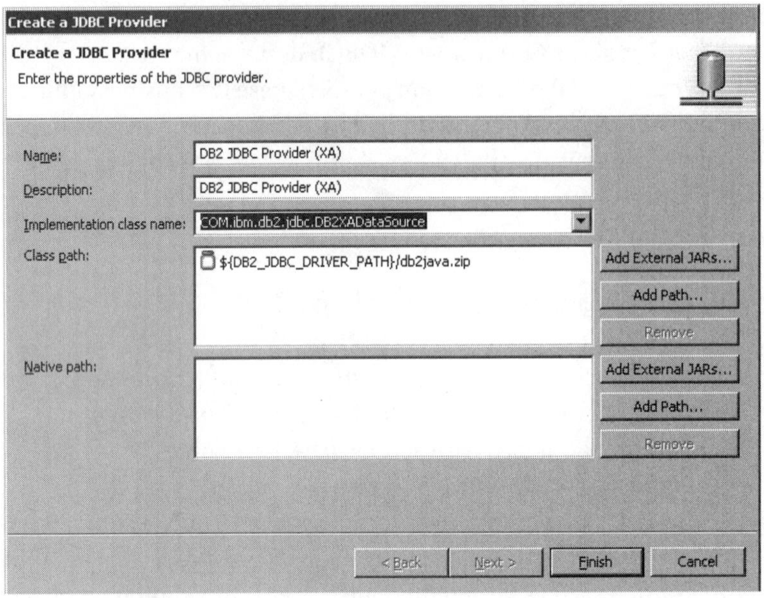

Figure 10-33. Selecting the XA-compliant DB2 driver

Click Finish. Next, select this JDBC provider and click the Add button next to the Data sources list. Select the new DB2 JDBC Provider (XA) and click Next. Enter DBDatasourceXA in the Name field and jdbc/DBDatasourceXA in the JNDI name field. Make sure that the Use this data source in container managed persistence (CMP) box is checked. Figure 10-34 shows the completed screen.

Click Finish. Finally, highlight the database name and enter TECHBOOK in the resource properties' Name field, as shown in Figure 10-35. Click Finish. Save and close the JMSServer configuration. Now, you need to change the transaction-related settings. Open the Deployment Descriptor for ReceivingJMSProjectEJB and click the Assembly Descriptor tab. Locate the "Container Transactions" section, highlight NotSupported, and click the Edit button. On the screen shown in Figure 10-36, replace NotSupported with Required.

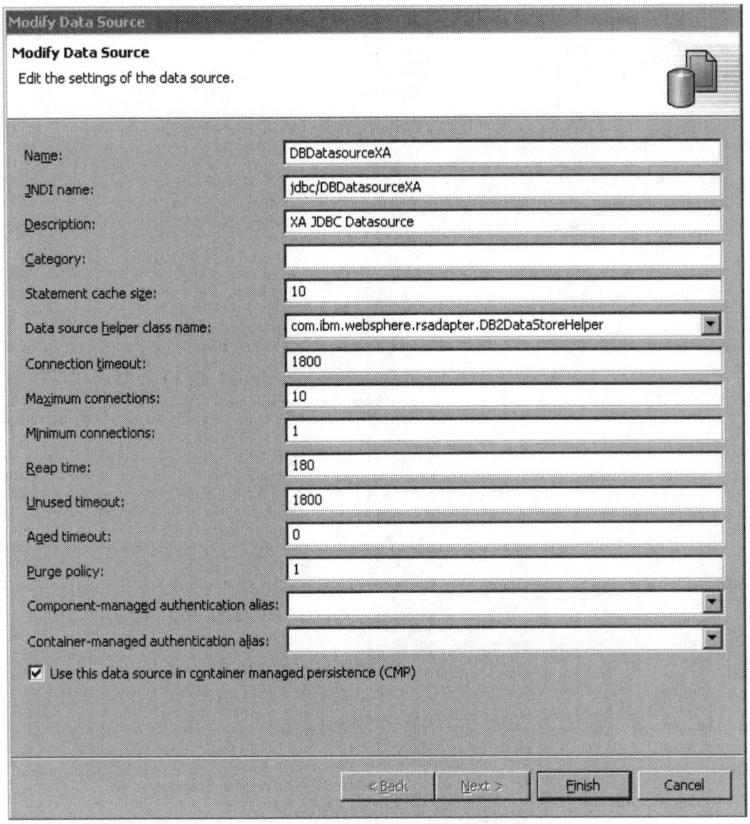

Figure 10-34. Setting the XA-compliant Datasource

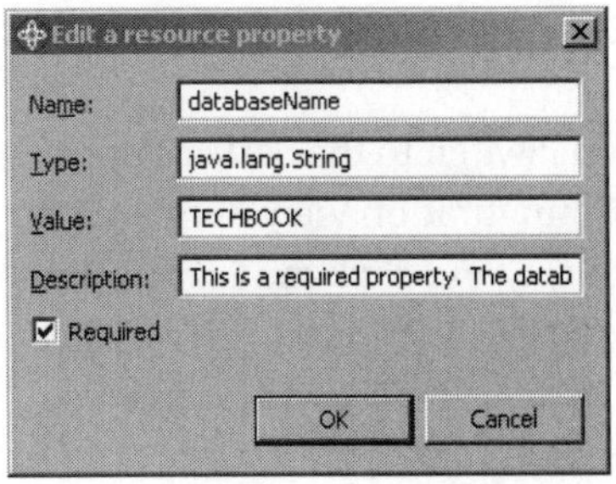

Figure 10-35. Setting the database name for the XA-compliant Datasource

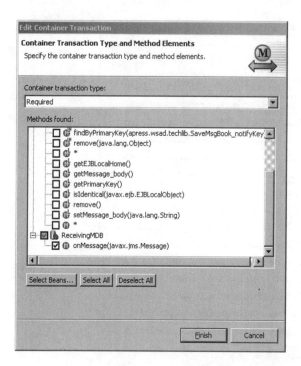

Figure 10-36. Changing the transaction setting to Required

You also need to change the Book_notify entity bean Datasource reference. Click the References tab. You will see the screen shown in Figure 10-37. Expand Book_notify, highlight the ResourceRef DBDatasourceXA reference, and change the Name field to DBDatasourceXA. Change the JNDI name field to jdbc/DBDatasourceXA and change the Isolation Level field to TRANSACTION_READ_COMMITTED.

Save the results and close the editor.

Now it's time to get back to the P2P JMS domain. Switch to the Server Perspective and double-click JMSServer in the Server Configuration View to open it for editing. Click the EJB tab, highlight TechLibListenerPort, and click the Edit button. Replace jms/NotifyTCF with jms/NotifyQCF and jms/NotifyT with jms/NotifyQ. Click OK. Also, make sure that DBDatasourceXA is selected in the Default data source field, as shown in Figure 10-38.

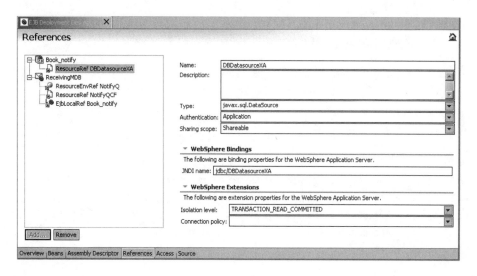

Figure 10-37. The processing results

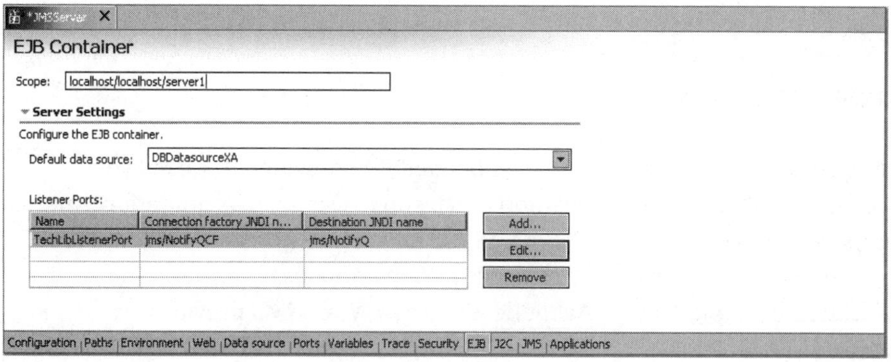

Figure 10-38. Setting the listener port

In addition, open the Deployment Descriptor for the ReceivingJMSProjectEJB, click the Beans tab, and select ReceivingMDB. Locate the "Message Driven Destination" section and change the DestinationType from Topic to Queue. Save and close the editor.

Now, you will test the two-phase commit application.

With this Datasource setting, the receiving side will run under the two-phase commit transaction mode. The execution results are as follows:

```
Database Connection Information
Database server      = DB2/NT 7.2.4
SQL authorization ID = c6023
Local database alias = TECHBOOK


08:56:28      The book Enterprise Java is due to be returned.
08:56:33      The book Using HTML is due to be returned.
04:56:38      The book Java in a Nutshell is due to be returned.
04:56:43      The book EJB Design Patterns is due to be returned.
04:56:48      The book Hacking Java is due to be returned.
5 record(s) selected
```

You need to make similar changes to the Pub/Sub application. This concludes the examples of developing JMS applications for the WAS 5.0 embedded JMS provider.

Summary

This chapter covered the WSAD 5.0 embedded JMS provider. It walked you through the JMS provider installation and testing, discussed its limitations, and compared it to WebSphere MQ as a JMS provider. Next, you developed two J2EE applications utilizing the JMS P2P and Pub/Sub domains.

The next chapter covers WebSphere MQ as a WSAD JMS provider.

CHAPTER 11

Using WebSphere MQ as the JMS Provider

THE PREVIOUS CHAPTER discussed the embedded WebSphere Java Message Service (JMS) provider, which is now part of the WebSphere Studio Application Developer (WSAD) package. You also learned that although the embedded WebSphere JMS provider is a useful tool, it has some serious limitations and is mostly suitable for application development and simple runtime environments because it is merely a subset of the full WebSphere MQ package. Java 2 Enterprise Edition (J2EE) JMS applications using the embedded WebSphere JMS provider can only communicate with other J2EE JMS applications that also use the embedded WebSphere JMS provider and that run on a node that belongs to the same WebSphere cell.

The main limitation of the embedded WebSphere JMS provider is its lack of support for MQ channels. JMS applications that use the embedded WebSphere JMS provider cannot communicate with remote MQ applications, so they are unable to support legacy applications. Furthermore, the embedded WebSphere JMS provider does not support encrypted communication.

Fortunately, both WSAD 5.0 and WebSphere Application Server (WAS) 5.0 allow close integration with MQ messaging middleware and can use MQ as a JMS provider. J2EE JMS applications that use the MQ JMS provider are able to communicate remotely over MQ communication channels with J2EE and non-J2EE applications running on a variety of platforms. These applications are even able to communicate with non-Java (legacy MQ) applications; however, it requires more programming efforts to reconcile JMS and native MQ message formats.

This chapter introduces you to MQ messaging middleware, shows you how to install MQ, and explains how to configure it as the WSAD JMS provider. You will also see that JMS applications that use the MQ JMS provider are capable of using JMS objects built by the embedded WebSphere JMS provider. You will also learn how to use native MQ tools (such as MQ Explorer and JMSAdmin) for building JMS objects. Finally, you will develop and test Point-to-Point (P2P) and Publish/Subscribe (Pub/Sub) JMS applications that use MQ as the JMS provider.

The chapter begins by introducing MQ.

Introducing WebSphere MQ

Among the messaging middleware software packages currently available, IBM's WebSphere MQ controls more than 80 percent of the market. WebSphere MQ was called *MQSeries*, but IBM renamed it recently, emphasizing its importance for the J2EE technology (the package became a member of the WebSphere family of enterprise products).

MQ supports more than 36 platforms and is capable of providing assured one-time message delivery to the target destination. With MQ, programs involved in a communication session are loosely coupled; in other words, they do not communicate directly with each other but via virtual channels called *queues* and *topics*. In the simple scenario shown in Figure 11-1, a sending program puts messages on the Q1 queue, and a receiving program reads messages from this queue.

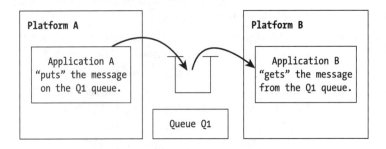

Figure 11-1. Simplified MQ message processing

Two fundamentally important features of MQ are asynchronous communication and assured message delivery based on store-and-forward technology. For two applications involved in asynchronous communication, the receiving side of the communication session does not need to be up and running. Even if a network is down, the sending side can continue to work.

Messages targeting a remote destination are held on a special queue called a *transmission queue*. They stay there until the opposite side of the communication session becomes available. At that point, all messages accumulated in the transmission queue are sent to the target destination. For persistent messages, MQ assures (notice that it does not guarantee) one-time message delivery to the targeted destination.

Understanding MQ Messages

Programs communicate via *messages*. When MQ operates in native mode, a message is a string of bytes organized in a specific structure. A message consists of application data (the *message body*) and the part that is mostly used by the system itself for controlling message delivery and other functions (the *message descriptor*). The message body keeps free-form data prepared by the sending application. The receiving application should be able to interpret this data. The message descriptor keeps the message control information (such as message type, destination, priority, and so on). When MQ operates as a JMS provider, it supports all types of JMS messages.

Understanding Queue Managers, Queues, and Channels

A *queue manager* maintains the messaging environment by providing queuing services to applications and by managing queues and other objects that belong to the messaging environment. MQ supports multiple queue managers on the same machine (the mainframe platform is an exception). *Queues* are data structures that store messages. Queues that reside in the main storage are *nonpersistent* queues, and they do not survive an MQ or operating system crash (all messages located in the queue at that time are lost). Queues that reside on disk are called *persistent* queues, and they are recoverable. Persistent queues are slower because they require disk Input/Output (I/O); they also need to maintain a logging mechanism for recovery (a tradeoff between performance and data integrity).

Each queue belongs to a single queue manager that is responsible for its maintenance. A queue has a set of attributes that determines the queue's structure. Queue attributes determine whether an application can retrieve messages from a queue (get enabled), put messages onto a queue (put enabled), and access a queue in an exclusive or shared mode. They also determine the maximum number of messages that can be stored on a queue, the maximum size of the queue message, and so on. Queues can be local (when they belong to a local queue manager) or remote (when they belong to a queue manager located on another machine).

Channels support communication between remote queues (queues that belong to different queue managers). There are two types of channels: message channels and Message Queue Interface (MQI) channels. You use message channels for transmitting messages between queue managers. Each message channel maintains communication in one direction. For two-way communication, you need two message channels. In contrast, you use MQI channels for connecting MQ clients to queue managers running on remote machines.

Each message channel is closely associated with a remote queue. The remote queue is the mechanism for delivering messages between two queue managers. A remote queue has a local definition on the machine on which the queue manager that owns that remote queue resides. The remote queue is not a physical queue; it is a local definition of a queue on another (remote) queue manager. The local transmission queue associated with the remote queue temporarily stores messages destined for the queue on the remote queue manager. The sender channel is responsible for retrieving messages from the transmission queue and sending them over the wire to the remote queue manager.

The following is an example of WebSphere MQ installed on two network machines: On machine A, you have a queue manager called QueueManagerA and a local queue called QueueA. On machine B, you have a queue manager called QueueManagerB and a remote queue called QueueB, which is linked to the local transmission queue and points to QueueA. Both queue managers communicate via a message channel.

When a program on a local machine connects to a local queue manager and puts messages on a remote queue, the messages are initially placed on the associated transmission queue and subsequently delivered to a targeted remote queue (defined as a local queue on a remote queue manager). Messages are delivered over message channels.

Understanding MQ Clients

An MQ *client* is a program that runs on a machine without a queue manager. It remotely connects to a queue manager that runs on a server machine to use its services via MQI channels. MQ also supports a message-triggering mechanism. For a queue with the triggering attribute turned on, a message that arrives on the queue triggers the execution of a program specified in the process definition (however, the triggering conditions must be satisfied).

When a program "gets" a message from a queue, the message is removed from that queue. Alternatively, a program can "browse" a message, which is a nondestructive operation (the message remains in the queue). MQ also supports clustering —a set of queue managers combined in a network group, or *cluster*. Inside the MQ cluster, queue managers communicate using a reduced number of channels. An MQ cluster is a flexible architecture that allows for simplified maintenance of queue managers and their channels (adding them to a cluster and removing them from a cluster).

As you can see, MQ's main advantage over the embedded JMS provider is its ability to connect programs running on different machines in a heterogeneous environment with the staged assured delivery of messages, which are automatically translated to the native code of the receiving application.

Downloading and Installing WebSphere MQ

Next, you will learn how to download and install the WebSphere MQ package.

 CAUTION *WebSphere MQ does not support machine names that include spaces. If your machine name contains a space, you need to rename the machine before installing MQ.*

Part of the MQ software runs as a Windows service responsible for user authentication. As part of the user authentication, the service must be able to verify the group to which the account that attempts to access MQ belongs. The MQ service itself runs under the local account MUSR_MQADMIN, which is created during the MQ installation. This local account (depending on the Windows 2000 domain controller configuration) could be unable to perform this security check. Therefore, if your machines are on a network that uses Windows 2000 domain controllers, you must configure each installation of MQ to run its service under a domain user account (rather than a local account) that has a special authority.

Configuring Your Windows Account

On a network, you must be a domain administrator (or you need a domain administrator's participation) to install MQ. Follow the steps in this section to assign your account the required special authority—to query the group membership of any account.

First, log on to a domain controller as the domain administrator (or ask your domain administrator to do so). Second, create a special global domain group for MQ called domain mqm (two words are separated by a space). Finally, check Security as the group type. Give members of this global group the authority to query the group membership of any account.

To set up the required authority level, follow these steps:

1. Right-click the domain name and select Delegate Control. Click Next.

2. On the subsequent screen, select domain mqm, click Add, and then click OK.

3. Highlight domain mqm on the following screen and click Next.

4. On the screen that appears, select Create a custom task to delegate and click Next.

5. On the next screen, select `Only the following objects in the folder` and then check `User objects`. Click `Next`.

6. On the next screen, select `Property-specific` and then check `Read group membership` and `Read groupMembershipSAM`. Click `Next`.

7. Finally, click `Finish`.

Quite a procedure!

Next, create one or more domain accounts and add them to the `domain mqm` group. You will be using the `MQAdmin` domain account for MQ installation, so you need to add it to the `domain mqm` group. When you install MQ on any network machine, the MQ installation detects the existence of the `domain mqm` group on the Local Area Network (LAN) and adds it to the local `mqm` group created during the MQ installation on each machine where MQ was installed. However, you still need to provide this special account when prompted during the MQ installation in order to configure MQ to use this account. You must enter this account into the `Prepare MQSeries Wizard` screen at the end of the installation.

Finally, you are just about ready to start installing MQ. Log on to the machine where you want to install MQ as the administrator but with an account that is different from `MQAdmin`. Later, when you are prompted for the account with special authorization, you will enter the `MQAdmin` account you have prepared.

 NOTE *Make sure you log in with an account different from* `MQAdmin`. *This is an MQ requirement.*

Until now, this section has discussed a stand-alone MQ installation. However, this is not your goal. You need to install MQ as the WSAD 5.0 JMS provider. A similar integration task exists in a production environment, where MQ should be installed as the WAS 5.0 JMS provider. The next section discusses it in more detail.

Installing MQ as the WSAD JMS Provider

You need to consider two situations for installing MQ as the WSAD JMS provider. If MQ was installed on the machine before the WSAD 5.0 installation, then during WSAD installation MQ automatically becomes the WSAD JMS server. In this case, you should not install the embedded WSAD JMS server during the WSAD 5.0 installation, but installing the embedded client is recommended. On the other hand, if WSAD 5.0 was installed first, you can install the embedded JMS provider (the server and the client parts). Later, you can install MQ on top of the embedded JMS provider, completely replacing it as the WSAD JMS provider. Before starting the installation, read the `Readme` file supplied with the MQ installation.

Insert the MQ installation disk or download the latest MQ release (5.3 or later) from the following IBM Web site: http://www-3.ibm.com/software/ts/mqseries/ downloads/. If you downloaded MQ from the IBM site, unzip it, and double-click setup.exe (because autorun will not work).

Follow the installation instructions and select Custom Installation (when prompted) to avoid a potential problem with using MQ. Specifically, the default MQ installation installs the package under the Program files directory, which requires administrative access. I do not recommend installing MQ into the default directory (also, avoid *Program files* as the installation directory). As previously mentioned, it is a good idea to keep the installation path as short as possible.

NOTE *On my machine, I install MQ in the* G:\WSMQ *directory. If your installation is different, please make the appropriate adjustments when following the instructions.*

Start the installation. On the WebSphere MQ Installation Launchpad screen, click Software Prerequisites (see Figure 11-2).

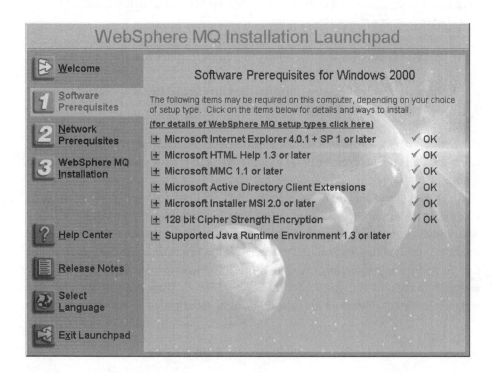

Figure 11-2. Checking software prerequisites

If everything is marked as OK, your software environment is ready for installation. If not, follow the installation recommendations and install all the necessary software packages. Next, click Network Prerequisites. Here, if your machine is on a network with Windows 2000 domain controllers, you should click Yes. The installation screen will display the requirements for setting a special user ID account. (You already did this at the beginning of this chapter.)

Before installing MQ, you need to stop MQ services (in case the embedded JMS provider was installed during the WSAD 5.0 installation). First, close WSAD. Next, open the Services panel, scroll to the bottom, and locate WebSphere Embedding Messaging. Stop it (if it is not already stopped) and make sure its status is Manual. In addition, stop IBM Agent Controller and change its status to Manual. Still, some services (DLLs) with an amq prefix are loaded in memory. You can see them by starting the Windows 2000 Task Manager. You can stop them manually, but it is better to reboot the machine (to flush any loaded DLLs out of memory). Now, if you start the Task Manager, you should not see any services with the amq prefix running.

To start installing MQ, click WebSphere MQ Installation ➤Launch WebSphere MQ Installer and follow the installation instructions. Because the embedded JMS provider (which is based on the simplified MQ version) is installed on the machine, the installation recognizes it as another MQ version that is already installed locally. It presents two options:

- Modify, which gives you the ability to modify/replace installed MQ features

- Uninstall, which lets you uninstall the current MQ installation and then start a new installation

Select Modify and click Next. On the next screen, select Server and JMS Messaging. Click Next. The next screen displays a summary of the requested installation (see Figure 11-3).

Notice that this installation keeps the WAS_localhost_server1 queue manager created by the embedded JMS provider. Click Modify to start the installation. After installation, verify that <MQ_Install_Directory>\Java\lib (in this case, G:\WSMQ\Java\lib) has been added to the PATH system variable and add it if not. To verify the installation, check that there are no error messages in the amqmjpse.txt installation log file located in <MQ_Install_Directory> (in this example, g:\WSMQ). This indicates a successful installation.

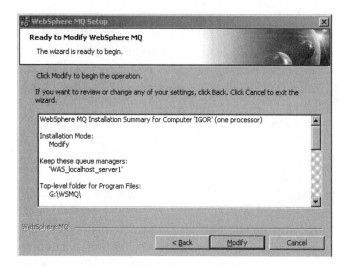

Figure 11-3. Summary of installation options

Extending the WebSphere MQ Middleware

All MQ releases prior to 5.3 install a version of MQ in native mode. In other words, you can use the installed MQ software with stand-alone application programs (written in C/C+ and some other languages) that use MQ native Application Programming Interfaces (APIs) to communicate. It supported neither Java programs nor JMS programs because it was developed long before Java and JMS were introduced.

To support developing MQ applications in Java and the JMS P2P domain, IBM released the support pack MA88, which contains the MQSeries classes for Java and the MQSeries classes for JMS. For all releases prior to MQ 5.3, you need to download MA88 from the following IBM Web site: http://www-3.ibm.com/software/integration/support/supportpacs/individual/ma88.html.

NOTE *This download may require you to register with IBM, which is free.*

Starting from MQ 5.3, MA88 became part of the base package and automatically installs during the MQ installation. If you are still using MQ 5.2.*x*, you need to install MA88 on top of the base installation.

To install MA88, download `ma88_win.zip` into some directory on your machine, unzip it, and run `setup.exe` from this directory. If MQ is not to be installed in the default location (as in this case), then when prompted, select the `Custom` install and indicate the installation folder as `G:\WSMQ\java` (where `G:\WSMQ` is the MQ installation directory). After that, follow the installation instructions. The next section discusses how to install MA0C, a second service pack.

Installing MA0C

JMS introduces two modes of communication: the P2P and Pub/Sub domains. However, MQ originally was developed to operate only in the P2P mode with the triggering feature. To accommodate the Pub/Sub domain requirements, IBM introduced a second service pack called MA0C that adds the Pub/Sub functionality to MQ. To install MA0C, download the `ma0c_ntmq52.exe` file from the following IBM Web site: `http://www.ibm.com/software/integration/support/supportpacs/individual/ma0c.html`.

Run this file from the download directory and follow the installation instructions. This pack also installs MQ Broker 2.1, which is necessary for supporting the JMS Pub/Sub mode.

NOTE *MQ Broker 2.1 is also present in the embedded JMS provider. IBM now recommends a separate, more sophisticated MQ broker package: WebSphere MQ Event Broker.*

With the necessary support pack installed, MQ becomes capable of supporting Java and JMS (both P2P and Pub/Sub domains), and it can function as the WSAD 5.0 JMS provider. (The native MQ mode is still available and should be used outside of the J2EE environment.) JMS-based Java applications can also send messages to native MQ applications (mostly legacy systems still using the native MQ APIs); however, this type of communication is more complicated because IBM changed the structure of the native MQ message descriptor to accommodate the additional control fields and attributes required by JMS. Thus, developers of JMS applications that send messages to the native mode should clearly understand the issue of mapping JMS messages to native MQ messages.

NOTE *You can find out more about this in the IBM online book* Using Java *at* `http://www-3.ibm.com/software/integration/library/manualsa/csqzaw06/csqzaw06tfrm.htm`.

MQ 5.0 already has a PTF for fixing recently discovered problems. You will install this PTF in the next section.

Installing PTF CSD03

CSD03 is the current PTF that you install after installing MQ 5.3. This PTF brings MQ to the level 5.3.3. You can check the installed version of MQ by issuing the following command: `mqver`. You can also locate information about this maintenance release by browsing the following file: `<MQ_Install_Directory>\PTF\en_us\memo.ptf`. You can download this CSD03 PTF from `https://www6.software.ibm.com/dl/wsmqcsd/wsmqcsd-p`.

Unzip the downloaded file and run the `U200187A.exe` program. Follow the installation instructions. Before installing the CSD03 support pack, make sure you stop all programs and services related to MQ. To do this, select `Start` ➤`Programs` ➤`IBM WebSphere MQ` ➤`WebSphere MQ Services`. On the screen that appears, right-click any running queue manager or service and select `Stop`. Close the `WebSphere MQ Services` window.

Next, open the Windows `Services` window. Locate the `IBM MQSeries` service and stop it. In addition, scroll to the bottom, find the WebSphere `Embedded Messaging Publish and Subscribe WAS_localhost_server1` entry, and stop it. Finally, right-click the Windows taskbar and select `Windows Task Manager`. Click the `Processes` tab. You will see a list of service tasks currently running. Any task name that starts with the `amq` prefix belongs to MQ and must be stopped. Right-click it and select `End Process`. Confirm that you want to stop the process. Now, start `setup.exe` and follow the installation instructions.

 NOTE *Sometimes, even after stopping all the MQ-related programs and services, CSD03 is still unable to install, complaining that some MQ-related tasks are still running. These are DLLs running in memory. In this case, you need to reboot the machine to clear these DLLs from memory. However, before rebooting, change the status of the MQ-related services from* Automatic *to* Manual *so they will not start automatically at boot time.*

Next, open the Windows 2000 `Services` window, locate the MQ-related services previously discussed, double-click them, and change the `Start Type` field from `Automatic` to `Manual`. Reboot the machine, install the CSD03 support pack, and change `Manual` back to `Automatic`. Then, start them by right-clicking and selecting `Start Service`.

Starting from CSD01, IBM moves the `mqji*.properties` files from their original location in the `<MQ Install root>\/java/lib` directory to the `com.ibm.mq.jar` file.

IBM recommends removing `../java/lib` from the CLASSPATH and deleting the following files from the `../java/lib` directory:

`mqji.properties, mqji_de.properties,`
`mqji_en.properties, mqji_en_US.properties,`

`mqji_es.properties, mqji_fr.properties,`
`mqji_it.properties, mqji_ja.properties,`
`mqji_ko.properties, mqji_pt.properties,`
`mqji_zh_CN.properties, mqji_zh_TW.properties`

Now, with the WebSphere MQ installation made on top of the embedded JMS provider, MQ replaces the embedded JMS provider and now functions as the WSAD 5.0 MQ JMS provider. The interesting part of this transformation is that the WSAD 5.0 MQ JMS provider recognizes JMS objects previously defined under the embedded JMS provider.

In the next section, you will run `ReceivingJMSProjectApp` and `SendingJMSProjectApp` (the same applications you developed in Chapter 10) under the new MQ-based JMS provider without making any changes.

Running the Example with the MQ JMS Provider

Start `JMSServer` in the debug mode (to see messages printed by the running application—sometimes they are not visible outside the debugging mode. WSAD automatically switches to the Debug Perspective. Switch back to the Server Perspective, right-click `SendingServlet`, and select `Run on Server`. Figure 11-4 shows the Console View, where you should see messages being produced by the running application.

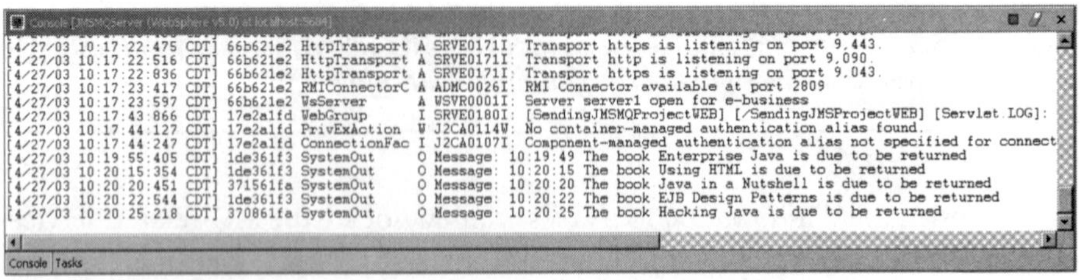

Figure 11-4. Messages produced by the running application

You can also use the DB2 command-line processor to browse the BOOK_NOTIFY table and see that the messages have been added to the table.

Figure 11-5 shows the content of the BOOK_NOTIFY table after processing the following SQL: SELECT * FROM LIB.BOOK_NOTIFY.

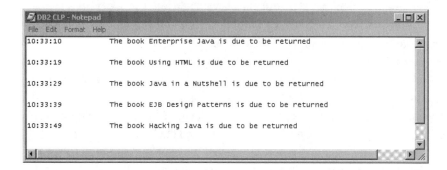

Figure 11-5. Messages written in the BOOK_NOTIFY table

As you can see, you get the same results as in the previous chapter without making any changes.

Using the MQ JMS Provider

Next, you want to run this example against the new JMS objects (queue connection factory, queue, topic connection factory, and topic) created under MQ 5.3 outside of the WSAD 5.0 environment. You will create new JMS objects (with the embedded MQ characters in the middle of each JMS object name): Notify_MQ_QCF, Notify_MQ_Q, Notify_MQ_TCF, and Notify_MQ_T, respectively. In addition, you will modify the source code of your applications to use these new MQ-based JMS objects.

You do not want to change the two existing applications (SendingJMSProjectApp and ReceivingJMSProjectApp) originally developed for running under the control of the embedded JMS provider; therefore, you will build two new applications (SendingJMSMQProjectApp and ReceivingJMSMQProjectApp) that closely mimic the original applications but use the new MQ-based JMS objects. You can do this with minimum effort by exporting the original SendingJMSProjectApp and ReceivingJMSProjectApp applications as EAR files to some temporary directory.

Next, you will import them back to the Workbench; however, during import, you will assign them new project names. After that, you will make some minor modifications to make them work with the new MQ-based JMS objects.

With this explanation under your belt, let's start developing. In the next section, you will build these two new applications.

Building the New Application Examples

Switch to the J2EE Perspective, right-click SendingJMSProjectApp, and select Export. On the next screen, select EAR file and click Next. Then, click Browse and select a temporary directory where you will save the exported EAR file. On the dialog that appears, make sure to check all three boxes (Export Source Files, Overwrite existing files without warning, and Include project build path and meta-data files). Click Finish. This exports the SendingJMSProjectApp.ear file. Repeat the same steps to export the ReceivingJMSProjectApp application.

Now you will do the opposite process. Select Import from the main menu. On the next screen, select EAR file as the Import type and click Next. On the next screen, navigate to the directory where you saved the exported files and select the ReceivingJMSProjectApp.ear file. In addition, enter the name of the new application as ReceivingJMSMQProjectApp. Click Next. Accept the defaults on the next screen and click Next. On the subsequent screen, change the original name of the EJB module from ReceivingJMSProjectEJB to ReceivingJMSMQProjectEJB. Click Finish.

Repeat the same steps to import the SendingJMSProjectApp.ear file. Again, assign a new name to the application: SendingJMSMQProjectApp.ear. Also, change the name of the Web module from SendingJMSProjectWEB to SendingJMSMQProjectWEB.

Now you have two new enterprise applications: SendingJMSMQProjectApp and ReceivingJMSMQProjectApp. They still show the corresponding old names as display names (because they are internally coded). So, in the J2EE Perspective (J2EE Hierarchy View), double-click SendingJMSMQProjectApp to open its Deployment Descriptor. Correct the Display Name. Save the results and close the editor. Repeat the same steps for the ReceivingJMSMQProjectApp. Save the results and close the editor.

Next, you will make some minor source code changes so that your new applications use the MQ-based objects: Notify_MQ_QCF, NOTIFY_MQ_Q, Notify_MQ_TCF, and Notify_MQ_T.

No source code changes are necessary for the receiving application because both the ReceivingMDB Message Driven Bean (MDB) and Book_notify entity bean do not directly manipulate JMS objects. You will need to make changes later for the Deployment Descriptor and the Unit Test Server (UTS) configuration.

For the sending application, you need to make some limited source code changes. In the J2EE Perspective (Navigator View), expand the SendingJMSMQProjectWEB project and open the SendingServlet.java servlet. Find the following two statements that define the queue connection factory name and the queue name. They are located near the top of the file:

```
String QueueConnectionFactoryName = "java:comp/env/NotifyQCF";
String QueueName = "java:comp/env/NotifyQ";
```

Change `NotifyQCF` to `Notify_MQ_QCF` and change `Notify_Q` to `Notify_MQ_Q`. Now, the `SendingServlet` will perform a lookup for the new MQ-based administered objects. After these changes, the two statements should read like this:

```
String QueueConnectionFactoryName = "java:comp/env/Notify_MQ_QCF";
String QueueName = "java:comp/env/Notify_MQ_Q";
```

That is all you need to do for the `SendingServlet` servlet. Save the changes and close the editor. Open the `PublishingServlet` servlet and make similar changes for the names of the topic connection factory and topic. They should read like this:

```
String topicConnectionFactoryName = "java:comp/env/Notify_MQ_TCF";
String topicName = "java:comp/env/Notify_MQ_T";
```

Save the changes and close the editor. In the next section, you will build a new server project called `JMSMQServerProject` and make it the default server for running the new applications.

Building the Unit Test Server Project

Switch to the Server Perspective and create a new UTS project called `JMSMQServerProject`. Right-click `JMSMQServerProject` and select `New` ➤ `Server` and `Server Configuration`. Enter `JMSMQServer` in the `Name` field and select `WebSphere version 5.0` ➤ `Test Environment`. Click `Finish`.

In the Server Configuration View, right-click `JMSMQServer` and click `Add` ➤ `ReceivingJMSMQProjectApp`. Repeat the same steps and add the second new enterprise application: `SendingJMSMQProjectApp`. Now, `JMSMQProject` is the default test server for both the `ReceivingJMSMQProjectApp` and `SendingJMSMQProjectApp` application projects. Double-click `JMSMQServer` to open it in the Editor View. Click the `Configuration` tab and check the `Enable administration console` box.

In the next two sections, you will configure the UTS environment for running your applications.

Configuring the Datasource

Double-click `JMSMQServer` in the server configuration, click the `Data Sources` tab, select `DB2 JDBC Provider`, and click the `Add` button. On the `Create a JDBC Provider` dialog, select `DB2 JDBC Provider (XA)` in the `Name` field. Select `COM.ibm.db2.jdbc.DB2XADataSource` as the `Implementation class name`. Enter `DBDatasourceXA` in the `Datasource name` and `jdbc/DBDatasourceXA` in the `JNDI name` field. Make sure that the Use this data source in container managed persistence (CMP) box is checked. Click Finish. Finally, highlight the databaseName field and enter TECHBOOK. Save the results and close the editor.

Building MQ-Based JMS Objects

In contrast with the embedded JMS provider, filling the corresponding WSAD screens for the MQ JMS provider builds only the administered objects. You must build the real JMS objects (queue connection factories, queues, topic connection factories, and topics) by using the MQ native tools. The same is true for any generic JMS provider.

MQ provides several different tools for building MQ objects. This section uses the Graphical User Interface (GUI) tool MQ Explorer. To activate MQ Explorer, select the following from the Windows taskbar: Start ➤ Programs ➤ IBM WebSphere MQ ➤ WebSphere MQ Explorer.

Figure 11-6 depicts the MQ Explorer main window. The tool allows you to create and view MQ objects.

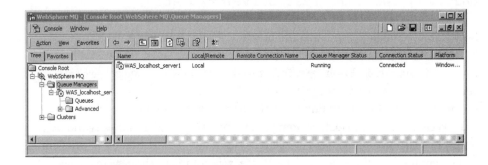

Figure 11-6. MQ Explorer's main window

Expand WebSphere MQ and click Queue Managers. You will see the WAS_localhost_server1 queue manager. The Queue Manager Status field indicates Running if the WSAD UTS has been started, which automatically starts a queue manager at startup. It also starts a broker, which is necessary for supporting the Pub/Sub domain. You can also manually start the queue manager by right-clicking a nonrunning queue manager and selecting Start. To build a new queue, right-click the Queues folder and select New ➤ Local Queue. On the dialog that appears, enter Notify_MQ_Q in the Queue Name field and select Persistent in the Default Persistence field. Persistent queues are written on disk and are recoverable during the system crash. Leave the rest of the queue properties as they are and click OK.

Now you are back to the MQ Explorer main window, as shown in Figure 11-7. Click the Queues folder. You should see a new queue in the list of existing queues.

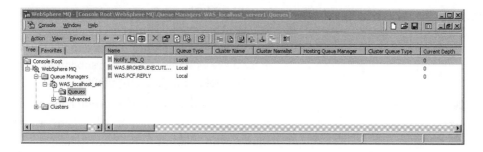

Figure 11-7. The default queue manager that is running

Notice that the Current Depth field is 0. This field shows the number of messages in the corresponding queue. The two other queues you see belong to the Pub/Sub broker. You have built your queue. Next, you need to build the rest of the MQ objects and register them using the JMSAdmin utility. However, first you need to learn how the JMSAdmin utility works, which is the subject of the next section.

Using the JMSAdmin Utility

The J2EE 1.3 specification requires that all JMS vendors provide a tool for creating the administered objects and placing them in the Java Naming and Directory Interface (JNDI) namespace. MQ comes with the JMSAdmin utility to meet these requirements.

The JMSAdmin utility builds the administered objects and places them in the JNDI namespace. The JMSAdmin configuration file called JMSAdmin.config controls the JNDI namespace used for placing the administered objects. The file named JMSAdmin.config is the default filename that the JMSAdmin utility uses as its configuration file. It is possible to use a different file as the JMSAdmin utility's configuration file by specifying the file as a command-line parameter:

```
JMSAdmin  -cfg MyJMSAdmin.config
```

Table 11-1 shows the JMSAdmin commands you can use for building administered objects and placing them in the JNDI namespace. The utility always starts at the JNDI root context. You use the commands for creating and maintaining the JNDI subcontext.

Table 11-1. JMSAdmin Commands

COMMAND	DESCRIPTION
DEFINE ctx(ctxName)	Attempts to create a new child subcontext of the current context.
DISPLAY ctx	Displays the current context or subcontext. Administered objects are annotated in the JNDI namespace with the a prefix. In a subcontext they are prefixed with the [D] prefix.
DELETE ctx(ctxName)	Deletes the subcontext of the current context.
CHANGE ctx(ctxName)	Switches to the subcontext of the current context. The ctxName can have two special values: =UP move to the parent context of the child and =INIT to move to the initial context (root).
ALTER TYPE (name) [property]	Updates the given property of the administered object.
DEFINE TYPE (name)[property]	Attempts to create an administered object of type TYPE with supplied properties.
DISPLAY TYPE (name)	Displays the property of the administered object.
DELETE TYPE (name)	Attempts to delete the administered object of type TYPE.
COPY TYPE (name A) TYPE (name B)	Makes a copy of the administered object of type TYPE with the source as nameA and the destination as nameB.
MOVE TYPE (name A) TYPE (name B)	Moves or renames the administered object of type TYPE.
END	Exits the utility.

NOTE *Any attempt to execute a JNDI command will fail if the subcontext indicated by* ctxName *cannot be found (because of a security violation or some invalid information). Also, substitute the word* TYPE *with the keyword that represents the required administered object.*

To set up the JMSAdmin environment, you will update both the JSMAdmin.bat and JMSAdmin.config files located in the <MQ_Installation_Directory>\Java\ bin directory.

NOTE *Before updating the* JMSAdmin.config *file, save the original version of the file in a different directory or just rename it to, say,* JMSAdmin_OLD.config *in the same directory.*

Open the JSMAdmin.config file by using any text editor and find the section shown in Listing 11-1, which is located near the top of the file.

Listing 11-1. Fragment of the JMSAdmin.config *File*

```
#INITIAL_CONTEXT_FACTORY=com.sun.jndi.ldap.LdapCtxFactory
#INITIAL_CONTEXT_FACTORY=com.sun.jndi.fscontext.RefFSContextFactory
#INITIAL_CONTEXT_FACTORY=com.ibm.ejs.ns.jndi.CNInitialContextFactory
INITIAL_CONTEXT_FACTORY=com.ibm.websphere.naming.WsnInitialContextFactory
#
#PROVIDER_URL=ldap://polaris/o=ibm,c=us
#PROVIDER_URL=file:/%MQ_JAVA_INSTALL_PATH%/JNDI
PROVIDER_URL=iiop://localhost/
```

The file comes preconfigured for using Sun Microsystem's Lightweight Directory Access Protocol (LDAP) naming service. The problem is that the Web-Sphere-based naming service loses its context each time that the WSAD UTS stops. Therefore, it requires rebuilding the naming context each time the UTS starts. A better approach is to use the file-based naming context that does not depend on the WSAD UTS. To do this, comment out (using the character #) the current setting for INITIAL_CONTEXT_FACTORY and PROVIDER_URL and uncomment the corresponding setting for the file-based naming context. Also, for PROVIDER_URL, indicate the directory where the naming context will reside (see Listing 11-2).

Listing 11-2. Fragment of the Changed JMSAdmin.config *File*

```
#INITIAL_CONTEXT_FACTORY=com.sun.jndi.ldap.LdapCtxFactory
INITIAL_CONTEXT_FACTORY=com.sun.jndi.fscontext.RefFSContextFactory
#INITIAL_CONTEXT_FACTORY=com.ibm.ejs.ns.jndi.CNInitialContextFactory
#INITIAL_CONTEXT_FACTORY=com.ibm.websphere.naming.WsnInitialContextFactory
#
#PROVIDER_URL=ldap://polaris/o=ibm,c=us
PROVIDER_URL=file:/%MQ_JAVA_INSTALL_PATH%/JNDI
#ROVIDER_URL=iiop://localhost/
```

Save and close the file. Next, update the JMSAdmin.bat procedure located in the <MQ_Installation_Directory>\Java\bin directory. Add one additional parameter that sets the value of the WSAD java.ext.dirs directory:

```
-Djava.ext.dirs="%MQ_JAVA_DATA_PATH%"\lib
```

Listing 11-3 shows the modified JMSAdmin.bat file.

Listing 11-3. The Modified JMSAdmin.bat *File*

```
@echo off
rem -------------------------------------------------
rem  IBM Websphere MQ JMS Admin Tool Execution Script
rem  for Windows NT
rem
rem  Licensed Materials - Property of IBM
rem
rem  5648-C60 5724-B4 5655-F10
rem
rem  © Copyright IBM Corp. 2002.  All Rights Reserved.
rem
rem  US Government Users Restricted Rights - Use, duplication or
rem  disclosure restricted by GSA ADP Schedule Contract with IBM Corp.
rem
rem  Note that the properties passed to the java program are defaults,
rem  and should be edited to suit your installation if necessary
rem -------------------------------------------------

cls
java -Djava.ext.dirs="%MQ_JAVA_DATA_PATH%"\lib -
DMQJMS_LOG_DIR="%MQ_JAVA_DATA_PATH%"\log -
DMQJMS_TRACE_DIR="%MQ_JAVA_DATA_PATH%"\errors -
DMQJMS_INSTALL_PATH="%MQ_JAVA_INSTALL_PATH%"
 com.ibm.mq.jms.admin.JMSAdmin %1 %2
%3 %4 %5
```

Save and close the file. Finally, create the JNDI directory where the file-based naming context will reside. In this environment, you will build the g:\WSMQ\JNDI directory to hold the file-based JNDI naming context.

In the next section, you will use the JMSAdmin utility to build the following JMS objects for your projects: the queue connection factory called Notify_MQ_QCF, the queue called Notify_MQ_Q, the topic connection factory called Notify_MQ_TCF, and the topic called Notify_MQ_T.

Using JMSAdmin for Building Administered Objects

Because JMSAdmin runs outside WSAD, it needs an environment that supports JMS. Adding multiple sets of directories and files to the global system PATH and CLASSPATH environment variables is not a good idea. It makes them quite long, impacting to some extent the operating system performance. In addition, these environment variables are limited in their length, which is another reason to keep them reasonably short.

A much better approach is to create a batch procedure, which (when executed from the command prompt) builds the necessary environment locally. This environment stays in place as long as this command prompt window remains open, and it disappears when you close the command prompt window.

Listing 11-4 shows the procedure for building the combined WSAD/MQ JMS environment necessary for running JMSAdmin. It is called SetJMSAdminEnv.cmd, and you can download it from the Downloads section of the Apress Web site (http://www.apress.com). Copy any procedures and files discussed in this chapter to the <MQ_Install_Directory>\Java\lib directory before using them.

Listing 11-4. SetJMSAdminEnv.cmd

```
@echo off
set WAS_HOME=g:\WSAD\runtimes\base_v5

@rem ==== Java runtime =====
set JAVA_INSTALL_PATH=g:\WSMQ\java
set JAVA_HOME=g:\WSAD\runtimes\base_v5\java\bin

@rem ==== MQ JMS ===========
set MQ=%MQ_JAVA_INSTALL_PATH%\lib
set MQ=%MQ%;%MQ_JAVA_INSTALL_PATH%\lib\com.ibm.mq.jar
set MQ=%MQ%;%MQ_JAVA_INSTALL_PATH%\lib\com.ibm.mqjms.jar
set MQ=%MQ%;%MQ_JAVA_INSTALL_PATH%\lib\jms.jar
set MQ=%MQ%;%MQ_JAVA_INSTALL_PATH%\lib\connector.jar

set MQ=%MQ%;%MQ_JAVA_INSTALL_PATH%\lib\com.ibm.mq.amt.jar
set MQ=%MQ%;%MQ_JAVA_INSTALL_PATH%\lib\com.ibm.mqbind.jar
set MQ=%MQ%;%MQ_JAVA_INSTALL_PATH%\lib\jta.jar

@rem ==== LDAP JNDI ===========
set MQ=%MQ%;%MQ_JAVA_INSTALL_PATH%\lib\ldap.jar

@rem ==== File System JNDI ===========
```

```
set MQ=%MQ%;%MQ_JAVA_INSTALL_PATH%\lib\providerutil.jar
set MQ=%MQ%;%MQ_JAVA_INSTALL_PATH%\lib\fscontext.jar

@rem ==== WebSphere JNDI ===========
set MQ=%MQ%;%MQ_JAVA_INSTALL_PATH%\lib\jndi.jar

set WebSphereCP=%WAS_HOME%\lib\naming.jar
set WebSphereCP=%WebSphereCP%;%WAS_HOME%\lib\namingclient.jar

set CLASSPATH=%WebSphereCP%;%MQ%;%CLASSPATH%
set PATH=%JAVA_HOME%;%JAVA_INSTALL_PATH%\bin;%JAVA_INSTALL_PATH%\lib;%PATH%
```

 TIP *To check if the environment for the JMSAdmin utility is set correctly, open a command line, switch to* <MQ_Install_Directory>\Java\bin, *and run the* SetJMSAdminEnv.cmd *procedure. After the necessary environment is set, enter* JMSAdmin -t -v. *If you have a clear cursor line, that is the JMSAdmin prompt and you are okay. Enter* End *to exit JMSAdmin. On the other hand, if you get an exception, open the file* <MQ_Install_Directory>\Error\mqjms.trc *to see the problem.*

With all these preparations done, you are ready to build the required administered objects. To run the SetJMSAdminEnv procedure, open the command prompt window and switch to the <MQ_Install_Directory>\Java\lib directory. Type SetJMSAdminEnv and press Enter. This builds the necessary environment. Keep this command prompt window open because it provides the supporting environment for running JMSAdmin. Next, you will execute the second procedure that actually registers your administered objects by placing them in the JNDI environment specified by the JMSAdmin.config file. The procedure is called RegisterMQAdminObjects.cmd; it is as follows:

```
@echo on
JmsAdmin < CommandsForJMSAdmin.txt
```

This procedure calls the JMSAdmin utility, which reads the CommandForJMSAdmin.txt file as standard input. Commands coded within this file define administered objects to be processed by the JMSAdmin utility. Listing 11-5 shows the content of the CommandsForJMSAdmin.txt file.

Listing 11-5. CommandsForJMSAdmin.txt

```
# === Delete existing MQ objects just in case ====
del q(Notify_MQ_TCF)
del q(Notify_MQ_QCF)

# Delete Queue
del q(Notify_MQ_Q)

# Delete QueueConnectionFactory
del qcf(Notify_MQ_QCF)

# Delete Topic
del t(Notify_MQ_T)

# Delete QueueConnectionFactory
del tcf(Notify_MQ_TCF)

# ========== Define new MQ objects =============
# Define QueueConnectionFactory
def qcf(Notify_MQ_QCF) qmgr(WAS_localhost_server1)

# Define Queue
def q(Notify_MQ_Q) qu(Notify_MQ_Q)

# Define Topic Connectin Factory
def tcf(Notify_MQ_TCF) qmgr(WAS_localhost_server1)

# Define Topic
def t(Notify_MQ_T) topic(Book)


# Display the current context
dis Ctx
end
```

Before examining this file, you should know about two additional JMSAdmin commands that are not present in the file but can be useful in other situations. By default, JMSAdmin places the administered objects in the root of the JNDI namespace. To place these objects in the subcontext of the root, you use the following commands:

```
def ctx(jms)
chg ctx(jms)
```

The first command builds a new naming subcontext called jms, and the second command switches to this subcontext, making it current. All commands that follow will place the administered objects in the jms subcontext. Consequently, you reference these administered objects with the subcontext prefix in front of their names (for example, jms/Notify_MQ_Q). It is always a good idea to use different subcontexts for different applications to eliminate potential naming conflicts.

The reason you do not place your administered objects in any naming subcontext is because the file-based JNDI namespace you use has a bug and does not currently support subcontexts. Therefore, all names must be flat (for example, instead of jms/Notify_MQ_Q, you must use the flat name Notify_MQ_Q). Please note that this naming restriction is only applicable to the external names of the administered objects and has nothing to do with the names used by programs inside the WSAD environment. You will return to this subject shortly when you configure the UTS environment for running your applications.

Now you are ready to examine the commands coded in the CommandsForJMSAdmin.txt file. First, you delete the existing identically named administered objects (just in case they are present in the naming context). Then you define your administered objects. You define queue connection factories and topic connection factories for a specific queue manager (in this case, it is WAS_localhost_server1). The last command just displays the current naming context or subcontext. You are ready to execute the RegisterMQAdminObjects procedure. Just remember that you should use the same command prompt that you kept open before.

Execute the RegisterMQAdminObjects procedure by typing RegisterMQAdminObjects and pressing Enter. Figure 11-8 shows the execution results; you will see your four administered objects in the root of the namespace.

```
Command Prompt                                                    _ □ ×
InitCtx> InitCtx> InitCtx> InitCtx>
InitCtx> InitCtx> InitCtx>
InitCtx> InitCtx> InitCtx>
InitCtx> InitCtx> InitCtx>
InitCtx> InitCtx> InitCtx> InitCtx> InitCtx>
InitCtx> InitCtx> InitCtx>
InitCtx> InitCtx> InitCtx>
InitCtx> InitCtx> InitCtx>
InitCtx> InitCtx> InitCtx> InitCtx>
  Contents of InitCtx

      .bindings                java.io.File
  [D] jms                      javax.naming.Context
   a  Notify_MQ_QCF            com.ibm.mq.jms.MQQueueConnectionFactory
   a  Notify_MQ_Q             com.ibm.mq.jms.MQQueue
   a  Notify_MQ_T             com.ibm.mq.jms.MQTopic
   a  Notify_MQ_TCF           com.ibm.mq.jms.MQTopicConnectionFactory

  6 Object(s)
    1 Context(s)
    5 Binding(s), 4 Administered

InitCtx>
Stopping Websphere MQ classes for Java(tm) Message Service Administration

G:\WSMQ\Java\bin>
```

Figure 11-8. Registered administered objects

With the necessary administered objects prepared, you will now return to the
WSAD Workbench. The next step is to configure the WSAD UTS environment for
running your applications, which is covered in the next section.

Configuring the Unit Test Server Environment

Switch to the Server Perspective and double-click JMSMQServer to open its configuration file in the Editor View. Click the Configuration tab and make sure the Enable
administration console box is checked. Next, click the Paths tab. The Paths screen
will display. Click the Add Path button inside the was.ext.dirs section and enter the
<MQ_Install_Directory>\Java\lib directory—in this case, it is g:\WSMQ\Java\lib, as
shown in Figure 11-9. Click OK.

Figure 11-9. Setting the PATH

Click the JMS tag and locate the "Server Settings" section. Click the Add button and enter your queue name: Notify_MQ_Q. The UTS needs to be aware about all queues that are under its control. Save the results and close the editor. You will continue to configure the UTS environment, but in contrast with the embedded JMS provider, you will do this part of the configuration using the Administrative Console.

Right-click JMSMQServer and select Start. Wait until the server has started. Right-click JMSMQServer again and select Run Administrative Console. Enter your user ID to log in. On the left pane, expand Resources. You should see entries for Generic JMS Providers, WebSphere JMS Provider (this is the embedded JMS provider), and WebSphere MQ JMS Provider. It would be reasonable to use the WebSphere MQ JMS Provider, but that is not the case here.

You should remember that you selected the file-based JNDI namespace while modifying the JMSAdmin.config file. So, you need to set the WSAD UTS environment to use the same file-based JNDI namespace. The problem with the available WebSphere MQ JMS provider is that it is preconfigured to use the WSAD JNDI namespace, and you cannot modify its setting. For that reason, you will use the generic JMS provider and configure it as the MQ JMS provider that uses the file-based namespace.

Click Generic JMS Providers. Click New. Figure 11-10 shows the next screen where you will configure the JMS provider. Enter MyMQProvider in the Name field and enter MQ as Generic JMS Provider in the Description field. Enter the following JAR files in the Classpath field:

```
g:\WSMQ\Java\lib\fscontext.jar
g:\WSMQ\Java\lib\providerutil.jar
g:\WSMQ\java\lib\
g:\WSMQ\java\lib\com.ibm.mq.jar
g:\WSMQ\java\lib\com.ibm.mqjms..jar
g:\WSMQ\java\lib\mqjms.jar
```

The first two libraries support the file-based JNDI namespace. Enter com.sun.jndi.fscontext.RefFSContextFactory in the External Initial Context Factory field and file:/g:WSMQ/Java/JNDI in the External Provider URL field.

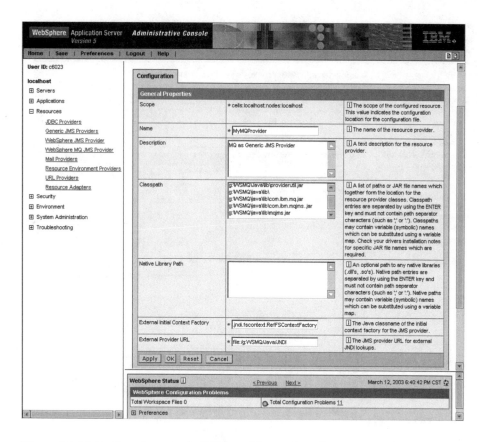

Figure 11-10. Setting the generic JMS provider as the MQ JMS provider

Click Apply. Next, scroll down to the "Additional Properties" section and click JMS Connection Factories. Click New. Figure 11-11 shows the next screen. Enter Notify_MQ_QCF in the Name field, select QUEUE in the Type field, and enter jms/Notify_MQ_QCF in the JNDI Name field. Enter Notify_MQ_QCF in the External JNDI Name field. Notice that this field points to the JNDI name of the queue connection factory that you set using the JMSAdmin utility—the flat name without the jms prefix.

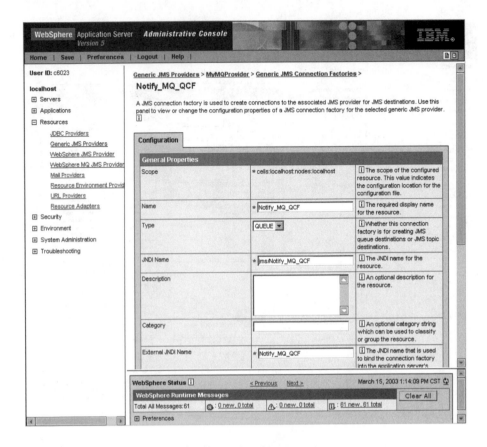

Figure 11-11. Setting the queue connection factory

Click OK. Get back to the "Additional Properties" section and click JMS Destinations. Click New. On the next screen, shown in Figure 11-12, enter Notify_MQ_Q in the Name field, select QUEUE in the Type field, and enter jms/Notify_MQ_Q in the JNDI Name field. Enter Notify_MQ_Q in the External JNDI Name field.

Figure 11-12. Setting a queue

Click OK. Get back to the "Additional Properties" section and click
JMS Connection Factories. Click New. Figure 11-13 shows the next screen that
appears. Enter Notify_MQ_TCF in the Name field, select TOPIC in the Type field, and
enter jms/Notify_MQ_TCF in the JNDI Name field. Enter Notify_MQ_TCF in the External
JNDI Name field.

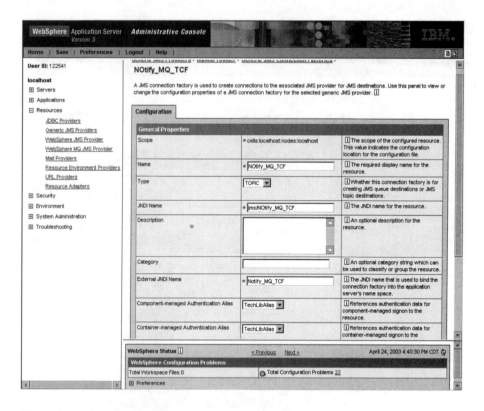

Figure 11-13. Setting the topic connection factory

Click OK. Get back to the "Additional Properties" section and click
JMS Destinations. Click New. On the next screen, shown in Figure 11-14,
enter Notify_MQ_T in the Name field, select TOPIC in the Type field, and enter
jms/Notify_MQ_T in the JNDI Name field. Enter Notify_MQ_T in the
External JNDI Name field.

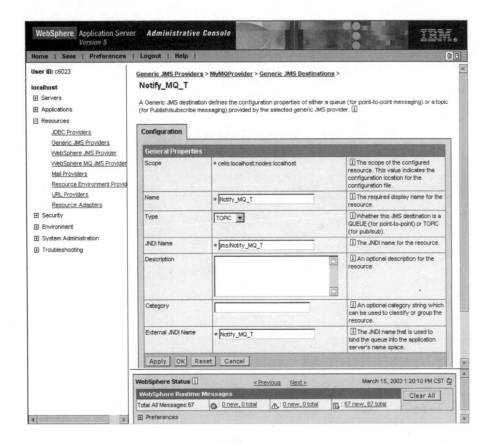

Figure 11-14. Setting the topic

Click OK. Next, you need to set the listener port. On the left pane, click Servers ►Application Servers ►server1. Scroll down to the "Additional Properties" section and click Message Listener Service ►Listener Ports. Click New. Figure 11-15 shows the screen that will appear. Enter TechLibMQListenerPort in the Name field. Enter jms/Notify_MQ_QCF in the Connection factory JNDI name field; enter jms/Notify_MQ_Q in the Destination JNDI name field. Select Started in the Initial State field. You have now mapped this listener port to the queue connection factory and queue JMS objects.

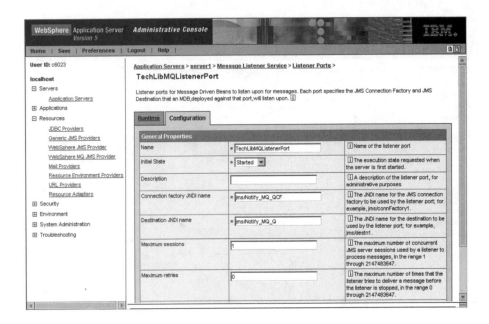

Figure 11-15. Configuring the listener port for the P2P domain

Click OK. Save the configuration and log out of the Administrative Console. Close the Web browser. Let's stop here for a moment and discuss what you have done and what the difference is in setting the administered objects for the embedded JMS provider vs. the MQ JMS provider.

For the embedded JMS provider, you expanded Resources, clicked WebSphere JMS Provider, and went through a series of screens to set the administered objects. For the MQ JMS provider, you selected WebSphere MQ JMS Provider and went through a set of similar screens to set the administered objects.

The Deployment Descriptor configuration is the last part; you will do this in the next section.

Configuring Deployment Descriptors

The final step is to configure the Deployment Descriptors for both applications. In the J2EE Perspective (J2EE Hierarchy View), double-click ReceivingJMSMQProjectEJB to open its Deployment Descriptor.

First, you want to define the listener port for the ReceivingMDB MDB. This is the port that the MDB delegates the container to list on its behalf. Click the Beans tab. Figure 11-16 shows the next screen that appears. Highlight ReceivingMDB. In the "WebSphere Bindings" section, enter TechLibMQListenerPort in the ListenerPort name field.

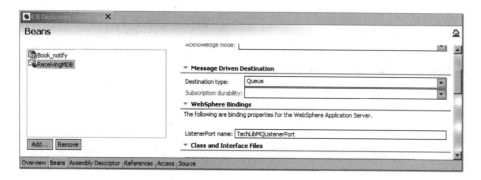

Figure 11-16. Setting the listener port

The Book_notify entity bean indirectly manipulates the TECHBOOK database, so you need to set a reference to the DBDatasource object here. Click the References tab, expand Book_notify, and click ResourceRef DBDatasourceXA. Make sure your screen looks like the one in Figure 11-17.

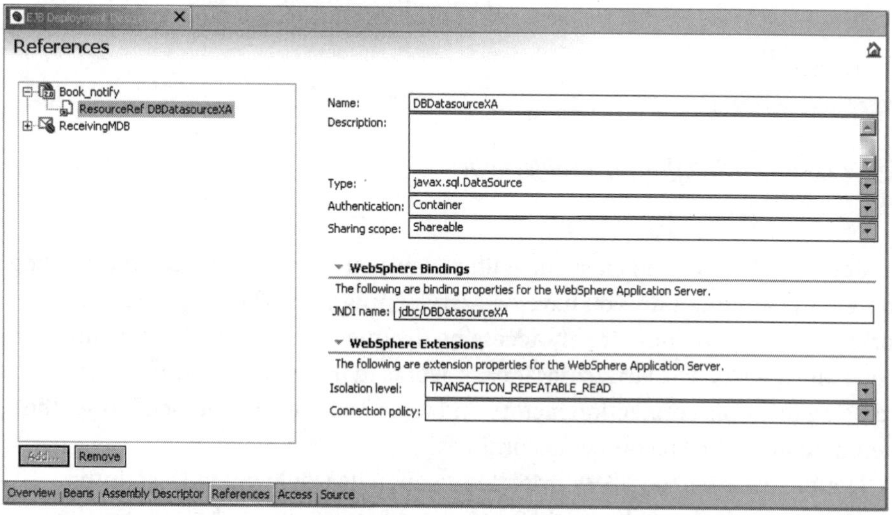

Figure 11-17. Setting a Datasource *resource*

The ReceivingMDB MDB calls the create method of the Book_notify entity bean. In addition, this module indirectly uses the administered objects; therefore, you need to set the reference to all these objects.

Expand `ReceivingMDB` and click `ResourceRef`. Set the `Name` field to `Notify_MQ_QCF` and the `JNDI Name` field to `jms/Notify_MQ_QCF`. Click `ResourceEnvRef`. Set the `Name` field to `Notify_MQ_Q` and the `JNDI Name` field to `jms/Notify_MQ_Q`. Click `ResourceRef`. Set the `Name` field to `Notify_MQ_TCF` and the `JNDI Name` field to `jms/Notify_MQ_TCF`. Click `ResourceEnvRef` again. Set the `Name` field to `Notify_MQ_T` and the `JNDI Name` field to `jms/Notify_MQ_T`. Your screen should look like the one shown in Figure 11-18.

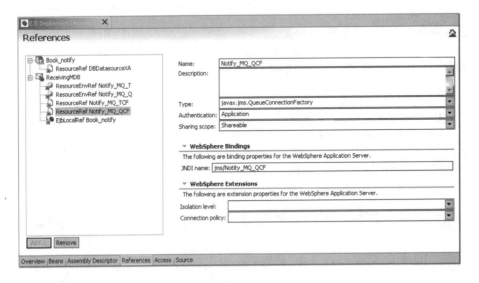

Figure 11-18. Setting the queue object reference

Save the changes and close the editor. Now you need to configure the sending side. On the sending side, you have two servlet programs. The `SendingServlet` works in the P2P domain directly accessing the queue connection factory and queue MQ objects. The `PublishingServlet` works in the Pub/Sub domain directly accessing the topic connection factory and topic MQ objects. You need to set the references to the MQ resources accordingly.

Double-click `SendingJMSMQProjectWEB` to open its Deployment Descriptor. Select the `References` tab, highlight `Resources`, and click the `Add` button. Set the `ResourceRef` name to `Notify_MQ_QCF` and enter `jms/Notify_MQ_QCF` in the `JNDI Name` field. Click the `Add` button again. Set the `New ResourceRef` name to `Notify_MQ_TCF` and enter `jms/Notify_MQ_TCF` in the `JNDI Name` field. Figure 11-19 shows how your final screen should look.

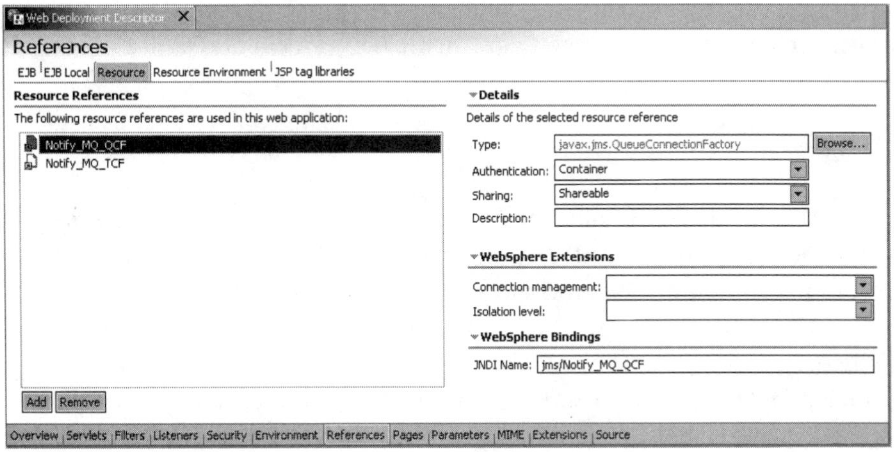

Figure 11-19. Setting the new queue connection factory reference

Highlight Resource Environment and click the Add button. Set the New ResourceEnvRef name to Notify_MQ_Q and enter jms/Notify_MQ_Q in the JNDI Name field. Click the Add button again. Set the ResourceEnvRef name to Notify_MQ_T and enter jms/Notify_MQ_T in the JNDI Name field. Figure 11-20 shows how your final screen should look.

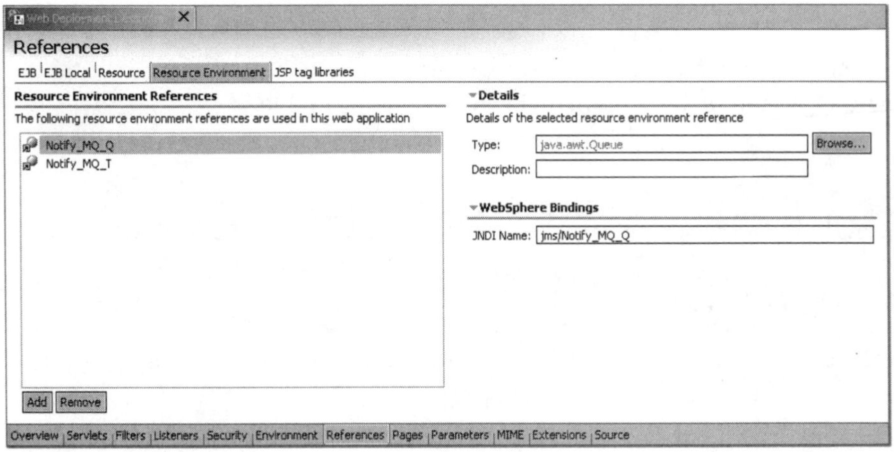

Figure 11-20. Setting the new queue reference

Save the changes and close the editor. You are ready to test your projects. In the next section, you will test how your two projects work in the P2P JMS domain.

Testing the Projects for the Point-to-Point Domain

Stop the UTS (if it is still running). Start the server again but in debug mode (so you can see the messages printed by the program during execution). When the server is up and running, the workspace automatically displays the Debug Perspective. Click the `Server Perspective` button on the vertical Perspective Bar to switch to the Server Perspective. Right-click `SendingServlet` and select `Run on Server`. Figure 11-21 shows the messages printed during the application execution that are displayed in the Console View.

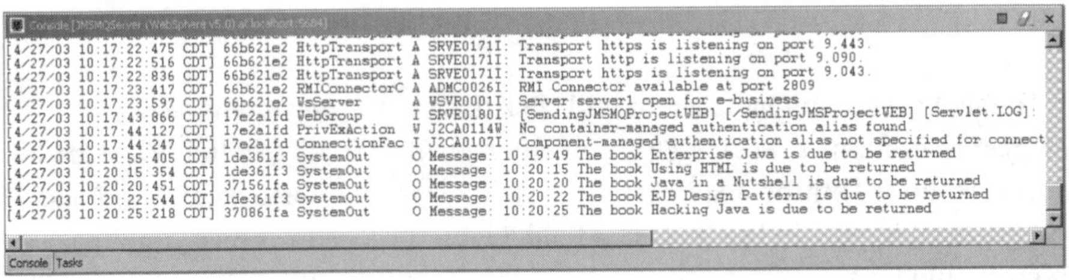

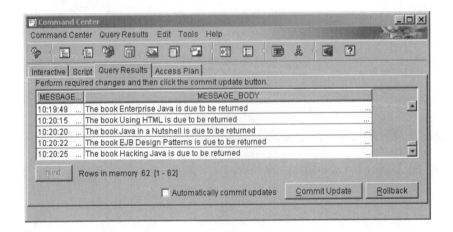

Figure 11-21. P2P execution results displayed in the Console View

Next, you use the DB2 Command Center to browse the BOOK_NOTIFY table. Figure 11-22 shows the content of the BOOK_NOTIFY table.

Figure 11-22. P2P messages in the BOOK_NOTIFY table

In the next section, you will test how your two projects work in the Pub/Sub domain.

Testing the Projects for the Publish/Subscribe Domain

The only change you need to do before testing the Pub/Sub domain is to change the TechLibMQListenerPort. You need to switch it from listening on a queue to listening on a topic. Stop JMSMQServer (if it is still running in debug mode) and start it again (but in run mode). When the server is started, right-click JMSMQServer and select Run administrative console. Enter your user ID to log in. Click Servers ►Application Servers ►server1. Scroll down to the "Additional Properties" section and click Message Listener Service ►Listener Ports. Enter jms/Notify_MQ_TCF in the Connection factory JNDI name field and jms/Notify_MQ_T in the Destination JNDI name field. You have now mapped this listener port to the topic connection factory and topic JMS objects. Figure 11-23 shows how your final screen should look.

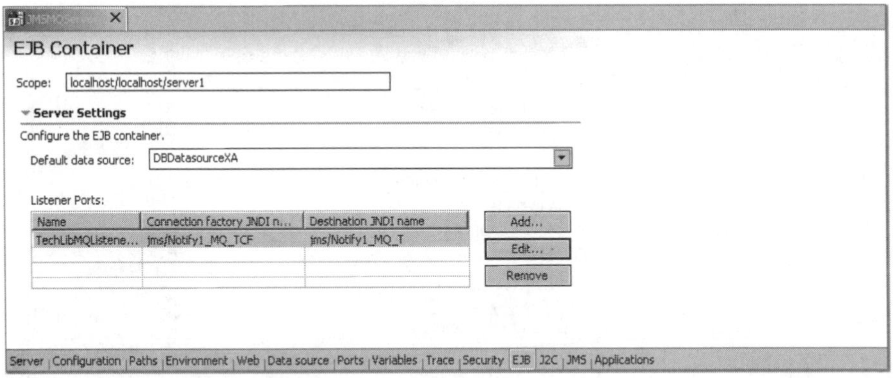

Figure 11-23. Listener port changed to topic

Save the server configuration and log out from the Administrative Console. Close the Web browser.

You also need to open the deployment descripter for the receiving project. Click the Beans tab and change the type of the JMS object for the listener port from Queue to Topic. Save and close the editor.

Start the JMSMQServer. Switch to the Server Perspective, right-click PublishingServlet, and select Run on Server. Figure 11-24 shows the messages that the running application displays in the Console View.

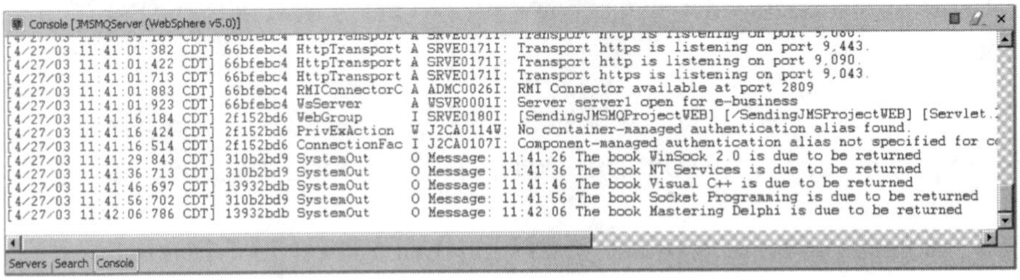

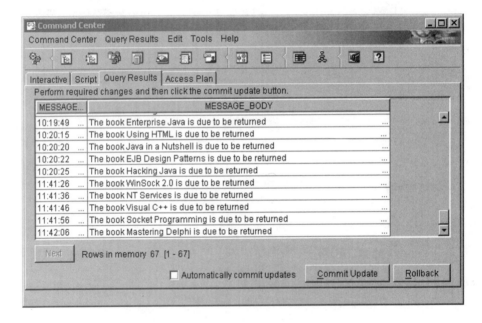

Figure 11-24. Messages printed during program execution

Next, you use the DB2 Command Center to browse the BOOK_NOTIFY table. Figure 11-25 shows the content of the BOOK_NOTIFY table.

Figure 11-25. Pub/Sub messages in the BOOK_NOTIFY table

Setting Administered Objects for the JMS MQ Provider Simply

Now that you have learned the hard way of this type of development (and sometimes the only way), there is good news: WSAD 5.0 now supports a simplified way of setting the JMS objects for the MQ JMS provider—similar to the way you set them for the embedded JMS provider. Just set your JMS objects and the listener port within the Administrative Console and run the project. If at runtime WSAD 5.0 (WAS 5.0) determines that a necessary JMS object is not present, it automatically builds a default configuration of this object.

You can download the two exported project files (`ReceivingJMSMQProject1App.ear` and `SendingJMSMQProject1.App.ear`) and the `JMSMQServer.zip` server configuration file from the Apress Web site. This version of the example uses the MQ objects that were set using the Administrative Console without the JMSAdmin utility. Of course, there are situations when the default configuration being set in the Administrative Console is not appropriate for production. In this case, you need to use one of the available MQ tools for setting the more sophisticated MQ objects.

Summary

This chapter discussed how to integrate the WSAD and MQ environments to use MQ as the WSAD JMS provider. It also covered how to install MQ on top of the WSAD embedded JMS provider and showed how to use the MQ Explorer and JMSAdmin utilities for building and registering MQ objects. Next, it discussed how to set the UTS environment and the Deployment Descriptor configuration. Finally, you developed the sending and receiving sides of the J2EE 1.3 JMS application and tested it for both JMS domains (P2P and Pub/Sub).

Deploying This Book's J2EE Examples

In this appendix, you will learn how to deploy the Java 2 Enterprise Edition (J2EE) 1.3 applications on WebSphere Application Server (WAS) 5.0. You will deploy some of the application examples that you developed in this book.

The runtime environment discussed in this appendix resides on a network server machine called JULIA. On this machine, the following software packages have been installed: WAS 5.0, DB2 Universal Database (UDB) 7.2 with Fixpack 6, and WebSphere MQ 5.3.1 with all the necessary service packs. Installation of the DB2 and MQ packages for the runtime and development environments is very similar. (See Chapter 3 where it is covered for the development environment.)

 NOTE *The installation of the WAS 5.0 package is beyond the scope of this book. Please consult the vendor documentation.*

The installation documentation for the Windows NT/2000 platform comes in the WAS 5.0 downloadable files. Unzip the Readme.zip file and read two documents: Installation.html and InstallGuide_en.PDF. Similar documentation is available for other platforms. In addition, you can refer to several books written for WAS, such as *IBM WebSphere Application Server V5.0 System Management and Configuration*, which is available from IBM Redbooks at http://www.redbooks.ibm.com.

These packages are installed on the runtime machine in the following directories:

- C:\SQLLIB: DB2 database 7.2

- C:\WSMQ: WebSphere MQ 5.3.1

- C:\WAS: WAS 5.0

This appendix frequently mentions these directories (or their subdirectories). Make the appropriate adjustments if your installation is different.

Avoiding Port Conflicts

If you install both the WSAD 5.0 and WAS 5.0 packages on the same machine, you will not be able to run them concurrently because of a conflict in the ports. One solution is to always stop WAS and the IBM HTTP Server before activating WSAD (and vice versa). Another solution is to modify the ports WAS uses. A typical WAS 5.0 installation uses the following ports: 80, 443, 900, 2809, 5557, 5558, 5559, 7873, 8008, 8880, 9000, 9043, 9080, 9090, and 9443. Issue the network command `netstat -an` to display the ports currently used on your machine.

To change the ports that WAS 5.0 uses and avoid the port conflicts, go to the WAS `config` directory and change the default ports that have been set within several configuration files. Be careful when directly modifying the WAS configuration files (back up them first). You can make the same modifications using the WAS Administrative Console: Expand `Nodes` all the way until you see `Application Servers` ➤`Web Containers` and `EJB Containers`. Check and change (if necessary) all the default ports. Also, expand `Virtual Hosts` ➤`Aliases` to examine (and change if necessary) the port assignments.

Preparing the WAS Environment for Deployment

In this section, you will deploy the database application developed in Chapter 4. The first task is to install the TECHBOOK database and its tables in the runtime environment (in the same way you installed it in the development environment). You will use the same procedure (used in the development environment in Chapter 4) for building the TECHBOOK database in your production environment. The procedure is called `BuildTechbookDatabase.sql`, and you can download it from the Downloads section of the Apress Web site (`http://www.apress.com`).

Listing A-1 shows the procedure. Make the appropriate adjustments if your runtime environment is different. Finally, remember to copy this procedure to the `<DB2-Install-Directory\bin` directory.

Listing A-1. `BuildTechbookDatabase.sql`

```
-- Build TECHBOOK database and tables --
DROP DB TECHBOOK;
CREATE DB TECHBOOK;
```

```
UPDATE DB CFG FOR TECHBOOK USING APPLHEAPSZ 256;
-- Commit to Save Work
COMMIT WORK;


GRANT ALL ON TECHBOOK TO PUBLIC;


CREATE SCHEMA LIB;


-- Commit to save work
COMMIT WORK;


CONNECT RESET;


-- Create the BOOK_CATALOG table


CONNECT to TECHBOOK;


-- DROP TABLE LIB.BOOK_CATALOG;


CREATE TABLE LIB.BOOK_CATALOG
  (CATALOG_NUMBER CHARACTER(5) NOT NULL,
   AUTHOR VARCHAR(50) NOT NULL,
   BOOK_TITLE VARCHAR(100) NOT NULL,
   LOCATION VARCHAR(50) NOT NULL,
   PLATFORM CHARACTER(2),
   LANGUAGE CHARACTER(2),
   PRIMARY KEY(CATALOG_NUMBER));


-- GRANT ALL ON BOOK_CATALOG TO PUBLIC;


-- Commit to save Work
COMMIT WORK;


-- Load BOOK_CATALOG Table Data


INSERT INTO LIB.BOOK_CATALOG (CATALOG_NUMBER, AUTHOR,
 BOOK_TITLE, LOCATION, PLATFORM, LANGUAGE)
VALUES('00001', 'Developer Journal', 'Windows NT
 Programming in Practice', 'Library', '04', '02');


INSERT INTO LIB.BOOK_CATALOG (CATALOG_NUMBER, AUTHOR,
 BOOK_TITLE, LOCATION, PLATFORM, LANGUAGE)
VALUES('00002', 'Chris Hare', 'Inside Unix', 'AAA_Company', '00', '02');
```

```
INSERT INTO LIB.BOOK_CATALOG (CATALOG_NUMBER, AUTHOR,
 BOOK_TITLE, LOCATION, PLATFORM, LANGUAGE)
VALUES('00003', 'David Flanagan and a team', 'Java Enterprise
 in a Nutshell', 'Library', '00', '01');

INSERT INTO LIB.BOOK_CATALOG (CATALOG_NUMBER, AUTHOR,
 BOOK_TITLE, LOCATION, PLATFORM, LANGUAGE)
VALUES('00004', 'Danny  Ayers and a team',
 'Java Server Programming', 'BBB_Company', '00', '01');

INSERT INTO LIB.BOOK_CATALOG (CATALOG_NUMBER, AUTHOR,
 BOOK_TITLE, LOCATION, PLATFORM, LANGUAGE)
VALUES('00005', 'Bill McCarty', 'Learn Red Hat Linux', 'Library', '05', '01');

INSERT INTO LIB.BOOK_CATALOG (CATALOG_NUMBER, AUTHOR,
 BOOK_TITLE, LOCATION, PLATFORM, LANGUAGE)
VALUES('00006', 'Lisa Donald and a team', 'MCSE Windows 2000
 Professional', 'BBB_Company', '04', '02');

INSERT INTO LIB.BOOK_CATALOG (CATALOG_NUMBER, AUTHOR,
 BOOK_TITLE, LOCATION, PLATFORM, LANGUAGE)
VALUES('00007', 'Harry M. Brelsford', 'Windows 2000
 Server Secrets', 'BBB_Company', '04', '02');

-- Commit to save work
COMMIT WORK;

-- Create the BOOK_ACTIVITY table

-- DROP TABLE LIB.BOOK_ACTIVITY;

CREATE TABLE LIB.BOOK_ACTIVITY
  (TXN_DATE    CHARACTER(10) NOT NULL,
   TXN_TIME    CHARACTER(8) NOT NULL,
   TXN_TYPE    CHARACTER(4) NOT NULL,
   BOOK_CAT_NUM CHARACTER(5) NOT NULL,
   COMPANY_NAME VARCHAR(50) NOT NULL,
   PRIMARY KEY(TXN_DATE,TXN_TIME));

-- GRANT ALL ON BOOK_ACTIVITY TO PUBLIC;

-- Commit to save Work
COMMIT WORK;
```

```
-- Load the BOOK_ACTIVITY table data

INSERT INTO LIB.BOOK_ACTIVITY (TXN_DATE, TXN_TIME,
 TXN_TYPE , BOOK_CAT_NUM, COMPANY_NAME)
VALUES('01-01-2002', '09:17:25', 'RENT', '00001', 'AAA_Company');

INSERT INTO LIB.BOOK_ACTIVITY (TXN_DATE, TXN_TIME,
 TXN_TYPE , BOOK_CAT_NUM, COMPANY_NAME)
VALUES('01-10-2002', '10:11:66', 'RETR', '00001', 'AAA_Company');

INSERT INTO LIB.BOOK_ACTIVITY (TXN_DATE, TXN_TIME,
 TXN_TYPE , BOOK_CAT_NUM, COMPANY_NAME)
VALUES('02-20-2002', '11:12:55', 'RENT', '00002', 'AAA_Company');

INSERT INTO LIB.BOOK_ACTIVITY (TXN_DATE, TXN_TIME,
 TXN_TYPE , BOOK_CAT_NUM, COMPANY_NAME)
VALUES('01-15-2002', '12:12:12', 'RENT', '00003', 'BBB_Company');

INSERT INTO LIB.BOOK_ACTIVITY (TXN_DATE, TXN_TIME,
 TXN_TYPE , BOOK_CAT_NUM, COMPANY_NAME)
VALUES('01-31-2002', '13:26:33', 'RETR', '00003', 'BBB_Company');

INSERT INTO LIB.BOOK_ACTIVITY (TXN_DATE, TXN_TIME,
 TXN_TYPE , BOOK_CAT_NUM, COMPANY_NAME)
VALUES('03-05-2002', '14:22:11', 'RENT', '00003', 'CCC_Company');

INSERT  INTO LIB.BOOK_ACTIVITY (TXN_DATE, TXN_TIME,
 TXN_TYPE , BOOK_CAT_NUM, COMPANY_NAME)
VALUES('04-05-2002', '15:44:31', 'RETR', '00003', 'CCC_Company');

INSERT INTO LIB.BOOK_ACTIVITY (TXN_DATE, TXN_TIME,
 TXN_TYPE , BOOK_CAT_NUM, COMPANY_NAME)
VALUES('02-11-2002', '16:32:33', 'RENT', '00004', 'BBB_Company');

INSERT INTO LIB.BOOK_ACTIVITY (TXN_DATE, TXN_TIME, TXN_TYPE,
 BOOK_CAT_NUM, COMPANY_NAME)
VALUES('02-17-2002', '17:12:22', 'RENT', '00005', 'BBB_Company');

INSERT INTO LIB.BOOK_ACTIVITY (TXN_DATE, TXN_TIME, TXN_TYPE,
 BOOK_CAT_NUM, COMPANY_NAME)
VALUES('03-11-2002', '18:23:44', 'RETR', '00005', 'BBB_Company');
```

```
INSERT INTO LIB.BOOK_ACTIVITY (TXN_DATE, TXN_TIME, TXN_TYPE,
 BOOK_CAT_NUM, COMPANY_NAME)
VALUES('03-15-2002', '19:27:11', 'RENT', '00005', 'DDD_Company');

INSERT INTO LIB.BOOK_ACTIVITY (TXN_DATE, TXN_TIME, TXN_TYPE,
 BOOK_CAT_NUM, COMPANY_NAME)
VALUES('04-A-2002', '20:43:21', 'RETR', '00005', 'DDD_Company');

INSERT INTO LIB.BOOK_ACTIVITY (TXN_DATE, TXN_TIME, TXN_TYPE,
 BOOK_CAT_NUM, COMPANY_NAME)
VALUES('05-01-2002', '20:11:21', 'RENT', '00006', 'BBB_Company');

INSERT INTO LIB.BOOK_ACTIVITY (TXN_DATE, TXN_TIME, TXN_TYPE,
 BOOK_CAT_NUM, COMPANY_NAME)
VALUES('05-02-2002', '21:11:21', 'RENT', '00007', 'BBB_Company');

-- Commit to save work
COMMIT WORK;

-- Create the BOOK_NOTIFY table

-- DROP TABLE LIB.BOOK_NOTIFY;

CREATE TABLE LIB.BOOK_NOTIFY
  (MESSAGE_DATE CHARACTER(10) NOT NULL,
   MESSAGE_TIME CHARACTER(8) NOT NULL,
   COMPANY_NAME VARCHAR(50) NOT NULL,
   USER_NAME VARCHAR(50) NOT NULL,
   MESSAGE_TEXT VARCHAR(200) NOT NULL,
   PRIMARY KEY(MESSAGE_DATE,MESSAGE_TIME));

-- GRANT ALL ON BOOK_NOTIFY TO PUBLIC;

-- Commit to save work
COMMIT WORK;

-- End the connection
CONNECT RESET;
```

To build the TECHBOOK database and its tables, start the DB2 command prompt window and enter the following command:

```
db2 -tf BuildTechbookDatabase.sql
```

You can verify that TECHBOOK database (and its tables) has been created by performing the same tasks you used for the database verification in the development environment (see Chapter 3).

Defining the Datasource for WAS 5.0

Next, you will define the Datasource that you use in many of this book's examples for the WAS 5.0 environment. Other WAS 5.0 applications can use this Datasource (once set). First, you need to start WAS 5.0 and then start the WAS Administrative Console. To start WAS 5.0, select Start ➤Programs ➤IBM WebSphere ➤First Steps ➤Start Server. You can start the Administrative Console from the Windows 2000 taskbar in two ways:

- Start ➤Programs ➤IBM WebSphere ➤Administrative Console

- Start ➤Programs ➤IBM WebSphere ➤First Steps ➤Administrative Console

On the Login screen, enter your user ID and click OK. In the WAS Administrative Console, expand Resources and click JDBC Providers. Then, click New. On the next screen, shown in Figure A-1, select DB2_JDBC_Provider from the list.

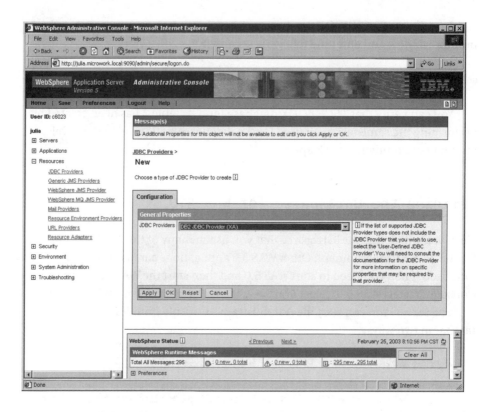

Figure A-1. Defining the JDBC provider

Click Apply. The subsequent screen, shown in Figure A-2, presents the DB2 provider attributes. Enter c:\SQLLIB\Java/db2java.zip in the Classpath field, where c:\SQLLIB is the DB2 installation directory.

NOTE *Alternatively, you can leave this field as it is:* $(DB2_JDBC_DRIVER_PATH)/ db2java.zip. *The problem is that this variable value is not set (it must point to the Java subdirectory of the DB2 installation directory). To set the value of this environment variable, expand* Environment *and click* Manage WebSphere Variables.

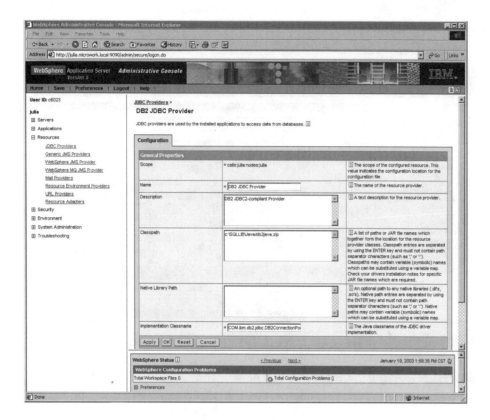

Figure A-2. Attributes of the DB2 JDBC provider

Click the Data Sources link at the bottom of the screen. Click New and on the next screen, enter DBDatasource in the Name field and jdbc/DBDatasource in the JNDI Name field. Click Apply. Click the Custom Properties link at the bottom of the screen. On the next screen, click databaseName and enter TECHBOOK in the Value field. Click OK.

You now need to set the authentication alias. Click J2C Authentication Data Entries at the bottom of the screen. Click New. On the next screen, shown in Figure A-3, enter DBDatasourceAlias in the Alias field, enter the user ID and password of the account authorized to access the database, and, optionally, enter a description of the alias.

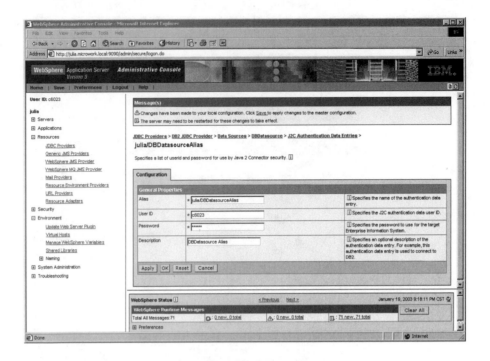

Figure A-3. Creating the authentication alias

Click OK, click the Data Sources link, and then click the DBDatasource link to return to the Datasource settings screen, depicted in Figure A-4. Select Julia/ DBDatasourceAlias for both the (Component-managed and Container-managed) Authentication Alias fields.

Click Apply. Click Connection Pool near the bottom. On the screen that appears, accept the defaults and click OK twice. Figure A-5 shows the configured Datasource object.

A message at the top of the screen reminds you to save the WAS configuration. Click the Save button on the main menu bar. Click the Save button again on the confirmation screen. Click the Logout button on the Administrative Console toolbar to exit the Administrative Console. Use the First Steps dialog to stop and restart the server so the WAS configuration changes take effect.

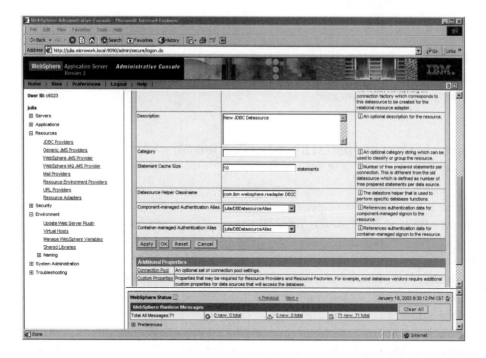

Figure A-4. Setting the authentication alias for the Datasource

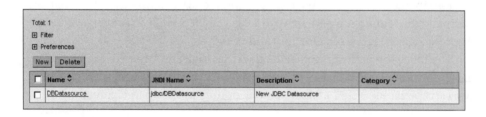

Figure A-5. The configured DBDatasource *object*

NOTE *Always wait until the application server completely stops or starts before using it again.*

Deploying the DBDatasourceProjectApp Application

You are now ready to deploy the DBDatasourceProjectApp application that you developed in Chapter 4. First, you need to export the application from the WSAD development environment.

Exporting the DBDatasourceProjectApp Application from WSAD

On the development machine, export the DBDatasourceProjectApp project from the WSAD Workbench. Switch to the J2EE Perspective (J2EE Navigator View), right-click the DBDatasourceProjectApp project, and select Export. On the next screen, select EAR file as the type of the exporting resource and click Next. On the next screen, the What resource do you want to export field should already be DBDatasourceProjectApp. If it is not, click the Browse button and locate DBDatasourceProjectApp.

You want to export the application in the installableApps subdirectory inside the WAS installation directory located on the runtime machine. Click the Browse button attached to the Where do you want to export resources to field and navigate to the installableApps subdirectory inside the WAS installation directory. Because in this case the installableApps subdirectory resides on another machine, I mapped the remote drive where WAS 5.0 is installed as the Z: drive. Navigate to the Z:\WAS\installableApps directory and click Open.

The following path appears in the field that indicates where to export the application: Z:\WAS\installableApps\DBDatasourceProjectApp.ear. Select the Overwrite existing files without warning option, as shown in Figure A-6.

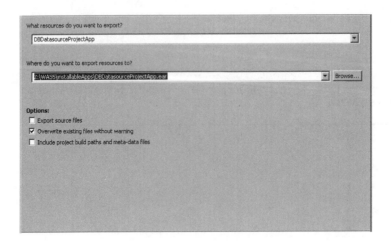

Figure A-6. Exporting the DBDatasourceProjectApp *application*

Click Finish. The DBDatasourceProjectApp.ear file will be placed in the WAS installedApps directory.

In the next section, you will install the exported application.

Installing the DBDatasourceProjectApp Application

Switch to the runtime machine JULIA (where WAS 5.0 is installed) and activate the WAS Administrative Console. Enter your user ID to log in. Expand Applications and click the Install New Application. Figure A-7 shows the next screen. Click Browse, navigate to the WAS installableApps directory, and select the DBDatasourceProjectApp.ear file.

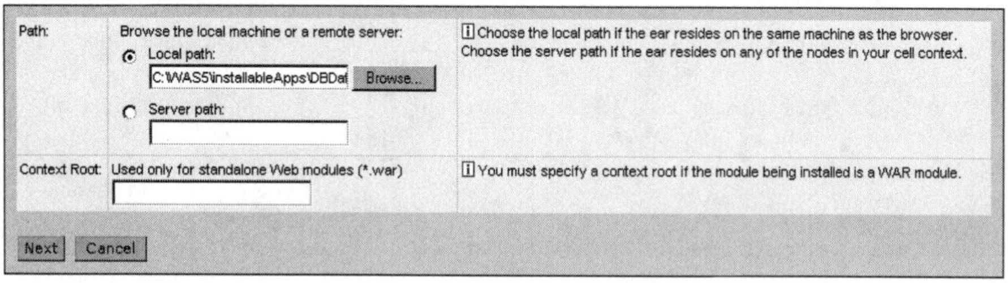

Figure A-7. Installing the DBDatasourceProjectApp *application*

Click Next. Figure A-8 shows the next screen.

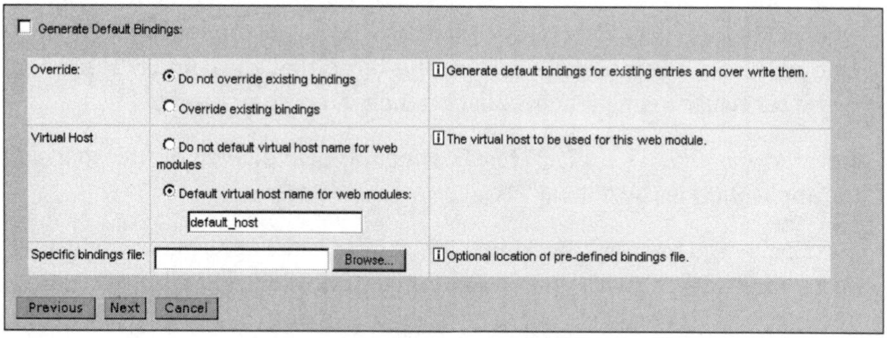

Figure A-8. Generic installation options

Checking the Generate Default Bindings box instructs WAS to automatically generate the default binding data. In this case, WAS will find all unmapped references in the EAR file and attempt to resolve them with the resources defined in the EAR file. You want to manually control this process, so leave this box unchecked. Accept all the defaults and click Next. The next screen, shown in Figure A-9, appears.

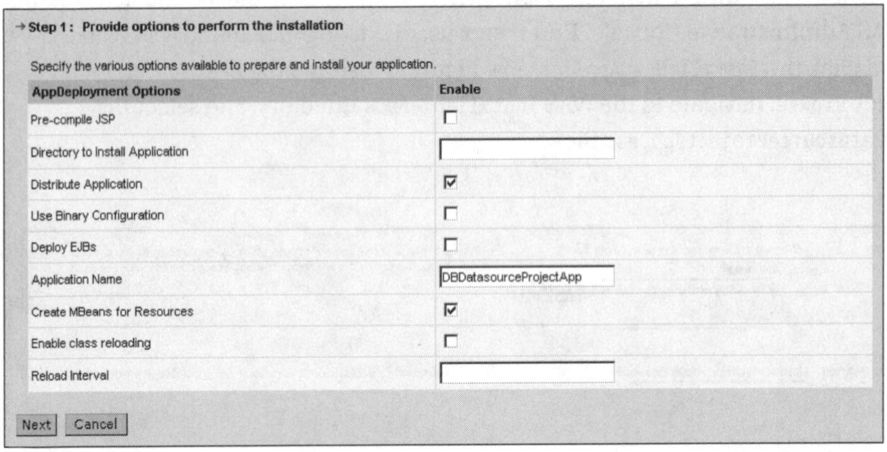

Figure A-9. Additional installation options

Figure A-9 allows you to set some additional options:

Pre-compile JSP: This instructs WAS to compile all JavaServer Pages (JSPs) during the application installation. Checking this box speeds up the response when a JSP is first activated, but it increases the application installation time. One additional advantage of checking this box is that any compilation errors in the JSPs will be caught at installation time rather than runtime.

Directory to Install Application: Leaving this field blank indicates to install the application in the default installedApps directory.

Distribute Application: Checking this box installs the application in the multiserver networked environment. The application will be distributed to all node servers. You really do not need to set this option, but you can leave this box selected for demonstration purposes.

Use Binary Configuration: If selected, this indicates that the setting done within WSAD should be used here as the predisplayed default. Otherwise, default values will be used.

Deploy EJBs: If this option is selected, the Enterprise JavaBean (EJB) deployment code will be generated during installation.

Application Name: This is the name of the installed application.

Create MBeans for Resources: If selected, this creates the Java Management Extension (JMX) modules used for the JMX resource management.

Enable class reloading: If selected, this automatically reloads objects that have been changed.

Reload interval: This defines the interval of reloading objects.

Accept the default on this screen and click Next. The screen shown in Figure A-10 appears.

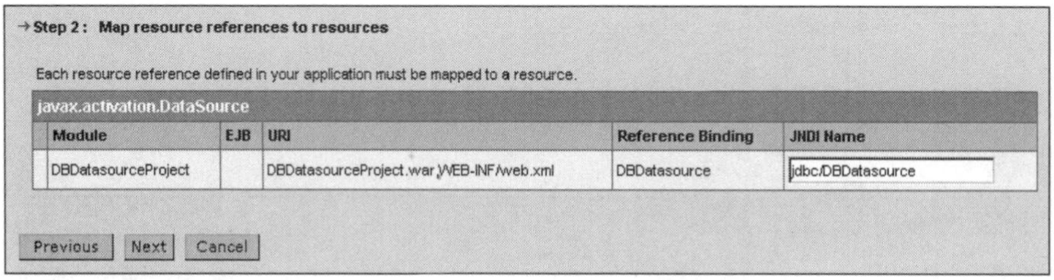

Module	EJB	URI	Reference Binding	JNDI Name
DBDatasourceProject		DBDatasourceProject.war,/WEB-INF/web.xml	DBDatasource	jdbc/DBDatasource

Figure A-10. Mapping a resource reference to the resource

Remember that you installed the TECHBOOK Datasource object for WAS with the name jdbc/DBDatasource; therefore, you do not have to make any changes on this screen. Instead, click Next. Figure A-11 shows the subsequent screen.

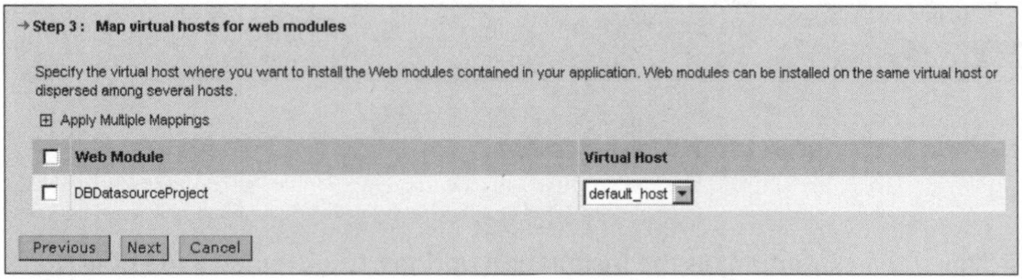

Figure A-11. Mapping a virtual host to a Web module server

Again, you do not have to make any changes on this screen. Click Next. On the subsequent screen, shown in Figure A-12, highlight the server and check the DBDatasourceProject.

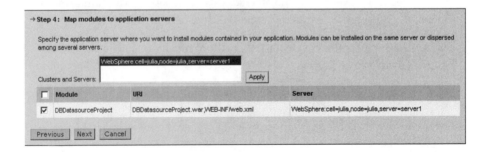

Figure A-12. Mapping modules to application servers

Click Apply and then click Next. Figure A-13 shows the next screen.

→ Step 5 : Summary

Summary of Install Options

Options	Values
Distribute Application	Yes
Use Binary Configuration	No
Cell/Node/Server	Click here
Create MBeans for Resources	Yes
Enable class reloading	No
Deploy EJBs	No
was.policy.data	was.policy file does not exist
Application Name:	DBDatasourceProjectApp
Reload Interval	
Directory to Install Application	
Pre-compile JSP	No
Application Name	DBDatasourceProjectApp

Previous Finish Cancel

Figure A-13. The installation Summary *screen*

This screen summarizes the installation options. Click Finish. WAS now starts installing the application. When it is done, the screen shown in Figure A-14 appears.

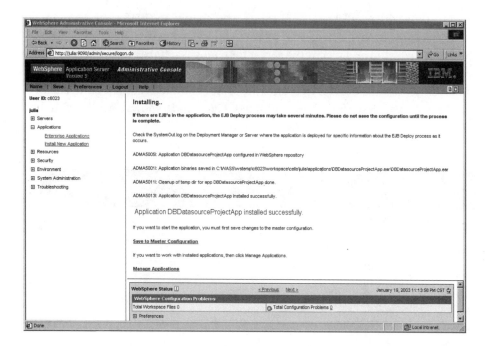

Figure A-14. The installation results

You should see a message stating that the application has been installed
successfully. Click the Save to Master Configuration link. Click Save again on the
confirmation screen. On the next screen, depicted in Figure A-15, you should
see that the DBDatasourceProjectApp application appears in the list of installed
applications. However, the application has not started yet (indicated in the Status
column). (You may need to click the Enterprise Applications link, shown in
Figure A-14, to get to this screen.)

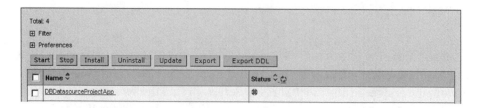

Figure A-15. List of installed applications

Any time you install a new application, you change the WAS configuration. You should always save changes in the WAS configuration (you have already done this), and then stop and restart the server for changes to take effect. Click the Logout button to exit the Administrative Console. Activate the WAS First Steps utility. Click Stop the Server. Wait until the server completely stops. Next, click Start the Server. Wait until the server starts. Figure A-16 shows a screen with the started server.

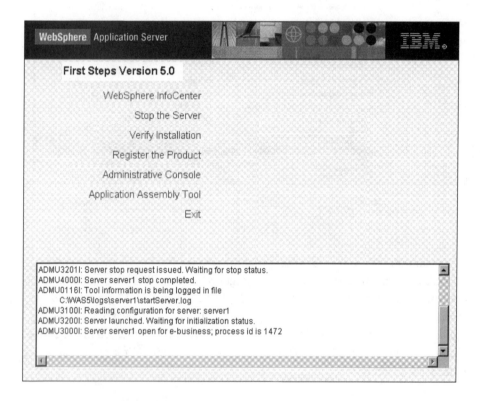

Figure A-16. Restarting the server

If you are using an external Web server (such as the IBM HTTP Server) to activate the application, you also need to regenerate the Web server plug-in file by stopping and restarting the IBM HTTP Server. To stop the server, select Start ➤Programs ➤IBM HTTP Server 1.3.26 ➤Stop HTTP Server. To start the IBM HTTP Server, select Start ➤Programs ➤IBM HTTP Server 1.3.26 ➤Start HTTP Server.

Start the Administrative Console again. Log in, expand Applications and click Enterprise Applications. Figure A-17 shows the next screen. You should see that the DBDatasourceProjectApp application is not only included in the list of installed applications but it has also successfully started (indicated by the green arrow on the Status column).

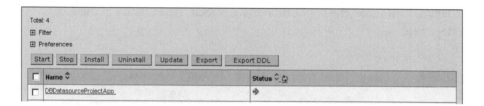

Figure A-17. The started `DBDatasourceProjectApp` *application*

You are ready to run the application. To invoke the application under the Web browser, you need to know how to construct the invocation Uniform Resource Locator (URL) for your application. The URL includes the node name where the server is running (which is `localhost` in this case). You also need to know the `Context-root` of the Web module. In the Administrative Console, click the `DBDatasourceProjectApp` application. In the "Additional Properties" section, click `View Deployment Descriptor`. Figure A-18 shows the application-level Deployment Descriptor. Expand `Web Modules` all the way down. You should see `Context-root: DBDatasourceProject`.

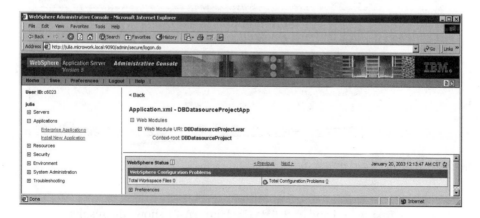

Figure A-18. The application Deployment Descriptor

To construct the URL, you concatenate the node (which is `localhost` in this case) with the `Context-root` and with the module name to be invoked (`BookSearchInputForm.html`). The final URL is `http://localhost/DBDatasourceProject/BookSearchInputForm.html`.

You are ready to run your application. Start your Web browser and enter the following URL in the command line: `http://localhost/DBDatasourceProject/BookSearchInputForm.html`.

Figure A-19 shows the application input screen. Type Library in the Book location field.

Figure A-19. The user input screen

Click Submit. Figure A-20 shows the processing results.

Figure A-20. The main processing results

Select the first record and click Details. Figure A-21 shows the results.

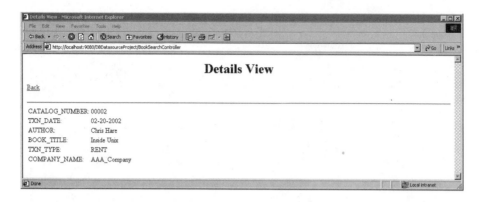

Figure A-21. The Details View *page*

This is the end of the DBDatasourceApp application deployment example. In the next section, you will deploy the full J2EE application called TechLibApp. Chapters 6 and 7 cover the development of this application.

Deploying the TechLibApp Application

To deploy the TechLibApp application, you need to export the application from your WSAD 5.0 development environment and then install it on WAS 5.0 in your runtime environment.

Exporting the TechLibApp Application from WSAD

On the development machine, you need to export the TechLibApp project from the WSAD Workbench. Again, in the J2EE Perspective, right-click TechLibApp and select Export. On the next screen, select EAR file as the type of export. Click Next. Figure A-22 shows the next screen. TechLibApp should already appear as the resource to be exported. Click the Browse button and navigate to the directory where you want to place the exported resource. You want to place the TechLibApp application in the WAS install subdirectory called installableApps.

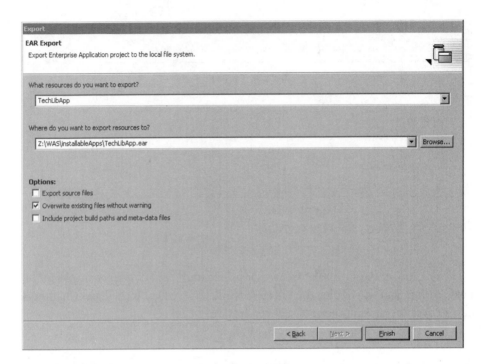

Figure A-22. Exporting the TechLibApp *application*

Click Finish. The TechLibApp.ear file will be placed in the WAS installableApps directory. In the next section, you will install the TechLibApp application.

Installing the TechLibApp Application

Now, switch to the runtime machine JULIA (where WAS 5.0 is installed) and activate the WAS Administrative Console. Enter your user ID and click OK. Expand Applications and click Install New Application. On the next screen, shown in Figure A-23, click Browse, navigate to the WAS installableApps directory, and select the TechLibApp.ear file.

Click Next. Figure A-24 shows the first screen of the installation wizard.

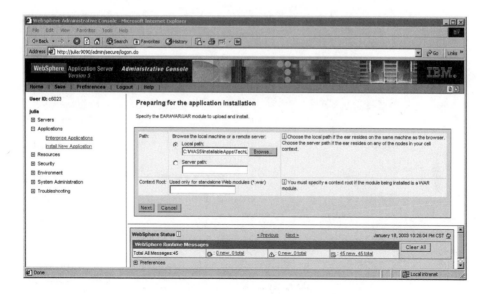

Figure A-23. Installing the TechLibApp *application*

Figure A-24. Preparing for the application installation screen

Accept the defaults and click Next. You will see the screen depicted in Figure A-25.

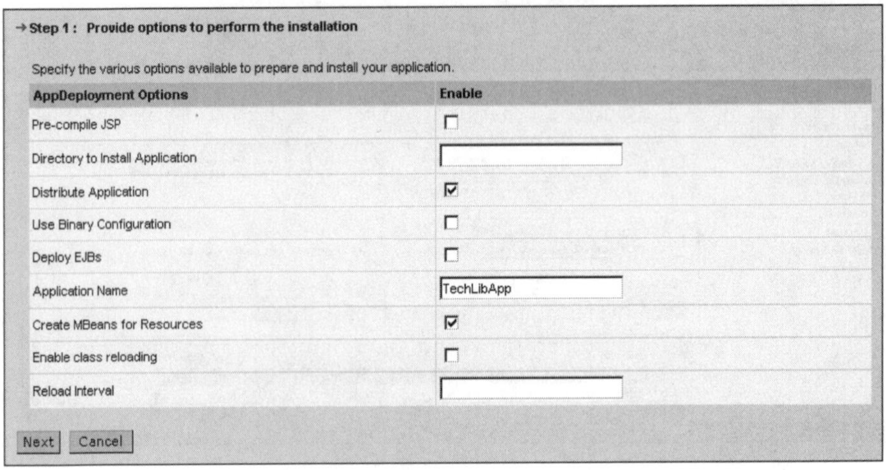

Figure A-25. Installation options

Again, accept the default and click Next. The next screen, shown in Figure A-26, allows you to change the mapping of the EJB modules to their JNDI names.

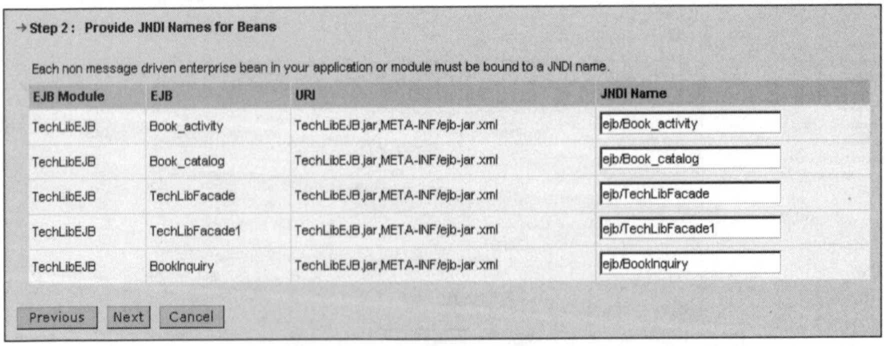

Figure A-26. Mapping EJB modules to JNDI names

All the names are already filled in correctly, so you do not need to change anything on this screen. Click Next. The subsequent screen, shown in Figure A-27, allows you to change the mapping of the TECHBOOK Datasource to its external JNDI name. Enter jdbc/DBDatasource in the JNDI Name field. This is the EJB module-level Datasource mapping that applies to every EJB 2.0 Container Managed Persistence (CMP) component within the EJB module.

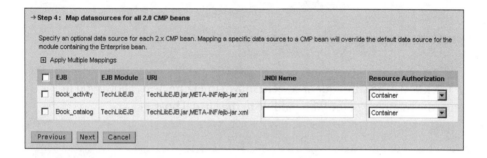

Specify the default data source for the EJB 2.x Module containing 2.x CMP beans.

⊞ Apply Multiple Mappings

	EJB Module	URI	JNDI Name	Resource Authorization
☐	TechLibEJB	TechLibEJB.jar,META-INF/ejb-jar.xml	jdbc/DBDatasource	Per connection factory ▾

OK   Cancel

Figure A-27. Mapping the Datasource *to the JNDI name*

Click OK. Figure A-28 shows the next screen, where you can optionally map each individual EJB 2.0 CMP module to a specific Datasource.

→ **Step 4 : Map datasources for all 2.0 CMP beans**

Specify an optional data source for each 2.x CMP bean. Mapping a specific data source to a CMP bean will override the default data source for the module containing the Enterprise bean.

⊞ Apply Multiple Mappings

	EJB	EJB Module	URI	JNDI Name	Resource Authorization
☐	Book_activity	TechLibEJB	TechLibEJB.jar,META-INF/ejb-jar.xml		Container ▾
☐	Book_catalog	TechLibEJB	TechLibEJB.jar,META-INF/ejb-jar.xml		Container ▾

Previous   Next   Cancel

Figure A-28. Mapping individual CMP modules to the Datasource *JNDI names*

You do not need to map individual CMP components to different Datasources, so click Next. The next screen, shown in Figure A-29, allows you to change the mapping of the EJB module references.

→ **Step 5 : Map EJB references to beans**

Each EJB reference defined in your application must be mapped to an Enterprise bean.

Module	EJB	URI	Reference Binding	Class	JNDI Name
TechLibEJB	TechLibFacade	TechLibEJB.jar,META-INF/ejb-jar.xml	Book_catalog	apress.wsad.techlib.TechLibBook_catalogLocal	ejb/Book_catalog
TechLibEJB	TechLibFacade1	TechLibEJB.jar,META-INF/ejb-jar.xml	Book_catalog	apress.wsad.techlib.TechLibBook_catalogLocal	ejb/Book_catalog
TechLibEJB	TechLibFacade1	TechLibEJB.jar,META-INF/ejb-jar.xml	Book_activity	apress.wsad.techlib.TechLibBook_activityLocal	ejb/Book_activity
TechLibWEB		TechLibWEB.war,WEB-INF/web.xml	Book_catalog	apress.wsad.techlib.TechLibBook_catalogLocal	ejb/Book_catalog
TechLibWEB		TechLibWEB.war,WEB-INF/web.xml	TechLibFacade1	apress.wsad.techlib.TechLibFacade1Local	ejb/TechLibFacade1

Previous   Next   Cancel

Figure A-29. Mapping EJB module references

All names are already filled in correctly, so click Next. Figure A-30 shows the next screen, which allows you to change the mapping of the resource references to the actual resources. Make sure TechLibEJB is checked, expand the Select box, and select the Datasource called julia:jdbc/DBDatasource. Enter jdbc/DBDatasource in the JNDI Name field.

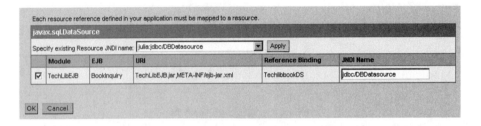

Figure A-30. Mapping EJB module references

Click Next. The subsequent screen, shown in Figure A-31, allows you to change the mapping of the Web module to the virtual host.

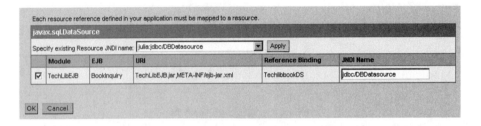

Figure A-31. Mapping the Web module to the virtual host

This screen does not require any changes, so click Next. Figure A-32 shows the next screen, where you can map modules to the application server.

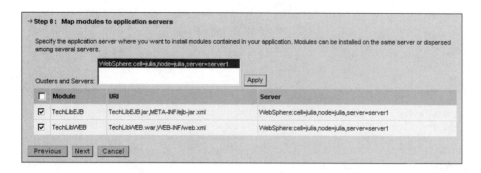

Figure A-32. Mapping modules to the application server

Click Next. The next screen, depicted in Figure A-33, allows you to define declarative security to protect the EJB methods.

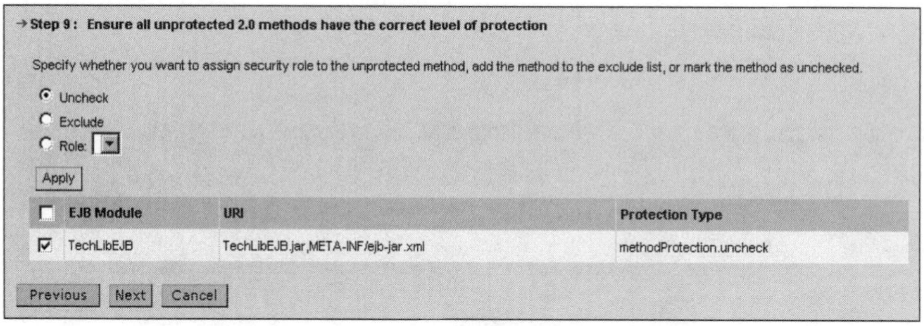

Figure A-33. Setting EJB module protection

You do not want to define declarative security for this application example, so click Next. Figure A-34 displays the installation summary.

Options	Values
Distribute Application	Yes
Use Binary Configuration	No
Cell/Node/Server	Click here
Create MBeans for Resources	Yes
Enable class reloading	No
Deploy EJBs	No
was.policy.data	was.policy file does not exist
Application Name:	TechLibApp
Reload Interval	
Directory to Install Application	
Pre-compile JSP	No
Application Name	TechLibApp

Figure A-34. The installation summary

Click Finish. WAS starts installing the application. When it is done, the installation results look like Figure A-35.

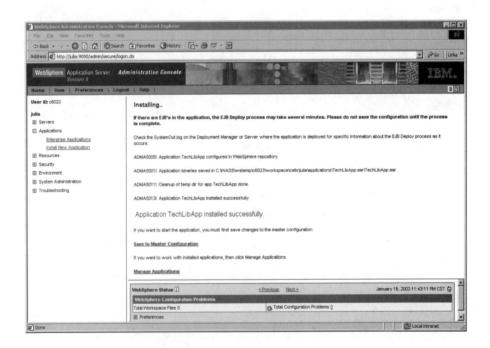

Figure A-35. Installation results

The installation is done. Expand `Applications` on the left part of the screen and click `Enterprise Applications`. Figure A-36 shows a list of the installed applications.

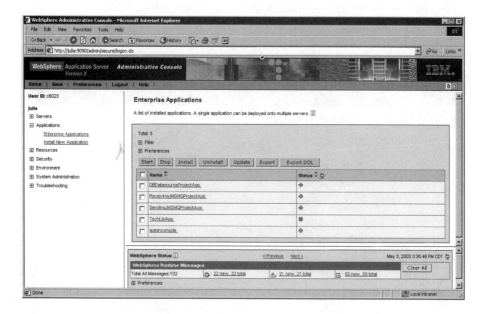

Figure A-36. List of installed applications

You should see the TechLibApp application in the list of installed applications, but you can see that its status shows that it has not been started yet. Figure A-37 shows a message on the top of the screen reminding you that the server configuration has been changed.

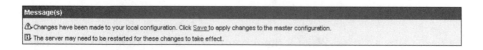

Figure A-37. WAS message

You need to save the server configuration and then stop and restart WAS. Click the Save button on the Administrative Console toolbar. Click Save on the confirmation screen. Click the Logout button to exit the Administrative Console. Activate the WAS First Steps utility. Figure A-38 shows the main utility screen.

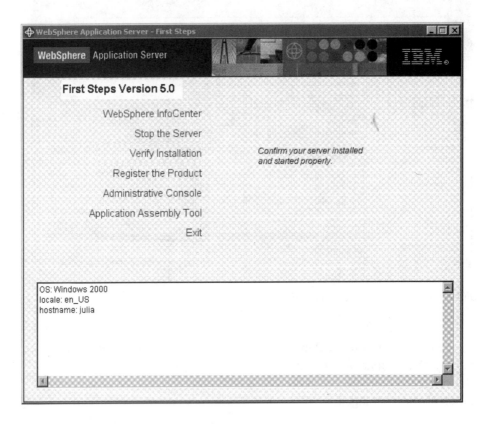

Figure A-38. The WAS Fist Steps utility's main screen

Click Stop the Server. Wait for the server to completely stop. Click Start the Server and wait for the server to start. Figure A-39 shows the started server.

Figure A-39. The WAS First Steps utility, after the server has started

Start the Administrative Console again and enter your user ID. Expand
Applications and click Enterprise Applications. Figure A-40 shows that the
TechLibApp application has been started.

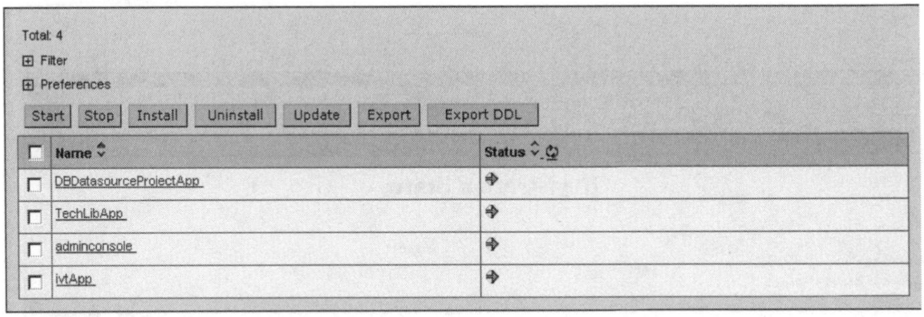

	Name ⇕	Status ⇕ ↻
Total: 4		
⊞ Filter		
⊞ Preferences		
Start Stop Install Uninstall Update Export Export DDL		
☐	DBDatasourceProjectApp	⇨
☐	TechLibApp	⇨
☐	adminconsole	⇨
☐	ivtApp	⇨

Figure A-40. The started TechLibApp *application*

Click the Logout button to exit the Administrative Console. You are ready to
run your application.

601

Running the TechLibApp Application

To run the TechLibApp application, you will execute two business functions. First, you want to register a new book in the library catalog. Start your Web browser and enter the following URL in the command line:
http://localhost:9080/TechLibWEB/BookBookRegisterInputForm.html.

Figure A-41 shows the user input screen. Enter 00008 in the Catalog number field, enter Maximum Java 1.1 in the Book title field, enter Vanderburg and a team in the Author field, enter BBB_Company in the Location field, enter 00 in the Platform field, and enter 01 in the Language field.

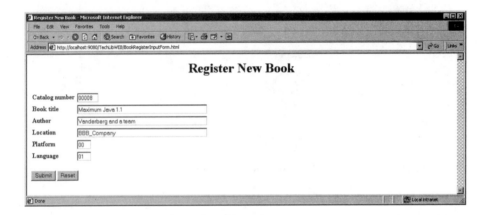

Figure A-41. Registering a new book

Click Submit. Figure A-42 shows the book's registration results.

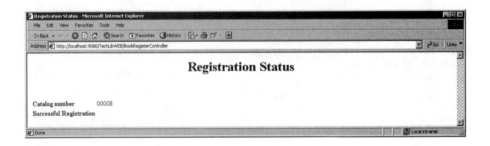

Figure A-42. The book's registration results

Next, you will execute the second business function that searches for all books written for a specific platform. Enter the following URL in the Web browser command line: `http://localhost:9080/TechLibWEB/BookByPlatformInputForm.html`.

On the user input screen, shown in Figure A-43, select `Cross platform` as the platform in question.

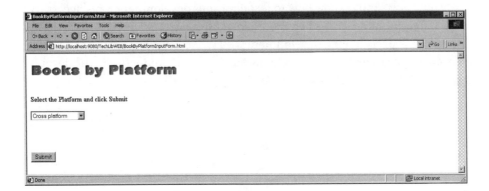

Figure A-43. Searching for all books written for `Cross platform`

Click `Submit`. Figure A-44 shows the processing results.

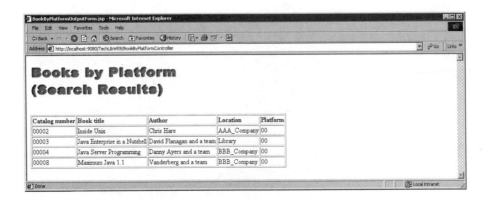

Figure A-44. The cross-platform search results

This completes the `TechLibApp` installation example.

Summary

This is the end of a long journey to J2EE development using WebSphere technology. The main goal for the book is to make the reader to become familiar with J2EE development using WSAD 5.0 and with the subsequent process of installing J2EE applications on WAS 5.0. This book has covered a lot of ground.

By now, you should know how to install various development tools necessary for building your development environment, and you should feel comfortable with various aspects of J2EE development with WSAD 5.0. I hope this book has achieved its goal to make you more knowledgeable and productive in the development of J2EE applications with WSAD 5.0.

Index

A

acknowledgment mode, JMS, 459
addBookActivity method, 123–124
Administrative Console
  Datasource, defining and, 577
  embedded WAS and, 36–37
  enabling, 495
  mapping listener port and, 502
  saving WAS configuration and, 580
  starting TechLibApp application and,
    601–602`
Aged timeout property, JMS, 500
Agent Controller, 14
ALTER TYPE (name) [property]
  command, 548
Application Client project, 43, 45
Application Name WAS installation
  option, 585
application servers
  classloader and, 145
  IBM WebSphere Application Server.
    See WebSphere Application
    Server (WAS)
  IBM WebSphere Application Server
    V5.0 System Management and
    Configuration, 571
  mapping modules to, 586, 596
  restarting, 581
applications. *See also* database
    applications development; J2EE 1.3
    framework; J2EE, deploying
    examples; Web application
    development
  building new application examples,
    WebSphere MQ, 544–545
  P2P applications. *See* Java Message
    Service (JMS), developing P2P
    applications
  Pub/Sub applications, developing,
    515–525
    administered objects, setting,
      516–518
    administered objects, setting
      references to, 522–524
    sending part, building, 518–522
    testing, 524–525
Apress Web site
  downloading
    BuildTextbookDatabase.sql file, 65
  downloading exported project files
    from, 569

  downloading SetJMSAdminEnv.cmd,
    551
  for information, 155, 339
  for source code, book examples, xx
asterisk (*), and bean methods, 161
asynchronous communication
  asynchronous message receipt, 464
  basics of, 447–448
  MDBs and, 468
  WebSphere MQ and, 532
attributes
  creating, Top Down method, 219
  dynamic attributes, setting, 352–353
  entity bean attributes, mapping to
    database tables, 225–226
  Web pages and
    processing for input field, 315–316
    selecting for, 291–292
  XML
    adding, 391
    of XML namespaces, 380–381
    XML Schemas and, 377, 383
authentication alias, 579–580, 581
AUTHOR table field, 64

B

BMP entity beans, 227–251
  introduction to, 227–229
  testing, 249–251
  transport object, building
    BookInquiryHome.java: Home
      Interface Class (code listing),
      244–245
    BookInquiry.java: Remote
      Interface Class (code listing),
      245
    BookInquiryKey.java: Primary Key
      Class (code listing), 245–246
    introduction to, 229–230
    methods, 231–233
    source code for book modules,
      233–246
    TransportBean.java (code listing),
      230–231
BOOK_ACTIVITY table
  Book_activity and, 188
  structure, 65
BookByPlatformController servlet, 348
BookByPlatformController.java (code
  listing), 346–348

W